LIFE-CYCLE COSTING

USING ACTIVITY-BASED COSTING AND MONTE CARLO METHODS TO MANAGE FUTURE COSTS AND RISKS

Jan Emblemsvåg

WILEY

JOHN WILEY & SONS, INC.

Library of Congress Cataloging-in-Publication Data
Emblemsvåg, Jan.
    Life-cycle costing : using activity-based costing and Monte Carlo methods to manage future costs and risk / Jan Emblemsvåg.
        p.   cm.
    Includes bibliographical references and index.
    ISBN 13: 978-0-4713-5885-5
    1. Costs, Industrial. 2. Life cycle costing. 3. Risk management. I. Title.
    HD47.E58 2003
    657'.42—dc21
    2002014328

10 9 8 7 6 5 4 3 2 1

To my son Nikolai and my wife Navita

CONTENTS

PREFACE

If you think predicting the future is risky, try ignoring it.

The Economist

When I first thought about writing this book, I briefly searched the global online bookstores to find out what other books concerning Life-Cycle Costing (LCC) are available. I was stunned to learn that only a dozen books have been published concerning LCC. Those that are available are highly specialized, too, such as infrastructure construction.

How can it be that one of the few concepts that systematically tries to eliminate costs before they are incurred gets so little attention, while an enormous body of work concerns how to assess and cut costs after the costs are incurred? After all, what counts the most: being cost effective or knowing what prevented us from being cost effective in the past?

I believe one of the prime reasons for this lack of interest in LCC is that it has mainly been associated with engineering; life-cycle costs are the costs of some technical "stuff" sometime in the future that the engineers worry about. But who cares about a distant future when most decision-makers are either in a new position, retired, or even fired? In fact, according to *The Economist,* an average American CEO only has a position for 18 months before he or she is removed. Or equally common, who cares about the impact on other people's budgets? Apparently, LCC concerns many issues that stretch beyond most organizational short-term needs, functional barriers, and present issues.

I believe that such fragmented thinking is becoming more and more a thing of the past. As product life cycles become increasingly shorter and product development become increasingly capital intensive, the point of decision-making and the point of measuring the effect of the decision-making are becoming increasingly closer, and the consequences of erroneous decisions are becoming increasingly grave. Also, more and more customers think beyond the purchase price; they want to know total costs. However, the best argument is that the very idea of LCC can be utilized in cost management and help turn cost management from hindsight to dealing with costs even before they are incurred. This is a much more effective approach than today's cost cutting and it will produce results much more efficiently than the traditional LCC. Also, it will more easily form the basis of systematic work toward gaining sustainable profitability for the long term.

Some would say that LCC is to help engineers "think like MBAs but act like engineers." That is true and important, but I think of LCC in a broader sense. I believe the main purpose of LCC should be to help organizations apply knowledge about past performance and their gut feelings to future issues of costs and risks. This should be done not in the traditional sense of budgeting, but in meaningful predictions about future costs of products, processes, and organization, and their associated business risks.

In order to turn LCC from being an engineering tool hidden in the cubicles in an engineering department to a more useful and widely accepted engineering *and* management tool, some changes must be made. The purpose of this book is to present and illustrate one such approach that can bridge the gap between past and future costs, engineering and management decisions, and direct and overhead resource usage. To do that, I have taken two well-known concepts, Activity-Based Costing and LCC, and merged the best parts while adding the usage of Monte Carlo simulations, uncertainty, and some additional insight.

It should be noted that Activity-Based LCC is similar to the Activity-Based Cost and Environmental Management approach, but as the saying goes, the devil is in the details. The Activity-Based Cost and Environmental Management approach does not explicitly detail how to do cost forecasting, financial analysis, and so forth, issues that are pertinent to LCC. Also, it leaves the reader with little explicit support on assessing and managing risks. This book therefore concerns how to turn the Activity-Based Cost and Environmental Management approach into an LCC approach, which for simplicity is referred to as Activity-Based LCC.

The result is an approach that in my opinion is flexible, highly effective, and efficient for most cost management considerations (including LCC) and that can handle risk and uncertainty in a credible fashion. This is evident both from its theoretical foundations and also from the three case studies provided in the book. For those who are particularly interested in the theoretical foundations, I have provided references to every chapter in the back of the respective chapter.

The book is organized into nine chapters. In Chapter 1, you will find the basic premises for the book and the key characteristics of Activity-Based LCC. In Chapter 2, the basics of LCC are discussed. It starts out by discussing what a life cycle is, because that is not obvious and numerous definitions exist in the literature. Then cost as concept is defined and contrasted to expense and cash flow. This distinction is important to understand because LCC models can be cost, expense, and cash flow models, and it is important to understand which is which, and what to use when.

Due to the inherent uncertainty in LCC, it is important to discuss how to handle risk and uncertainty, and that is done in Chapter 3. Risk and uncertainty will be defined and discussed in sufficient detail for LCC purposes. Situations where an increase in uncertainty can reduce risks will be discussed and even shown in the case study in Chapter 8. This finding links directly to the Law of Incompatibility, which has important implications for all management efforts. Some of these implications are discussed throughout the book. Finally, a brief overview of a traditional risk management approach is provided. It is intended as a basic introduction for those who are not already fluent in risk management.

Chapter 4 is about Activity-Based Costing (ABC). ABC is an integral part of Activity-Based LCC, as the name indicates. ABC has several indispensable characteristics that are invaluable in cost management in general. Chapter 4 discusses the background of ABC, how it compares to traditional, volume-based costing systems, what the basic concepts behind ABC are, how it can be implemented, and so on. Like the two preceding chapters, Chapter 4 is intended as an introduction to some vital concepts that must be understood in order to understand Activity-Based LCC. Illustrative examples are also provided.

Then, in Chapter 5, the Activity-Based LCC approach is presented, which consists of 10 steps that are discussed in detail. The best way to learn the approach is, however, by carefully studying the case studies because they are organized according to the steps of Activity-Based LCC.

The first case study is found in Chapter 6, which is coauthored with Randi Carlsen. It concerns a tire disposal problem in the County of Ullensaker, north of Oslo, Norway. A do-nothing approach to the problem is unlikely to succeed in the long run because of the near proximity of Oslo Gardermoen International Airport. Thus, something must be done. In the case study, we look at the feasible options using both traditional LCC and Activity-Based LCC. Even in this simple case study, it is evident that Activity-Based LCC provides additional value by its superior tracing capabilities and flexible uncertainty handling.

The second case study, found in Chapter 7, concerns the operation of a Platform Supply Vessel (PSV) owned by Farstad Shipping ASA in Ålesund, Norway. Operating a PSV is not easy due to the very narrow margins, and an LCC model can be useful both in terms of providing decision support during bidding and cost forecasting. Chapter 7 also shows how to provide decision support in relation to choosing fuel and types of machinery, issues that have major structural impacts on costs. Here an Activity-Based LCC model shows how both issues can be handled effectively and efficiently.

In Chapter 8, the WagonHo!, Inc. case study is found, the most complex case study in the book. Its complexity derives from the facts that:

- It incorporates multiple products and cost objects.
- It includes credible overhead cost considerations.
- It includes the entire life cycle of the products.
- It includes both a cash flow analysis and a costing analysis.
- It shows how Monte Carlo simulations can effectively be used in terms of handling uncertainty as well as risks and in enhancing tracing.

This case study is, unlike the two other case studies, functional. That may be viewed as a limitation. However, given the complexity of similar real-world case studies, I am happy to use a simpler version because it is more than sufficient enough to illustrate the potential of Activity-Based LCC. For example, the case study clearly illustrates how Activity-Based LCC can handle multiple cost objects at the same time, how Activity-Based LCC handles overhead costs in a credible fashion, and that Activity-Based LCC is in fact a costing analysis and not just a cash flow analysis. Another advantage of this case study is that it is also used in Chapter 4 as an extensive example of an ABC implementation. By contrasting that implementation to the model in Chapter 8, readers can easily see both the differences and similarities between ABC and Activity-Based LCC.

In Chapter 9, some key concepts and findings are revisited. Whereas Chapter 1 focuses on the problems Activity-Based LCC must overcome and how they relate to traditional cost management approaches, including traditional LCC to a large extent. Chapter 9 focuses on the building blocks of Activity-Based LCC. The earlier chapter helps readers to understand what LCC ideally should be about and how Activity-Based LCC overcomes the problems of traditional approaches. Chapter 9 explains how Activity-Based LCC can be applied. Both Chapters 1 and 9 tell the same story, although they tell it differently. Finally, some future issues are discussed.

The book also includes two appendices. Appendix A contains a Monte Carlo example. This example is handy to read for those who do not quite understand the power of Monte Carlo methods. It clearly illustrates how Monte Carlo methods can be used for three purposes: (1) uncertainty and risk assessment/management, (2) the tracing of critical success factors, and (3) information management. Appendix B provides an overview of a ship component classification system, which is applicable to the case study in Chapter 7.

As outlined in the last chapter of the book, Activity-Based LCC opens up a completely different way of conducting cost management. Instead of depending on hindsight and chasing the deceptive accuracy of past figures to look forward into the future, ask what causes costs and what are the risks? Everybody jokes about the hindsight of cost accounting. Why not do something about it?

Please note that the views presented in this book are solely those of the author and do not represent those of Det Norske Veritas (DNV) Consulting.

Jan Emblemsvåg
Høvik, Norway
www.emblemsvag.com

ACKNOWLEDGMENTS

It is difficult to mention one person before the other. However, I undoubtedly owe much to Professor Bert Bras at the Systems Realization Laboratory (SRL) at the Georgia Institute of Technology. Apart from being my supervisor, and an excellent one, he and I worked together during my master studies in 1993 and 1994 to develop a new Life-Cycle Costing method called Activity-Based Costing with Uncertainty. Then we embarked on a new Life-Cycle Assessment method in 1996 through 1999 as a part of my Ph.D. studies, which upon completion turned out to be useful for integrated cost and environmental management. In 2000, a popularized and edited version of the Ph.D. dissertation was published as a book titled *Activity-Based Cost and Environmental Management: A Different Approach to the ISO 14000 Compliance.*

I also am highly indebted to Professor Farrokh Mistree also at the SRL for his mentoring of both me and his former student Bert Bras. In recent years, I have found his insight concerning identifying "hidden assumptions" particularly interesting because it turns out that they are literally everywhere. Now, working as a consultant, identifying such hidden assumptions can be the difference between a mediocre project and a great one.

Another great thing I learned from Farrokh and Bert was to articulate my thoughts. Without such training, I would probably never even have written a single paper. I have truly learned a lot from the two of you, Bert and Farrokh, more than I can ever express. When I came to the SRL, I hated writing, but I came to love it, and it is mostly due to your efforts. Because I can never repay you, I hope that by completing this book without your help, you will think "yes, Jan has graduated," and you should know that it is largely due to your efforts through the years. Meeting and working with the two of you has been a defining moment in my life. Thank you!

After writing some hundreds of pages, it is virtually impossible to have a fresh view of the book. I would therefore very much like to acknowledge the tremendous effort made by Senior Partner John Erik Stenberg at Considium Consulting Group AS and my colleague Lars Endre Kjølstad in reviewing, providing constructive comments, and simply making the book better. The proofreaders and Sheck Cho at John Wiley & Sons also have done a great job in making this book presentable.

Regarding the case studies, I would like to thank Randi Carlsen from Sagex Petroleum AS, who wrote Chapter 6; Jan Henry Farstad of Farstad Shipping ASA, Annik Magerholm Fet of the Norwegian University of Science and Technology (NTNU), and Greg Wiles of the Center for Manufacturing Information Technology. Without their help, none of my case studies would have materialized.

I would also like to thank Det Norske Veritas (DNV) Consulting for allowing me to pursue writing this book and spend some time on its completion. Moreover, the insight I have gained through DNV projects has been valuable.

Finally, I would like to thank my family for their support. In particular, my wife has been very patient with me.

1

INTRODUCTION

Which of you, intending to build a tower, sitteth not down first, and
counteth the cost?

Jesus
Luke 14:28

This book concerns the age-old question, "What does it cost?" But not just in monetary terms. Not understanding the uncertainties and risks that divide an organization from its desired results is also a "cost" because it can, and often will, result in
a loss. Therefore, if we were to build a tower, we should also consider the risks and
uncertainties of building it when counting the costs.

Despite the fact that cost management has been around as a field of study for
more than 150 years, the answers we have found so far to this simple question have
obvious shortcomings. That is evident from the fact that virtually all cost management systems only concern the costs incurred within the four walls of the
organization. Even worse, we try to control costs after they are incurred instead of
eliminating them before they are committed. The result is a massively wasteful
economy.[1]

In this book, a new approach is presented that deals with estimating future costs
and directing attention toward its root causes so that companies and organizations
can get useful decision support for solutions both inside and outside the organization. The approach, called Activity-Based Life-Cycle Costing (LCC), is presented
by theory, argumentation, and illustrative case studies.

WHAT DOES IT COST?

Most businesses, if not all, live by buying something, adding some value to it, and
then selling it for a higher price to someone. The organization cashes in the difference between the price charged and the costs incurred as a profit. Whereas the
price is given in the marketplace and is ideally a function of suply and demand, the
incurred costs are a result of a series of decisions throughout the organization that
started long before the product was even conceived. This chain of decisions leads

to costs being committed before they are incurred. Managing costs effectively and efficiently thus implies that costs must be eliminated in the commitment stage and not reduced in the incurring stage. Many organizations realize this, but is few practice it. The costing methods employed by most companies simply do not take such notions into account as they embark on cost cutting. This happens for many reasons, but it might simply be a matter of bad habits or because we dislike to learn new things unless the consequences of not learning are worse than those of learning, as world-renowned psychologist Edgar H. Schein claims.[2]

The points argued so far are illustrated in Figure 1.1. The numbers are heuristics from manufacturing. In the literature, we typically find that the number is somewhere between 70/30 and 90/10; the most often quoted numbers are along the 80/20 ratio. Figure 1.1 shows that although about only 20 percent of the costs are actually incurred in the activities prior to production, these activities actually commit 80 percent of the costs. The production costs, however, incur about 80 percent of the costs, but production improvement efforts impact only about 20 percent of the cost commitment. This has been a well-known fact for many years. In fact, LCC came about in the early 1960s due to similar understanding concerning weapons systems procurement in the U.S. Department of Defense.

The first to use such ideas extensively in cost management on a continuous basis and on extensive scale, however, were the Japanese. After World War II, Japan was in ruins, and to rise, the Japanese had to be more clever than the rest. American industry, in contrast, saw no need to become smarter because they were already doing so well—for the time being. It is therefore not strange that a Japanese cost management concept, target costing, has most clearly emphasized the need for the elimination of costs through design. Such emphasis leads to *proactive* cost management, as opposed to reducing costs after they are incurred, which is *reactive* cost management.

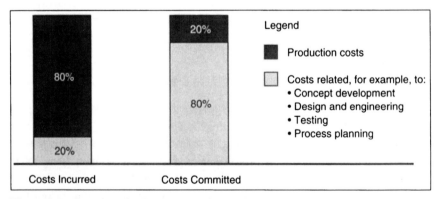

Figure 1.1   Cost committed versus costs incurred.

Unfortunately, even today, more than 30 years after Japanese industry became world class, most companies still manage costs reactively. While they try to eliminate costs via design, unless cost management follows suit, it will be two paradigms fighting each other. Thus, the most established paradigm will usually prevail unless the challenger can present a convincing case.

The traditional, reactive paradigm is a challenge for the new, proactive paradigm because this paradigm inevitably incurs more costs up front, which traditionally is thought to be bad for business since traditional accounting regimes treat Research and Development (R&D) costs as period costs and not investments. Then design departments will get insufficient funding to eliminate costs before they are incurred. The intended results do not materialize, which in turn will be used as an argument against the new paradigm. Therefore, what is needed is a change of mindset and a change of cost management approaches. We simply cannot achieve the results promised by the proponents of cost elimination via design unless we commit wholeheartedly to it. As Michael Porter argued concerning strategic positioning, middle positions are never successful.[3] The traditional paradigm has some other unwanted side effects that the new paradigm can overcome. The best-known side effect is quality. Just as the Japanese designed products that were less costly than their American counterparts, they also produced products that many considered better in terms of quality. The overall value of Japanese products was in other words greater, at least if we use the definition of value that the European Committee for Standardization uses.[4]

Value[5] is defined as proportionate to the satisfaction of needs divided by the use of resources. In other words, value is proportionate to quality divided by costs. Value-driven organizations must therefore be both quality driven and cost conscious, something traditional management systems simply cannot deliver, as explained in Chapter 4. On top of that, despite the fact that traditional cost management systems are partially designed to satisfy external needs for reporting, they have completely missed the concept of shareholder value and its measure of economic profit, or Economic Value Added (EVA).[6]

Costs like quality and other important aspects of the product, such as image and branding, cannot be fixed after the product is manufactured, as is traditionally done. They can be successfully handled only during an effective and efficient design process supported by relevant cost management systems and value-driven strategies. The new paradigm of cost elimination through design has far-reaching implications that must be taken seriously if the intended results are to materialize. Quick fixes and shortcuts, which have often been the rule of the day in many companies,[7] will not sustain a change toward the new paradigm. A change must occur in both the culture of business and the performance measures, because those two factors are the most important ones in change management efforts, as shown by the two large surveys carried out by A.T. Kearney and Atticus.[8]

One such change in performance measures is to expand the horizon of the cost management efforts from the four walls of the company to the relevant parts of the life cycle where value is created and to employ foresight instead of hindsight. In this context, LCC can play a far greater role than traditionally thought, and that is one of the main messages of this book.

THE ROLE OF LIFE-CYCLE COSTING

As discussed in Chapter 2, LCC serves mainly three purposes today:

1. To be an effective engineering tool for use in design, procurement, and so on. This was the original intent.
2. To be applied proactively in cost accounting and management.
3. To be a design and engineering tool for environmental purposes.

Numerous publications are available on how LCC can be used as an engineering tool, and I therefore give this little attention. This book focuses on how LCC can be a managerial tool because most organizatins seem to forget to use LCC in cost accounting and management despite its great potential. Some attention is also given to the use of LCC in the environmental domain because much confusion exists in that area (see Chapter 2).

Nonetheless, the three purposes have a common denominator, which is the role of LCC to provide insight in future matters regarding *all* costs. Furthermore, since the future is always associated with uncertainty and risks, truly proactive cost management should also handle all sorts of risks that can incur losses to the organization. Such risks are commonly referred to as business risks and have become a new focal point of corporate governance. In fact, due to the many corporate scandals in the 1980s and 1990s, large institutional investors have demanded better financial transparency, integrity, and accountability.[9] This push toward improved corporate governance has resulted in the Turnbull Report, published in 1999 in the United Kingdom, which was made at the request of the London Stock Exchange (LSE). In fact, the Listing Rules disclosure requirements of the LSE demand full compliance with the reporting requirements stated in the Turnbull Report for accounting periods ending on or after December 23, 2000. It has been said that "non-compliance with the Turnbull guidance would result in an embarrassing disclosure in the annual report, which could attract the attention of the press, shareholder activists and institutional investors."[10]

In this light, it is evident that cost management should ideally be expanded to *risk-based* cost management as well as a focus on total costs. In fact, just as "The (Turnbull) guidance is about the adoption of a risk-based approach toward establishing a system of internal control and reviewing its effectiveness,"[11] LCC must take risks and uncertainties into account in order to be really useful for decision-makers. LCC should therefore be an important way to help companies eliminate costs before they are incurred *and,* to manage some crucial business risks related to costs, cash flow, and profitability.

Unfortunately, as discussed in Chapter 2, most LCC methods cannot handle these issues credibly, except cash flows, and that is why a different LCC method was needed. Professor Bert Bras of the Georgia Institute of Technology and I first came up with an approach called Activity-Based Costing with Uncertainty.[12] Then, based on my growing experience and insight from other areas of cost management, I saw the need to improve it further. This book is about this new improved approach called Activity-Based LCC.

WHY ACTIVITY-BASED LIFE-CYCLE COSTING?

On the one hand, Activity-Based LCC is a result of research spurred by dissatisfaction with existing LCC methods; on the other hand, during my consulting work I have seen that using the life-cycle cost idea purely for LCC purposes is a gross devaluation of the idea. Many cost management efforts are ineffective because cost management traditionally is performed after the fact. Although hindsight is 20/20, it gives little room for effective decision-making.

Now, suppose we want to look at cost management from a different perspective. This perspective should be one in which we look forward in time, we look farther than the four walls of the organization, and we reduce the wasteful activities of the annual budgeting ritual of chasing the numbers. Cost management and budgeting of the future should concern itself with identifying the underlying drivers of business performance, manage these, then settle for ballpark numbers, and manage the risks: This is the ultimate goal of Activity-Based LCC. After all, costs are statistical in nature and cannot be managed unless we understand the underlying drivers.

This can be achieved by using the basic LCC idea (not the methods), coupling it with the Activity-Based Costing (ABC) concept, and being more flexible in our definitions of what constitutes a life cycle. To power the whole thing, we use Monte Carlo simulations to handle uncertainty and risks much more efficiently and effectively than traditional methods, besides also effectively identifying critical success factors. This is also done much faster than traditional approaches.

In short, this new perspective on the LCC idea entails three shifts and an improvement:

1. From a partial focus to holistic thinking
2. From structure orientation to process orientation
3. From cost allocation to cost tracing
4. Managing risk and uncertainty realistically

From a Partial Focus to Holistic Thinking

Several issues spring to mind when we talk about partial focus versus holistic thinking in the context of cost management, notably:

- Making cost management relevant.
- Linking costs to quality. This linkage is important because value is a function of cost and quality.
- Linking costs to uncertainty and risks.

Making Cost Management Relevant

As discussed, cost management is predominantly concerned about costs in a very fragmented way. Roughly speaking, in traditional cost management as performed by most companies today:

- Downstream costs are largely ignored despite the fact that we know they are of considerable importance.
- Historic costs are studied because the future costs are believed to be unknown.
- The focus is mostly on variable costs because fixed costs are assumed to be fixed.
- Direct costs are better understood than indirect costs because traditional cost accounting systems virtually ignore overhead costs.
- The distinction between costs and expenses cannot be captured and is ignored.

In sum, traditional cost management focuses only on some aspects of an organization's costs. It has been described in many unflattering ways, but essentially it has lost its relevance.[13]

When LCC first was developed in the early 1960s, the first three of these "partialities" were remedied; namely, one started to look beyond the four walls of the organization, think of future costs, and treat all costs as costs or to think in terms of *total* costs. Unfortunately, such thinking has not progressed much outside of LCC. In parallel, however, ABC brought an elegant solution to the latter two points in addition to the first and third ones. Activity-Based Budgeting (ABB), a step further in the development of Activity-Based Management (ABM), whose roots are ABC, also provides a sort of remedy to the third point. The point is that remedies exist for the aforementioned shortcomings of traditional cost management.

These remedies can be put together—synthesized—and that is essentially what Activity-Based LCC is about. Whether the name of the method should incorporate LCC or not is a matter of perspective. I have chosen to do so because the underlying idea of LCC—managing all relevant costs throughout the life cycle of a product—is so intuitive, basic, and paramount. However, one can probably argue convincingly for another name, such as value chain costing, (see Glossary).

Activity-Based LCC also incorporates effective and efficient handling of uncertainty and risk, which neither ABC nor most LCC methods can do. This is discussed more in the sections "Linking Costs to Uncertainty and Risks" and "Managing Risk and Uncertainty Realistically."

Linking Costs to Quality

Everybody finally realized the importance of quality as the Japanese industry swept the globe. What is less recognized is the enormous impact quality has on the *operating* costs of the company. In the distribution industry, for example, it is estimated that up to 25 percent of operating expenses stem from internal quality problems.[14] Unfortunately, traditional costing systems have little, if any, chance of estimating the cost of quality, that is, what it costs to provide a certain level of quality.

The cost of quality is important to assess because "Too much quality can ruin you," as former vice chairman of Chrysler Corporation, Robert Lutz, puts it.[15] The other extreme version of quality commitment would be organizations that simply seek ISO 9000 certification to comply to pressure. Such work is not expensive, but it does not have any clear, measurable improvements on the organization according to several surveys.[16]

In any case, what is needed is a cost management system that can link cost and quality together. A well-designed ABC system can handle this challenge because ABC is transaction based, and one significant group of transactions is related to quality, as discussed in Chapter 4. This explains the large potential for quality-driven organizations to implement ABC and total quality management (see "Activity-Based Costing and Total Quality Management in Chapter 4). Therefore, ABC can be used as a quality-enforcing system, not just as the cost-cutting tool for which it has been criticized.[17]

By extending ABC to Activity-Based LCC, we benefit from having the opportunity to think of quality in life-cycle perspectives, which is difficult for traditional LCC because traditional LCC methods are not transaction based. The traditional LCC method can at best handle what is referred to as grade,[18] which is defined by the product's features. Since quality and process performance is closely linked, the structure orientation of traditional cost management approaches (see "From Structure Orientation to Process Orientation") inhibits the effective cost of quality management.

Linking Costs to Uncertainty and Risks

In cost management, except LCC and some special areas, uncertainty and risk are completely forgotten topics. It is as if future costs can be determined with certainty, although they are largely unknown at the time. However, as we shall see later, both costs are statistical in nature, as is quality. Statistical quality control and statistical process control are cornerstones of Total Quality Management.[19] In cost management, however, the world is still deterministic and determinable by simple averages. We hear, for example, about how executives rush into implementing integrated cost systems but that "some (real-time cost information) will cause confusion and error, delivering information that is far less accurate than what managers currently receive."[20] The reason for such confusion and error is lack of understanding in the statistical nature of costs because "there will always be fluctuations in spending, volume, productivity and yield."

It is time to internalize the fact that costs simply cannot be determined with certainty and act accordingly. Basically, while it is important to avoid cost management practices that act on random variation, information about cost fluctuations should be incorporated in forecasts to provide uncertainty and risk measures for budgeting and so on.

From Structure Orientation to Process Orientation

Structure orientation refers to the fact that costs are categorized according to their types or structure. Examples of this would be marketing costs, direct labor costs, depreciation, and so on. This thinking is not very effective because it does not consider the underlying demands for jobs to be done. Cost effectiveness in such a setting will inevitably lead to cost cutting, starting with the largest costs. Such cost cutting can be highly damaging, as many in the literature report, because one might cut costs for jobs that are in high demand rather than the intended idle capacity. Then the company has reduced its ability to produce value and will consequently be worse off. Further ill-founded cost cutting can further aggravate the situation, and the organization may approach a so-called death spiral.

The only way to get around this problem is by thinking in terms of processes: process orientation. The costs should be categorized according to the processes, activities, tasks, jobs, or whatever desirable process element. Then a manager can see that a particular machine costs such and such, with all costs included (depreciation, energy, labor, tools, and so on). Then it is a lot easier to measure the time the machine is idle, estimate what that idleness costs, and find out whether this activity should be performed or not, or how it should be changed. A further advantage of the process orientation is that a direct link is made to quality management, as noted earlier. Cost of quality can be realistically estimated, and cost management will become a quality and continuous improvement enforcer. Today, however, quality management in many companies is done despite the cost management systems.

Unfortunately, the general ledger is structure oriented. It should be reorganized to become object oriented (in terms of organizing the data) or process oriented (in terms of its relation to the work processes), but this is probably not legal due to Generally Accepted Accounting Principles (GAAP). Sound cost management will entail having a costing system for internal control and management and another one for external reporting and compliance. This is, in fact, what many leading companies do.

As of today, ABC is the costing method that has captured process orientation the best, in my opinion. Activity-Based LCC enjoys the same benefits as ABC does because it piggybacks on ABC in this context.

A more subtle part of process orientation is to also think about continuous improvement when implementing or designing a costing system or model. That is, it is important to steadily improve the costing model. When this is done, it is crucial to notice that the cost estimates inevitably will change as well. Such changes should not be interpreted as a sign of error, but rather a sign of improvement or inevitability. Costs are, after all, statistical in nature. Hence, an estimate of $100 for something might be equally correct as $90, or vice versa. In fact, both are probably correct at some time, but not at the same time. The problem is that we will never know when this "some time" occurs. Cost should therefore be treated according to its nature, statistical and uncertain, as discussed earlier.

From Cost Allocation to Cost Tracing

Cost allocation refers to the process of assigning costs to cost objects using arbitrary allocation bases (see Glossary), whereas tracing is based on the establishment of cause-and-effect relationships (drivers) between costs and cost objects. The basic difference between allocation and tracing is therefore that allocation is arbitrary while tracing relies on cause-and-effect relationships.

Traditional cost management allocates costs in a single step, whereas ABC traces costs using two stages of cause-and-effect relationships. The result of this apparent small difference is enormous; it is in fact reported that the difference in product costs can shift several hundred percent.[21] In Chapter 4, this fact, along with the theory of ABC, is explained in detail.

Traditionally, this difference would, however, play no role in LCC because most LCC models concern only one cost object at a time. By performing LCC like this, overhead costs are grossly mistreated, as in traditional, volume-based cost accounting systems, or simply ignored. When overhead costs constituted up to 35 percent of total costs in a typical U.S. company in the mid-1980s,[22] it is clear that ignoring such a large proportion of total costs is a large risk in itself. For advanced technological systems, the error of this approach is even larger. Activity-Based LCC aims at handling overhead costs as realistically as possible, using ABC principles, also in the context of LCC.

To do that, LCC cannot be performed product by product but must incorporate the entire system whose cost base can be clearly defined. In order to clearly define the cost base, however, the purpose of the LCC must be defined and an appropriate life cycle chosen. Often it is more work limiting an analysis than performing a complete analysis for the entire organization. The reason is that much work must be spent trying to understand the consequences of limiting the analysis. Also, if people know that many assumptions have been made to limit the analysis, they may try to undermine the results, particularly if they do not like them.

Managing Risk and Uncertainty Realistically

When discussing risks and uncertainty, it is important to be aware of two things: (1) assessing risks and uncertainties, and (2) reducing risks and uncertainties. Both are important when it comes to managing risks and analyzing uncertainties. This is discussed in the two subsequent sections. Then the topics of forecasting and how to forecast are discussed because LCC is an attempt to forecast, or predict, the future, and such predictions are always subject to risks and uncertainties.

Assessing Uncertainty and Risks Realistically

As will be evident from Chapter 3, the most common approaches of handling uncertainty and risks have many problems. In fact, some people do not even distinguish between risk and uncertainty, and that is probably a reason why they have never challenged some of the common approaches toward risk and uncertainty assessments.

Many risk assessment methods are unnecessarily limiting, as explained in detail in Chapter 3. On top of that, many of the most popular sensitivity analyses are incapable of measuring the consequences of interplay between variables. For example, what happens if a variable has a high value, another variable has a medium value, and a third has a low variable? Popular methods have a great difficulty in answering this simple question, especially if we do not find discrete choices (high, low, and so on) satisfactory, but rather think in terms of continuous ranges (all real numbers).

What is truly amazing in my opinion is that even though the remedy for all these unnecessary limitations, and much more, have been known for more than 30 years, few seem to care or even know about them. The remedy for all these problems is Monte Carlo simulations, and why they are applicable in this context can be explained by both fuzzy logic and probability theory. This is discussed in detail in Chapter 3, but here it is sufficient to recognize that with Monte Carlo simulations, no limitations exist on how risk and uncertainty can be assessed. In fact, due to the simple crudeness of Monte Carlo simulations, it does not matter if a variable is probabilistic, statistic, stochastic, or fuzzy in nature; it will all be solved in the same way. Moreover, as a by-product of the Monte Carlo simulation, you get a sensitivity analysis that outperforms any form of sensitivity analyses. It is not without reason that Monte Carlo methods have been referred to as "the perfect tool of numerical theories and applications."[23]

Some may argue that they do not like the Monte Carlo methods because they involve the problem of random errors. Random errors occur as a consequence of Monte Carlo methods being statistical in nature, and all statistical measures are associated with some random errors. However, since costs are statistical in nature, surely using a statistical method to handle the associated risks and uncertainties is most appropriate. Also, the random errors are not a problem as long as you have a computer that enables you to run enough trials to reduce the errors to acceptable levels. As the clock speed of chips still seems to double every 18 months, it is safe to assume that the problem of random errors is one of the past. In fact, most PCs today have more than enough Random Access Memory (RAM) and high enough clock speed to handle even large LCC Monte Carlo simulations. Add to that the possibility of running Monte Carlo simulations over a local area network (LAN) or a similar system, and the use of such simulations is virtually endless for any practical cost-modeling purpose.

Reducing Risks and Uncertainty

Once the risks and uncertainties are assessed, the next step is to handle them. Uncertainties should be handled with particular care, as explained in Chapter 3, because an apparent reduction in uncertainty can in fact increase risks. This fact ties nicely into the earlier discussions; excessive simplification of cost assessments and management to reduce the uncertainty in the cost assessment—that is, making it "simple"—in fact increases the risks associated with cost management.

When it comes to managing the risks, numerous, well-known, and road-proven methods are available, as discussed in Chapter 3. But any analysis, regardless of how well it is done, is worth nothing if it does not lead to action. This is possibly the largest risk of all the risks, because nonaction is in many cases worse than wrong action. As one of the great executives of Ford put it:

> If you've got ten decisions to make and you spend all your time making just four, then you've made six wrong decisions.[24]

If we can act sensibly, we should be in good shape. In order to act sensibly, we need to act on facts and not on whims, myths, and erroneous information. Here the role of a good performance measurement system becomes crucial. When discussing performance measurement systems, it is important to emphasize that research shows that in many cases of cost system implementation, success is strongly correlated with behavioral and organizational variables, but not with technical variables, such as the type of software used.[25] In fact, two large studies point out that in the context of change management, changes in the performance measurement system and in culture are the two most important factors of success.[26]

How to Forecast the Future

LCC is essentially the art of forecasting future costs, but any forecast is uncertain. Being capable of assessing uncertainty and managing the associated risks is important, but it is not sufficient. We must also decide what kind of mental model of forecasting we want to choose. Figure 1.2 shows four ways of performing forecasting (in relation to economic performance):

1. The most common one is probably *extending a trend line*. The assumption is that the future will roughly follow this trend line. That can be true, but that approach completely misses new opportunities and threats.
2. Another common approach is to use *experiments* of some sort and, based on the experiment, make generalizations concerning the future.
3. Basing the work on *general economic forecasts* is another approach, but then you are in the hands of those who made the forecast. Also, it may be the case that your organization will not follow the industry forecast.
4. The last approach is the *grassroots approach* where those facing the issues are asked, surveyed, interviewed, and so forth, and based on this set of information a forecast is made. Note that front-line representatives are the people who work the closest with the issue under investigation. For example, if

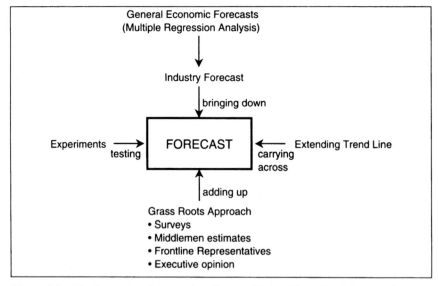

Figure 1.2 The four ways of forecasting. Source: Adapted from F. Allvine, *Marketing: Principles and Practices*. Boston, MA: Irwin/McGraw-Hill, 1996.

we want to make a sales forecast, the front-line representative will be the sales representative. If we want to make a technology forecast, the front-line representative will be a technology worker who has a good overview of all possible technologies. This approach is probably the most flexible in that it is not necessarily based on past data or performance. We are allowed to guess.

When innovations are the subject of the LCC, only the grassroots approach is flexible enough to allow a wide-enough scope for the forecast. Extending a trend line and performing experiments are not feasible options since an innovation is by definition something new. Innovations are therefore more risky, but it is better to make a forecast about the future than to ignore it. This is even truer when we talk about the improvements of existing products and systems.

From this discussion, it follows that we need a way to handle uncertainty and risks that is so flexible that guesses can be made, historical data can be utilized when available, and so on. Otherwise, the approach will become a limitation in terms of assessing uncertainty and risks and also in supporting forecasting. Basically, we want no limitations.

Luckily, as explained in Chapter 3, modeling uncertainty and risks as probability distributions, fuzzy numbers, and/or fuzzy intervals, and solving the problem using Monte Carlo simulation are the most flexible approaches for both assessing uncertainty and risks and for forecasting. Of course, the usefulness of the Monte Carlo simulations cannot go beyond the meaningfulness of the mathematical modeling, and some uncertainties and risks are simply impossible to formulate mathematically. Consequently, there are limitations, as Albert Einstein put it:

> As far as the laws of mathematics refer to reality, they are not certain; and as far as they are certain, they do not refer to reality.

Outside of this, no limitations exist. However, even if we can guess as much as we want, and use as much historical data as we want, we are ultimately affected by the past, because even a guess is made with the past in mind to some extent or the other. To forecast the future, we must understand the past, which further emphasizes the need to make cost management relevant. ABC can be used to understand the past, but Activity-Based LCC can be used to both understand the past and forecast the future just as easily. This is because uncertainty and Monte Carlo simulations work both ways, past and future.

I would like to point out that although this book builds on well-known subject matter, and thus offers little new information per se, it is the unique synthesis of that provides the real value. In the words of Robert Frost:

> Two roads diverged in a wood, and I—I took the road less traveled by. And that has made all the difference.

NOTES

1. P. Hawken, A.B. Lovins, and L.H. Lovins, *Natural Capitalism: The Next Industrial Revolution*. London: Earthscan Publications, 1999, p. 396.

2. D.L. Coutu, "Edgar H. Schein: The Anxiety of Learning." *Harvard Business Review* 80, March 3, 2002, pp. 100–106.

3. M.E. Porter, *Competitive Advantage: Creating and Sustaining Superior Performance*. New York: The Free Press, 1985, p. 557.

4. Technical Committee CEN/TC 279, "EN 12973:2000 Standard: Value Management." Brussels: European Committee for Standardization, 2000, p. 61.

5. In the CEN 12973 Standard.

6. See J. Pettit's, *EVA & Strategy*. New York: Stern Stewart & Co., 2000, p. 17.

7. See, for example, R.G. Eccles, "The Performance Measurement Manifesto," *Harvard Business Review*, January-February 1991, pp. 131–137, and R. Ernst and D.N. Ross, "The Delta Force Approach to Balancing Long-Run Performance," *Business Horizons*, May-June 1993, pp. 4–10.

8. "Change Management: An Inside Job." *The Economist* 356 (8179), 2000, p. 65.

9. See Graham Ward's speech on corporate governance at INSEAD at www.icaew.co.uk.

10. M.E. Jones and G. Sutherland, "Implementing Turnbull: A Boardroom Briefing." London: The Center for Business Performance, The Institute of Chartered Accountants in England and Wales (ICAEW), 1999, p. 34.

11. Ibid.

12. B. Bras and J. Emblemsvåg, "Designing for the Life-Cycle: Activity-Based Costing and Uncertainty." *Design for X: Concurring Engineering Imperatives*, ed, G.Q. Huang. London: Chapman & Hall, 1996, pp. 398–423.

13. H.T. Johnson and R.S. Kaplan, *Relevance Lost: The Rise and Fall of Management Accounting*. Boston, MA: Harvard Business School Press, 1987, p. 269 and Chapters 2 and 4.

14. N. Shepherd, "The Bridge to Continuous Improvement." *CMA*. March 1995, pp. 29–32.

15. R.A. Lutz, "Lutz's Laws: A Primer for the Business Side of Engineering." The George W. Woodruff Annual Distinguished Lecture, 1998. Atlanta, GA: Georgia Institute of Technology.

16. N. Bowie and H. Owen, "An Investigation into the Relationship Between Quality Improvement and Financial Performance." United Kingdom: Certified Accountants Educational Trust, 1996. Häversjö, T, "The Financial Effects of ISO 9000 Registration for Danish Companies." *Managerial Auditing Journal* 15 (No. 1 & 2), 2000, pp. 47–52.

17. H.T. Johnson, "It's Time to Stop Overselling Activity-Based Concepts." *Management Accounting*, September 1992.

18. H.P. Barringer, "Why You Need Practical Reliability Details to Define Life Cycle Costs for Your Products and Competitors Products!" New Orleans, LA: The 16th International Titanium Annual Conference & Exhibition, October 9–10, 2000.

19. S.M. Hronec and S.K. Hunt, "Quality and Cost Management," *Handbook of Cost Management*, ed, J.B. Edwards. Boston, MA: Warren, Gorham & Lamont, 1997, pp. A1.1–A1.42.

20. R. Cooper and R.S. Kaplan, "The Promise—and Peril—of Integrated Cost Systems." *Harvard Business Review,* July/August 1998, pp. 109 –119.

21. M. O'Guin, "Focus the Factory with Activity-Based Costing." *Management Accounting*, February 1990, pp. 36–41.

22. J.G. Miller and T.E. Vollmann, "The Hidden Factory." *Harvard Business Review,* September-October, 1985, pp. 142–150.

23. A. Kaufmann, "Advances in Fuzzy Sets: An Overview." *Advances in Fuzzy Sets, Possibility Theory, and Applications*, ed. P.P. Wang. New York: Plenum Press, 1983.

24. D.N. James, "The Trouble I've Seen." *Harvard Business Review* 80, March 3, 2002, pp. 42–49.

25. M.D. Shields, "An Empirical Analysis of Firms' Implementation Experiences with Activity-Based Costing." *Journal of Management Accounting Research* 7, Fall 1995, pp. 148–166.

26. For details, see "Change Management: An Inside Job." *The Economist* 356 (8179, 2000), p. 65.

2

BASICS OF LIFE-CYCLE COSTING

A cynic is one who knows the price of everything and the value of nothing.

Oscar Wilde

Before we start thinking about Life-Cycle Costing (LCC), a very basic concept must be clarified, namely the *life cycle*, and that is the topic in this chapter. After that, the purpose of LCC is discussed followed by a discussion on what cost is, because many people confuse cost with expense and even cash flow. An overview of the various LCC approaches is also provided.

WHAT IS A LIFE CYCLE?

The interpretation of the term *life cycle* differs from decision-maker to decision-maker, as is evident from the literature. A marketing executive will most likely think in terms of the *marketing perspective,* which consists of at least four stages[1]:

1. Introduction
2. Growth
3. Maturity
4. Decline

A manufacturer, on the other hand, will think in terms of the *production perspective,* which can be described using five main stages or processes:

1. Product conception
2. Design
3. Product and process development
4. Production
5. Logistics

When the product has reached the customer (user or consumer), a different perspective occurs: the *customer perspective*. This perspective often includes five stages or processes:

1. Purchase
2. Operating
3. Support
4. Maintenance
5. Disposal

Because the purchase price the customer pays is equal to the cost of the producer plus an add-on (profit), the life-cycle costs of the consumer perspective will most often be the most complete. This is important to realize and to turn into a competitive advantage, as Toyota did, for example. Over the years, Toyota has systematically worked toward minimizing total life-cycle costs, and this is something its customers have benefited from, as Toyota's cars are virtually problem-free after purchase. Toyota can actually charge a higher price than its competitors and increase its profits because its customers know that they also save money and hassles, a win-win situation for both customer and manufacturer. Unfortunately, traditional cost accounting methods give no decision support for such considerations, but that will be discussed later. In fact, most accounting regimes require that spending for intangibles like Research and Development (R&D) be treated as period costs. As a result, the current profit is reduced and financial measures like earnings per share drop despite the fact that such spending is essentially investments that take place into the future.[2] Traditional accounting practices therefore distort the picture and promote shortsightedness. In fact, it has been argued that "accounting practices often drive major business decisions despite—and not because of— the economics."[3]

That the customer perspective also incorporates the most costs is probably more often the case in relation to infrastructure than in relation to any other type of produce or service. For example, it has been estimated that "the operating costs of a school can consume the equivalent of its capital costs every 4 to 5 years and remain in service for a century."[4]

The three perspectives only consider "private" costs, that is, costs that directly impact a company's bottom line. The *societal perspective,* however, includes those activities (and associated costs) borne by society, such as:

- Disposal
- Externalities (see Glossary)

Concerning disposal costs, the trend now internationally is that they are becoming the cost of the manufacturer or the user. For example, in both Germany and Norway, various take-back legislation exists. Thus, as societies become more affluent and knowledgeable, it is likely that it will become increasingly difficult for companies to escape from their social responsibilities.

Finally, we have the most comprehensive perspective, namely that of the product itself, as shown in Figure 2.1. The product life cycle is essentially all the activ-

ities that the product, or parts of the product, undergo regardless of which decision-makers are involved. It may therefore involve all the proceeding perspectives
except one: the marketing perspective. The reason is that the product life cycle is
on the *individual* level of each product unit, whereas the marketing perspective is
on the *type* level of a product. By the same token, if we compare the product life
cycle depicted in Figure 2.1 to the life cycle illustrated in Figure 2.3, we see that
the product life cycle always consists of processes and activities, whereas the market life cycle in does not. Of course, underlying activities in addition to factors in
the business environment are needed to sustain or improve a product in a specific
stage or to move it to another stage. The stages themselves, however, are neither
processes nor activities. They are related to the market situation as characterized
by being new or old (introduction or decline) or the amount of sales (growth, maturity, and decline), as shown later in Table 2.2.

In this book, this life cycle is therefore denoted as the *market life cycle* and not
product life cycle, which is the common denomination, particularly in management literature. In my opinion, the term *product life cycle* logically fits the life
cycle shown in Figure 2.1 better than the one shown in Figure 2.3. Furthermore,
this book focuses on the product life cycle and not so much on the market life
cycle. However, because the underlying mechanisms of the market life cycle are
processes and activities, the approach presented in this book can easily be adopted
to market life-cycle issues. In any case, two genuinely unique life cycles exist: one
on the individual product level (the product life cycle) and one on the product-type
level (the market life cycle).

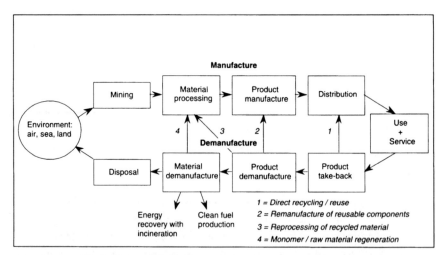

Figure 2.1   Generic representation of a product life cycle. Source: J. Emblemsvåg and
B. Bras, *Activity-Based Cost and Environmental Management: A Different Approach to
the ISO 14000 Compliance.* Boston: Kluwer, 2000, p. 317.

Product Life Cycle

The product life cycle is comprised of the activities an individual part of the product, or parts of the product, undergoes regardless of which decision-makers are involved, as shown in Figure 2.1. For each activity, or process, in Figure 2.1, more detailed activities can be defined depending on the specific products and processes involved. A manufacturer will typically focus on the upper half of the figure, whereas the customer typically thinks of the right-hand side of the figure. Until recently, the lower half of the figure was left to society to handle, while nobody thought of the left-hand side. But as environmental problems have increased, from the 1950s on, more and more laws and regulations have been made to respond to public demands. In fact, in 1991 the United Nations Environmental Program (UNEP) listed 141 global, legally binding treaties concerning the environment that add to the several thousand agreements, conventions, and protocols on environmental issues. Today the number is probably much higher.

All these new laws and regulations have created a compliance pressure for the industry, but they have also opened up potential liabilities in the future, such as the liabilities the tobacco industry is facing. Many companies have realized that the only way to manage this situation is to be proactive, and in fact many are way ahead of laws and regulations because they are convinced this is a great investment opportunity for those who are prepared. For example, the world-leading carpet tile manufacturer, Interface, Inc., is aiming toward becoming the first sustainable enterprise in history[5] and Percy Barnevik, the CEO of ABB, the Swedish-Swiss engineering giant, claimed that "industry is the driving force these days" in an interview with *Newsweek* in 1998. Other companies have also made great progress, and many of their initiatives have one common denominator: They involve product and/or process (re)design. Many of them also involve the lower half of Figure 2.1.

To achieve such success, companies must think in terms of design. Many new design methods and approaches have therefore been developed in the last 10 to 15 years, such as life-cycle design and design for X. Also, many new terms have been coined, such as *cradle to grave*, *reincarnation*, and *end of life*. In fact, some refer to LCC in this context as environmental LCC (see also the discussion in Chapter 1). This is because LCC has other roots than in the environmental domain, which will be discussed later, but it has seen almost a renaissance in recent years due to the environmental issues.

What is important about the lower half of the product life cycle is that several different end-of-life strategies exist and each strategy has advantages and disadvantages. The first end-of-life issue to discuss is whether to take back the products or not and, if so, what to do with them. Some companies will be forced to take back their own products due to laws and regulations, as mentioned earlier. Others may do this voluntarily, as Interface, Inc., did because it is good business. The third option is that a third party takes back the products. If none of the above options occur, the product will be disposed of.

After a product has been retrieved from the marketplace, it can be either directly reused or demanufactured. Direct reuse is the best option in terms of both costs and environmental impact, but selling directly reused products may be difficult. Ironically, the farther to the left we come in the lower half of Figure 2.1, the easier it seems to be to sell the product, but the more downgraded it is. So typically a product would have to be demanufactured in order to be economically interesting.

As the term indicates, demanufacturing is the opposite of manufacturing, that is, it involves taking the product apart. During demanufacturing, several different paths must be taken:

- **Disassembly** The product is taken apart *without* destroying any parts or components. Some products may undergo only this process, which occurs if the reusable parts are sold (the product loop is closed) whereas the rest is recycled.
- **Remanufacturing** This is an industrial process that restores worn products to like-new condition. A retired product is first completely disassembled, and its usable parts are then cleaned, refurbished, and put into inventory. Finally, a new product is reassembled from both old and new parts, creating a unit equal in performance to the original or a currently available alternative. In contrast, a repaired or rebuilt product usually retains its identify, and only those parts that have failed or are badly worn are replaced.[6] Remanufacturing is therefore a systematic way of closing the product loop.
- **Material demanufacture** Products and components that cannot be reused or remanufactured are broken down further into either simpler products (polymers are broken down into smaller polymers) or incinerated for energy recovery purposes. The simpler products can be either consumed (as fuel, for example) or used in material regeneration (the material loop is closed).
- **Recycling** In this process, material is reprocessed into "new" raw material. This is, in other words, the same as closing the materials loop. Recycling is perhaps the most common strategy to closing the loop, but it is the least effective one in the sense that it is the most wasteful strategy (except disposal).
- **Disposal** The last resort is disposal, which ideally should not happen at all. In fact, Interface, Inc. aims toward totally eliminating disposal from its value chain.[7] But in the grand scale, disposal is the most common of all end-of-life strategies. In fact, less than 2 percent of the total waste stream is actually recycled, primarily paper, glass, plastic, aluminum, and steel. Over the course of a decade, 500 trillion pounds of American resources have been transformed into nonproductive solids and gases.[8]

Once an end-of-life strategy has been chosen, the design job begins. Of course, the strategy is chosen in relation to what is feasible given the current product mix, but over time the products and their value chains should be designed concurrently to fit each other. In any case, depending on the scale of the temporal and organizational concerns, seven major umbrella terms are pertinent to look at, both from a strategic and a design-related perspective (see Figure 2.2). It is, after all, a quite different task to become sustainable than to run environmental engineering programs, and this must be reflected in everything in the company (vision, strategy, product mix, suppliers, and so on).

Under each umbrella are a huge variety of methods, approaches, and tools. All these approaches, however, can be grouped into three according to their relation to the product life cycle: those that are applied *within* a single product life cycle and focus on *specific* life-cycle stages, those that focus on a *complete* product life cycle and cover *all* life-cycle stages, and those that go *beyond* single product life cycles.

For this book, it suffices to acknowledge that these methods exist and that LCC should be used in conjunction with useful design methods. LCC and other performance measurement techniques can, after all, only direct attention and indicate paths of improvements; they cannot actually improve anything.

Market Life Cycle

The marketing perspective is the background for the market life cycle. This life-cycle concept may be defined as the "progression of a specific product (service) from mar-

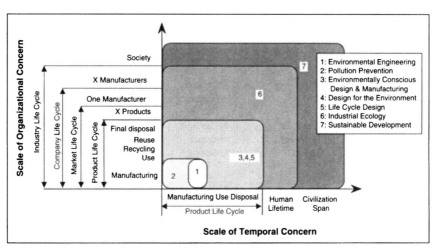

Figure 2.2 Environmental and organizational scales of environmental impact reduction approaches. Source: Adapted from S. Coulter, B.A. Bras, and C. Foley, "A Lexicon of Green Engineering Terms," 10th International Conference on Engineering Design (ICED 1995), Praha, Heurista, Zürich, 1995, pp. 1033–1039.

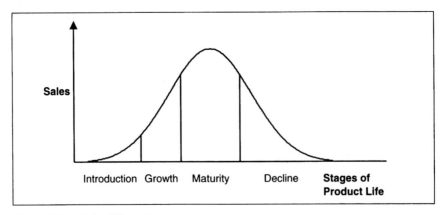

Figure 2.3 Market life cycle.

ket development to market decline."[9] The market life cycle is therefore also conceptually strikingly similar to industry life cycles, business life cycles, and even human life cycles as they all go through the same four generic stages (see Figure 2.3). The shape of the curve will of course depend on many different situational factors.

Although, Figure 2.3 is symmetric, this situation is not likely to occur in reality. The figure should only be interpreted schematically. As noted earlier, seven-stage models can also be found in the literature, but the crux is the same.

In Table 2.1, the different typical characteristics and responses related to the four stages are shown. It is important to be aware of the fact that a product in the

Table 2.1 Market Life Cycle: Characteristics and Responses

Stages of Cycle	Introduction	Growth	Maturity	Decline
Characteristics:				
Sales	Small	Substantial	Maximum	Falling
Profit	Loss	Accelerating	Declining	Low or negative
Cash flow	Negative	Negligible	Large	Low
Customers	Innovative	Early user	Mass market	Laggards
Competitors	Few	Increasing	Stable	Fewer
Responses:				
Strategic focus	Expand market	Develop share	Defend share	Retrenching
Marketing expenditures	Highest	High	Falling	Low
Promotion	Product attributes	Brand preference	Brand loyalty	Eliminated
Distribution	Limited	Broad	Maximum	Selective
Price	Highest	High	Lower	Lowest
Product	Basic	Extensions	Quality	Narrower

Source: Adapted from F. Allvine, *Marketing: Principles and Practices*. Boston, MA: Irwin/McGraw-Hill, 1996.

decline stage can be repositioned in the market, but if it has gone too far, only two options are available. The best is usually to discontinue the product as soon as other products can more profitably utilize the resources earlier allocated to that particular product, but often companies keep their products too long. However, products can be made profitable for some time by using a retrenching program. Such programs would typically attempt to appeal to customers' sentimental attachments to the products and increase the price up front to an announced discontinuation of the product. Volkswagen, for example, increased the price of its convertible as the company announced plans to drop the product.[10]

Clearly, "What is a life cycle?" is not possible to answer straightforwardly using a simple definition. All life-cycle terminology is subject to considerable confusion. The U.S. Environmental Protection Agency (EPA), for example, states that "some people view life-cycle costing as referring only to private costs, while others view it as including both private and societal costs." Hence, it is important to define the purpose of the analysis in order to define an appropriate life cycle and consequently a suitable cost base.

Luckily, Activity-Based LCC is a process-oriented method, and defining the correct life cycle is therefore quite easy. The difficulty lies in defining the activities so that reliable data can be found, but this and more will be discussed in Chapters 4 and 5.

In the "Purpose of LCC" section, the purpose of LCC is discussed, but first the difference between a life cycle and a value chain must be explained.

Differences between the Life Cycle and the Value Chain

The definitions of a life cycle (product/market life cycle) may seem elusive, whereas value chain was defined quite straightforwardly as a basic tool for systematically examining all the activities a firm performs, and how the firm interacts is necessary for analyzing the sources of competitive advantage.[11] Yet the value-chain idea became "one of the most discussed and misunderstood in the whole of the management area"[12] in the decade after its launch in 1985.

Later the term *value chain* has come to mean three things (see Glossary). Its original definition was simply as a tool, but it came to be seen as any set of value-creating activities up to the final consumer. It is also defined as the set of activities required to design, procure, produce, market, distribute, and service a product or service. Value chain is therefore no longer so crisply defined as it once was.

Regardless of what definition we choose for the value chain, we see that at least one major difference exists between life cycle and value chain: The value chain takes the perspective of a specific company. The life-cycle definitions, however, follow the product, which has significant implications in the case of the product life cycle. In a product life cycle, many decision-makers are normally involved, such as suppliers, the producer, customers, and so on. The life cycle has also a longer chain of activities, from cradle to grave, and consequently the time horizon is also longer. The life cycle is therefore a more generic, less limiting concept than the value chain, and that is why I prefer the concept life cycle to value chain. However, in many cases an Activity-Based LCC implementation will essentially be a value-chain costing implementation.

Purpose of LCC

As most concepts, LCC has evolved over time, and today LCC serves three main purposes:

1. LCC can be an effective engineering tool for providing decision support in the design and procurement of major open systems, infrastructure, and so on. This was the original intent for which it was developed.
2. LCC overcomes many of the shortcomings of traditional cost accounting and can therefore give useful cost insights in cost accounting and management.
3. LCC has reemerged as a design and engineering tool for environmental purposes.

LCC as an Engineering Tool

LCC is a concept originally developed by the U.S. Department of Defense (DoD) in the early 1960s to increase the effectiveness of government procurement. Two related purposes were to encourage a longer planning horizon that would include operating and support costs and increase cost savings by increasing spending on design and development. The traditional approaches of making decisions on the initial procurement costs, often derived from simple rules, "are so cheap that they are not affordable."[13] From the very beginning, LCC has therefore been closely related to design and development because it was realized early that it is better to eliminate costs before they are incurred instead of trying to cut costs after they are incurred. This represents a paradigm shift away from cost cutting to cost control during design.

In fact, the Institute for Defense Analyses (IDA) has estimated that 70 percent of the costs during the life of a weapons system are determined during the design and development phase.[14] Others claim that 80 to 90 percent of the manufacturing costs are committed during the design and testing phases, as discussed in Chapter 1. In any case, the traditional approach of cost cutting is a very ineffective one.

Since the beginning of LCC roughly 40 years ago, the concept has spread from defense-related matters to a variety of industries and problems. The common denominator seems to be that LCC is mostly applied by companies and public institutions that either procure or manufacture large capital goods, facilities, weapons systems, and other products (or systems) that are *open*. An open system is a system that evolves over time and changes with its environment. For example, the aircraft carrier the *USS Enterprise* was first commissioned in 1961 but is still in service. During those 40-plus years, it has naturally undergone many updates, repairs, major maintenance jobs, and so on. The costs of building the *USS Enterprise* therefore was minor compared to the costs incurred during its life span, and this illustrates why it is so important to perform LCC analysis before making decisions. Many, if not most, open systems incur *more* costs during their life span than the purchasing costs. For example, the cost of sustaining equipment is frequently 2 to 20 times the acquisition costs.[15] Assessing, eliminating by design, or managing the downstream costs as well as their associated risks and uncertainties are therefore vital for both the manufacturer and the purchaser because:

- The downstream costs after purchasing will most likely be very significant and should therefore play a major role in purchasing decisions.
- The knowledge about downstream costs and their associated risks and uncertainty can be used during negotiations both when it comes to costs/pricing and risk management.
- The simulation of downstream costs can be very useful in designing the products so that the costs are eliminated even before they are incurred.

Essentially, LCC in an engineering context helps engineers think like MBAs but act like engineers. But why was it necessary to come up with a new concept to assess the life-cycle costs?

LCC as Decision Support for Management

Historically, engineers were heavily involved in managing the costs in companies. For example, the well-known Standard Costing method was developed in the 1870s by the American Society of Mechanical Engineers (ASME), although it was not commonly in use until the 1920s or even later.[16] At the time, factories were technologically simple and labor intensive and product variety was very limited. We have all heard a version of Henry Ford's famous statement that "you can have any color Model T that you'd like—as long as it is black." The degree of overhead was therefore very low, and it made perfect sense to allocate costs according to direct labor hours. The costing systems at the time consequently had sufficient managerial relevance.

Around 1920, however, laws were passed that required companies to provide various estimates for tax purposes. After this, cost management became more and more externally and financially oriented. Consequently, it gradually lost its managerial relevance particularly when major business environmental changes came about after World War II.

Arguably, one of the most important is the invention of the digital computer, which in the simplest form is known as Programmable Logic Controllers (PLCs), and PLCs are the precursors to the personal computer (PC). The result was an explosion in product variety at affordable prices due to the new manufacturing technologies that enabled mass production at an unprecedented scale. This required more support in the companies, and overhead grew increasingly. These days, surveys indicate that overhead costs constitute roughly 35 percent of an average American company, whereas 100 years ago it was somewhere around 10 percent. This should indicate that the costing systems invented more than 100 years ago are long outdated, and indeed they are; they have lost their relevance in managerial accounting, as H. Thomas Johnson and Robert S. Kaplan argued in their famous book, *Relevance Lost: The Rise and Fall of Management Accounting*.[17]

Traditional cost accounting is capable of handling only a relatively small part of the costs, despite the fact that a company's bottom line incorporates total costs. In other words, traditional cost accounting can focus only on partial costs, not total costs.

Companies simply cannot afford to segregate cost accounting from design, engineering, production, and other core business processes as in the good old days. Nowadays, even the customer relationships must be scrutinized by cost accounting because keeping the customers satisfied has both an upside and a downside (costs). The four walls of the company are basically no longer the borders. This puts new challenges on management that traditional cost accounting techniques have little chance of handling well.

These facts were unpleasantly revealed to many western companies in the 1980s due to the tough competition from primarily Japanese companies. The Japanese had long realized that it is better to eliminate costs via design than to cut costs during production, which was pretty much the western approach. But because many studies concluded that up to 85 percent of production costs are committed before even a single unit of the product is manufactured, new approaches were needed. One of the approaches people turned to was LCC. In fact, it was said that "LCC is an accounting methodology that became very popular in the 1980s, when the increasing competitive pressure on most markets forced firms to improve their capability to control and reduce manufacturing costs."[18] Hence, the LCC principles of the 1960s became pertinent during the 1980s for a quite larger context than procurement, and in this book I try to take it a step further.

LCC in the Environmental Domain

Over the years many approaches have been presented to assist environmental management. Recently, the ISO 14000 Environmental Management System standard has received much attention. Although this set of 14 distinct standards is comprehensive and covers many interesting topics, they have failed to provide something basic for the industry, namely comparability. In fact, some researchers themselves admit that "it is not possible to give a general rank of priorities of strategies and options for improvements." This is a serious problem that lies inherently in their performance measurement standards (particularly the ISO 14040 series) and will not be remedied by more accurate data and scientific understanding.[19]

Despite such dedicated and thorough attempts in managing environmental issues that ISO and others can show, LCC has remained one of the premier environmental management tools. LCC has the potential of being a more effective decision-making tool than conventional LCA for reasons such as:

- Cost is often a more reliable indicator of resource consumption than any physical analysis because the economic system systematically captures many more difficult-to-trace subtle interactions than an ad hoc approach can.
- Costs provide a more direct measure compared to scientific measures (such as gigajoules of energy) that do not reflect marginal economic effects relating to resource scarcity.
- Priority setting in environmental improvement projects can be very difficult in view of the profusion of available options. The environmental improvements combined with cost reduction can greatly facilitate this process.
- It is easy to promote the results of environmental studies if related cost savings can be demonstrated.
- The data needed for LCC calculations are generally easily accessible. In fact, they are much easier to access than the detailed process data needed for carrying out Life-Cycle Assessment (LCA) studies, as several in the literature have pointed out.
- The LCC information regarding a product can be a real eye-opener to management by revealing hitherto unidentified cost drivers.[20]

Thus, not only can LCC aid in making cost management more relevant and proactive, which was the original intent, but LCC can be useful in aiding companies toward "doing (economically) well by doing (environmentally) good." Thus, LCC has grown substantially in scope over the 40 years the concept has been around.

Before proceeding, it should be noted that these points do not apply to all LCA methods, except for the point about data being easily accessible. A method called Activity-Based Cost and Environmental Management can be used for conducting integrated cost and environmental management according to Activity-Based Costing (ABC) principles.[21] The result is that environmental issues can be managed just as closely as economic issues, given that data are available. In fact, Activity-Based LCC can be viewed as a subset of the Activity-Based Cost and Environmental Management method. In this book, it is therefore focused on LCC, cost management (as a managerial tool), and related issues.

We have now discussed what a life cycle is as well as the purpose of studying it and assigning costs to it. We need to understand the concept of costs, because a great deal of confusion exists in the literature and among practitioners, particularly in the field of environmental management.

WHAT IS A COST?

Two terms are often used incorrectly or interchangeably, both in the literature and among practitioners, including the undersigned, namely cost and expense. This is probably partly due to language simplifications but also to ignorance. Let us therefore look at what a cost is and what an expense is.

Cost is a measure of resource consumption related to the demand for jobs to be done, whereas expense is a measure of spending that relates to the capacity provided to do a job.[22] For example, a stamping machine costs $100 daily to operate and it can stamp 10,000 coins per day. One day, only 5,000 coins are stamped. The expense is $100 because that is the capacity provided, which shows up in the books, but the cost of stamping the coins is only $50. Hence, this day there was a surplus capacity worth $50.

It is the resource consumption perspective that counts, because management must match capacity to demand and not the other way around. In our example, management must consider if the excess capacity should be kept or removed, not stamp more coins than demanded because that only drives costs, and the risks of producing obsolete coins increase. However, in most companies, the latter is the case because "producing to capacity rather than to demand often appears to reduce costs."[23] This in turn leads to overinvestment and surplus capacity for companies with significant free cash flow, which further erodes profits. In such cases, debt is a greater good because their cost systems foster erroneous decisions but debt introduces spending discipline.

While the logical consequence of this is that an LCC model should represent the cost/resource consumption perspective, from the literature we see that most LCC models are actually cash flow models or expense models at best.

Cash flow models are necessities in situations where revenues and their related costs occur in different time periods. Cash flow models are important to ensure sufficient liquidity, but they cannot replace cost models. Also, it is important to take the time value of money into account using a discounting factor, because, as we have all heard, "it is better to earn one dollar today than one dollar tomorrow." The time value of money is, however, not confined to cash flow models, but this will be discussed in greater detail in Chapter 3 because risk and uncertainty is closely related to time and value. In any case, such models are always used in investment analyses, which in some ways are like LCC analyses. But what is the difference?

In the wide sense, an investment is a sacrifice of something now for the prospect of something later. Furthermore, "we see two different factors involved, *time* and *risk*. The sacrifice takes place in the present and is certain. The reward comes later, if at all, and the magnitude may be uncertain."[24] Depending on the type of sacrifice, we are talking about *financial investment* and *real investments*. Financial investments typically involve assets that can be quickly liquidated (cash, stocks, and bonds). Financial investment analyses therefore include cash flow analyses and financial performance measures. Real investments, on the other hand, concern physical (real) assets that depreciate over time, such as buildings and equipment, and their economic evaluation is variously referred to as economic analysis, engineering economy, and economic decision analysis. Hence, real investment analyses *can* in principle be the same as LCC, whereas financial investment analyses are not. Furthermore, LCC may or may not include consideration of the time value of money. That depends on the scope of the LCC, which is discussed in Chapter 5.

Expense models typically support environmental initiatives and policies by including the expenses and benefits that are derived from the effects of the environment on the General Ledger while expenses outside the four walls of the organization are included when possible or desirable. Such practices go under many names in the literature, such as environmental accounting, environmental cost accounting, life-cycle accounting, total cost accounting, green accounting, full-cost accounting, and full-cost environmental accounting. Depending on whom you ask, these practices can be anything from essentially financial reporting and analysis of environmental aspects as they show on the General Ledger to a national income accounting. The managerial relevance therefore varies considerably.

This proliferation of terminology and the associated confusion has also led to many different definitions of what a life-cycle cost is. Some of the better definitions are:

- The sum total of the direct, indirect, recurring, nonrecurring, and other related costs incurred, or estimated to be incurred, in the design, development, production, operation, maintenance, and support of a major system over its anticipated useful life span.[25]
- The amortized annual cost of a product, including capital costs, installation costs, operating costs, maintenance costs, and disposal costs discounted over the lifetime of a product.[26]
- The total cost throughout its (an asset's) life, including planning, design, acquisition and support costs, and any other costs directly attributable to owing or using the asset.[27]

To keep things simple, in this book the life-cycle cost for a product is defined as "the total costs that are incurred, or may be incurred, in all stages of the product life cycle." This simple definition relies on the definition of the product life cycle and will therefore vary from product to product. It must be so, because LCC is a decision-support tool that must match the purpose and not an external, financial reporting system that should obey rigid principles, such as the U.S. GAAP.

LCC is therefore defined more widely in this book than what is common. That is by intention, because LCC should be just as much an approach to capture future costs as it is a technique to compute *the life-cycle cost* for a specific product. After all, ABC goes well beyond assessing the costs of the activities. Thus, just as ABC employs activities as a core element in its costing assignment, I suggest using a specific life-cycle definition as a premise for a specific LCC analysis. By doing it this way, we do not have to use all the different acronyms and terms that plague the environmental accounting field in particular.

It is not, as some seem to believe, that having many accurate terms makes life easier, because as Hegel said, "Theories conceal as much as they reveal." It is better to keep things simple and rather concentrate on understanding the essentials and how they relate to reality. As Nanquan explains to Zhaozhou in *Case 19* of *Gateless Barrier*:

> Zhaozhou asked Nanquan, "What is the way?"
> Nanquan said, "Ordinary mind is the way."
> Zhaozhou asked, "Shall I try for that?"
> Nanquan said, "If you try, you'll miss it."
> Zhaozhou asked, "How do I know it's the way if I don't try?"
> Nanquan said, "The way has nothing to do with knowing or not knowing. Knowing is illusion; not knowing is ignorance. If you penetrate the way of no-trying, it will be open—empty and vast. What need is there to affirm this or deny it?"
> Zhaozhou was suddenly enlightened upon hearing this.

To better understand the costs in a life-cycle perspective, the next two sections provide discussions and some examples regarding *categories* of costs (and expenses) and business activities that create cost, that is, a demand for jobs to be done.

Categories of Life-Cycle Costs

Costs can be categorized in numerous ways, and some are more useful than others, at least on a general basis. Two main categories exist: (1) acquisition costs and (2) sustaining costs. These categories are then broken down into some generic *cost trees* that are memory joggers. This way of categorizing costs is handy for a certain type of LCC problem, such as the replacement and procurement of equipment, but it does not work on a general basis.

In general, four types of costs must be considered (usual, hidden, liability, and less tangible) in a product life cycle, regardless of the scale of the organizational concern (discussed in Figure 2.2). The costs and expenses referred to as usual costs include, for example:

- Capital costs:
  - Buildings
  - Equipment
- Expenses:
  - Labor
  - Supplies
  - Raw materials
  - Utilities
  - Disposal
- Revenues:
  - Primary product
  - Marketable byproducts

As the name indicates, these are the costs—or expenses, to be accurate—that traditional accounting methods usually handle. Traditional cost-cutting exercises often cut such costs, and not without reason; they are usually the largest costs in a company.

The second cost category is the hidden costs. These costs are typically associated with regulation of some sort. In traditional cost accounting, these costs are lumped together in the big bag of overhead costs that is usually allocated to products normally using direct labor or direct machine hours as allocation bases. This way of allocating costs leads to large cost distortions and wrong cost allocation, which is why a new method called ABC (see Chapter 4 for a full description) was designed in the 1980s. ABC has overcome these shortcomings and proved highly useful (see Table 4.12), yet a few years later surveys reported that 94 percent of the surveyed companies still used direct labor as an allocation base. Basically, the companies went on as before. Nonetheless, these costs should be found and eliminated or reduced because they are usually nonvalue-added costs. Some examples of such hidden costs are:

- Capital costs:
  - Monitoring equipment
  - Preparedness and protective equipment
  - Additional technology
- Expenses:
  - Reporting
  - Notification
  - Monitoring/testing
  - Record keeping
  - Planning/studies/planning
  - Training
  - Inspections

- ○ Manifesting
- ○ Labeling
- ○ Preparedness and protective equipment
- ○ Closure/postclosure care
- ○ Medical surveillance
- ○ Insurance/special taxes

The third type of costs is liability costs, or costs that arise due to noncompliance and potential future liabilities. These costs are also referred to as contingent costs by some. Depending on the type of costs, these costs traditionally will either be handled as overhead costs and be put in the big bag of poorly allocated costs, or be handled as extraordinary costs. An example of these costs would be the cleanup costs of the so-called Superfund sites in the United States, which were estimated to be between $300 and $700 billion as of 1991.[28]

Since liability costs include future liabilities, it is difficult to estimate them; environmental liability costs are particularly difficult to estimate and hence probably understated. Nonetheless, here are some examples:

- Legal staff and/or consultants
- Penalties and fines
- Future liabilities from customer injury
- Future liabilities from hazardous waste sites:
  - ○ Soil and waste removal and treatment
  - ○ Groundwater removal and treatment
  - ○ Surface sealing
  - ○ Personal injury (health care and insurance ramifications)
  - ○ Economic loss
  - ○ Real property damage
  - ○ Natural resource damage
  - ○ Other

The last category of less tangible costs, or image and relationship costs, as some denote such costs, are very difficult to estimate. They are, however, far from unimportant as is evident from the following examples:

- Customer acceptance
- Customer loyalty
- Worker morale/union relations
- Corporate image
- Brand name
- Stakeholder relations

One of the classic examples of such less intangible costs and the effect on a company is the introduction of New Coke by the Coca-Cola Company on April 23, 1985.

Preliminary taste tests concluded that New Coke was "better" than the old Coke because during blind testing they found that people preferred the New Coke taste. But this was a classic market research error, because what Coca-Cola completely failed to take into account was the fact that people ascribed a certain taste to the brand Coca-Cola. Thus, when New Coke was released on the market, it became an instant failure. The sweeter and less carbonated New Coke was to many more like Pepsi-Cola than Coca-Cola. Suddenly, millions of customers thought that Pepsi, not Coke, was the "Real Thing." After New Coke spent only 77 days on the market, Coca-Cola had to quickly reintroduce the old Coca-Cola under the new name Classic Coke. Most will agree this was a huge embarrassment for Coca-Cola. But according to chairman Roberto Goizueta, the introduction of New Coke was the best thing that ever could have happened for Coca-Cola because it taught management a valuable lesson as to why the company has one of the highest returns on investment of any U.S. company today.[29] This goes to show that although the costs of a catastrophe can be great, if handled properly, the lessons taken from it can be a turning point for the better. Indeed, *catastrophe* is a Greek word that originally means turning point.

An example from the environmental domain is the *Exxon Valdez* accident in Alaska in 1989. Prior to the accident, Exxon said it saved $22 million on building the *Exxon Valdez* with a single hull (as opposed to a double hull). But then came the accident in Prince William Sound. Exxon spent roughly $2 billion just on cleaning up, yet it captured only 12 percent of the 11 million gallons spilled. Law suits followed from both the state of Alaska and a group of 14,000 fishermen and citizens in the region. The state demanded compensatory and punitive damages possibly in excess of $1 billion, while the people in the region sought punitive damages of $15 billion. In September 1994, Exxon was ordered to pay $5.3 billion, with $4 billion for environmental costs and $1 billion as retribution for insensitivity. But Exxon appealed both damage awards, won, and avoided paying both the damages and any interest on them. In the end, the fishermen and fisheries were awarded $286 million as compensatory damages for losses incurred as a result of not being able to fish in the area of the spill. In any case, Exxon ended up paying in excess of $2 billion as almost a direct result of saving $22 million. But these are only tangible costs. What about the costs related to the corporate image or loss of confidence?

These various types of costs are associated with various degrees of quantification difficulty, as illustrated in Figure 2.4. On the right, we have the so-called externalities or costs that are external to the economic system. Basically, we just know that they exist but cannot really provide any meaningful cost quantification. Many in the literature refer to external costs or externalities as societal costs. I do not subscribe to that view because it does not acknowledge the fact that some costs are simply incomprehensible in an economic sense; they are external to the economic system, hence the name. For example, what is the cost of clearing 1,000 km^2 of

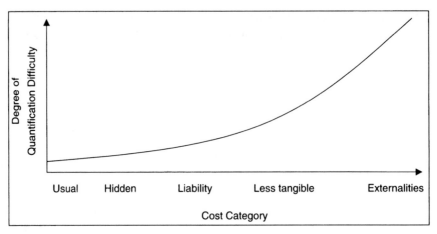

Figure 2.4   The difficulty of quantifying costs.

rain forest? Clearly, we can identify the labor costs, the costs of machinery, admin-istrational costs, the costs to the local society, and so on, but what is the cost of the potential loss of an indigenous species? Maybe we lost a plant that could provide cancer medicine. What cost is that?

From my point of view, four economic cost categories exist (usual, hidden, lia-bility, and less tangible) as well as an external category (externalities). These five different categories exist in all organizational concerns and even individual con-cerns. For example, a manufacturer has usual, hidden, liability, less tangible, and external costs. The external costs of a manufacturer are in many cases societal costs, but some will also be externalities (this is the point that I feel many in the literature miss).

The same logic applies to society as well as an individual. The cost categoriza-tion is therefore two-dimensional: (1) the obvious cost category dimension, as shown in Figure 2.4, and (2) the less obvious organizational concern dimension. These two dimensions are inseparable. Thus, we should not talk about a cost cat-egory without also specifying the organizational concern. For example, if we talk about a hidden cost, we must say "hidden" with respect to what? The department? The company? The society? Nature?

Business Activities That Create Costs

Most companies work with environmental issues in some form or another. Typically, they implement product stewardship programs, pollution prevention con-trol programs, and/or environmental accounting systems, particularly the latter two. Table 2.2 lists possible costs associated with a pollution prevention program.

Table 2.2 Examples of Production and Environmental Costs Firms May Incur

Labor	Materials	Equipment	Other
Production work	Raw materials	Production equipment	Depreciation
Material handling	Solvents	Cleansing/degreasing	Waste disposal
Inspection	Process water	Material-handling machinery	Insurance
Record-keeping	Cleaning water	Waste treatment	Utilities
Manifesting	Office supplies	Wastewater treatment	Regulatory fees
Labeling	Training materials	Air pollution control	Taxes
Stocking	Safety materials	Painting equipment	Maintenance
Training	Parts	Protective equipment	Lab fees
Permitting		Storage equipment	

Source: Adapted from S. Perkins and T. Goldberg, *Improving Your Competitive Position: Strategic and Financial Assessment of Pollution Prevention Investments.* Boston, MA: The Northeast Waste Management Officials' Association, 1998, p. 81.

The importance of environmental accounting can be exemplified by a study in which "one major US oil company was found to have environmental costs equal to 20% of its operating costs, far in excess of the 2–3% initial estimate."

Lately, Corporate Social Responsibility (CSR) has been added to the list. Such programs will inevitably create the need for environmental compliance activities and related oversight activities to be performed. These activities will come in addition to all the other activities, and thus managing environmental costs seems to become more and more important.

An organization that has an effective environmental cost accounting system, however, will reap greater benefits from having the system than the costs of keeping the system. As one study claimed, "environmental cost accounting is an appropriate instrument to ensure legal compliance at lower costs." In fact, another study estimated in 1997 that companies could reduce their total costs by 5 percent with a decision-oriented environmental management system, showing more than 1,000 examples of how companies could reduce costs through environmental protection. Why companies have not understood these potential reductions, and some of them are very obvious, is probably a product of accounting systems that push for over-investment in capacity, as explained in "What Is a Cost?"

Environmental cost accounting most frequently explicitly reports and analyzes the costs in the two right columns of Table 2.2 as they appear in the General Ledger, in addition to the traditional costs in the left column that are always analyzed. This has the advantage of making the environmental compliance costs and the related oversight costs visible; normally they are just lumped together in the big sack of general overhead costs, which makes environmental cost accounting, and ultimately environmental management impossible.

Concerning the discussion we had earlier about expenses versus costs, we see that even the heading of Table 2.2 speaks solely of costs, although in fact a mixture of costs and expenses exists. This may be confusing, but it is common and almost unavoidable. The point, however, is not to get stuck in terminology but to realize that a fundamental difference exists between costs and expenses, namely the measure of the demand for jobs to be done versus the capacity provided to do the jobs, respectively. This is important for cost management purposes, but it is also important in relation to challenging the ruling theory of the business. The reason is that faulty cost management sustains this theory by indirectly creating myths about what is profitable and what is not. Challenging these theories is vital for companies to sustain long-term profitability: "What underlies the malaise of so many large and successful organizations worldwide is that their theory of business no longer works."[30]

FOUR WAYS OF LCC

Depending on the amount of resources available, the time available, the degree of accuracy, and other factors such as data availability, four main different ways of performing LCC exist: analogy, parametric, engineering cost methods, and cost accounting.[31] The different ways are, as everything, suspect to different advantages and disadvantages.

Analogy Models

An LCC estimate made by an analogy identifies a similar product or component and adjusts its costs for differences between it and the target product. This way of conducting LCC is common in shipbuilding, for example, where mass is the factor they relate costs to.

In the energy sector, we find approaches such as exergy costing, which is a part of exergoeconomics or thermoeconomics. The essence of exergoeconomics is that it "combines a detailed exergy (exergy is the availability to do work) analysis with appropriate cost balances to study and optimize the performance of energy systems. The analyses and balances are usually formulated for single components of an energy system. Exergy costing, one of the basic principles of exergoeconomics, means that exergy, rather than energy or mass, should serve as a basis for costing energy carriers."[32] In the literature, exergy costing has also been used in the complete life cycle of an energy system.

This way of handling costs may sound utterly crude, and it is. It says nothing about direct labor or overhead costs. It simply looks at what the costs have been historically and scales them according to the most important cost driver, which in shipbuilding is mass and in some energy systems is exergy. Such methods can serve well when extensive historical material is available, the products are produced unit by unit (such as a shipyard producing ferries), one dominant cost driver is used, and the products do not differ much (such as in size, technology, use patterns, and operational characteristics). It is crucial that the products are produced unit by unit because that effectively reduces cost allocation issues to virtually nothing. By the same token, the existence of a dominant cost driver is paramount because otherwise the analogy has no basis. To ensure the relevance of historical data, it is vital that the products do not change much. Thus, such methods have limited usage.

This book does not discuss such ways of performing LCC because it is simple and well established. You don't need to read this book to do analogy LCC, although Chapter 3 on uncertainty and risk management may be useful.

Parametric Models

Parametric models are in many ways more advanced analogy models. A parametric LCC model is based on predicting a product's or a component's cost either in total or for various activities by using several models describing the relationships between costs and some product- or process-related parameters. The predicting variables typically include:

- Manufacturing complexity
- Design familiarity
- Mass
- Performance
- Schedule compression

Compared to the analogy models, three main differences exist. First, an analogy model depends on one single, dominant cost driver, whereas a parametric model can use several parameters. Second, an analogy model is based on linear[33] relationships between costs and cost drivers, while parametric models rely on one or more nonlinear regression models. Third, whereas analogy models use an analogy (such as mass) as a driver, parametric models are essentially regression, or response surface, models that can be linear, quadratic, multidimensional, and so on.

Like the analogy models, parametric models do not handle overhead costs in a credible fashion, nor do they go beyond simply presenting an assessment number without any further insight, except what is a direct consequence of their parameters. Parametric modeling, like analogy modeling, has clear limitations, but under some circumstances they are sound approaches. However, when some propose parametric approaches to *optimize* the economic performance of a manufacturing system, they seem to stretch the validity of parametric modeling beyond its limits. It is clear that parametric models are easy to use in optimization algorithms. However, one must remember that open systems cannot really be optimized because they interact with the environment and because implementing a solution can take so much time that the solution is no longer the optimum by the time it is implemented. It is not without reason that Nobel laureate Herbert Simon invented the terms *bounded rationality* and *satisficing*. Basically, what he said was that in most real-life circumstances, we must search for a solution that is good enough and not necessarily "the best."

Since parametric models can offer more insight and higher accuracy than analogy models, they are often found in the engineering literature. Parametric models can also perform well as models *within* a cost accounting system, preferably one that can handle overhead costs well, such as ABC (see "Cost Accounting Models"). For example, if an ABC model discovers that a particular product incurs too many disposal costs related to cutting raw materials, a parametric model can be used to investigate how to reduce the need for disposing of waste. In such a model, it would be useful to look at the direct labor costs, the machine times, and the associated overhead costs, for example.

Engineering Cost Models

According to the New South Wales Government Asset Management Committee in Australia, "The Engineering Cost Method is used where there is detailed and accurate capital and operational cost data for the asset under study. It involves the direct estimation of a particular cost element by examining the asset component-by-component. It uses standard established cost factors (e.g. firm engineering and/or manufacturing estimates) to develop the cost of each element and its relationship to other elements (known as Cost Element Relationships—CER)." This type of model is probably what some refer to as an industrial engineering approach.

Numerous methods in the literature probably mix the three aforementioned methods, particularly parametric and engineering cost models. None of these approaches, however, handles overhead costs correctly because none captures the complexity of modern organizations, and many of them include only simple mathematical manipulations of already identified costs. These cost estimates that are taken as input are probably generated by traditional cost accounting systems and are therefore likely to be distorted.

The importance of handling overhead costs correctly is increasing due to the increased automation and use of advanced technologies in companies. If a company cannot manage 35 percent[34] of its costs properly, it will soon find itself in a severe situation, as many companies found themselves in the 1980s. For the same reason that the fraction of overhead costs is increasing, the complexity that a costing system must handle is increasing.

Engineering cost models, although offering much more insight than analogy and parametric models, are therefore also limited in usage. But as the name indicates, they are particularly useful in engineering and development situations to give an early cost estimate. However, as information becomes more and more available, the next type of models is preferable: cost accounting models.

Cost Accounting Models

The literature contains numerous cost accounting models and systems. Here these systems are grouped into three groups for simplicity:

1. Volume-based costing systems
2. Unconventional costing methods
3. Modern cost management systems

As noted earlier, LCC cost accounting models came about during the 1980s, a point further supported by the fact that in 1979, Benjamin Blanchard, in his book, *Design and Manage to Life Cycle Cost,* only speaks of three LCC methodologies. Some of the most important cost accounting approaches are discussed briefly in the next three sections.

Volume-Based Costing Systems

In the literature, volume-based costing systems are often referred to both as conventional costing systems and traditional costing systems; an example is standard costing. Volume-based costing systems have been thoroughly discussed since ABC arrived in the mid-1980s because their limitations became increasingly apparent to companies and ABC provided a solution to it. In the much-acclaimed book, *Relevance Lost: The Rise and Fall of Management Accounting,* Johnson and Kaplan explain how early costing systems were focused toward decision-making, but then they became more and more focused toward external, financial reporting. This legacy, combined with an unsurpassed technological development and the subsequent increase in organizational complexity and therefore in overhead costs, is an important reason why volume-based costing systems perform relatively poorly today.

In a survey in 1987, 94 percent of the companies contacted reported that they used labor hours to allocate overhead costs. This is shocking news given the known limitations of using only direct labor as an allocation base. Thus, it can be argued to some extent that most in the industry do not know what their products cost and that many companies therefore have survived *despite* their cost management systems. Obviously, this is not a desirable situation, and in the recession in the 1980s many companies learned this the hard way. Hence, volume-based costing systems are not attractive under any circumstances for LCC purposes because they perform too poorly.

Unconventional Costing Methods

The term *unconventional* is used to signify that the approaches discussed here are either quite different from most cost management approaches or not popular. Probably many more approaches deserve to be mentioned, but these two are sufficiently illustrative for this book.

The first is called Attribute-Based Costing, which is a development of ABC and hence is simply denoted ABCII. The purpose is to provide a detailed cost-benefit analysis of customer needs aimed at improving effectiveness. Moreover, "the focus of ABCII is on planning rather than analyses of past costs which can have little impact since 60 to 80 percent of costs are already locked in at the design stage."[35]

ABCII uses the standard ABC approach to cost product attributes, that is, it uses drivers and the like, but the problem arises when a one-to-one relationship no longer exists between a certain attribute and a certain activity. Quality Function Deployment (QFD) can be interfaced with costing, and in the recorded applications of QFD that involve costing, target costs are "deployed" or broken down to product attributes, components, and parts and then compared with current quoted costs. This is apparently a possible bridge in cases where the one-to-one relationship does not exist, which I believe is common. In other words, ABCII appears to be a hybrid between ABC, Target Costing (TC, which is discussed later), and QFD. However, QFD brings in a lot of subjectivity and caution is advised, which probably explains why such an interesting idea has received so little attention in the literature.

The second unconventional costing method is Feature Costing (FC) and is another spin-off from the ABC methodology. Instead of focusing on the product attributes, as in ABCII, the product features are the focal point.[36] Since features are easier to link to specific activities, FC seems to be more realistic than ABCII. FC can be an improvement over ABC in that it leads to a more direct reduction of costs and an improvement of performance. Nonetheless, how FC is an improvement over ABC in general cases is unclear.

Modern Cost Management Systems

By *modern*, I am referring to costing systems that are commonly discussed in positive ways in the current cost management literature and some of their derivatives. Four such systems are discussed here:

1. ABC
2. Just-in-Time (JIT) Costing
3. Target Costing (TC)
4. Strategic Cost Management (SCM)

These methods will be explained in more detail, starting with ABC. It is evident that valuable lessons can be learned from all the concepts, with respect to cost management in general but also with respect to LCC in particular.

Activity-Based Costing

Activity-Based Costing (ABC)[37] is a significant improvement over the volume-based systems for reasons explained in Chapter 4. However, ABC alone cannot handle the design needs in the twenty-first century for at least four reasons:

1. ABC does not handle uncertainty. Since uncertainty is inherent in design, it is vital to understand how uncertainty can affect the solutions.
2. By using large cost pools, the direct association of costs with their respective activities leads to a lack of process information.
3. The relationships among products, processes, and production costs are not clearly delineated.
4. ABC does not facilitate any ways of simulating changes to see how the changes work. This is also true for virtually all cost accounting approaches because they are invariably hindsight oriented. To look forward instead of backward (hindsight) is clearly important since design is upstream of manufacturing and other activities in the life cycle, yet it has a tremendous impact on the final solution, Therefore, one of the most important aspects of this book, is turning cost accounting around from hindsight to foresight.

Before we continue, it should be noted that the second and third reasons are more due to the way ABC is commonly implemented and not because of a conceptual limitation of ABC, which will be evident from the discussions in Chapter 4. Nonetheless, these common limitations associated with many ABC implementations have led people to develop ABC methods for use in process design. Unfortunately, the frameworks presented are not easy to understand nor do they handle uncertainty. As some note, "The framework presented . . . is not simple. Indeed, this framework is likely unworkable except in an advanced manufacturing environment."[38] This unworkability is a good reason for trying to come up with a better method, which is one reason why I wrote this book.

Others have taken ABC and tried to extend it to deal with the environmental issues; however, only a slight improvement (at best) of what has been done earlier is achieved, and uncertainty is ignored. The fact that linear goal programming is used also ruins the credibility of the ABC implementation since one of the great benefits of ABC is to capture nonlinear phenomena by choosing nonlinear drivers. Linear drivers, such as the number of units produced, are the basis for volume-based costing methods, but only product material costs (direct material) are truly linear.

Interested readers and readers not fluent in ABC are referred to see Chapter 4, where ABC is presented and contrasted to volume-based costing systems.

Just-in-Time Costing

In contrast to volume-based costing systems that focus on products, Just-in-Time (JIT) Costing is oriented toward process and time, as measured by the cycle time. Compared to all other costing systems I am aware of, JIT Costing has special ways of finding the cycle time cost and also treating direct labor. More specifically, in JIT Costing[39]:

- Only *one single* cost driver is used: cycle time.
- The cycle time cost formula is unique.
- Direct labor is considered an overhead cost.

In most costing systems, the unit cost formula is given as a process flow cost formula:

$$\frac{Overhead\ Expenses\ +\ Direct\ Labor\ Costs}{Number\ of\ Units\ Produced} \tag{2.1}$$

The focus on cycle time in JIT costing, however, has led to a slightly different definition but nevertheless a significant cycle time cost formula:

$$\frac{Overhead\ Expenses\ +\ Direct\ Labor\ Costs}{Cycle\ Time\ in\ Hours} \tag{2.2}$$

The big difference between these two definitions is that the JIT Costing uses *time* as a basis for cost absorption. The cycle time includes:

- Process time (machine, direct labor, total quality control in line inspection) (value added)
- Queue (nonvalue added)
- Setup (nonvalue added)
- Wait (nonvalue added)
- Move (nonvalue added)
- Inspection (nonvalue added)

Cycle times exclude line stops for quality, direct delivered parts, and training. Evidently, line stops are not included in the cycle time. Consequently, in a JIT environment, a very unique practice is employed: JIT encourages manufacturing to stop production immediately whenever a quality problem is discovered!

Although defining cycle time is straightforward, tracing cost contributors is more complicated. A common method is the Average Unit cycle time Method (AUM), which is based on First-In, First-Out (FIFO) product flow (see Equation 2.3). Another requirement is a line audit at least twice a day, where an actual count of the number of products at each process step is performed.

$$AUM = \frac{Daily\ Production\ Hours}{Number\ of\ Units\ Produced} \tag{2.3}$$

Total Product Cycle Time = Average Number of Units in Process × AUM   (2.4)

Because of this heavy focus on time, to avoid serious cost distortions, it is clear that the product diversity cannot be too large. Thus, some claim that JIT is best suited for the manufacture of *closely related standardized products* in which homogeneity (rather than heterogeneity) is a dominant characteristic of the output.

Yet some disagreement exists as to what extent cycle time is *the* cost driver. This disagreement seems to be mainly due to how people *envision* the JIT manufacturing environment, that is, the degree of automation and hence *time* focus. For example, some explain that JIT environments *normally* operate with automated equipment but not necessarily, and the product costs are classified as either materials costs (including all materials-related costs) or conversion costs (the rest of production-related costs). The allocation procedure is mostly based on cycle time, except materials costs, which are allocated in a traditional way. Clearly, this way of doing JIT Costing is less radical than what is proposed here.

A third view holds that JIT Costing distinguishes itself mainly in three aspects:

1. Costs associated with raw materials and in-process inventory are put in a Raw and In-Process inventory (RIP) account.
2. The usage of conversion costs (see above).
3. Overhead costs are not included in the product costs *until* the products are finished. Thus, no Work In Process (WIP) accounts are needed.

Regardless of what view we take, JIT Costing is almost like a subset of ABC in the sense that volume-based drivers are not *necessarily* used at all. In JIT Costing, however, the main cost driver is *predetermined*—time—while ABC enables complete flexibility in cost driver definitions. Other similarities exist as well. For example, ABC was originally designed to improve the accuracy of product costing while JIT was conceived as a method for eliminating all forms of wasteful activity in an organization, yet both focus on value adding with ABC as a side benefit.

Essentially, while ABC is designed to manage (eliminate or reduce) the complexity of modern organizations, JIT seeks to simply eliminate this complexity. Clearly, time is a very important factor when it comes to utilizing the production resources as efficiently as possible, because the less time spent per product unit, the higher the throughput and the more likely it is to be profitable. However, time is not the only possible cost driver that could be employed, and in some cases a heavy focus on time can even be counterproductive, as shown in the literature. Therefore, ABC seems to provide a more general approach than JIT Costing does.

It is evident that ABC will work well in a JIT environment; however, since the JIT environment seeks to eliminate the complexities ABC is good at handling, one might as well settle for the simpler JIT Costing system. Thus, the ultimate question is whether the complexity is needed or not, which is a strategic issue (diversification versus cost effectiveness, for example).

How JIT Costing would work for LCC purposes is not discussed in the literature I have reviewed, but since time estimates will be very difficult to obtain realistically, particularly in the use phase of the product, it is not likely that JIT Costing would work in LCC. Also, JIT Costing seems to be too specialized for manufacturing environments.

Target Costing

The conceptual idea behind Target Costing (TC) is to balance the needs of the customers with the profit need of the company. The Consortium for Advanced Manufacturing—International utilizes the following definition:

> *Target Costing is a system of profit planning and cost management that is price driven, customer focused, design centered and cross functional. Target Costing initiates cost management at the earliest stages of product development and applies it throughout the product life-cycle by actively involving the entire value chain.*

The earliest (late 1960s and early 1970s) implementers of TC were Japanese automotive manufacturers. TC was a logical outgrowth of their analysis of the causes of cost. As they sought ways to reduce or eliminate costs, the influence of the design of manufacturing costs became apparent. The Japanese recognized that profitability depends on marketplace success, which is the result of developing cogent business strategies, satisfying customers, and confronting competitors. The costing process becomes interdependent with the business management process and provides a common focus for the activities of the enterprise. Hence, TC is process oriented, but, more important, TC is employed in strategic management. Thus, TC can, for example, be combined with ABC and JIT Costing if desired.

However, TC provides two concepts that ABC does not offer explicitly. One is the way products are being priced and the other is to turn away from cost cutting to cost elimination via design and planning. These two points are important paradigm shifts:

1. **From cost-plus pricing[40] to market-based pricing** In TC, customers and competitors drive market prices. The company sets the target profit and the resulting cost (target price − target profit) is the targeted cost the company must meet. In the literature, this approach is also referred to as the market-based approach or the deductive method, and it is a fundamentally different way of looking at pricing. It is rooted in the fact that in the marketplace, customers have many high-quality products to choose from; the price of these products may therefore be the only significant competitive edge for a company. It should be noted that the other popular method in TC, called the additive method, is essentially a cost-plus approach, but it is less attractive in my opinion because it is less customer focused.

2. **From cost-cutting during production to cost control during design** As we have seen, it is widely noted in the literature that during the design phase (concept, design/engineering, and testing), most of the basis for the costs is formed (refer to Figure 1.1). TC takes this into account and is proactive rather than reactive in its management focus.

TC also requires a shift (1) from an internal to an external focus, (2) from an internal vantage point to listening to the customer, and (3) from independent efforts to interdependent efforts, but these shifts are not limited for TC. Indeed, these paradigm shifts were probably preceded by the work of Deming and others like Juran and Crosby. These thoughts and more were popularized in the "If Japan Can, Why Can't We" TV show on NBC in 1980 and were articulated for the general public in Deming's 1986 book, *Out of the Crisis*. The focus on quality is an idea adopted by all modern cost management approaches, since quality affects customer satisfaction substantially, as noted in a wide array of management and design literature.

What is less known is the enormous impact the focus on quality has on the *operating* costs of the company. As Taiichi Ohno, the former vice president of Toyota, said, "Whatever an executive thinks the losses of poor quality are, they are actually six times greater."[41] In the distribution industry, for example, studies indicate that up to 25 percent of operating expenses stem from internal quality problems. But former vice chairman of Chrysler Corporation Robert Lutz warns us that "too much quality can ruin you." Indeed, in the literature we can read about many companies that have received quality awards soon after getting into serious financial difficulties. For example, many Baldrige Award winners have encountered severe financial difficulties. In fact, 14 out of the 43 supposedly best-run companies in the United States that Peters and Waterman reported on in their book *In Search of Excellence* "were in financial trouble within two years of the book's completion."[42] Hence, a cost management system that can also capture internal quality is essential.

Strategic Cost Management

One of the major concerns in Strategic Cost Management (SCM) is how the firm organizes its thinking about cost management.[43] To answer this question, Michael Porter introduced the notion of value chain in his highly acclaimed book, *Competitive Advantage: Creating and Sustaining Superior Performance*. In several ways, this is the root to the value-added notions that can be found in ABC, for example. It also is remarkably close to the product life-cycle concepts discussed earlier in "Differences between the Life Cycle and the Value Chain."

The value-added concept focuses on internal activities, while the value chain focuses on external activities. This has significant implications from a strategic perspective because the value-added concept (1) *starts too late* and (2) *stops too soon*. As a result, a large proportion of the entire value chain in which significant improvement opportunities exist is missed. This argument also emphasizes why LCC should be important.

The methodology of the value chain concept can be summarized into three steps:

1. Identify the value chain and then assign costs, revenues, and assets to the value activities.
2. Diagnose the cost drivers regulating each value activity.
3. Develop sustainable competitive advantage either through controlling cost drivers better than competitors or by reconfiguring the value chain.

In the value-chain concept, the cost drivers are diagnosed by grouping them into two different groups: (1) structural cost drivers and (2) executional cost drivers. The structural cost drivers are derived from a company's choices of economical structure:

- **Scale**   What is the size of the investment to be made in manufacturing, R&D, and marketing resources (horizontal integration)?
- **Scope**   What is the degree of vertical integration?
- **Experience**   How many times in the past has the firm already done what it is doing again?
- **Technology**   What process technologies are used in each step of the firm's value chain?
- **Complexity**   How wide a line of products or services is being offered to customers?

The executional cost drivers determine a firm's cost position, which hinges on its ability to execute successfully. In contrast to the structural cost drivers, more is *always* better:

- **Workforce involvement**   Is the workforce committed to continuous improvement?
- **Total Quality Management (TQM)**   Is the workforce committed to total product quality?
- **Capacity utilization**   What are the scale choices on maximum plant construction?
- **Plant layout efficiency**   How efficient against current norms is the plant's layout?
- **Product configuration**   Is the design or formulation of the product effective?
- **Linkages with suppliers or customers**   Is the linkage with suppliers or customers exploited according to the firm's value chain?

Attempts have been made to create a comprehensive list of cost drivers. In the strategic management literature in particular, good lists of cost drivers exist. The grouping of the cost drivers is particularly interesting as a way of helping management focus on the correct aspects of the company from a strategic perspective.

The last two lists are good preliminary checks for management before a more elaborate analysis is undertaken. However, as indicated by the very name *Strategic Cost Management*, this methodology is intended for strategic purposes only. Hence, SCM is not very useful in design except when it comes to identifying goals and objectives. Most important, it introduces the notion of value-chain analysis, which is essential in three ways:

1. *Supplier linkages*, which are vital to consider every time major changes are made to make sure that suppliers can handle the changes.
2. *Customer linkages*, which basically mean that an LCC for the customer should be performed to make sure long-term relationships with customers are a win-win situation.
3. *Missed opportunities*, which must be avoided primarily by being aware of what is going on in the value chain. For example, if technology changes in one of the links in the value chain, both downstream customers and upstream suppliers must evaluate the effects on their business.

Furthermore, SCM does not focus much on risk and uncertainty and is suited for strategic issues only. Also, the last two steps in the approach seem too generic to provide any help for many practitioners.

Before Activity-Based LCC can be introduced along with pertinent LCC discussions, we need to discuss how to deal with risk and uncertainty, which is done in chapter 3. Risk and uncertainty are, after all, inherent in LCC. Also, the brief discussion on ABC in this chapter must be expanded upon significantly, which is done in Chapter 4. Without understanding ABC, at least conceptually, there is little hope of understanding Activity-Based LCC.

NOTES

1. Other models also exist for the marketing perspective, such as the seven-stage model presented by H.G. Adamany and F.A.M. Gonsalves in "Life Cycle Management," *Handbook of Cost Management*, ed. B.J. Brinker, Boston, MA: Warren, Gorham & Lamont, 1997, pp. D5-1–D5-26. However, they all essentially say the same; only the degree of refinement varies.
2. More details are provided in M. Schwartz's, *The Value of R&D: Creating Value Growth through Research & Development,* London: Stern Stewart Europe, Ltd., 1999, p. 11.
3. J. Pettit, *EVA & Strategy*, New York: Stern Steward & Co., 2000, p. 17.
4. Government Asset Management Committee, "Life Cycle Costing Guideline," Sydney, New South Wales: Government Asset Management Committee, 2001, p. 15.
5. According to its CEO and Chairman of the Board, Ray C. Anderson. See R. C. Anderson's, *Mid-Course Correction,* Atlanta, GA: The Peregrinzilla Press, 1998, p. 204.

6. An excellent discussion on remanufacturing is provided by R.T. Lund in "Remanufacturing," *Technology Review* 87, 1984, pp. 18–23.

7. See note 5.

8. For more details, see P. Hawken, A.B. Lovins, and L.H. Lovins, *Natural Capitalism —The Next Industrial Revolution,* London: Earthscan Publications, Ltd., 1999, p. 396.

9. T. Levitt, "Exploit the Product Life Cycle," *Harvard Business Review,* November-December 1965, pp. 81–94.

10. According to F. Allvine's, *Marketing: Principles and Practices,* Boston, MA: Irwin/McGraw-Hill, 1996.

11. M.E. Porter, *Competitive Advantage: Creating and Sustaining Superior Performance,* New York: The Free Press, 1985, p. 557.

12. According to T. Hindle's, *Guide to Management Ideas* (London: The Economist Books, 2000, p. 241).

13. H.P. Barringer and D.P. Weber, "Life Cycle Cost Tutorial," Fifth International Conference on Process Plant Reliability. Houston, TX: Gulf Publishing Company and Hydrocarbon Processing, 1996.

14. R.I. Winner, J.P. Pennell, H.E. Bertrand, and M.M.G. Slusarczuk, *The Role of Concurrent Engineering in Weapons System Acquisition*, Alexandra, VA: Institute for Defense Analyses, 1988.

15. See note 13.

16. A thorough discussion is found in R.K. Fleischman's, "Completing the Triangle: Taylorism and the Paradigms," *Accounting, Auditing & Accountability Journal* 13 (5), 2000, pp. 597–623.

17. For a more complete discussion on the developments in management accounting, see H.T. Johnson and R.S. Kaplan's, *Relevance Lost: The Rise and Fall of Management Accounting,* Boston, MA: Harvard Business School Press, 1987, p. 269.

18. P. Maccarrone, "Activity-based Management and the Product Development Process," *European Journal of Innovation Management* 1 (3), 1998, pp. 148–156.

19. A thorough discussion of these problems is provided by J. Emblemsvåg and B. Bras, "LCA Comparability and the Waste Index," *International Journal of Life Cycle Assessment* 4 (5), September 1999, pp. 282–290.

20. A complete discussion is found in E.F. Finch's, "The Uncertain Role of Life Cycle Costing in the Renewable Energy Debate," *Renewable Energy* 5, Part II, 1994, pp. 1436–1443.

21. J. Emblemsvåg and B. Bras, *Activity-Based Cost and Environmental Management: A Different Approach to the ISO 14000 Compliance,* Boston, MA: Kluwer Academic Publishers, 2000, p. 317.

22. R. Cooper, "Explicating the Logic of ABC," *Management Accounting (UK),* November 1990, pp. 58–60.

23. See note 2.

24. C.S. Park and G.P. Sharp-Bette, *Advanced Engineering Economics,* New York: John Wiley & Sons, 1990, p. 740.

25. OMB, "OMB Circular No. A-109," April 5, 1976.

26. Executive Order, "Federal Acquisition, Recycling, and Waste Prevention," Executive Order 12873, Section 210, October 20, 1993.

27. See note 4.

28. P. Passel, "Experts Question Staggering Costs of Toxic Cleanup," *The New York Times,* September 1991, p. A1.

29. See note 10.

30. P.F. Drucker, "The Theory of the Business," *Harvard Business Review,* September-October 1994.

31. For a comprehensive introduction to traditional LCC, review S.K. Fuller and S.R. Petersen's, *Life Cycle Costing Manual for the Federal Energy Management Program,* Washington, D.C.: U.S. Government Printing Office, 1996, p. 210. However, be aware that some of the terminology used is somewhat different than elsewhere. Good discussions are also provided by M.D. Shields and S.M. Young's, "Managing Product Life Cycle Costs: An Organizational Model," *Journal of Cost Management for the Manufacturing Industry* 5, No. 3, Fall 1991, pp. 39–51.

32. G. Tsatsaronis, L. Lin, and J. Pisa, "Exergy Costing in Exergoeconomics," *Journal of Energy Resources Technology* 115, March 1993, pp. 9–16.

33. Nonlinear relationships between two variables can often be approximated linearly by using, for example, logarithmical functions.

34. This is the amount of overhead costs of typical American companies, as mentioned earlier.

35. See both M. Walker's, "Activity Based Costing Using Product Attributes," *Management Accounting* (UK), October 1991, pp. 34–35, and "Attribute Based Costing," *Australian Accountant,* March 1992, pp. 42–45.

36. J.A. Brimson, "Feature Costing: Beyond ABC," *Journal of Cost Management for the Manufacturing Industry,* January/February 1998, pp. 6–12.

37. With ABC here, it is referred to the costing part *including* the value-added analysis (see Chapter 4).

38. T.G. Greenwood and J.M. Reeve, "Activity Based Cost Management for Continuous Improvement: A Process Design Framework," *Journal of Cost Management for the Manufacturing Industry* 5 (4) Winter 1992, pp. 22–40.

39. Most of this section is based on A.J. Dodd's, "The Just-in-Time Environment" in *The Handbook of Cost Management,* ed. by B.J. Brinker, Boston, MA: Warren, Gorham & Lamont, 1997, pp. A3-1–A3-35. Others sources of information include C.T. Horngren and G. Foster's, "Cost Accounting and Cost Management in a JIT Environment" in *Emerging Practices in Cost Management,* ed. by B.J. Brinker, Boston, MA: Warren, Gorham & Lamont, 1990, p. 200; J.B. MacArthur's, "The ABC/JIT Costing Continuum," *Journal of Cost Management for the Manufacturing Industry,* Winter 1992, pp. 61–63; H.H. Anderson, B.E. Needles, J.C. Caldwell, and S.K. Mills', *Managerial Accounting,* Boston, MA: Houghton Mifflin Company, 1996, p. 657; and H.M. Sollenberger and A. Schneider's, *Managerial Accounting,* Cincinnati, OH: South-Western College Publishing, 1996, p. 822.

40. Cost-plus pricing is based on calculating the price as the cost plus a profit. Various companies use different cost as a basis, but often the cost of goods sold is the basis.

41. G. Taguchi and D. Clausing, "Robust Quality," *Harvard Business Review,* January-February 1990, pp. 65–75.

42. J. Kandampully and R. Duddy, "Competitive Advantage Through Anticipation, Innovation and Relationships," *Management Decision* 37 (1), 1999, pp. 51–56.

43. J.K. Shank and V. Govindarajan, "Strategic Cost Management and the Value Chain," *Handbook of Cost Management,* ed. B.J. Brinker, Boston, MA: Warren, Gorham & Lamont, 1997, pp. D1-1–D1-37.

3

UNCERTAINTY ANALYSIS AND RISK MANAGEMENT

I have seen something else under the sun:
The race is not to the swift
or the battle to the strong,
nor does food come to the wise
or wealth to the brilliant
or favor to the learned;
but time and chance happen to them all.

King Solomon
Ecclesiastes 9:11

"Time and chance happen to them all." It is the death of certainty and simple, clear-cut, cause-and-effect relations. It is a nightmare for engineers, for managers, and for decision-makers in general. Yet many systems will not function without uncertainty. In fact, if you reduce the uncertainty to zero, the risk may increase, but if the uncertainty is balanced, the risks may be acceptable. Indeed, risk and uncertainty are formidable opponents for any decision-maker, because when we make decisions, we expose ourselves to the risks that lurk in uncertainty as it were. But luckily we are not left to our own devices.

In this chapter, a discussion of risk and uncertainty is provided along with a simple yet powerful way of analyzing risk and uncertainty to support effective uncertainty analyses and risk management.

WHAT ARE RISK AND UNCERTAINTY?

Dictionary definitions of risk and uncertainty provide some good hints to start with, but often risk and uncertainty are used interchangeably. In fact, for auditors "risk is uncertainty."[1] It may be that distinguishing between risk and uncertainty makes little sense for auditors, although I doubt it because the fact is that many, and very interesting, differences exist, which are discussed in this chapter.

Risk: The Chance of Loss

The word *risk* derives from the early Italian word *risicare*, which means "to dare." In this sense, risk is a choice rather than a fate.[2] This idea is also found in recent definitions, such as the 1989 edition of *Webster's Encyclopedic Unabridged Dictionary of the English Language*, where *risk* as a general noun is defined as "exposure to the chance of injury or loss; a hazard or dangerous chance." In fact, in statistical decision theory, risk is defined as "the expected value of a loss function." It is important to emphasize that risk is not just bad things happening, but also good things not happening; in any case, we are talking about loss. Thus, various definitions of risk imply that we expose ourselves to risk by choice, and that is an important point: Risk arises from choice.

Risk is commonly measured, however, in terms of consequences and likelihood, where likelihood is understood as a qualitative description of probability or frequency. Frequency theory, however, is dependent on probability theory.[3] Thus, risk is ultimately a probabilistic phenomenon as it is defined in most of the literature.

We see from this that it is important to discuss two aspects: Risk gives negative associations and risk is a probabilistic phenomenon. These aspects are discussed in the two subsequent sections.

But first, a third aspect to discuss is that the source of risk is uncertainty. This follows as a logical consequence of the fact that risk is a choice rather than a fate, as already stated, because choices can occur only if things are not decided, and undecided things are uncertain. Risks arise when we make decisions because we expose ourselves to uncertainty in which the risks lie. This is discussed more in the "Uncertainty, the Lack of Information and Knowledge" section.

Risk and Our Negative Associations

We see from the definition that risk is always associated with negative things such as a loss, a hazard, or an injury. This coincides well with a survey that indicates that people in business view risk as primarily associated with the probability of not achieving a target return.

Also, risk is perceived differently in terms of gender, age, and culture. In fact, another survey found that women are more risk averse than men and that older, more experienced managers are more averse to risk than younger managers. Furthermore, evidence suggests that successful managers take more risks than unsuccessful managers.

As already emphasized, risk is not just bad things happening, but also good things not happening, a clarification that is particularly crucial in a business context, because many companies do not fail from primarily taking wrong actions but from not capitalizing on their opportunities. Combining traditional business development approaches and risk management is important because traditional approaches can be outright dangerous as they may ignore risks (positive and negative). This is further emphasized as "The effective business focuses on opportunities rather than problems."[4] Thus, risk management is ultimately about being proactive, and that must be a part of all other management activities. It is therefore important that risk goes beyond the directly negative associations. The loss of opportunities is just as bad for business as direct losses. The difference in my opinion lies in that direct losses have mostly a short-term effect and therefore get more attention, whereas losses of opportunities have mostly a long-term effect.

Also, it may be useful to be aware of cultural differences. In a survey, for example, 49 countries were studied for more than 20 years by questioning over 100,000 respondents. Hence, the study is without any doubt statistically significant; that is, the chance of error is low. The results are shown in Table 3.1.

With uncertainty avoidance, the degree to which cultures feel uncomfortable with uncertainty is understood. Whether the questions are risk oriented and/or uncertainty oriented I do not know, but the respondents are probably mainly thinking in terms of risk; that is what most people are concerned about, because it involves loss and other negative associations. In any case, what is interesting is that very few of the really risk-averse cultures are also doing very well. The only exceptions seem to be France, Japan, and South Korea, whereas many of the most successful economies are risk takers, such as Canada, the United States, Great Britain, Hong Kong, and Singapore. We also understand from Table 3.1 that being eco-

Table 3.1 Uncertainty Avoidance by Selected Countries

Country	Uncertainty Avoidance	Country	Uncertainty Avoidance	Country	Uncertainty Avoidance
Argentina	86	Indonesia	48	Portugal	104
Australia	51	India	40	South Africa	49
Austria	70	Iran	59	San Salvador	94
Belgium	94	Ireland	35	Singapore	8
Brazil	76	Israel	81	Spain	86
Canada	48	Italy	75	Sweden	29
Chile	86	Jamaica	13	Switzerland	58
Colombia	80	Japan	92	Taiwan	69
Costa Rica	86	South Korea	85	Thailand	64
Denmark	23	Malaysia	36	Turkey	85
Ecuador	67	Mexico	82	Uruguay	100
Finland	59	Netherlands	53	U.S.A.	46
France	86	Norway	50	Venezuela	76
Germany	65	New Zealand	49		
Great Britain	35	Pakistan	70	**Score Ranges**	
Greece	112	Panama	86	Low	8-53
Guatemala	101	Peru	87	Medium	54-84
Hong Kong	29	Philippines	44	High	85-112

Source: Adapted from P.C. Brewer, "Managing Transnational Cost Management Systems," *Journal of Cost Management for the Manufacturing Industry,* November/December 1997, pp. 35–40.

nomically successful consists of more than taking risks because although Jamaica is a risk taker, but it does not perform well.

Because risk and success seem to follow each other in many cases, it is important that organizations have a consistent attitude toward risk. According to some research, the risk-taking strategy is an essential part of the total strategy, and furthermore, risk acceptance characteristics are essential to the success of many strategies. This is particularly crucial in organizations where innovation and creativity are important, because innovation and creativity are uncertain and often associated with great financial risk as the capital needs are often substantial. One way to accomplish this is to consider failure as "enlightened trial and error," which essentially means that we must learn from our mistakes. That can be a source of success as well. According to former chairman of the Coca-Cola Company, Roberto Goizueta, the disastrous New Coke "was the best that could ever happen to Coca-Cola because this gave a valuable lesson to management. That is why the company has one of the highest returns on investment of any U.S. company today."[5] This goes to show that although risk is a negative thing, it can be a source of great success as long as we learn from our failures.

Sources of Risk

Of course, too many sources of risks exist to mention them all, but in Tables 3.2 and 3.3 provided some examples that may be helpful to consult when doing risk analysis. It is important to limit oneself to such tables or checklists. Often, the greatest risks are due to the inherent belief system in an organization, *the theory of the business.* When this system no longer reflects reality, the organization runs a great danger of becoming outdated. This is what caused many large multinationals to succumb in the last 20 years; their theory of business no longer worked.[6] Take the American car makers, for example. For decades, they provided affordable cars to a vast number of customers, but they failed to recognize the quality drive initiated by Japanese car makers; their theory of business no longer worked.

Of course, not all the aforementioned sources of risks are equally important. A 1999 Deloitte and Touche survey identified the following five risks as significant (on a scale of 1 to 9):

- Failure to manage major projects   (7.05)
- Failure of strategy   (6.67)
- Failure to innovate   (6.32)
- Poor reputation/brand management   (6.30)
- Lack of employee motivation and poor performance   (6.00)

The survey basically indicates that the most significant risks were frequently operational or strategic in nature. For example, the problems that ABB, the Swedish-Swiss engineering giant, is in today are due to "its exposure to operating

Table 3.2 Examples of Sources of Risk

Commercial and Strategic	Economic	Environmental
1. Competition	1. Discount rate	1. Amenity values
2. Market demand levels	2. Economic growth	2. Approval processes
3. Growth rates	3. Energy prices	3. Community consultation
4. Technological change	4. Exchange rate variation	4. Site availability/zoning
5. Stakeholder perceptions	5. Inflation	5. Endangered species
6. Market share	6. Demand trends	6. Conservation/heritage
7. Private sector involvement	7. Population growth	7. Degradation or contamination
8. New products and services	8. Commodity prices	8. Visual intrusion
9. Site acquisition		

Political	Social	Contractual
1. Parliamentary support	1. Community expectations	1. Client problems
2. Community support	2. Pressure groups	2. Contractor problems
3. Government endorsement		3. Delays
4. Policy change		4. *Force majeure* events
5. Sovereign risk		5. Insurance and indemnities
6. Taxation		6. Joint venture relations

Financial	Project Initiation	Procurement Planning
1. Debt/equity ratios	1. Analysis and briefing	1. Industry capability
2. Funding sources	2. Functional specifications	2. Technology and obsolescence
3. Financing costs	3. Performance objectives	3. Private sector involvement
4. Taxation impacts	4. Innovation	4. Regulations and standards
5. Interest rates	5. Evaluation program	5. Utility and authority approvals
6. Investment terms	6. Stakeholder roles and responsibilities	6. Completion deadlines
7. Ownership		7. Cost estimation
8. Residual risk for government		
9. Underwriting		

(continues)

Table 3.2 Examples of Sources of Risk (*Continued*)

Procurement and Contractual	Construction and Maintenance	Systems
1. Contract selection	1. Buildability	1. Communications or network failure
2. Client commitment	2. Contractor capability	2. Hardware failure
3. Consultant/contractor performance	3. Design and documentation	3. Linkages between subsystems
4. Tendering	4. Geotechnical conditions	4. Software failure
5. Negligence of parties	5. Latent conditions	5. Policies and procedures
6. Delays: weather or industrial disputes	6. Quality controls	
7. Damages and claims	7. Equipment availability and breakdowns	
8. Errors in documentation	8. Obsolescence	
9. *Force majeure* events	9. Industrial action	
10. Insurance and indemnities	10. Materials availability	
	11. Shutdown and startup	
	12. Recurrent liabilities	
	13. Health and safety	
	14. Accidents, injury	
	15. OH&S procedures	
	16. Contamination	
	17. Noise, dust, and waste	
	18. Disease	
	19. Irradiation	
	20. Emissions	

Human Factors	Natural Events	Organizational
1. Estimation error	1. Landslide/subsidence	1. Industrial relations
2. Operator error	2. Earthquake	2. Resource shortage
3. Sabotage	3. Fire	3. Scheduling
4. Vandalism	4. Flood	4. Operational policies
	5. Lightning	5. Management capabilities
	6. Wind	6. Management structures
	7. Weather	7. Personnel skills
		8. Work practices

Source: Adapted from Government Asset Management Committee, "Risk Management Guideline," Sydney, New South Wales: Government Asset Management Committee, 2001, p. 43.

Table 3.3 Examples of Sources of Risk

Business	Operational and Other
1. Wrong business strategy	1. Business process not aligned to strategic goals
2. Competitive pressure on price/market share	2. Failure of major change initiative
3. General economic problems	3. Loss of entrepreneurial spirit
4. Regional economic problems	4. Stock out of raw materials
5. Political risks	5. Skills shortage
6. Obsolescence of technology	6. Physical disaster (including fire and explosion)
7. Substitute products	7. Failure to create and exploit intangible assets
8. Adverse government policy	8. Loss of intangible assets
9. Industry sector in decline	9. Breach of confidentiality
10. Takeover target	10. Loss of physical assets
11. Inability to obtain further capital	11. Lack of business continuity
12. Bad acquisition	12. Succession problems
13. Too slow to innovate	13. Year 2000 problems (not applicable anymore)
	14. Loss of key people
	15. Inability to reduce cost base
	16. Major customers impose tough contract obligations
	17. Overreliance on key suppliers or customers
	18. Failure of new products or services
	19. Poor service levels
	20. Failure to satisfy customers
	21. Quality problems
	22. Lack of orders
	23. Failure of major projects
	24. Loss of key contracts
	25. Inability to make use of the Internet
	26. Failure to outsource provider to deliver
	27. Industrial action
	28. Failure of big technology-related projects
	29. Lack of employee motivation or efficiency
	30. Inability to implement change
	31. Inefficient/ineffective processing of documents
	32. Poor brand management
	33. Product liability
	34. Inefficient/ineffective management process
	35. Problems arising from exploiting employees in developing countries
	36. Other business probity issues
	37. Other issues giving rise to reputation problems
	38. Missed business opportunities

(continues)

Table 3.3   Examples of Sources of Risk (*Continued*)

Financial
1. Liquidity risk
2. Market risk
3. Going concern problems
4. Overtrading
5. Credit risk
6. Interest risk
7. Currency risk
8. High cost of capital
9. Treasury risk
10. Misuse of financial resources
11. Occurrence of types of fraud to which the business is susceptible
12. Misstatement risk related to published financial information
13. Breakdown of accounting system
14. Unrecorded liabilities
15. Unreliable accounting records
16. Penetration and attack of IT system by hackers
17. Decision based on incomplete or faulty information
18. Too much data and not enough analysis
19. Unfilled promises to investors

Compliance
1. Breach of listing rules
2. Breach of financial regulations
3. Breach of Compliance Act requirements
4. Litigation risk
5. Breach of competition laws
6. VAT problems
7. Breach of other regulations and laws
8. Tax penalties
9. Health and safety risks
10. Environmental problems

Source: Adapted from *Implementing Turnbull: A Boardroom Briefing* with the kind permission of the Institute of Chartered Accountants of England & Wales.

risks that have been poorly understood."[7] The major projects that have been identified often had an element of technology.

However, be aware that risks often are industry specific and are closely related to the circumstances of the company. In other words, only use Tables 3.2 and 3.3 as a starting point from which to get some ideas. Then input ideas in a process of identifying/analyzing risks, because that must be done before we can even start thinking about managing risk.

Identifying risks is often a creative exercise in which a process framework is commonly used. There are probably as many ways of doing this as there are companies, but according to the 1999 Deloitte and Touche survey, the following techniques are the most useful (on a scale from 1 to 9) for identifying business risks:

- Roundtable debates on key risks   (6.92)
- Interactive workshops   (6.62)
- Strategic risk reviews   (6.58)
- Specific studies/surveys   (6.42)
- Structured interviews   (6.04)
- Management reports   (5.60)
- Checklists/questionnaires   (4.43)

It is important to recognize that the previous list is valid only for business risks and not for technical risks, for example. Of course, these techniques must be applied to the core areas of the company to have the desired effects. That includes areas such as strategy, product development, market understanding, service and product development, the quality of the company's management, changes both within and without, and so on.

Risk as a Probabilistic Phenomenon

Risk is based on a certain chance of an occurrence, according to the definition in this book. Furthermore, we have said that risk is commonly measured in terms of consequences and likelihood. Likelihood is understood as a qualitative description of probability or frequency, and frequency theory is dependent on probability theory. But what is probability?

In the literature, two major directions claim to have the best approach toward modeling uncertainty, namely, *probability theory* and *possibility theory*, which is based on fuzzy sets. But as Kaufmann points out, "We can probabilize the fuzzy sets as well as fuzzify the events (in probability theory)."[8] I believe that the reason for this unfruitful discussion between the two camps is due to the fact that "theories conceal as much as they reveal" as Hegel put it.

Basically, it is important to realize that neither probability theory nor possibility theory came out of the blue; that is, they must be seen in a historical context. Also, much of the argumentation is based on logic, but logic does not ensure anything beyond itself. This follows as, for example, Wittgenstein pointed out, logic is merely a tool that is consistent *within* itself but is "content free." Hence, objectivity is an illusion and logic cannot provide relevance to anything but itself.

As with risk, it is in my opinion important to distinguish between the concept of probability and the measure of probability. Furthermore, it is important to realize that probability has always carried a double meaning: "one looking into the future, the other interpreting the past, one concerned with our opinions, the other concerned with what we actually know."[9] It is the former interpretation of probability that is relevant for this book and concerns most theories of probability, and fuzzy sets,[10] or possibility theory.

In the former sense, probability refers to a "degree of belief or an approvability of an opinion,"[11] but it should be noted that "the nature of its (probability) subject-matter is still in dispute" and that "its logic runs into 'circularity'."[12] However, by investigating the roots of the word *probability*, we find that the previous interpretation is probably useful because the word εικοζ (*eikos*), which means "plausible" or "probable," was used by Socrates in ancient Greece to describe "likeness to truth."[13] When we try to forecast the future, we are essentially trying to express our opinion and belief about the future as it likens truth. Thus, this interpretation of probability seems to be what we are looking for.

Evidently, the concept of probability in the former sense refers to a *degree of belief*, but with respect to what? It is here that the probability camp and the possibility camp stumble into each other, in my opinion. The opponents of possibility theory and fuzzy logic uses Cox's proof, saying that "if one wishes to represent 'plausibility' of a proposition by a real number and require consistency in the resulting calculus, then the 'axioms' of probability follow logically."[14] The proponents of possibility theory claim that the most limiting aspect of probability theory is "that it is based on two-valued logic."[15] I believe the points these disputes miss are that:

- Internal logic consistency does not prove anything with respect to reality, as discussed earlier.
- Probability theory is not a complete representation of probability.

Probability theory is, as its opponents claim, digital, but that is more due to the fact that the theory developed from gambling, and dice cannot have any intermediate values. But from the original concept of probability, as discussed earlier, we see that probability is a measure of the degree of belief. Thus, the point is that probability theory simply does not capture entirely the term *probability*.

I believe much of the disagreement between the probability camp and the possibility camp is that both are unaware of these philosophical roots of probability theory. They have to a large extent been comparing the various forms of measuring probability to each other and claiming that one is superior to the other. What they have missed is that both are trying to measure the degree of belief, but that probability theory has often an absolute approach and always a digital approach, while possibility theory has a relative approach based on measures of degree. This will be clarified in "Increase Uncertainty to Lower Risks" section. For now, it suffices to understand that probability theory requires more information than possibility theory.

Of course, probability theory is a sound approach in many cases and it provides the most insight, but as explained later in "Probability Theory Versus Possibility Theory," cases do occur when this approach may prove deceptive. In such cases, the possibility camp view is more useful because for them the point is to compare the outcomes against each other; that is, the solution space does not matter. This eliminates several problems, but we lose precision. My point is simply that we must understand that the two theories complement each other and that we must understand which theory fits under which circumstances.

However, a genuine difference exists between the probability view and the possibility view, and that is the interpretation. In probability theory, an outcome will either occur or not, whereas in fuzzy logic and possibility theory degrees of occurrence exist. Possibility theory is therefore closer to the concept of probability than probability theory, but this is simply due to historical reasons.

In all situations where Monte Carlo simulations take place, the calculus part of the theories matters the most in terms of operationalizing the difference, which is explained in the "Probability Theory Versus Possibility Theory" section. From that discussion, it is evident that because Activity-Based Life-Cycle Costing (LCC) relies on such numerical approximation methods, this difference between probability theory and possibility theory evaporates in the realm of theory.

Monte Carlo methods are, however, not the most common approach in economic analyses. Rather, the most common way is to assign probabilities to the outcomes, including LCC (as far as I have seen), and the use of decision trees or similar techniques, as illustrated in the example below, is common.

Decision Tree Example

The decision-maker in Figure 3.1 is facing a decision (the $\square$ node, a decision node) whether to reuse or recycle some glass bottles she is receiving next year, but the number of bottles (the O node, an event node) is associated with some risks (10,000 units or 30,000 units) as shown. The probability for receiving 10,000 units is 40 percent, while the probability for receiving 30,000 units is 60 percent.

If the decision-maker chooses to reuse the bottles but receives only 10,000, she is facing a loss, whereas 30,000 will give her the highest potential profit, namely

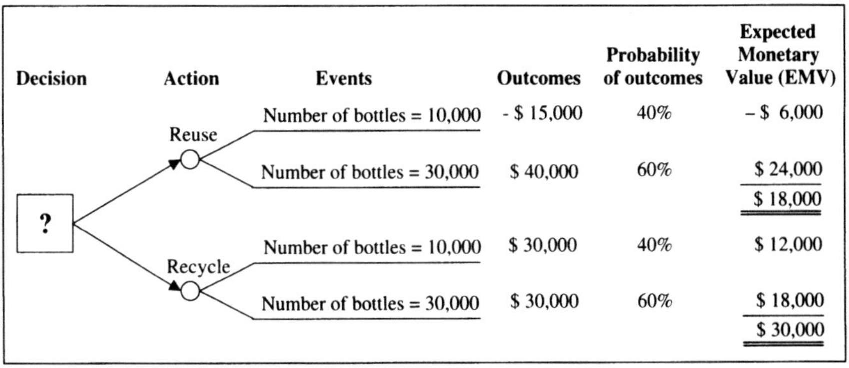

Decision	Action	Events	Outcomes	Probability of outcomes	Expected Monetary Value (EMV)
		Number of bottles = 10,000	- $ 15,000	40%	– $ 6,000
	Reuse				
		Number of bottles = 30,000	$ 40,000	60%	$ 24,000
					$ 18,000
?					
		Number of bottles = 10,000	$ 30,000	40%	$ 12,000
	Recycle				
		Number of bottles = 30,000	$ 30,000	60%	$ 18,000
					$ 30,000

Figure 3.1 Decision tree example.

$40,000. Recycling, however, is always guaranteed to be profitable because during the recycling process, no process loss exists (all the glass is broken before recycling), but the process is more costly, hence less profits on average.

To decide what to do, the decision-maker designs a decision tree, as shown in Figure 3.1. The Expected Monetary Value (EMV) of an action is calculated by multiplying the outcome values by the associated probabilities and then summing the values for each action. We see that Reuse has the lowest EMV and consequently the bottles should be recycled.

Or have we missed something? Yes, we forgot to find out whether the decision-maker is *risk averse, risk seeking,* or simply *indifferent.* In this example, as often, the choice with the best outcome has a high risk associated with it. Maybe she should reuse the bottles and gamble on receiving 30,000 units. That would give her the best profit, but if she receives only 10,000, the costs are too high to be balanced by the revenues and she may lose her job. Thus, deciding how to react to risks, which is discussed in the "Uncertainty, Risk, and Utility" section, is more complex than simply choosing the option with the highest EMV. But first we must discuss uncertainty.

Uncertainty: The Lack of Information and Knowledge

Uncertainty as a general noun is defined as "the state of being uncertain; doubt; hesitancy" in the 1989 edition of *Webster's.* Thus, neither loss nor chance is *necessarily* associated with uncertainty; it is simply *what is not known with certainty,* not the unknown.

Others define uncertainty as "the inability to assign probabilities to outcomes and risk is regarded as the ability to assign such probabilities based on differing perceptions of the existence of orderly relationships or patterns."[16] In most cases, however, relationships or patterns are not orderly; they are complex. Thus, uncertainty and complexity are intertwined, and interestingly in real life we can find many examples of how we depend on uncertainty to function and even survive. Not only that, by increasing the uncertainty, risk can be reduced and vice versa. This needs some explanation, and that is done in the following two sections.

Dependency on Uncertainty

Uncertainty exists in all situations that are unknown, unpredictable, open ended, or complex, but matters that are unknown or unpredictable are too difficult for analysis. I believe uncertainty can be best described as a subset of unpredictability, which in turn is a subset of the unknown. The reason is that an uncertain matter is not unknown or unpredictable. We simply lack information and knowledge about it; we lack certainty. In other words, unpredictability can be reduced to uncertainty given enough knowledge. Uncertainty is therefore best described in relation to complexity, which arises in open systems.

An open system is a system that interacts with its environment to various degrees and evolves over time. An open system is therefore a complex system because the interplay with the environment is complex; that is, only *loose couplings* exist between the open system and the different parts of the environment. A loose coupling can be thought of as an unclear or partial cause-and-effect relationship. Uncertainty, complexity, and openness are therefore intertwined and complementary; we cannot have one without the others.

Before I continue, I would like to clarify a common mix of terms: complex versus complicated. Complicated situations refer to situations where the cause-and-effect relations are well established (strong couplings) but where the sheer amount of information makes it difficult to comprehend. For example, clockwork is complicated, whereas sailing a boat is complex. Computers are therefore ideal in handling complicated issues. Also, complicated issues are not uncertain in themselves, but they may appear uncertain to us due to human ignorance.

When the complexity becomes large enough, we can talk about chaos. Possibly the most famous example of loose couplings (complexity) is the butterfly effect often cited as chaos theory in a nutshell. According to chaos theory, minute changes in the initial state of a system will over time lead to large-scale consequences, and the butterfly effect is a funny way of saying the same thing. A butterfly stirring the air today in Beijing can cause a storm in New York next month. Basically, a small change in a system can, but not necessarily, lead to a set of cascade effects that may build up to something large. This fact was first established by Edward Lorenz, who "realized that any physical system that behaved non-periodically would be unpredictable."[17] This unpredictability means that the behavior of the system is uncertain because we do not know how the system will react to change. Ironically, most complex systems are robust *because* of this unpredictability.

Take nature, for example, arguably the pinnacle of complex systems. Would nature as a system exist if it was predictable? I believe that the only systems that are predictable are dead systems. In fact, not even a completely dead system is completely predictable because of erosion and other degrading processes. But back to nature: Let us hypothesize that nature *is* predictable and then discuss the consequences. Any living organism tends to act in the easiest way possible (as seen by the organism; others may consider the way ridiculous). Then, if nature is predictable, organisms would evolve in certain ways to improve their own situation. In other words, the organisms would shed unneeded features and abilities. For example, abilities related to responsiveness would not be needed since there is nothing to respond to (because everything is already known and predicted). Yet one of Charles Darwin's most famous quotes is "It is not the strongest that survive, nor the most intelligent, but the ones most responsive to change." From this, we can reach two possible preliminary conclusions of our discussion: (1) Darwin is wrong or (2) our hypothesis is wrong. From our experience, I think it is fairly safe to say that it is the hypothesis that is wrong. Nature is not predictable; nature is unpredictable, but only within certain limits as defined by the laws of nature.

But how does that secure robustness? Because nature is unpredictable, all organisms contain latent features or abilities in order to face the unpredictable. This is not necessarily by purpose and design, but at least as a consequence over time due to the continuous changes in nature. This information resides in the organism's genes and cells, and it contains much more information than needed for its daily life. Essentially, every organism has an overkill of genetic information for its own purpose, but this overkill makes nature robust. If a major cataclysm takes place, someone will always benefit from it. For example, in the very early history of our planet, oxygen was a toxic by-product of the bacteria that ruled the world. Eventually, the amount of oxygen in the atmosphere rose above a certain level and the number of bacteria was vastly reduced (something like 99 percent of bacteria died), yet this gave room for life that thrived on oxygen, which ultimately led to the dawn of *Homo sapiens*—us.

Another example is the stock market. If the stock market was predictable, there would be no point trading stocks because everybody would know what was going to happen. Hence, there would be no market. Likewise, if the stock market was completely unpredictable, nobody would gain anything because no way would exist for establishing an advantage of some sort. Again, there would be no market.

A third example is democracy. If democracy was predictable, what would be the point of voting? There would be no democracy. Yet if democracy was completely unpredictable, what would be the point of election campaigns and politics? In other words, several examples support the claim that uncertainty is necessary for the survival of open systems.

What determines whether something is unknowable, unpredictable, or uncertain is our current level of knowledge. Something that appears to be unpredictable can therefore be reduced to uncertainty given an increased amount of knowledge. Thus, for a system that is as complex as nature, an uncertainty analysis is applicable but quite unreliable because we currently understand too little about nature. As Göthe said:

Nature goes her own way, and all that to us seems an exception is really according to order.

In far less complex systems than nature, such as corporations, it may be useful to create uncertainty in lieu of sufficient uncertainty in order to more effectively respond to the overall environmental unpredictability. Without this uncertainty, the system would gravitate toward one solution and hence lose its flexibility to respond to environmental unpredictability. This supports large corporations in using competing brands. Although they compete against each other and thereby create uncertainty within the corporation, they tend to make the corporation as a whole a more adaptable entity and therefore more competitive in the long run.

In other words, uncertainty is necessary for us. We depend on it because otherwise we would get lazy and rigid. Those who can manage uncertainty thrive on it, while those who cannot manage uncertainty face problems, and this is a source of great risks for organizations. In fact, uncertainty has become a tradable "asset" by using financial instruments such as derivatives. Thus, not only do we depend on uncertainty, uncertainty can also be a very profitable phenomenon for those who understand how to harvest its fruits.

Increase Uncertainty to Lower Risks

Risk and uncertainty are closely linked. As argued in the preceding section, adding uncertainty can actually reduce risks and vice versa. This is due to the fact that uncertainty and complexity are so closely linked and produce an unpleasant side effect for decision-makers, namely, lack of precision. Lotfi A. Zadeh formulated this fact in a theorem called the *Law of Incompatibility*:

> *As complexity rises, precise statements lose meaning and meaningful statements lose precision.*

Since all organizations experience some degree of complexity in their decision-making, this theorem is crucial to take seriously and act accordingly. Nobel laureate Kenneth Arrow warns us that "[O]ur knowledge of the way things work, in society or in nature, comes trailing clouds of vagueness. Vast ills have followed a belief in certainty." Basically, this means that ignoring complexity and/or uncertainty is risky. Luckily, the reverse is also true; increasing the uncertainty in the decision-making process and associated analyses to better reflect the *true* uncertainty actually will lower the risk, as argued in the previous section. Thus, striking a sound balance between meaningfulness and precision is crucial and can be achieved only by possessing a relatively clear understanding of uncertainty and risk.

Uncertainty is essentially inherent in a system due to knowledge or information deficiency. The former is due to the simple fact that some things are unknowable, whereas the latter arises due to information incompleteness or limited cognition. However, uncertainty can be categorized in order to make it clearer. One such way is shown in Figure 3.2. We see that two main types of uncertainty exist: fuzziness and ambiguity.

Fuzziness occurs whenever definite, sharp, clear, or crisp distinctions cannot be or are not made. For example, "Let's eat lunch around noon" is a fuzzy statement, because what is "around noon"? Is it 11:55, 12:05, 12:30, or something else? We do not know; the timing is fuzzy. Eleven sources of fuzziness exist,[18] but the three main sources are:

1. Fuzziness due to inexact conditions of observations
2. Fuzziness due to classification in an under- or overdimensioned universe
3. Fuzziness due to the intersubject differences with respect to the membership function

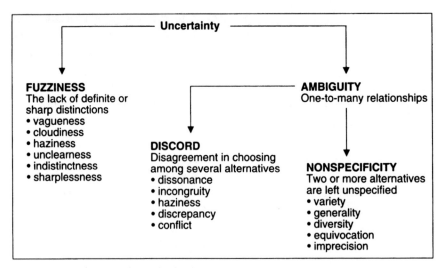

Figure 3.2 Basic types of uncertainty. Source: Adapted from G.J. Klir and B. Yuan, *Fuzzy Sets and Fuzzy Logic: Theory and Applications.* New York: Prentice-Hall, 1995, p. 268.

The first fuzziness is essentially the error we make when making estimates from observations. The second fuzziness revolves around our inability either to include (exactly) everything or to simplify, while the third basically deals with the differences in human perceptions.

Ambiguity, however, results from unclear definitions of the various alternatives involved. For example, "See you tomorrow at 7:00" is an ambiguous statement because you will wonder whether it is A.M. or P.M. The alternatives involved can be in conflict with each other or they can be left unspecified. The former is ambiguity resulting from discord, whereas the latter is ambiguity resulting from nonspecificity. The ambiguity resulting from discord is essentially what the probability theory revolves around because "probability theory can model only situations where there are conflicting beliefs about mutually exclusive alternatives."[19] In fact, neither fuzziness nor nonspecificity can be conceptualized by probability theory. In other words, uncertainty is too wide-ranging a concept for probability theory.

In fact, one study discussed the various methods used in risk analysis and classified them as either classical (probability based) or conceptual (fuzzy sets based):

. . . probability models suffer from two major limitations. Some models require detailed quantitative information, which is not normally available at the time of planning, and the applicability of such models to real project risk analysis is limited, because agencies participating in the project have a problem with making precise decisions. The problems are ill-defined and vague, and they thus require subjective evaluations, which classical models cannot handle.[20]

Zadeh therefore launched the concept of fuzzy logic, the first new method of dealing with uncertainty since the development of probability. Another product of Zadeh's mind is *possibility theory*, which will be discussed in "Theory of Fuzzy Numbers and Fuzzy Intervals." With respect to the discussion in "Probability Theory Versus Possibility Theory," we see here that it is important to distinguish the concept of probability, which has not been discussed earlier, and the measures of probability, which have been scrutinized previously.

Both fuzzy logic and possibility theory are used to examine and reduce uncertainty in areas as diverse as washing machines and environmental problems. Many are therefore starting to believe that everything is a matter of degree. This is a lost point in probability theory because in it everything is crisp and clear; an event will either occur or not. This is not strange since probability theory was developed from games of dice and gambling, and in such settings logic is crisp. That is, a dice will produce a 1, 2, 3, 4, 5, or 6, and nothing in between. Over time, probability distributions have reduced this problem of discreteness to some extent, but they rely on hard data, something we often do not have the luxury of possessing.

Probability Theory versus Possibility Theory

For my work, the crux of the difference between classic probability theory and possibility theory lies in the estimation of a probability. For example, consider the Venn diagram in Figure 3.3. The two outcomes A and B in outcome space S overlap; that is, they are not mutually exclusive. The probability of A is in other words dependent on the probability of B, and vice versa. In Figure 3.2, this was referred to as a nonspecific ambiguous situation.

In probability theory, we look at A in relation to S and correct for overlaps so that the sum of all outcomes will be 100 percent (all exhaustible). In theory, this is unproblematic, but in practice determining the probability of A ∩ B is difficult at best because A and B are interdependent; that is, they overlap. Thus, in cases

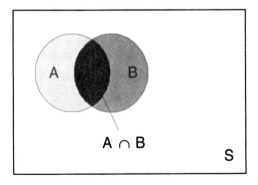

Figure 3.3   Two nonmutually exclusive outcomes in outcome space S.

where this interdependency is important, the larger the probability of A ∩ B is, the larger becomes the mistake of using probability theory. In possibility theory, however, we simply look at the outcomes in relation to each other, and consequently S becomes irrelevant and overlaps do not matter. The possibility of A will simply be A to A + B in Figure 3.3. Hence, at some point it is wise to use possibility theory.

In other words, probabilistic approaches are based on counting, whereas possibilistic logic is simply based on relative comparison. Clearly, possibility theory is intuitive and easy, but we pay a price: loss of precision (an outcome in comparison to outcome space). This loss of precision, however, is truer to high levels of complexity, and that is crucial in a business context.

Before we continue, it should be noted that the term *event* applied in probability theory requires a certain level of distinctness in defining what is occurring and what is not. The term *sensation* has therefore been proposed; a sensation is something weaker than an event. Also, although sensations have some probability of happening, we introduce possibility, in addition to the aforementioned reasons, to further emphasize that positive risks should be pursued actively (*risicare*), hence including all opportunities (possibilities). That cannot be achieved unless risks are connected to future, foreseen *sensations* and we capitalize on them.

But it is one thing to examine and reduce uncertainty and risk; it is another thing to decide what to do. Several theories for decision-making exist. Possibly the most popular one is the utility theory, at least in the face of risk and uncertainty.

UNCERTAINTY, RISK, AND UTILITY

The decision-maker in the example in "Sources of Risk" preferred to play it safe and accept a profit of $10,000 lower than what it could have been in 60 percent of the cases. Such behavior can be characterized as risk averse. This type of behavior is the most common,[21] but it has been argued that some people actually exhibit risk-seeking behavior in certain situations. The rationale is, for example, that poor people buy disproportionately more lottery tickets than wealthy people because a poor person is willing to take risks in order to get out of his or her situation. If this is true, people react to risk differently depending on their status, economic situation, and so on. Or as an economist would say, people would act in order to maximize their *utility*, not necessarily to maximize the EMV.

Utility can be defined in many ways, but if we turn to the 1989 edition of *Webster's* we find it defined as the "state or quality of being useful; usefulness." In other words, people will generally try to maximize whatever they think is useful. For some, this will mean that they aim for the highest profits while accepting a higher risk, whereas others may settle for a lower return knowing that it is relatively safe. Economists have defined utility somewhat differently, namely as "the ability to satisfy wants,"[22] and saying that utility is "the ultimate goal of all economic activity."[23]

In fact, Daniel Bernoulli (in 1738) and later economists devised an entire theory called *utility theory*. Utility theory, or expected utility theory, is important because it attempts to reconcile real behavior with EMV in decision-making, and it is in fact the theory that most economists rely on when dealing with risks and decision-making.[24] It is both a *prescriptive* and *descriptive* approach to decision-making, as we are told how individuals and corporations *should* make decisions, as well as predicting how they *do* make decisions.

The basic assumption in utility theory that Bernoulli developed is that people make decisions to maximize Expected Utility (EU). According to the theory, each decision-maker has a certain utility function that represents each outcome of an event in terms of utility value. The utility function is therefore derived from the decision-maker's attitudes toward risk and outcomes (refer to Figure 3.4) and is usually determined by the popular Certainty Equivalent Method, whereby information from an individual is elicited by asking questions about lotteries. Depending on the shape of the utility function, it is determined whether an individual is risk averse, risk seeking, or indifferent (risk neutral), as shown in Figure 3.4:

- Risk-averse person, concave utility function
- Risk-neutral person, linear utility function
- Risk-seeking person, convex utility function

As illustrated in Figure 3.4 and argued earlier, it is believed that the utility function is dependent on wealth. In fact, many economists argue that the logical thing to do for an intelligent investor is to give up a smaller risk premium when faced with the same risky option as those less fortunate.[25] But people do not necessarily act logically, as explained later.

The fact that decision-making can be described by such an apparently beautiful mathematical theory is very appealing, and some have therefore introduced utility theory into cost models. Thus, it may appear that utility theory can be very

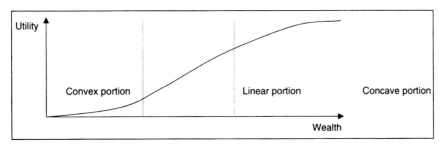

Figure 3.4   Example of a utility function.

straightforwardly and effectively applied in LCC because of its mathematical rigor. Three problems, in my opinion, make utility theory impractical in most situations, although it is useful in *explaining* behavior.

First, establishing a reliable utility function is, at best, difficult. In some cases, it is virtually impossible, whereas in others it is quite possible. The impossible cases are cases when laymen are involved (such as consumer products) because laymen are normally more irrational than experts. The most likely cases where utility theory can actually have merit are when highly technical decisions are made (technical products that are evaluated almost entirely by performance, such as power cables).

Second, and possibly profoundly important, Arrows' Impossibility Theorem states that "a group consisting only of rational individuals need not exhibit transitive preferences and in general will not." Thus, even though we could establish reliable utility functions for each individual, the outcome would still be irrational and hence unsuitable for mathematical modeling.

A third reason is that the theory in fact does not quite capture reality well: "Expected utility theory says risk attitudes drive solely from changes in marginal utility associated with fluctuations in lifetime wealth. Hence, the theory says that people will not be averse to risks involving monetary gains and losses that do not alter lifetime wealth enough to affect significantly the marginal utility one derives from that lifetime wealth."[26] The theory hence implies that people should be risk neutral to a gamble that involves small stakes, but people are not. Thus, utility theory is internally inconsistent, or illogical. It has, however, produced good results in, for example, financial markets in the shape of game theory. That might be because most financial experts would view themselves as rational, yet the overall financial market is often perceived as irrational, and that finance has a single objective. Hence, utility theory might be involuntarily correct concerning financial markets and some other special cases.

Nonetheless, for the aforementioned reasons, I believe that although we can give detailed decision support using utility theory, it is probably wisest in the general case to identify the risks and uncertainties, and estimate their impact on the outcomes. Then the decision-maker(s) can decide how to use this knowledge. After all, managerial thinking (especially at the more senior levels) in all organizations requires intuition and the exercise of subjective judgment. For example, in Figure 3.1, I think it would be sound to estimate the probabilities for the outcomes and to compute the EMVs, but it would be unwise to analyze what the decision-maker should do using EU or something similar. That follows from Arrows' warning that "Vast ills have followed a belief in certainty," because we would make something appear certain that in reality is not. Thus, from what I have seen and understood, it is a far greater risk to eliminate a risk than to manage it. Deception is a far greater risk than most risks in my opinion.

COMMON WAYS OF ANALYZING RISK AND UNCERTAINTY

Other sources provide many different ways of dealing with risk and uncertainty but since this book is not about risk management, but about managerial LCC, this discussion is confined to the approaches that are most common in management today and that may be pertinent to LCC. These are the decision tree and the what-if technique (and their derivatives), and they are discussed in the next two sections. After that, a more generic technique for determining significant risks is discussed.

These techniques, however, lack an important part of risk management and uncertainty analysis: how to develop and implement ongoing measures to deal with risk and uncertainty. Since that particular part of risk management is very generic, it is covered in "Traditional Risk Management" because it is always applicable, regardless of risk and uncertainty analysis methods.

Much of the management literature seems to ignore the difference between risk and uncertainty that is explained in this book. Risk and uncertainty are almost used interchangeably and are simply often defined as, in one textbook, "the possibility that an actual amount will deviate from a forecasted amount."

Decision Tree Technique

Figure 3.1 shows a decision tree is from which the EMVs can be found. The decision-maker can ultimately make a decision, unless she wants to buy additional information to further clarify issues that may be unclear. Whether she should pursue additional information or not is a matter of cost versus benefit. But before the decision tree is set up, a decision model must be designed.

As the name indicates, a decision model is a model that describes how the decision-maker is to arrive at a decision. The following five-step model illustrates a decision model behind decision trees:

1. Identify the objective function (choice criterion) of the decision-maker. The purpose of the objective function is to specify what the objective is; that provides the basis for choosing the best alternative.
2. Identify the set of actions that the decision-maker considers.
3. Identify the set of relevant events that can occur. It is important that this set is mutually exclusive and collectively exhaustible so that all bases are covered.
4. Assign probabilities for the occurrence of each event.
5. Identify the set of possible outcomes (payoffs) that are dependent on specific actions and events. Basically, for a given specific set of actions and the relevant events that can occur as a consequence of these actions, identify the possible outcomes. A decision table might be helpful to summarize the information before drawing the decision tree.

Others propose an eight-step model that includes obtaining additional information via experimentation, choice, and calculations of a desired profit function, but the generic steps are the same. In any case, you will end up with a tree such as the one shown in Figure 3.1, but how well does such a tree capture the *real* risk?

The best way to illustrate this method's capability to capture the real risk (as opposed to the calculated or assessed risk) is to plotting the results. If we look at the situation in Figure 3.1, we can plot it as shown in Figure 3.5. Clearly, many options have not been captured, such as the white box area compared to the four points. Why is that? This is mainly for two reasons:

1. The decision tree analysis is a discrete technique. That is, the outcomes are just points among a large area of possibility.
2. Only a very limited number of outcomes can be analyzed. This is partly a consequence of the former point, but it is simply due to the fact that performing an all-exhaustive search among all possibilities is too laborious even with a computer.

Our example was only two-dimensional (the number of units and profits) for each action. Now imagine a more real situation where profits depend on many variables. The situation in Figure 3.5 would be even worse. Hence, the reliability of the decision tree approach is rather low.

An elegant solution to this problem is shown in the *Reduce Risk by Introducing Uncertainty* section, but first another famous technique: the what-if technique.

What-If Technique

As the name indicates, the what-if technique is a technique where we ask ourselves or a computer model many "What if this happens?" types of questions. Instead of

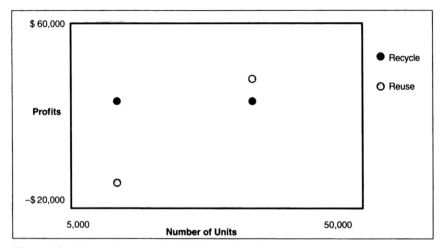

Figure 3.5   Captured versus all possible outcomes.

calculating the probabilities of the various events as in the decision tree method, we simply vary the input variables in the model and look at the response in the output variable(s). In other words, we are investigating the responsiveness, or sensitivity, of the output variable(s) to changes in the input variables. A what-if analysis is therefore essentially a sensitivity analysis technique and a more general approach to measuring the impact of uncertainty.

With respect to our example, we would not ask what is the probability of the number of units being 10,000, 30,000, or anything else. We would rather ask "What if the number of units received is 10,000?" and then use a model to assess the profits. We would proceed like that until the decision-maker found the risk (of making an erroneous decision) acceptable.

Although this technique is very simple, it is probably a better approach than the decision tree method because it is easier and enables us to more easily and more cost effectively study a larger amount of possible outcomes. Chapter 6 illustrates the what-if technique in a case.

Unfortunately, the technique does not overcome the basic problems of the decision tree method, although it is easier to try out many more scenarios. Rather, another problem has been added: We can only vary one variable at a time because otherwise we cannot measure its impact on the output variable. Thus, an implicit assumption exists, namely that for every new value of an input variable, *everything else remains constant*. But how many times can you recall where everything actually did remain the same? None? This approach is therefore based on a major flaw that makes it deceptively reliable. It simply ignores the fact that in reality some input variables may have a higher value than anticipated, some have a lower value, and others nobody knows.

In the "How Belief Sheds Light on Risk and Uncertainty" section, the solution to these problems is presented, but first we turn to a very simple and generic approach for determining significant risks.

Generic Risk-Ranking Technique

Both the what-if and the decision tree techniques rely on a common baseline of impact, which in LCC will normally be a monetary/economic measure with a unit such as U.S. dollars. But what if no common impact baseline exists? Then we must establish it, and to do that we need a so-called risk factor (RF) or risk value that can scale and aggregate the various risk estimates.

To calculate the RF for something, we need two things: a probability estimate and a consequence/impact estimate. Since we have no common baseline, the first impact statement is often expressed verbally; then we assign values that can be in the (0, 1) range or on a 1 to 5 scale, for example. Here we can estimate the values using probability theory, possibility theory, or something else, but often a very simple subjective assignment is used.

Table 3.4 Normalized Probabilities and Impacts due to Sea-Level Rise in the Next 50 Years

If Sea Level Rises	Risk Likelihood	Probability (p)	Risk Impact	Impact (i)
0.1 meters	Almost certain	0.95	Low	0.05
0.5 meters	Highly likely	0.70	High	0.50
1.0 meters	Likely	0.40	Extreme	0.80
2.0 meters	Unlikely	0.10	Catastrophic	0.95

Consider the example in Table 3.4. A sea-level rise is something we are actually facing, up to 3.0 mm per year, according to studies by the Intergovernmental Panel on Climate Change (IPCC), but what is the risk? Economic estimates of the consequences have probably already been done, so the impacts are measured in terms of money, but let us take another simpler approach.

Our job is to look at the consequences, but we do not want to use any economic approach because we think money cannot really capture a problem of this magnitude. We obtain probability estimates from a risk analysis, so all we have to do is find the impact and calculate the RFs.

First, we must identify the consequences. It is clear that a sea-level rise will affect everybody living by the sea, but it is fair to assume that cities will face the biggest challenges because they must build defenses for their harbors and/or raise the city in some way. We therefore ask a group of city development experts what they think the impact will be. Their answers are shown in the impact column in Table 3.4.

Then we convert the verbal impact statements to numerical measures. We ask the group to consider this: "On a scale of 0 to 1 (1 being the worst), how bad is catastrophic? How bad is extreme?" We are essentially asking the experts to transform the verbal statements to a baseline of their own liking. In other words, the impact measure has no units.

The answers are found in the rightmost column of Table 3.4. We see from the answers that the experts consider the rise in sea level from 0.1 meters to 0.5 meters to be relatively worse than the rise from 1.0 meters to 2.0 meters. Perhaps they think that once the water passes 0.5 meters, it is so bad that the impact curve starts to flatten toward the 1.0 asymptote already at the 0.5 meters rise or even before. Nevertheless, we now have both probability estimates and impact measures. Then we just need to combine them to calculate the RF.

The RF can be calculated in numerous ways. It is important to be consistent and document which method is used. The New South Wales Government Asset Management Committee provides two techniques for calculating RF. Out of those two techniques, the one I prefer is given by:

$$RF = p + i - (p \times i) \qquad (3.1)$$

The sea-level consequences can therefore be described as in Table 3.5. By ordering the RF in Table 3.5 in decreasing order, we can generate a so-called risk profile.

The purpose of the risk profile is to aid decision-makers in prioritizing. Priority should be given to the consequences with the highest RF values. In our simple example, we see from Table 3.5 that it is the extreme options that got the highest RF values. For city planners in coastal areas of the world, this would imply (if the data were real) that they should concentrate on small sea-level rises and very large rises. Those in between should have a lower priority.

We can also do it even more simplistically, but not necessarily less reliably. If we use a 1 to 5 scale for both probabilities and impacts (1 being very low and 5 being very high), we get a reworked Table 3.4 as shown in Table 3.6.

The consequences will therefore be measured on a 1 to 25 scale because the consequence is simply the product of the probability and the impact, that is:

$$RF = p \times i \qquad (3.2)$$

For this particular example, the consequences are shown in Table 3.7. Since Equation 3.2 is different from Equation 3.1, the consequences are, of course, calculated differently and hence the results are different, as is evident from comparing Table 3.5 to Table 3.7.

The immediate question that arises is naturally: Which method is most reliable? Equation 3.1 or Equation 3.2? Should we focus on an 0.5-meter sea-level rise (the

Table 3.5 Normalized Sea-Level Rise Risk Factors

If Sea Level Rises	Consequence (RF)
0.1 meters	0.95
0.5 meters	0.85
1.0 meters	0.88
2.0 meters	0.96

Table 3.6 Scaled Probabilities and Impacts Due to Sea-Level Rise in the Next 50 Years

If Sea Level Rises	Risk Likelihood	Probability (p)	Risk Impact	Impact (i)
0.1 meter	Almost certain	5	Low	1
0.5 meter	Highly likely	4	High	3
1.0 meter	Likely	2	Extreme	4
2.0 meter	Unlikely	1	Catastrophic	5

Table 3.7   Scaled Sea-Level Rise Consequences

If Sea Level Rises	Consequence (RF)
0.1 meters	5
0.5 meters	12
1.0 meters	8
2.0 meters	5

worst according to Table 3.7) or on the extreme versions, as are evident from Table 3.5? Since we have no common baseline from which we can argue which equation is the most logical, we cannot really say that one is better than the other. In many ways, it seems more intuitive to focus on the extreme version (see Table 3.5 and Equation 3.1), but on the other hand, it is difficult to understand why we should accept Equation 3.1 over Equation 3.2. I tend to prefer Equation 3.2 and use a scale of 1 to 5 because it is simple, easy to understand, and conceptually similar to the EMV. Because that approach does not rely on normalized probability assessments and impact statements, it is important to be consistent in the choice of scales.

This technique also works well in combination with monetary measures, but when monetary measures are present, other techniques perform better most of the time.

HOW BELIEF SHEDS LIGHT ON RISK AND UNCERTAINTY

Regardless of the assessment and management methods used, three main avenues exist for dealing with uncertainty (see Glossary).

The most common approach is to use either discrete probability estimates or continuous probability distributions. However, in complex models, not to mention in reality, the additional information needed to quantify probability estimates or probability distributions is often not obtainable at a reasonable cost if at all. Furthermore, because of the computational strengths of modern computers, it does not make much sense to simplify a problem that is already fairly easy to handle by making additional assumptions that only reduce the usefulness of the output from the models.

The second approach is Bayesian statistics. This is perhaps the approach that relies the most on hard data and consequently involves the least guesswork, but that also presents a problem. Historical data are often impossible to find when performing an original design, and they are hard to find in many other situations as well. Also, sometimes guesswork can be better than historical data because when using historical data, one implicitly assumes that the future will be somewhat like the past. This is true enough when minor changes or product improvements are involved, but it hardly applies to original products or major corporate decisions, simply because such decisions are almost by definition not made frequently enough to generate reliable historical data. Consequently, Bayesian statistics cannot be used in general. It should be noted, however, that in some areas, such as hydrogeology/hydrology, Bayesian statistics are commonly used.

The third approach is to employ the theory of fuzzy numbers and fuzzy intervals, which derives from fuzzy logic. This is a very flexible way of handling uncertainty, and it has two great advantages:

1. Fuzzy numbers and fuzzy intervals can be used with or without hard data. Bayesian statistics, on the other hand, need quite a large sample of hard data. However, it is always preferable to have as much *relevant* hard data as possible.
2. The use of fuzzy numbers and fuzzy intervals has very few, if any, restrictions. This is the perfect tool of numerical theories and applications.[27]

The good thing about fuzzy numbers and intervals is that they are an effective way to model gut instinct. This is crucial because gut instinct is important in managerial thinking (especially at the more senior levels), and experiments show that processing knowledge about uncertainty categorically—that is, by means of verbal expressions—imposes less mental workload on the decision-maker than numerical processing. Furthermore, the NRC Governing Board on the Assessment of Risk points out the "important responsibility not to use numbers, which convey the impression of precision when the understanding of relationships is indeed less secure. Thus, while quantitative risk assessment facilitates comparison, such comparison may be illusory or misleading if the use of precise numbers is unjustified."

An equally compelling reason, however, is that probabilistic approaches are based on counting, whereas possibilistic logic is based simply on comparing. Comparing is easier for people because, as experiments show, "one needs to present comparison scenarios that are located on the probability scale to evoke people's own feeling of risk." This is particularly true for low-probability risks, and many business risks are low-probability risks because the number of potential outcomes of a decision is so vast. Moreover, as the literature points out, given the increasingly complex and uncertain environment in which contemporary organizations operate, there is a need to be able to "embrace complexity and learn how to handle uncertainty." Thus, a method in which one can blend rationality with irrationality should be highly useful. In the words of a commercial lender:

> ... *basic credit decisions are often based solely on considerations of the heart (often biased), head (analytical) or gut instinct (experience). Using these guidelines, I have generally found that if my heart overrules my head, the loan has almost uniformly been a poor one. If my head overrules my gut instinct, the resulting loan may sometimes be a poor one. In looking back at poor loans, I should have followed my gut instinct more often.*[28]

The basic problem of probability theory is that it is too precise. Yet, in his acclaimed book *Against the Gods: The Remarkable Story of Risk*, Peter Bernstein does not mention fuzzy logic at all. Evidently, fuzzy numbers and intervals have many advantages over more conventional approaches; how this works is explained in the following section. Also, as discussed below, there are virtually no disadvantages if fuzzy numbers and fuzzy intervals are approximated numerically.

Note that the next section is theoretical and can be skipped without losing the thread of the book. However, it is helpful to understand the logic behind the use of uncertainty distributions, which is discussed at the end of the section.

Theory of Fuzzy Numbers and Fuzzy Intervals

In order to understand what fuzzy numbers and fuzzy intervals are, we must go back to the basics, to when we first started to learn mathematics. We looked at sets of things and determined what belonged where. The most basic was to look at five balls, three of which were green and two were blue, and then answer the question, "How many green balls do you see?" From this, we learned class membership; there were three balls that were members of the class of green balls. Furthermore, there were two circles, one with five cows inside and four in the other. We were asked to decide which set was greater than the other. We soon learned that five is larger than four. Thus, such sets, ordinary sets, provided a very clear and sharp definition of "much" versus "little." They provided a systematic framework for dealing with fuzzy quantifiers, such as many, few, and most, as well as linguistic variables like tall, small, old, and so on.

Fuzzy sets, in contrast, are of the vague type (more versus less). Fuzzy sets are therefore viewed as a generalization of ordinary sets and, according to Zadeh, "provide a natural way of dealing with problems in which the source of imprecision is the absence of sharply defined criteria of class membership rather than the presence of random variables." In other words, the occurrence of fuzzy sets is not due to randomness but to imprecision, lack of certainty, vagueness, ambiguity, and so on. This is a major difference from probability theory, but for Monte Carlo methods the difference in interpretation makes no difference to the calculations, because Monte Carlo methods are numerical approximation methods and, hence, treat probability distributions, fuzzy numbers, fuzzy intervals, and possibility distributions in the same way.

Although fuzzy sets are of the vague type, the theory is by no means vague. In set theory, an object (number) is either within the set or not, while in fuzzy set theory, it is not that simple. If X is a collection of objects denoted generically by x, then a *fuzzy set* $\tilde{A}$ in X is a set of ordered pairs:

$$\tilde{A} = \{(x, \mu_{\tilde{A}}(x)) \mid x \in X\} \tag{3.3}$$

where $\mu_{\tilde{A}}$ is the membership function that maps X to the membership space M and $\mu_{\tilde{A}}(x)$ is the grade of membership (also the degree of compatibility or degree of

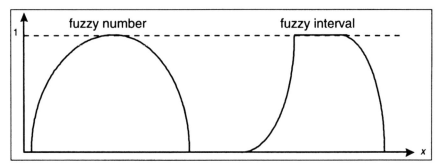

Figure 3.6 Fuzzy numbers versus fuzzy intervals. Source: Adapted from H. Bandemer and W. Näther, *Fuzzy Data Analysis*. Dordrecht, The Netherlands: Kluwer Academic Press, 1992, p. 341.

truth) of x in $\tilde{A}$. In other words, the real crux of the fuzzy set lies in the definition of $\mu_{\tilde{A}}(x)$ which describes to which extent (degree) a number is part of the membership space. In ordinary sets, it would be either zero or one, but in fuzzy sets, or fuzzy logic, it can be anything in between as well. In fact, $\mu_{\tilde{A}}(x)$ could be a probability distribution or a set of probabilities, or maybe we should say a *possibility distribution* and a set of possibilities. We can go both ways; we can probabilize the fuzzy sets as well as fuzzify the events (in probability theory). The possibilities are limited only by one's imagination and a mix is unavoidable. In fact, the role possibility theory plays for fuzzy sets is analogous to the role mathematical expectancy plays in probability theory. Thus, possibility theory and fuzzy logic match each other in much the same way that probability theory and ordinary crisp sets match each other.

Nahmias in the United States and Dubois and Prade in France have taken the notion of fuzzy sets and developed it further into fuzzy intervals and fuzzy numbers. Basically, fuzzy numbers provide the connection between the fuzzy set theory and the confidence theory. Fuzzy numbers and intervals define a multidimensional area of confidence, whereas confidence intervals in confidence theory are one-dimensional, as in Figure 3.6. A confidence interval would be like a slice in the x direction, thus missing the l direction totally. In other words, fuzzy numbers and intervals are less strictly defined, are associated with fewer assumptions, and are therefore more general approaches.

However, a difference also exists between fuzzy numbers and fuzzy intervals, because depending on the shape of the membership function, fuzzy numbers and fuzzy intervals are defined differently (see Figure 3.6). A fuzzy number has to be bounded and convex, while an interval is only bounded.

For example, a triangular fuzzy number on $\mathcal{R}$ (see Figure 3.7) is characterized by its membership function $\mu_N(x)$: $\mathcal{R} \rightarrow (0, 1)$ with:

$$\mu_N(x) = \begin{cases} \frac{1}{m-1}x - \frac{1}{m-1} & for \quad x \in [l, m] \\ \frac{1}{m-n}x - \frac{n}{m-n} & for \quad x \in [m, n] \\ 0 \; otherwise \end{cases}$$

(3.4)

Just like ordinary numbers and intervals, fuzzy numbers and fuzzy intervals can be added and multiplied. For a triangular number like the one in Figure 3.7, the computations involved in these two definitions are rather laborious. However, on the basis of the extension principle, the addition and multiplication of two fuzzy numbers, $\tilde{N}_1$ and $\tilde{N}_2$, for example, are defined as follows:

Addition:

$$\mu_{\tilde{N}_1 \oplus \tilde{N}_2}(z) = sup(min(\mu_{\tilde{N}_1}(x), \mu_{\tilde{N}_2}(y)))$$

$$(x, y) \in \mathcal{R}^2$$

$$z = x + y$$

$$= sup(min(\mu_{\tilde{N}_1}(x), \mu_{\tilde{N}_2}(z - x)))$$

$$x \in \mathcal{R}$$

(3.5)

Multiplication:

$$\mu_{\tilde{N}_1 \otimes \tilde{N}_2}(z) = sup(min(\mu_{\tilde{N}_1}(x), \mu_{\tilde{N}_2}(y)))$$

$$(x, y) \in \mathcal{R}^2$$

$$z = x \cdot y$$

$$= sup(min(\mu_{\tilde{N}_1}(x), \mu_{\tilde{N}_2}(z/x)))$$

$$x \in \mathcal{R}$$

(3.6)

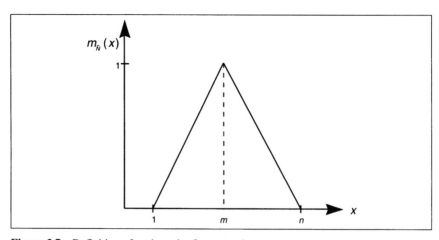

Figure 3.7 Definition of a triangular fuzzy number.

To reduce the amount of work associated with the aforementioned addition and multiplication procedures, some approximation methods have been designed. For example, one could approximate the addition but solve the rest of the computations exactly.

A step further from an exact solution and/or from approximating the exact solution is to approximate the entire solution by employing numerical approximation techniques. This is done by modeling the uncertainty as fuzzy numbers, as in Figure 3.8, and consequently solving the model numerically by employing a Monte Carlo simulation technique. This is the method I have worked with the most; I recommend it for reasons explained in the next section.

Since no difference exists between the various approaches of modeling uncertainty when employing numerical approximation techniques, it is more useful simply to talk about uncertainty distributions, given that we need not capture the difference in interpretation between the various approaches. In the rest of the book, I therefore simply talk about uncertainty distributions.

Handling Models with Many Variables

First, I would like to clarify why a numerical approach is chosen and not an exact approach when it comes to the mathematical aspects. The reason is simply that LCC in particular and cost management and performance measurement in general depend heavily on performing sensitivity analyses and handling uncertainty. Essentially, two distinct approaches to sensitivity and uncertainty analysis exist. One is the use of differential methods, whereas the other is the use of statistical methods.

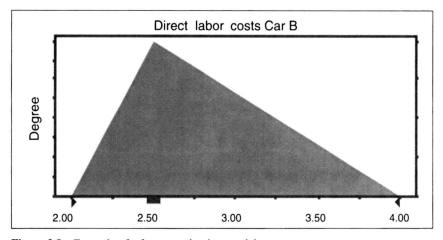

Figure 3.8   Example of a fuzzy number in a model.

Differential methods involve calculating partial derivatives and are therefore, in my opinion, very difficult to apply for large systems of variables because "one run of the code is required for *each* point at which partial derivatives are to be evaluated."[29] Add to that the efforts spent in handling the uncertainty.

Statistical methods, on the other hand, involve the use of regression (response surface) methods and related partial correlation coefficients, but they yield essentially the same results. Moreover, "an advantage of statistical methods is that the partial correlation coefficients are computed from model evaluations at *several* points in some region in the input space."[30] In plain words, a statistical method simulates what happens in the model for a sufficient number of points so that the overall simulation of the model is good enough, but not exact. It is like conducting a political survey; although you interview only 1,500 individuals, you have a pretty good idea about the overall opinion of the entire population.

Also, the sensitivity analysis and the uncertainty can be handled at the same time. In fact, the very mechanism behind many statistical methods is to *introduce* uncertainty on purpose in the model's input variables in order to measure statistically the impact this uncertainty has on the output's variables. Then you accurately measure the output's sensitivity to the input, given that the uncertainty is modeled consistently and as bounded symmetric uncertainty distributions throughout the model (see the simple example in Appendix A). So by adding uncertainty to the model, the risk is actually reduced. As discussed later, the Monte Carlo methods exploit this beautiful paradox for all it's worth.

Statistical methods are methods that rely on n-point evaluations in m-dimensional space to produce an approximate solution (because that is what we need since an exact approach will not work). In plain English, m is the number of variables, while n is the number of points used for an assessment. A point is a specific set of values for the m variables. "Among all numerical methods that rely on n-point evaluations in m-dimensional space to produce an approximate solution, the so-called Monte Carlo methods have an absolute error of estimate that decreases as $n^{-1/2}$ whereas, in the absence of exploitable special structure, all others have errors that decrease as $n^{-1/m}$ at best."[31] This is a crucial point because it says that the error in the approximation is smaller for Monte Carlo methods than for other comparable methods. The error is basically an estimate of how different the approximation is from the true answer. This can be assessed using standard statistical techniques.

Despite this fact, "Monte Carlo methods were considered mathematical blasphemy until as recently as 1970. Today, however, Monte Carlo methods are the *only* approaches capable of providing useful insights in several problems in physics."[32] Although the Monte Carlo method is now the most powerful and commonly used technique for analyzing complex problems, some are less enthusiastic about using it.

For example, some claim that "the computational burden precludes the use of standard[33] Monte Carlo analysis." This statement must be interpreted in relation to climate models that are comprised of hierarchical computer codes, because then the Monte Carlo analyses must be performed at several levels and provide input to each other, which is not the case in LCC or any management discipline. Clearly, a Simple Random Sampling (SRS) Monte Carlo method will be time consuming in such a situation. However, by using Latin Hypercube Sampling (LHS), the number of trials can be reduced drastically. The only problem with LHS is the difficulty in computing the mean output response. It is therefore suggested to break up the models into a hierarchy and run a simulation first to identify the most important variables. Then run Monte Carlo simulations including only the most important variables. However, this can be a dangerous approach because it neglects the "insignificant" variables. Delta Airlines' success over the past 20 years, for example, can be attributed to the fact that they have done all the little things—that is, the insignificant variables—right.[34] Doing the big things right is probably more a prerequisite for being in business than excelling in business. Excellence lies in the details. It should be mentioned that a large number of various sampling techniques is used with Monte Carlo methods and have certain advantages in certain situations, and some variations of LHS have been created that perform better.

In any case, the choice should be clear since LCC and cost management problems with many variables (large m) are *not* nested. In fact, I have not been able to find any numerical method that can even remotely compete with Monte Carlo methods for management purposes. Another issue is that Monte Carlo methods never go wrong. Thus, the only issue is what is fastest:

- To run a Monte Carlo simulation once and for all and be done, or
- To reduce the size of the problem and then solve the problem wondering if you missed something

The latter approach is a reductionist approach. Johnson and Kaplan argue, in their book *Relevance Lost: The Rise and Fall of Management Accounting,* that the reductionist approach was one of the main reasons for the loss of relevance in management accounting until the introduction of Activity-Based Costing (ABC). Researchers simply made the problems so simple that they could employ their theories; in the process they missed the point that reality is complex and cannot be sliced up into one problem here and another problem there. Everything is connected.

In any case, I believe that because modern software enables distributed computing over a web of computers, These methods will take over more and more in uncertainty analysis, sensitivity analysis, and optimization. Monte Carlo methods are already being used in an increasing number of areas, such as economics, biology, chemistry, and engineering. We have only seen the beginning.

REDUCE RISK BY INTRODUCING UNCERTAINTY: HOW MONTE CARLO METHODS WORK

Conceptually, Monte Carlo methods are simple, stemming from three distinct but related historical developments in the mathematical sciences:

1. Games of chance motivated seventeenth- and eighteenth-century mathematicians to regard outcomes on successive trials as forming a sequence of random events.

2. After observing that the mean of a function of continuous random variables took the form of an integral, nineteenth- and early twentieth-century statisticians subsequently recognized that, in principle, one could randomly draw numbers, transform them according to prescribed rules, and derive an approximate solution to an integral in a problem that intrinsically contained no probabilistic content whatsoever. Also see the publications by the National Bureau of Standards on Monte Carlo methods in 1951.

3. During the 1920s and 1930s, several new discoveries were made in solving differential equations, in the relationship between a Markov stochastic process and certain differential equations, and during the atomic energy developments after World War II in which large multidimensional problems proved too formidable for the differential equation approach. This development led to discoveries by John von Neumann and Stanislaw Ulam, which suggested that sampling experiments using random walk models executed on the newly developed digital computer could provide readily usable approximations to the desired solutions. This proposal reversed the direction of reasoning. Instead of using the cumbersome differential equation approach to provide solutions to probabilistic problems, one conducts sampling experiments to provide solutions to the differential equations, which did not necessarily have a probabilistic basis themselves.

Monte Carlo methods rely on introducing uncertainty into the models since no uncertainty exists in them. But a more obvious use of Monte Carlo methods exists, namely to assess the impact of uncertainty on the outcomes. The difference in the application of Monte Carlo methods lies solely in the way uncertainty is modeled (see Appendix A for a simple illustrative example):

- By modeling the uncertainty as it actually is, Monte Carlo methods can be used to assess the impact of uncertainty. By conducting a statistical sensitivity analysis on such a Monte Carlo simulation run, one can identify which input variables are most important with respect to managing the uncertainty. Such information is crucial if one wants to spend money on getting better information or to simply reduce risks via Critical Assumption Planning (CAP).

- By introducing uncertainty in the model, such as ±10 percent bounded and symmetric uncertainty distributions like the triangular numbers in Figure 3.7, we can measure and rank the relative impact the various input variables have on the output variables. This is critical for management purposes, CAP, and product and process design because it is a very effective way of identifying and ranking performance drivers, provided of course that the model is well designed.

Surprisingly, defining a Monte Carlo method (or a method of statistical trials, as some call it) is not straightforward, and a good deal of disagreement has taken place. Historically, the first example of a computation by a Monte Carlo method is Buffon's problem of needle tossing, which he described in his 1777 treatise, *Essai d'Arithmetique morale*. In 1908, the famous statistician Student used the Monte Carlo method for estimating the correlation coefficient in this *t*-distribution. The von Neumann–Ulam method, which is considered the original Monte Carlo method, seems to be that Monte Carlo specifically designates the use of random sampling procedures for treating deterministic mathematical problems. Some define Monte Carlo to be the use of random sampling to treat problems of a deterministic or a probabilistic sort. Others demand that the sampling be sophisticated (involving the use of some variance-reducing techniques or swindle) in order to qualify as Monte Carlo; they call those cases where simple random sampling is used "straightforward sampling," "experimental sampling," or "model sampling."

In 1954, the most common definition was that Monte Carlo is the use of random sampling to treat problems, whether of a deterministic or a probabilistic sort.[35] This is the definition I use because of its simplicity and because it covers all the areas of possible application in LCC, cost management, or management in general. A more elaborate definition is "The Monte Carlo method consists of solving various problems of computational mathematics by means of construction of some random process for each such problem, with the parameters of the process equal to the required quantities of the problem. These quantities are then determined approximately by means of observations of the random process and the computation of its statistical characteristics, which are approximately equal to the required parameters."[36]

In a stricter sense, the Monte Carlo method is defined as the construction of an artificial random process that possesses all the necessary properties but that is in principle realizable by a means of ordinary computational apparatus. After PCs were introduced, the focus on the computer became clear: "The Monte Carlo method provides approximate solutions to a variety of mathematical problems by performing statistical sampling experiments on a computer."[37]

Mathematics of Monte Carlo Methods

Given that x is the required quantity of the mathematical expectation of Mξ of a certain random variable, the Monte Carlo method of determining the approximate value of x consists of an N-fold sampling of the value of the variable ξ_N in a series of independent tests, $\xi_1, \xi_2, \ldots, \xi_N$, and the computation of their mean value:

$$\xi = \frac{\xi_1 + \xi_2 + \cdots + \xi_N}{N} \tag{3.7}$$

Then, according to the law of large numbers (Bernoulli's or Chebyshev's Theorem):

$$\xi \approx M\xi = x \tag{3.8}$$

with a probability that is close to unity for a sufficiently large N. A traditional example in statistics is the tossing of a die and calculating the probability of obtaining a total of three when tossing two ordinary dice. Simulating this problem using a Monte Carlo method is straightforward. Simulate the tossing (one can also physically toss the dice) in N trials (each trial representing a toss), count the number of trials when one gets threes, and then estimate the probability as

$$\hat{p} = \frac{n}{N} \tag{3.9}$$

The error in this estimate is measured by the standard deviation σ, where

$$\sigma = \sqrt{\frac{p(1-p)}{N}} \tag{3.10}$$

However, since we assume we do not know p, the error term can only be estimated statistically. In the general case, for every $\varepsilon > 0$ and every $\delta > 0$, there exists a number N of trials, such that with a probability greater than $1 - \varepsilon$, the frequency of occurrences of an event $\left(\frac{L}{N}\right)$ will differ from the probability p of the occurrence of this event by less than δ:

$$\left| \frac{L}{N} - p \right| < \delta \tag{3.11}$$

The degree of certainty of the error is $1-\delta$. By investigating the error term, we see that the accuracy is highly dependent on the number of trials (N) performed in the simulation. By simplifying Chebyshev's inequality, we can estimate the δ as

$$\delta \sim \frac{1}{\sqrt{N}} \tag{3.12}$$

We see that to improve an estimate tenfold, we need to run a hundred times more trials! This equation holds for all cases. However, if we assume that the distribution of the event is approximately Gaussian (follows a normal distribution), we get the following:

$$\delta \le \frac{3\sigma}{\sqrt{N}} \tag{3.13}$$

Thus, we see that in most cases (Gaussian behavior is most common, and all other behavior tends to approach the Gaussian behavior according to the Central Limit Theorem), the error also depends on the variance of each independent test (trial).

To sum up defining and discussing the error in Monte Carlo methods, Monte Carlo methods have three general key features:

1. It is necessary to perform a large number of trials.
2. The errors are smoothed out; thus, the method is stable against noise. This was particularly important before the digital computer came, because early computers had random defects. However, the problem with round-off errors is still present.
3. Monte Carlo methods use a comparatively small amount of memory to store intermediate results, which makes it well suited to multidimensional problems.

Variance Reduction Sampling Techniques

A large number of sampling methods are available. Briefly, some of them are:

- **Correlation and regression** This technique can be employed whenever we want to compare situations. By combining the comparisons into a single problem, a significant amount of work can be saved. We therefore assess the difference directly. Some claim that correlated sampling is one of the most powerful variance reduction techniques.
- **Extraction of the regular part** In this sampling method, we try to extract the regular part before running a Monte Carlo simulation, so that only the remainder needs to be estimated by the simulation.
- **Importance sampling** The basic idea is that accuracy increases by using more points (trials) in the important regions.
- **Group sampling** This concept is similar to importance sampling and divides the region of interest into groups so that each group has similar function values.
- **Russian roulette and splitting** The sampling is done in stages and is divided into two categories: interesting and uninteresting (splitting). The interesting samples are split further, while the uninteresting samples are given less effort or "killed off" if they do not seem interesting in a supplementary sampling (Russian roulette).
- **Systematic sampling** The region of interest is systematically sampled.

- **Control variates**   Instead of estimating a parameter directly, the difference between the problem of interest and some analytical model is considered.
- **Antithetic variates**   This method is based on seeking two unbiased estimators for some unknown parameter, which have a strong negative correlation.
- **Stratified sampling**   At least two different stratified sampling methods exist:
  - ○ **Quota sampling**   This is a combination of importance sampling and systematic sampling.
  - ○ **Latin hypercube**   The region of interest is divided into intervals of equal probability. This provides higher accuracy because the entire region is sampled in a more even and consistent manner.

Today many of these variance-reduction techniques are only of academic or even historic interest because of the new and powerful digital computers that enable us to do heavy calculations much more easily than in the 1950s and 1960s. In the literature, we therefore often find just SRS, LHS, or some variations of these. In some studies, however, we find a so-called modified LHS Monte Carlo and a so-called smart Monte Carlo. However, due to the high efficiency of LHS combined with powerful computers, I see little reason to explore many of the old sampling techniques, which were designed when the best computer was probably slower than an average calculator today.

LHS Technique

The LHS strategy was developed, in part, to overcome some of the difficulties with SRS. Roughly speaking, LHS involves dividing up the range of variables in sectors of equal probability, sampling each sector using SRS, and finally combining it all to form an LHS. The point is to ensure that the entire range of variables is sampled properly to avoid leaving large ranges blank, as shown in Figure 3.4.

In more mathematical terms, the steps in LHS to generate a sample size N from n variables $\xi = [\xi_1, \xi_2, \ldots, \xi_n]$ with the joint probability density function (pdf) $f_\xi(\xi)$ are:[38]

- The range of each variable is partitioned into N *nonoverlapping* intervals on the basis of equal probability size $1/N$. This step is illustrated in Figure 3.9.
- One value from each interval is selected and paired. The pairing may be random (if the variables are independent) or may reproduce a correlation in the input variables.
- The N values obtained for ξ_1 are paired with the N values of ξ_2. The N pairs are (randomly) combined with the N values of ξ_3 to form N triplets and so on, until a set of N n-tuples is formed. This set of n-tuples is called a Latin Hypercube sample.

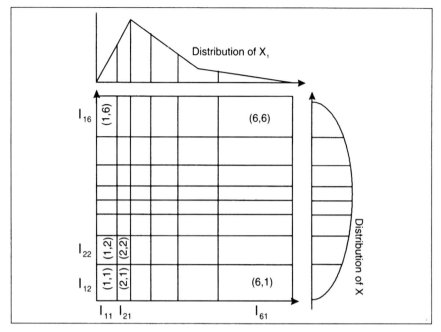

Figure 3.9 Example of the first key step in LHS. Source: Adapted from A.M. Liebtrau and M.J. Scott, "Strategies for Modeling the Uncertain Impacts of Climate Change," *Journal of Policy Modeling* 13(2), 1991, pp. 185–204.

As noted earlier, the LHS technique increases the accuracy of a Monte Carlo simulation and reduces the number of trials necessary to achieve a specified accuracy drastically. A rule of thumb is that "*the number of trials should be at least six times the number of variables* (emphasis added) to achieve satisfactory estimates."[39] Some researchers have even devised a smart Monte Carlo scheme that supposedly exceeds even the LHS for a low number of trials (10 to 200).

The biggest disadvantage of LHS is related to the mean output response since computing its variance is difficult. But this level of sophistication and accuracy is miles beyond what we need for cost management purposes and the like.

Before leaving the risk and uncertainty theme, I would like to provide a brief overview of how risks are often managed. Unless we have this basic knowledge, all our analyses of risk and uncertainty are wasted effort.

TRADITIONAL RISK MANAGEMENT

So far, I have talked about risk and uncertainty analysis techniques, that is, techniques that are used to identify risk and uncertainty to estimate their probability (or possibility) and to evaluate potential impacts (the outcomes). But all this is pointless unless we can manage the risks.

Risk management is about devising and implementing responses to the most critical risks—those that have the greatest RF. This stage consists of six steps:

1. Rank risks.
2. Identify feasible responses (to risks).
3. Select a satisfactory response.
4. Develop management measures and risk action schedules.
5. Report plans.
6. Implement plans if necessary.

Ranking risks is done by using the techniques described in the "Common Ways of Analyzing Risk and Uncertainty" and "Reduce Risk by Introducing Uncertainty: The Way of Monte Carlo Method," sections, but to communicate the results easily, a so-called risk-ranking matrix can be handy (see Figure 3.10). These are most often 2×2 or 3×3 matrices, but it has been reported that some companies use up to 6×6 matrices.

To use a ranking matrix, the decision-makers must first decide what constitutes a minor risk, a moderate risk, or a major risk. Here are some working definitions:

- A minor risk is simply accepted or ignored.
- A moderate risk is either likely to occur or to have large impacts, but not both.
- A major risk has both a high likelihood of occurrence and a large impact.

Other working definitions exist, such as A, B, C, and D ratings; these are illustrated in Figure 3.10, where they can be interpreted as follows:

- A. High impact, high probability—act immediately.
- B. High impact, low probability—consider action and have a contingency plan.
- C. Low impact, high probability—consider action.
- D. Low impact, low probability—keep under periodic review.

Whatever system we use, we can communicate risks, their importance, and what to do about them (management measures and risk action schedules), but before we know what to do, we must identify feasible responses. Risk has four generic responses or strategies:

1. **Risk prevention** Risk prevention is directed toward eliminating the sources of risk or substantially reducing their probabilities of occurrence.
2. **Impact mitigation** The purpose of impact mitigation is to reduce the consequences—the impacts—of risk occurrence.
3. **Risk transfer** Risk transfer involves transferring the risk to a third party such as an insurance company.

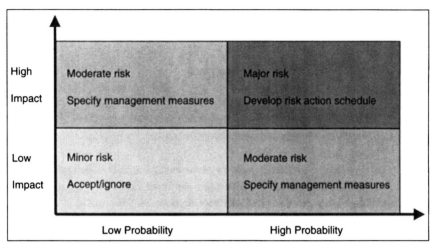

Figure 3.10 Risk-ranking matrix.

4. Acceptance of risk It is important to not forget such risks, because as environmental and internal factors change, the risk profile changes as well.

The responses are situational, and we must therefore select among several alternatives. To guide the selection process, a set of accepted criteria should be decided on first. In general, the selection will always revolve around costs versus benefits, unless no options exist, in which case we must accept the risks.

Once the response strategies are chosen, we must decide what to do in case something does not go as planned. For moderate risks, management measures should be prepared. These measures are simple action statements that specify the activities necessary to handle an event. Major risks, however, are more demanding due to the potential for large losses. They require, in addition to the management measures, clear definitions of who is responsible, what the time frame is, what the reporting requirements are, what resources are needed, and so on. This is often referred to as a risk action schedule.

During this process, it is important to document what is being done and create a concise report at the end that others can use later. This is important because the substantial lead time that many projects have or the long life cycle of many products makes it unlikely that the persons who worked with it during the design stage, for example, will still be present or even remember what they did.

Implementation of the plans requires that risks are monitored and that new ones are scanned for routinely and continuously so that deviations and problems can be swiftly identified and dealt with. The frequency and the responsibility of the monitoring depend on a variety of factors that must be decided on from case to case.

The true mastery of risk probably lies more in preparing for unidentified risks than in managing identified risks.

NOTES

1. G.T. Friedlob and L.L.F. Schleifer, "Fuzzy Logic: Application for Audit Risk and Uncertainty." *Managerial Auditing Journal* 14 (3), 1999, pp. 127–135.
2. P.L. Bernstein, *Against the Gods: The Remarkable Story of Risk*. New York: John Wiley & Sons, 1996, p. 383.
3. This is a topic of great philosophical discussion, but for this book it suffices to subscribe to the most accepted interpretation. See Honderich's, *The Oxford Companion to Philosophy*, New York: Oxford University Press, 1995, p. 1009.
4. P.F. Drucker, *Managing for Results: Economic Tasks and Risk-Taking Decisions*. New York: HarperInformation, 1986, p. 256.
5. F. Allvine, *Marketing: Principles and Practices*. Boston, MA: Irwin/McGraw-Hill, 1996.
6. P.F. Drucker, "The Theory of the Business." *Harvard Business Review*, September-October 1994.
7. "Barnevik's Bounty," *The Economist*, 362 (8262), 2002, p. 62.
8. A. Kaufmann, "Advances in Fuzzy Sets: An Overview." *Advances in Fuzzy Sets, Possibility Theory, and Applications*, ed. P.P. Wang. New York: Plenum Press, 1983.
9. See note 2.
10. Note that the term *fuzzy set* is the original term introduced by Zadeh, but that in the 1970s Richard C.T. Lee coined a new term, *fuzzy logic*, which is the same as fuzzy sets. Personally, I prefer the term *fuzzy logic* and that is what is used in this book.
11. See note 2.
12. T. Honderich, ed. 1995. *The Oxford Companion to Philosophy*. New York: Oxford University Press, p. 1009.
13. See, for example, Sambursky's "On the Possible and Probable in Ancient Greece," *Osiris* 12, 1956, pp. 35–48.
14. See, for example, Cheeseman's, "Probabilistic Versus Fuzzy Reasoning" in *Uncertainty in Artificial Intelligence*, eds. L.N. Kanal and J.F. Lemmer, New York: North-Holland, 1986, pp. 85–102.
15. L.A. Zadeh, "Is Probability Theory Sufficient for Dealing with Uncertainty in AI: A Negative View," *Uncertainty in Artificial Intelligence*, eds. L.N. Kanal and J.F. Lemmer. New York: North-Holland, 1986, pp. 103–116.
16. W.E. Gilford et al., "Message Characteristics and Perceptions of Uncertainty by Organizational Decision Makers." *Academy of Management Journal* 22 (3), 1979, pp. 458–481.
17. J. Gleick, *Chaos*. New York: Penguin, 1987.
18. E. Hisdal, "Infinite-valued Logic Based on Two-valued Logic and Probability, Part 1.1," *International Journal of Man-Machine Studies* 25, 1986, pp. 89–111; Hisdal,

E. "Infinite-valued Logic Based on Two-valued Logic and Probability, Part 1.2," *International Journal of Man-Machine Studies* 25, 1986, pp. 113–138; and Hisdal, E. "Are Grades of Membership Probabilities?" *Fuzzy Sets and Systems* 25, 1988, pp. 325–348.

19. G.J. Klir, "A Principal of Uncertainty and Information Invariance." *International Journal of General Systems* 17, 1991, p. 258.

20. R. Kangari and L.S. Riggs, "Construction Risk Assessment by Linguistics." *IEEE Transactions on Engineering Management* 36 (2), 1989, pp. 126–131.

21. According to C.S. Park and G.P. Sharp-Bette, *Advanced Engineering Economics,* New York: John Wiley & Sons, 1990, p. 740.

22. As defined by P. Wonnacott and R. Wonnacott, *Economics,* New York: John Wiley & Sons, 1990, p. 804.

23. According to G. Bannock, R.E. Baxter, and E. Davis, *Dictionary in Economics,* London: Profile Books, 1999, p. 439.

24. According to "Averse to Reality," *The Economist* 360 (8234), 2001, p. 61.

25. See note 20.

26. M. Rabin and R. Thaler, "Anomalies: Risk Aversion." *Journal of Economic Perspectives* 15 (1), 2001, pp. 219–232.

27. According to Kaufmann, see note 8.

28. S. Sailsbury, "Failures of My Lending Career." *Journal of Commercial Lending* 67 (2), 1984.

29. A.M. Liebtrau and M.J. Scott, "Strategies for Modeling the Uncertain Impacts of Climate Change." *Journal of Policy Modeling* 13 (2), 1991, pp. 185–204.

30. See note 29.

31. G.S. Fishman, *Monte Carlo Concepts, Algorithms, and Applications.* New York: Springer-Verlag, 1996, p. 698.

32. R.Y. Rubinstein, *Simulation and the Monte Carlo Method.* New York: John Wiley & Sons, 1981, p. 278.

33. A standard Monte Carlo method is a method that uses Simple Random Sampling (SRS). SRS means that the points are picked completely randomly without any plan or structure.

34. See note 5.

35. A.W. Marshall, "An Introductory Note." In *Symposium on Monte Carlo Methods,* ed H.A. Meryer. New York: John Wiley & Sons, 1954.

36. Y.A. Shreider, N.P. Buslenko, D.I. Golenko, I.M. Sobol, and V.G. Sragovich, *The Monte Carlo Method.* Oxford: Pergamon Press, 1966.

37. See note 31.

38. For details, see A.M. Liebtrau and P.G. Doctor, "The Generation of Dependent Input Variables to a Performance Assessment Simulation Code," an uncertainty analysis for performance assessments of radioactive waste disposal systems, which was part of the proceedings of a Nuclear Energy Agency workshop in Seattle in 1987. Also see M. Keramat and R. Kielbasa, "Efficient Average Quality Index Estimation of

Integrated Circuits by Modified Latin Hypercube Sampling Monte Carlo (MLHSMC)," from the IEEE International Symposium on Circuits and Systems in Hong Kong, 1997, pp. 1648–1651.

39. B.R. James, J.P. Gwo, and L. Toran, "Risk: Cost Decision Framework for Aquifer Remediation Design." *Journal of Water Resources Planning and Management* 122 (No. 6), November/December 1996, pp. 414–420.

4

ACTIVITY-BASED COSTING

Never ask for money spent
Where the spender thinks it went.
Nobody was ever meant
To remember or invent
What he did with every cent.

Robert Frost
"The Hardship of Accounting"

Activity-Based Costing (ABC) is one of the few management inventions that actually has its roots in industry, and that is interesting in itself because it shows that ABC has arisen out of real-life needs. To introduce this interesting concept, I start with a motivating example of ABC.[1] The theory is then discussed in order to explain why things turned out the way they did in the example. The following section provides even more comprehensive ABC examples, and the case study presented will be expanded on in Chapter 8 to provide a simple yet illustrative application of Life-Cycle Costing (LCC). Finally, some of the critiques of ABC are discussed.

MOTIVATING EXAMPLE

This motivating example illustrates how ABC can be employed in environmental management. Consider a hypothetical manufacturer, Chair, Inc., which produces two types of furniture: unfinished (UFIN) and finished (FIN) chairs. The difference between the chairs lies in the finish, the UFIN chair being the simplest. The production volume is 1 million chairs per year, divided equally between the two product lines. Management views the finished chairs as the most profitable of the two lines because it has a higher traditional margin. Recently, management has also given serious thought to phasing out the UFIN chair line, but is that a good decision?

To find out, we first take a brief look at the value chain. It turns out that the manufacturing process for the UFIN results in very little waste that has environmental consequences: sawdust and residual glue. The manufacturing process for the FIN, however, involves paints, stains, solvents, and other toxic adhesives in addition to sawdust and residual glue. But the way the traditional costing system treats the $5.4 million in environmental overhead does not reflect the fact that UFIN hardly incurs any environmental costs. In fact, the environmental overhead cost is allocated to the products by using direct labor as an allocation despite the fact that direct labor has nothing to do with the environmental overhead. This clearly indicates a faulty cost management system, but to truly answer the question we must analyze the costs for the products using both a volume-based approach and ABC. Then it will become evident why management wants to phase out UFIN and whether it is smart or not.

Chair, Inc.'s 1993 total overhead costs are $30 million. They are distributed as shown in Table 4.1. Forty-five percent of the corporate/plant administration costs are attributable to environmental costs, which are $5.4 million.

To keep the tables tidy, I use parentheses to denote which units I use. For example, (MUSD) indicates that we are discussing numbers whose units are in millions of U.S. dollars.

But we also need some information about the products. This is presented in Table 4.2. We see that the FIN chairs are more costly in terms of raw materials but also a little more labor intensive because of the finishing processes.

If we use a traditional *volume-based costing system,* the costs would be allocated as shown in Tables 4.3 and 4.4. Since a substantial difference seems to take place in the way environmental overhead and the other overhead costs are incurred

Table 4.1   Chair, Inc., Overhead Cost Distribution

Cost Category	Cost (MUSD)	Relative Importance
Corporate/plant adm.	12.0	40%
Indirect materials	4.5	15%
Marketing	4.5	15%
Miscellaneous	3.9	13%
Benefits	1.8	6%
Depreciation of equipment	1.8	6%
Utilities	1.5	5%

Table 4.2   Product Information

Product	Raw Materials ($/unit)	Direct Labor ($/unit)	Sales Price ($/unit)	Production (units/year)
UFIN	10.00	8.00	45.00	500,000
FIN	15.00	10.50	65.00	500,000

Table 4.3 Traditional Cost Allocation (MUSD)

Product	RM	DL	DC	EOH	OOH	TOH	TC	Sales	Profit
UFIN	5.00	4.00	9.00	2.34	10.64	12.98	21.98	22.00	0.02
FIN	7.50	5.25	12.75	3.06	13.96	17.02	29.77	32.00	2.23
Total	12.50	9.25	21.75	5.40	24.60	30.00	51.75	55.00	2.25

Table 4.4 Traditional Cost Allocation ($/unit)

Product	RM	DL	DC	EOH	OOH	TOH	TC	Sales	Profit
UFIN	10.00	8.00	18.00	4.76	21.28	25.95	43.95	44.00	0.05
FIN	15.00	10.50	25.50	6.13	27.92	34.05	59.55	64.00	4.45

in the process, the overhead costs are divided into two groups, namely environmental overhead and other overhead. These two groups are, however, allocated using the same allocation base, as shown in Tables 4.1–4.4.

RM	Raw materials costs
DL	Direct labor costs
DC	Direct costs = RM + DL
EOH	Environmental overhead costs
OOH	Other overhead costs
TOH	Total overhead costs = EOH + OOH
TC	Total costs = DC + TOH

We see that the volume-based cost system clearly supports the management decision, but is everything all right? If we look carefully, we will see that the two processes are treated in the same way and that all the overhead costs are just lumped together. The volume-based costing system simply does not discover the difference in activities in the two processes; it does not consider the fact that the UFIN product line triggers few environmental costs, while the FIN product line is responsible for triggering most of the environmental costs. This is reflected in the cost accounting by the fact that the cost assignment mechanism is the same for both EOH and OOH.

Convinced by this argument, the management of Chair, Inc. asks for an ABC analysis to see what is really the case. We start by identifying and studying the finishing activities. We learn that these activities are performed equally unit by unit, regardless of the amount of direct labor or anything else earlier on in the value chain. Hence, we choose annual production as an allocation key for the environmental overhead costs. Also, the UFIN chairs (together with the FIN chairs) only incur sawdust and residual glue disposal costs, which amounts to $30,000. The rest of the environmental overhead cost, $5.37 million, is solely attributable to the FIN chairs. This gives us the cost allocations shown in Tables 4.5 and Table 4.6.

With the same selling price as earlier, this gives a $4.69 profit for the UFIN chairs and a $0.19 *loss* for the FIN chairs. The situation has changed dramatically, and the management decision is, according to ABC, wrong.

Management also has another problem: the Clean Air Act (CAA), which imposes a $1.0 million investment to comply with the law. Management, realizing the mistakes of traditional costing, decides to shut the FIN product line down. That decision is apparently correct using ABC principles, assuming that the loss in volume can be compensated for by an increase in UFIN chair volume and/or a cut in the overhead costs. But that large investment will erode profits substantially. Why not try to modify the technology, establish Environmental Management Systems, and try to recycle and reuse?

The required environmental audit costs $1.67 million. This cost is carried by the FIN chair line since it directly triggers the need for an audit. Furthermore, it can be argued that the audit is part of an investment. Thus, the $1.67 million is depreciated linearly over five years, which gives an annual cost of $334,000.

Instead of eliminating the FIN, line management must employ a solvent recovery system that treats the used solvents and removes the paint by-products. This system will reduce hazardous waste disposal volumes so that only residual wastes are hauled away. The solvent recovery system will also reduce the expenditures for raw materials by $2 per FIN chair. In other words, we have saved:

Table 4.5   ABC Cost Allocation (MUSD)

Product	RM	DL	DC	EOH	OOH	TOH	TC	Sales	Profit
UFIN	5.00	4.00	9.00	0.015	10.640	10.655	19.655	22.00	2.345
FIN	7.50	5.25	12.75	5.385	13.960	19.345	32.095	32.00	-0.095
Total	12.50	9.25	21.75	5.400	24.600	30.000	51.750	55.00	2.250

Table 4.6   ABC Cost Allocation ($/unit)

Product	RM	DL	DC	EOH	OOH	TOH	TC	Sales	Profit
UFIN	10.00	8.00	18.00	0.03	21.28	21.31	39.31	44.00	4.69
FIN	15.00	10.50	25.50	10.77	27.92	38.69	64.19	64.00	-0.19

- $2 million a year in hazardous waste disposal costs.
- $1 million a year in material costs.

With these facts taken into account and the same production volumes as before, we get the cost allocations and results shown in Tables 4.7 and 4.8. Note that during the first five years, the results of the FIN line profit would be $334,000 lower than the results shown in Table 4.7 due to the depreciation of the environmental audit investment.

This program yields significant profit improvements for the FIN chair line, as can be seen by comparing Tables 4.8 and 4.6. Ultimately, a $3 million profit improvement in the bottom line for the company was achieved. This was good news for management.

Thus, we have seen how a firm actually made money by becoming more "environmentally friendly" when it was able to relate costs to environmental programs. The example ignored possible benefits arising from being environmentally friendly to customers and other stakeholders. These benefits, which are most likely to increase in years to come, would have increased profits further.

Of course, this is a simple example, but it clearly illustrates the dangers of volume-based cost accounting. These dangers increase as the complexity of the organization increases. Hence, even though we could have solved this particular case without using ABC and ended up with similar results, in real-life situations this rarely is the case. See, for example, the case of John Deere Component Works.[2]

John Deere had quite recently (in the early 1990s) adopted a strategy of competitively bidding for business and was now competing for the first time against other producers. The existing cost system (a volume-based costing system) was designed to report overall costs and not report accurate product costs, so it proved

Table 4.7 ABC Cost Allocation (MUSD) after the First Five Years

Product	RM	DL	DC	EOH	OOH	TOH	TC	Sales	Profit
UFIN	5.00	4.00	9.00	0.015	10.64	10.655	19.655	22.00	2.345
FIN	6.50	5.25	11.75	3.385	13.96	17.345	29.095	32.00	2.905
Total	11.50	9.25	20.75	3.400	24.60	28.000	48.750	55.00	5.250

Table 4.8 ABC Cost Allocation ($/unit) after the First Five Years

Product	RM	DL	DC	EOH	OOH	TOH	TC	Sales	Profit
UFIN	10.00	8.00	18.00	0.03	21.28	21.31	39.31	44.00	4.69
FIN	13.00	10.50	23.50	10.77	27.92	38.69	64.19	64.00	5.81

to be inadequate for the new strategy because the overhead costs that were treated inadequately represented about 27 percent of the total costs. Essentially, the volume-based costing system was telling management that low-volume, low-value-added parts were more profitable than high-volume, high-value-added parts. After implementing an ABC system, management realized that production should shift away from low-volume, low-value-added parts to the profitable high-volume, high-value-added parts. In fact, prior to the installment of ABC, one can claim to a certain extent that John Deere had systematically encouraged the production of unprofitable products and reduced or eliminated the production of the profitable products. Because John Deere was in a sheltered, competitive situation, however, it did well financially.

In retrospect, some of the findings from the ABC analysis seem obvious. But because common sense is not that common, sound cost management is needed. It is better to stop the guesswork and forget rules of thumb and act on facts instead.

ACTIVITY-BASED COSTING

Activity-based costing (ABC) is a big topic, but in this book we discuss these issues:

- The ABC concept and volume-based (traditional) concepts
- ABC compared to volume-based costing
- Cost-reduction opportunities using ABC
- The expansion of ABC into new areas
- Designing traditional ABC systems
- ABC and Total Quality Management (TQM)

ABC Concept

ABC is a costing system that is based on the formulations of resources, activities, and cost objects (see Glossary), as shown in Figure 4.1. Resources are everything the organization uses to operate, and the measure is cost. Activities are what are actually being done in the organization. Groups of activities with certain commonalties are usually referred to as processes, activity centers, departments, and so on, depending on the type of commonalty. Cost objects are the objects, typically products and customers, for which we want separate cost, revenue, and profit statements. These elements interact as follows: The cost objects consume activities, which in turn consume resources. Thus, ABC is a *two-stage* costing system.

The volume-based (traditional or conventional, as often denoted in the literature) costing systems, however, are one-stage costing systems without any process perspective, and hence the costs are allocated directly to the cost objects, usually using highly volume-related allocation bases such as direct labor hours and

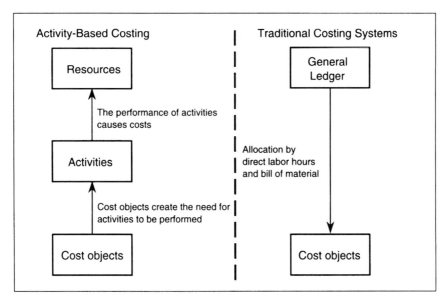

Figure 4.1   Main principles of ABC versus volume-based costing.

machine hours. This difference is important to notice because it implies that ABC is process oriented, whereas volume-based systems are not. Put differently, ABC is based on what *really* happens, while volume-based costing systems are based on the organizational structure and volume. Many implications of this are further discussed in the "Activity-Based versus Volume-Based" section, but first we should look a bit closer at the direction of the arrows.

We see that in ABC the arrows go upward, whereas the arrows in volume-based costing systems go downward. This is to signify that ABC is resource oriented and aims to direct capacity toward demand, which is estimated by upward aggregation, hence the upward arrows. Volume-based costing systems, however, simply allocate the capacity quite arbitrarily, in the sense that the allocation is not based on any cause-and-effect relationships. Thus, the arrows go downward. The cost assignment in ABC is, however, top-down (see Figure 4.2). To appreciate this difference, recall from Chapter 2 that cost is a measure of resource consumption that relates to the demand for jobs to be done, whereas expense is a measure of spending that investigates the capacity provided to do a job. The resource consumption perspective counts because management must match capacity to demand and not the other way around;[3] that is what ABC is based on. Volume-based costing systems, in contrast, are capacity oriented and in fact ignore the demand altogether.

In addition to the cost assignment view, ABC also offers a process view or a second dimension (see Figure 4.2), and a so-called two-dimensional ABC concept

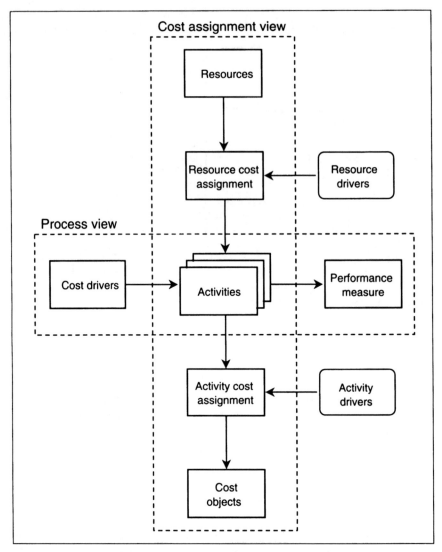

Figure 4.2   Two-dimensional ABC system. Source: Adapted from P.B.B. Turney,
Common Cents: The ABC Performance Breakthrough. Hillboro, OR: Cost Technology,
1991, p. 322.

emerges. The second dimension, the process view, is used for noneconomic performance measurement.

This type of ABC concept is also referred to as a second-generation ABC architecture since it is an improvement over the older version shown in Figure 4.1. The
core of the second-generation architecture is, however, the same as before, but the
process view is enhanced further.

The two views serve different purposes. The cost assignment view, which was the original perspective of ABC, deals with issues like:

- Pricing
- Product mix
- Sourcing
- Product design
- Setting priorities for improvement efforts

The process view, on the other hand, concerns matters such as:

- *Why* work takes place and *how much* effort must be expended to carry out the work, which is measured by *cost drivers*. Cost drivers include factors related to the performance of prior activities in the value chain as well as factors internal to the activity.
- *How well* the work was performed, which is measured by the *performance measures*. This includes such issues as quality, time, and efficiency.[4]

Notice that the process view and its performance measures provide an obvious link to Balanced Scorecards and similar performance measurement systems such as the performance prism.

Volume-based costing systems like standard costing, on the other hand, only produce product costs using a bill of materials (BOM) and then allocate the overhead costs using direct labor hours,[5] machine hours, or something similar as an allocation base. The process view is completely ignored.

From this discussion, it is clear that ABC has upward cost management, although the actual cost assignment is downward, as the ABC cost assignment has its roots in the actual ongoing processes; volume-based costing systems have downward cost management and a cost assignment according to a simple overhead allocation. Furthermore, ABC is process oriented (due to the formulation and dependency of activities), while volume-based costing systems are structure oriented (since costs are classified according to the current structure of the organization).

The difference between volume-based costing methods and ABC is therefore like day and night, yet the source of these differences lies in a few basic assumptions:

- Volume-based costing system:
  - Products consume resources.
  - Costs are allocated using unit-level allocation bases.
- ABC:
  - Products consume activities; they do not directly use up resources.
  - Costs are traced using multilevel drivers.

Clearly, two major differences exist: resource consumption versus activity consumption, and unit-level allocation bases versus multilevel drivers, which are discussed in the next section.

Activity-Based versus Volume-Based

Figures 4.3 and 4.4 illustrate volume-based costing systems and ABC systems. A volume-based costing system works as pictured in Figure 4.3. Volume-based costing systems have several essential features:[6]

- For product-costing purposes, the firm is separated into functional areas of activity, that is, manufacturing, marketing, financing, and administration.
- The manufacturing costs of direct material, direct labor, and manufacturing overhead are inventoriable costs; that is, they are accounted for in inventory assessments.
- Direct material and direct labor costs are considered to be traceable (or chargeable) directly to the product.
- Manufacturing overheads of both production and manufacturing service departments are treated as indirect costs of the product but are charged to the product by the use of predetermined overhead rates.
- When a single, plant-wide, predetermined overhead rate is used, overhead is charged indiscriminately to all products without regard to possible differences in resources utilized in the manufacture of one product versus another. As one plant manager expressed, "We spread overhead to all products like peanut butter."
- The functional costs of marketing, financing, and administration are accumulated in cost pools and are treated as costs of the period in which they are incurred. These costs are not treated as product costs.

Of course, the volume-based way of performing costing has advantages: It is widely used, understood well, simple, and fairly accurate when direct labor has a large portion of product costs. But unfortunately, these costing systems have lost their relevance.[7] In the literature, very negative phrases have been associated with volume-based costing systems. Examples are "number one enemy of production,"[8] "undermining production,"[9] and "systematically distorting product costs,"[10] and the question has been asked whether cost accounting was an asset or a liability.[11]

Although volume-based costing systems appear to be so inadequate, it is important to remember that when they were invented roughly 100 years ago, many important factors that determine the success of cost management systems today were completely different. For example, the business environment was far simpler in numerous ways, product mix complexity and organizational complexity were minute compared to today, and the various stakeholders of the organizations were

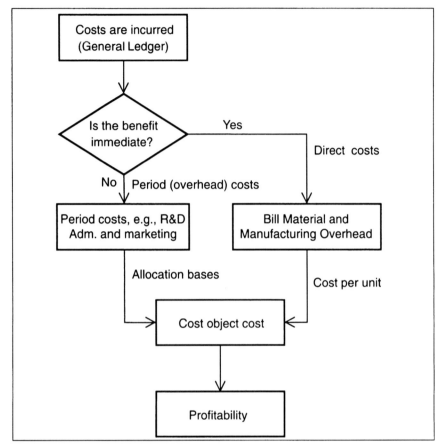

Figure 4.3   Volume-based costing system overview.

far less demanding. Thus, volume-based costing systems worked just fine when they were developed; however, the context in which they were developed around 1900 no longer exists. Thus, it is time to rethink, and ABC is the result.

Figure 4.4 shows a schematic overview of how the cost assignment in ABC works. For more details, see the "ABC Example and Case Study" section. ABC is often combined with other activity-related approaches under the wider umbrella of Activity-Based Management (ABM).

If we compare ABC, as shown in Figure 4.4, to the volume-based costing systems shown in Figure 4.3, we see that many aspects are opposite. For example, the various functions within a company are not found anywhere in Figure 4.4. That is because ABC is cross-functional and process oriented. Furthermore, the definition of activities, the process-orientation, is the central hub between ABC as a cost assignment tool and as a cost planning/control tool (see Figure 4.2). This is com-

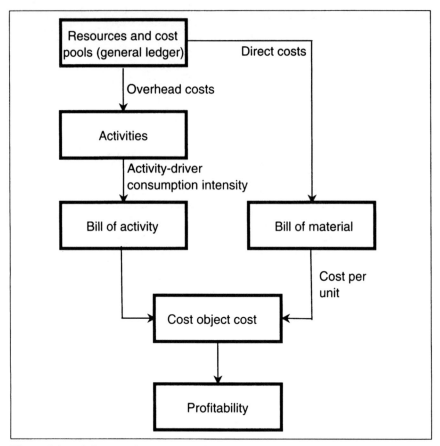

Figure 4.4   ABC cost assignment overview.

pletely missing in Figure 4.3. Equally important is the fact that while ABC provides an important link to nonfinancial performance measurement during cost planning/control, traditional approaches totally ignore nonfinancial aspects. The result is that ABC provides a link to, for example, quality management and a Balanced Scorecard that is completely missing in volume-based costing systems. This is discussed more in the "Activity-Based Costing and Total Quality Management" section.

However, all the differences between Figure 4.3 and Figure 4.4 are attributable to the two conceptual differences previously mentioned: (1) resource consumption versus activity consumption and (2) unit-level allocation bases versus multilevel activity and resource drivers. These are discussed in detail next.

It should be noted that the terms *resource driver* and *activity driver* are used in the second-generation ABC architecture (see Figure 4.2). In the first-generation

ABC architecture, the terms used were *first-stage cost driver* and *second-stage cost driver*, respectively, thus implicitly implying that ABC systems consist of two stages. But as ABC developed, it was recognized that the term *cost driver* could be used more accurately to describe what actually drives the costs of an activity. In this book, the term *driver* is used to encapsulate all three types of drivers in the second-generation ABC architecture.

Resource Consumption versus Activity Consumption

The basic assumption that volume-based costing systems rest on is that products consume resources, such as direct labor and material. This consumption is calculated using allocation bases, that is, the unit-level product characteristics of which resources are allocated. Thus, traditional allocation bases only measure attributes of a unit, such as the number of direct labor hours per product unit in making the product. In this context, it becomes important to classify costs as fixed or variable in an attempt to classify and manage the likely changes in spending or supply of a resource. An ABC system, however, traces costs to the activities that consume resources and then traces those activity costs to the cost objects that consume the activities. Thus, changes in spending or supply of a resource are related *not* to a change in the resources but rather to a change in activity consumption, which *in turn* causes a change in resource consumption. This is an upward cost tracing, as mentioned earlier. In other words, products consume resources *indirectly* via their consumption of activities. For this reason, the use of the terms *fixed* and *variable costs* has no meaning in ABC, except on an activity level. Also note that good product costing systems measure long-term costs, for which the distinction between fixed and variable costs is unwarranted.

As already mentioned, volume-based costing systems have a downward cost allocation, and the resources are simply spread out over the product units using, for example, direct labor as an allocation base. The distribution of overhead costs in a volume-based costing system (in particular) will therefore be highly distorted and arbitrary unless the overhead costs are directly proportionate to the chosen allocation base. The likelihood of that is minimal to say the least.

From a management perspective, the difference between ABC and volume-based costing systems is perhaps even larger. Traditionally, cost management is concerned with managing costs. In ABC, however, it is recognized that costs cannot be controlled. Rather, one must control activities that in turn cause costs. However, several papers attack all the activity-based panaceas, and it is true that *ABC is no miracle cure*. What is required is a change in mind-set. Hence, it is insufficient to implement ABC without promoting a culture of continuous improvement, bottom-up management, process thinking, and so forth. But although it is possible to implement ABC and continue with business as usual, this is rarely what happens.[12]

Just as ABC alone is not a guaranteed recipe for success, other practices also require decision support concerning the cost perspective. For example, as mentioned in Chapter 2, many Baldrige Award winners have encountered severe financial difficulties; thus, focusing on quality and continuous improvement is not enough by itself either. What is needed is a balanced approach, which can be achieved by realizing that ABC is process oriented in a wide sense and that it requires a paradigm shift to process thinking to be really successful. With process thinking, I do not mean the superficial act of implementing nonfinancial performance measures, which is important in its own right, but rather a much more profound process-orientation toward everything that happens within the four walls of the organization. This should include measures such as:

- Separating[13] external financial reporting systems from internal cost management systems and making the latter process oriented. A process-oriented cost management system will have all its costs assigned to processes. Today this is not easy because workers are organized according to departments and machines are often not treated as single objects, but rather broken down into individual components based on, for example, depreciation time, point of purchase, and so on.
- Extensive use of cross-functional teams and multidisciplinary teams.
- Implementing process-oriented information and quality management systems.
- Thinking about continuous improvement in everything that is done, and not just in relation to quality management.

Unit-Level Allocation Bases versus Multilevel Drivers

In a volume-based costing system, the cost drivers are referred to as allocation bases, which are a unit-level characteristic of the product, such as material costs per product unit. That is, an allocation base is not really a cost driver at all. When overhead costs are allocated using these unit-level characteristics, a major amount of distortion is introduced in the assessments. For example, it is reported that the difference in product costs can shift several hundred percent, and Robin Cooper, one of the ABC pioneers, found that:

> Conventional cost accounting systems systematically undercost small, low-volume products and overcost large, high-volume products.

In ABC, such distortion is reduced significantly by using multilevel drivers. These levels should be organized according to the processes, but usually four levels are present:

1. *Unit-level drivers,* which are triggered every time a unit of a product is produced, such as drilling a hole and painting a surface.

2. *Batch-level drivers,* which are triggered every time a batch of products is produced, such as machine setup time and the transportation of the production lot. The effect on unit costs is significant (see Figure 4.5).

3. *Product-level drivers,* which are triggered by the fact that products are produced, such as design changes and maintaining the BOMs.

4. *Factory-level drivers,* which are triggered by the fact that production occurs. An example would be kilowatt hours of electricity for lighting and cleaning hours for the factory. However, note that how the drivers are grouped depends on the focus of the model. In a plant where two products are competing for factory floor space, the kilowatt hours of electricity for a lighting resource driver should be treated as a product-level resource driver, because the focus is to identify how the floor space and its associated costs can best be used. In other words, which product can give the highest return of the floor space resource?

The choice of drivers will always determine the accuracy of the model. A good model should be capable of handling all the different cost-driving complexities of the company. Some examples are presented in Figure 4.6. That is, the cost of maintaining and designing the model must always be taken into consideration; simplicity versus accuracy is therefore a very important issue to address when designing a model. In any case, it is obvious that using only direct labor as an allocation base, which is the case for volume-based costing systems, will not handle all these sources of distortion well.

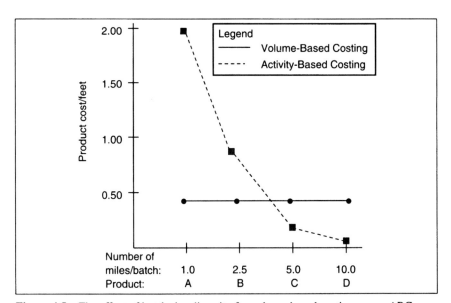

Figure 4.5   The effect of batch size diversity for volume-based costing versus ABC.

Volume complexity	Size complexity	Product design complexity	Distribution complexity
Number of units Machine hours Direct labor Direct material	Space Head count Equipment	Number of part numbers Number of material structure levels Number of engineering change orders Number of "special" parts	Number of customers National standards Number of manual customer orders Number of customer "e-orders" Number of internal orders

Procurement complexity	Process complexity	Product range complexity	Other complexity
Number of vendors National standards Number of purchase orders Number of parts inspected Number of "A" parts	Outsourcing Change transactions Logistics transactions Quality transactions Balancing transactions Cycle time Process flow Schedule changes	Number of products Number of variants Number of accessories Number of bundling options Number of new products Number of discontinued	Inventory levels Internal transportation Information system Rework Scrap Waste

Figure 4.6 Examples of complexity that drives costs. Source: Adapted from R.G. Eiler and C. Ball, "Implementing Activity-Based Costing," *Handbook of Cost Management*, ed., B.J. Brinker. Boston, MA: Warren, Gorham & Lamont, 1997, pp. B2.1–B2.33.

It is important to choose resource and activity drivers that reflect as closely as possible the way activities actually are consumed. When this has been achieved to a satisfactory degree, we can use the model to estimate costs, trace the costs, and thereby identify cost-reduction opportunities.

It should be noted that a costing model will never be 100 percent correct in the sense that not only can we never expect to estimate a cost 100 percent accurately, but doing so is in fact impossible. The reason is that costs are in nature uncertain because the underlying mechanisms for cost formation are complex. Thus, costs should ideally be measured statistically, just like quality, and the most accurate cost estimate cannot be more accurate than the inherent uncertainty. Cost estimates that are more accurate than that are deceptive.

From a conceptual point of view, the problem of distortion can be illustrated as in Figure 4.7, where it is one of three major sources of error in performance measurement. The two others are reliability problems during implementation and deficiencies concerning the method itself and the potential lack of data. The goal is to make the three circles overlap as well as possible since the best assessment is the intersection of the three circles.

The system of wrong costing caused by large amounts of distortion, explained earlier in the section on volume-based costing systems, makes it necessary to estimate the bias if we are to use such approaches. However, in a realistic situation

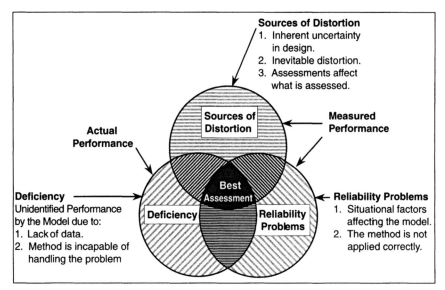

Figure 4.7   The challenge of performance measurement.

(many products, multiple sources of bias, and so on), it is impossible to find this bias before it is too late, that is, after a decision is made. In other words, it is impossible to predict either the direction or the magnitude of this bias in volume-based costing systems because the underlying source of cost formation is ignored. Thus, volume-based costing systems are inappropriate as cost management tools in most situations.

ABC, on the other hand, has superb characteristics and is an excellent tool in cost reduction studies. Also, because ABC is process oriented, we can quite reliably identify the direction of the cost distortion. Identifying the magnitude is more difficult, but not impossible.

Cost Reduction Opportunities Using ABC

What drives or triggers costs in ABC, how these costs can be reduced, and how resources can be utilized more effectively and efficiently are important issues not discussed so far. Before continuing, it should be emphasized that cutting costs is a last resort, because by cutting costs a company reduces its resource base and thereby its capability to launch successful strategies. To put it in a military context, no army commander will fire soldiers and sell their guns, even if only launching a limited attack, because the commander knows the value of reserves. Although sometimes cost-cutting is simply necessary and represents the only sound path, the point is to understand the difference between having too large an army and having necessary reserves.

Before we approach the issue of cost cutting, it is important to look at other options. That starts by realizing that, in general, *transactions* drive costs. Figure 4.6 presents some of the types of complexities that drive costs. Some of the many common transactions that drive costs in a manufacturing environment are:[14]

- Negotiating with vendors
- Ordering material and parts
- Scheduling receipts of material and parts
- Receiving incoming material and parts
- Inspecting incoming material and parts
- Moving inventory
- Tracking inventory
- Scheduling machines
- Setting up machines
- Inspecting parts after setup
- Performing quality assurance
- Expediting orders
- Assembling orders
- Shipping orders
- Paying for shipment received
- Billing customers
- Designing engineering change orders (ECOs)
- Implementing ECOs
- Reworking defective items
- Updating and programming the computer-based information system
- Designing products
- Processing customer orders

That transactions drive costs is old news. In 1963, Peter F. Drucker observed that:[15]

While 90% of the results are being produced by the first 10% of events, 90% of the costs are being increased by the remaining and result-less 90% events.

Economic events are, by and large, directly proportionate to revenue, while costs are directly proportionate by number of transactions.

Furthermore, . . . efforts will allocate themselves to the 90% of events that produce practically no results. . . . In fact, the most expensive and potentially productive resources (i.e., highly trained people) will misallocate themselves the worst.

These transactions can be grouped into four types of transactions:[16]

1. *Logistical transactions* order, execute, and confirm materials' movements. Personnel busy with such transactions include indirect shop floor workers as well as people engaged in receiving, shipping, data entry, electronic data processing (EDP), and accounting.
2. *Balancing transactions* match the supply of materials, labor, and machines with demand. These transactions are typically performed by people doing purchasing, materials planning, production control, forecasting, and scheduling.
3. *Quality transactions* validate that production is conforming with specifications. People in quality control, indirect engineering, and procurement perform quality transactions.
4. *Change transactions* update manufacturing information. Manufacturing, industrial, and quality engineers involved with engineering change orders (ECO), schedules, routings, standards, specifications, and BOMs perform change transactions.

A well-designed ABC system can by definition handle these transactions well since ABC is to a large extent transaction based. One group of transactions is related to quality, which explains the large potential for quality-driven organizations to implement ABC and TQM. Therefore, ABC is a quality-enforcing system if it is used as such and not just a cost-cutting tool.

A costing system, in addition to revealing status by keeping track of the transactions made, should also be useful for finding ways to *reduce* the costs or identify better ways to use the resources. In an ABC system, this is done in four ways:[17]

1. *Activity reduction* is one of the key elements in continuous improvement. This implies that the elapsed time and effort required to perform activities must be reduced.
2. *Activity elimination* is based on the fact that changes in the production process or products can eliminate the need to perform certain activities. Many activities in an organization do not contribute to customer value, responsiveness, or quality (nonvalue-added activities); however, it is wrong to conclude that those activities can be eliminated. An example of this would be all the cashiers; they perform nonvalue-added activities, but their jobs are not eliminated. Activity elimination is the only way to affect the fixed activity costs, and it is therefore the most effective way to reduce cost/increase resource utilization. This is an important angle for Business Process Reengineering (BPR). Unfortunately, BPR "became debased because many companies tried to boost productivity solely by reducing the number of people on payroll ('downsizing') rather than by improving the production process,"[18] and it became "a euphemism for cost-cutting"[19] in reengineering financial processes.

3. *Activity selection* is applicable when a product or a production process can be designed in several ways, with each alternative carrying its own set of activities and costs.

4. *Activity sharing* provides economies of scale as the designer of a product or process can choose design alternatives that permit products to share activities.

One way of reducing costs is to simplify the transaction flow. As we can see from Table 4.9, both product design and process design can be effective in this respect.

In Table 4.10, a fairly complete list of possible cost-reduction approaches is presented. ABC supports most of them, while volume-based costing systems give little aid.

Expansion of ABC into New Areas

ABC has been used in a growing number of arenas outside manufacturing, as shown in Figure 4.8, because of its capabilities in reducing costs and increasing the overall resource efficiency. This may seem surprising, but recall the fact that ABC is based on the formulation of resources, activities, and cost objects, something that all organizations possess. In other words, it would be surprising if ABC did not work in those new areas.

One study provides an even more comprehensive and updated overview of the areas in which companies utilize ABC and the wider concept of ABM. In Table 4.11, this information is summarized. The study investigated 25 sources in the literature and 25 different applications. The Occurrences column in the table refers to how many times the authors identified that particular way of applying activity-based principles among their 25 sources in the literature.

Others have extended the ABC principles to include environmental management in a broad sense. In fact, this book serves as a further extension of the list.

Table 4.9 Examples of Cost Reduction Possibilities Supported by ABC

How to Reduce Costs	Possible Process Design Changes	Possible Product Design Changes
Activity reduction	Reducing setup time	Reduce number of parts
Activity elimination	Eliminating material-handling activities	Outsource subassembly production
Activity selection	Separate high-volume from low-volume products	Choosing an insertion process
Activity sharing	Centralize functions	Using common components

Table 4.10   Examples of Cost Reduction Approaches

Design and Manufacturing Methods:
- Design to manufacture and assembly
- Group technology:
  - Standardizing and reducing the number of parts
  - Standardizing the manufacturing process
  - Manufacturing cells
  - Critical Path Planning (CPP)
  - High-volume/experience curve
- Just in Time (JIT) manufacturing
- Design for X
- Design for the life cycle
- Design for the environment
- Function analysis
- Value analysis and engineering
- Concurrent and systems engineering
- Reliability engineering
- TQM
- Quality Function Deployment (QFD)
- Design for maintainability
- Axiomatic design

Design and Manufacturing Organizational Structure:
- Early manufacturing involvement
- Manufacturing signoff
- Integrator
- Cross-functional and multidisciplinary teams
- Concurrent engineering team
- Simultaneous engineering
- Product-process design department

Material Sourcing:
- Vendor selection and certification
- Electronic data interchange and e-commerce
- Purchasing of materials and subcomponents
- TQC of incoming materials before arrival

Inventory Management:
- Manufacturing Resource Planning (MRP II)
- JIT

Advanced Manufacturing Technology:
- Computer-aided design and manufacturing (CAD/CAM)
- Robotics and automation
- FMS
- Computer-Integrated Manufacturing (CIM)
- Rapid prototyping

Capacity Utilization:
- Optimized production technology (OPT)
- CIM
- Total preventive maintenance
- MRP

Manufacturing Costs:
- Economies of scale:
  - Dedicated technology
  - Standardization
  - High volume/experience curve
- Economies of scope:
  - Flexible technology
  - Focused factories
  - Elimination of changeovers

Activity and Cost-Driver Analysis:
- Eliminating nonvalue-adding activities
- Reduction of value-adding cost drivers

Total Quality Control:
- Statistical process control
- Cost of quality
- Six Sigma

Customer Consumption Costs:
- Design for maintainability
- Design for the life cycle
- Design for reliability
- Design for serviceability

Performance Measures of Continuous Improvement:
- Constant flow of inventory and standing inventory
- Cost
- Simplicity
- Quality
- Grade
- Productivity, agility, and flexibility
- Time

Motivation:
- Target costing
- Motivational standards
- Ratchet productivity standards
- Design target accountability
- Design productivity standards
- Management by objectives
- Employee ownership
- Employee training
- Suggestion box systems
- Performance contingent compensation
- Skill contingent compensation

Accounting Control:
- Budget planning and control
- Cost planning and estimation
- Actual cost accounting
- Standard cost accounting

Source: Adapted from M.D. Shields and S.M. Young, "Managing Product Life Cycle Costs: An Organizational Model," *Journal of Cost Management* 5(3) Fall 1991, pp. 39–51.

Table 4.11 Application of Activity-based Approaches

Application	Occurrences	Application	Occurrences
Activity analysis	20	Output planning	8
Activity drivers	10	Performance measures	17
Activity-Based Budgeting (ABB)	12	Process reengineering	16
		Product costs	17
Benchmarking	10	Product design	9
Channel costs	6	Product pricing	10
Channel decision	4	Quality costing	13
Continuous improvement	17	Resource consumption	13
Cost drivers	7	Stock valuation	3
Cost modeling	6	Transfer pricing	1
Cost objects	17	Value chain analysis	5
Customer costs	10	VA/NVA analysis	18
Customer profitability	12		
Organization redesign	3		

Source: Adapted from M. Partridge and L. Perren, "An Integrated Framework for Activity-Based Decision Making," *Management Decision* 36(9), 1998, pp. 580–588.

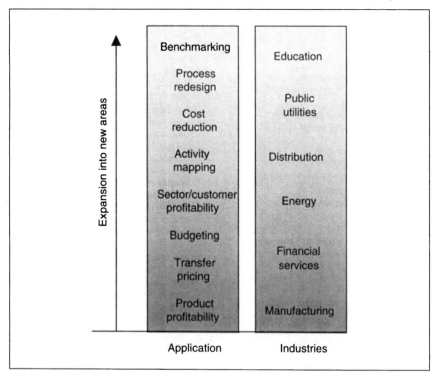

Figure 4.8 ABC expanding into new areas.

Also, the concept of Economic Profit (EP) from the 1920s, or possibly earlier, that Stern Stewart & Co. invented under the term Economic Value Added (EVA), can quite easily be incorporated into ABC.

The introduction of EP into an ABC framework has the advantage of further broadening the scope from operating costs and profits to operating costs and profits, *including* the cost of capital. The reason is that some products, customers, and processes may incur a disproportional cost of capital (in both positive and negative directions) and hence alter the picture provided by standard ABC to some degree. Also, EP correlates well with changes in stock prices, according to Stern Stewart & Co., and this provides an added benefit for publicly traded and listed companies.

How to include EP in ABC is beyond the scope of this chapter. It will, however, be explained in Chapter 5 because this extension is particularly important in the LCC context as LCC often is applied on large capital goods investments. Here it suffices to know that the extension is quite straightforward. It rests on two critical points:

1. The identification and usage of *capital* drivers whose purpose is to trace the cost of capital. The term *capital driver* is analogous to resource drivers, activity drivers, and cost drivers found in standard ABC.
2. The computation of the cost of capital. The most common way of calculating the cost of capital is to use the so-called Weighted Average Cost of Capital (WACC) method[20] and multiply that by the net worth of assets. The estimated cost of capital is a pure calculation; that is, it does not appear in any books.

From this brief discussion, it is apparent that activity-based approaches are becoming more and more encompassing. Judging from the literature, it does not appear that this will stop in the near future.

Note that ABC has limited utility in certain circumstances. For ABC to be useful, some degree of activity repetitiveness and complexity must exist. For example, organizations that manufacture products on a project basis, which is unique from time to time, such as a shipyard building specialty ships, have limited usage of ABC because the uniqueness of the project makes the activity consumption too unique. For a shipyard that produces the same types of ships, however, ABC can provide insight into the overhead costs that volume-based costing systems cannot.

Also, sufficient complexity must be present for ABC to be really useful. For very simple organizations such as food stores, gas stations, and very small organizations in general, ABC would simply be overkill.

Some Good Advice for ABC System Design

Since the formalized[21] ABC framework first arrived in the early 1980s, the framework has undergone quite substantial changes. In 1990, Robin Cooper provided a straightforward way of implementing an ABC system in a paper entitled "Five Steps to ABC System Design" in the journal *Accountancy*, while *The Handbook of Cost Management* provides some of the most up-to date discussions. Many books about the topic have been published, including some by notable authors such as Robin Cooper, Robert S. Kaplan, Gary Cokins, and Peter B.B. Turney. Lists of things that typically can go wrong and how to avoid such problems are also discussed at great length. These lists are applicable to most activity-based framework implementation, but only the main points are discussed here.

Not asking "the five why's" is the number one problem in these lists—they fail to define the scope of implementation properly. It is important to understand that in order to have good answers, we must have good questions. Basically, the general lack of asking why is a problem in itself. The five why's refer to a technique attributable to JIT concept developer Taichii Ohno that focuses on finding the root cause and not the symptoms. The Fishbone diagram and Pareto Analysis are also applicable.

A second important problem is *forgetting the three cost views:* strategic, operational, and financial. The problem arises when practitioners try to do all of them *simultaneously*. The three cost views are presented in Table 4.12. My experience is mostly linked to strategic ABC analyses, and Activity-Based LCC is mainly such a strategic approach, at least as long as organizations do not discover the blessing of foresight cost accounting over hindsight cost accounting.

A third problem is *looking at only manufacturing costs, not total costs,* and thereby omitting large areas of potential improvements. This happens easily if the practitioner thinks in terms of fixed and variable costs.

A fourth important problem is related to the team setup, *using a team solely from finance, not cross-functional*, which is rooted in three issues:

1. A group consisting solely of finance people will be stigmatized as being "just another accounting project" and therefore not get the necessary company-wide buy-in necessary for success.
2. A model implemented solely by finance people will inevitably have too much focus on the financial perspective.
3. Finance people do not have the knowledge to model the business processes accurately enough. This is crucial since ABC is process oriented. In fact, when Taichii Ohno implemented JIT at Toyota, he kept cost accountants out of the plant to "prevent the knowledge of cost accounting from entering the minds of his people."[22]

Table 4.12 Three Cost Views

	Operational	Strategic	Financial
User of information	Line managers, process improvement teams, quality teams	Strategic planners, cost engineers, capital budgeters, product sourcing	Financial controllers, tax managers, financial accounting, treasury
Uses	Key performance indicators, value/nonvalue-added indicators, activity analysis for process improvements	Activity-based product costing, Target Costing, investment justification, Life-Cycle Costing, make/buy analysis	Inventory calculation, external reporting, shareholders, lenders, tax authorities
Level of aggregation	Very detailed, little aggregation	Plan or product line aggregation, detailed based on what is needed for a specific decision	High aggregation, often company-wide data
Reporting frequency	Immediate, sometimes hourly or daily	Ad hoc, as needed, or usually a special study	Periodic, often monthly, or probably could be quarterly or annually if other needs were met

Source: Adapted from R.S. Player, "The Top Ten Things That Can Go Wrong with an ABM Project (And How to Avoid Them)," *As Easy As ABC*, Summer 1993, pp. 1–2.

In my experience, it is important that the ownership of the ABC implementation is secured by someone who is accountable, such as the chief executive officer (CEO) or chief operating officer (COO). Otherwise, the results of the analysis can easily be forgotten and nothing happens after the ABC implementation.

Another problem from one of the lists is, in my opinion, among the most important issues: *not addressing the changes.* An inherent resistance to change exists in organizations, as expanded on by Edgar H. Schein in a 2002 interview with *Harvard Business Review*, and such a resistance can be very damaging since changes typically are necessary after an ABC implementation. In fact, changes occur constantly, but in an organization where this is not acted on and the organizational myths are not being challenged thoroughly, the benefits of an ABC analysis will be severely reduced. The reason is that these myths—or the theory of business, as Drucker calls it—are the prime reason for the malaise of many large corporations.[23]

Activity-Based Costing and Total Quality Management

In the literature, an increasing proliferation of activity-based frameworks is employed for various purposes, as discussed in the previous section. Notably, Total Quality Management (TQM) is one of the most important approaches. TQM and ABC are complementary to each other in that they fulfill each other.

For ABC, some of the basic TQM notions are vital to avoid the business-as-usual syndrome attacked by several ABC authorities. When ABC implementations have failed, it is often attributable to a lack of understanding in management that fundamental changes are needed and that ABC is not just another cost-cutting tool, even though it works really well for that purpose too.[24]

For TQM, the cost perspective is important to ensure focus on what matters. Hence, ABC aids TQM, which puts ABC in the right context. After all, ABC is process oriented, and continuous improvement, which is a process, is one of the cornerstones of TQM. Furthermore, TQM focuses on quality, which is one of the four transaction types, and its importance in a long-term perspective can be illustrated by Figure 4.9. Quality is the basis for both dependability, speed, and cost efficiency.

A study of 187 European manufacturers, for example, showed that long-term cost improvements result from having first achieved improvements in quality, then dependability, and finally in speed (time). The peak of the model, cost efficiency, can only contribute up to 20 percent of the possible advantages.[25] Others estimate that traditional cost-efficiency improvement strategies can only affect circa 10 percent of manufacturing costs (see Figure 1.1).

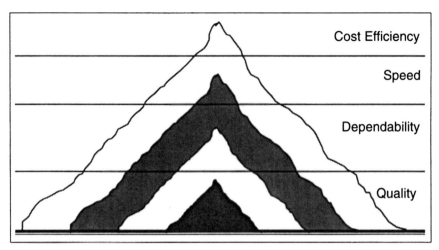

Figure 4.9 Model of cost reduction. Source: Adapted from K. Ferdows and A. DeMeyer, "Lasting Improvements in Manufacturing Performance: In Search of a New Theory," *Journal of Operations Management*, Vol. 9, pp. 168–184. Copyright 1991, reprinted with permission from Elsevier Science.

Intuitively, after contrasting ABC to the volume-based costing systems, ABC seems, and is, far more logical and better than the volume-based costing systems in my opinion. Yet a study shows that:

- Direct labor as an allocation base is still dominant in product costing.
- These product costs are used for a wide range of strategic and competitive decisions.
- Nonmanufacturing costs are rarely (if ever) included as a part of product or product line costs.
- However, the worst finding was that most people were confident with the situation.

These findings illustrate that even faced with a remarkable amount of information and evidence, business as usual still prevails five years after the ABC concept became well known. It is as a former colleague of mine, Tor Schaathun, liked to put it: "Corporations' ability to change is inversely proportionate to its distance from bankruptcy negotiations." This gives innovative companies an advantage in sharpening and sustaining their competitive edge.

ABC EXAMPLE AND CASE STUDY

The following example is a pure comparison between ABC and a volume-based approach to illustrate the computational differences. It is a reworking of an example found in the much-debated paper "ABC: A Need, Not an Option," authored by Robin Cooper in 1990. Then, a more comprehensive case study is presented that will be further expanded on in Chapter 8.

ABC Example

Suppose we were invited by company XYZ to estimate the profitability of its four products, P1, P2, P3, and P4. We are told that the products are produced on the same equipment and use similar processes, but that they differ in physical size and in production volumes, as indicated in Table 4.13. From this table, we also see the various cost information available.

Furthermore, three types of information are available for the costs related to direct inputs: (1) material costs, (2) direct labor hours, and (3) machine hours. When it comes to the costs related to setting up equipment and planning production, XYZ can also provide a threefold set of information: (1) the number of setups,

Table 4.13 Company XYZ Consumption Patterns and Overhead by Product

Product	Size	Volume	Material Costs ($)	Direct Labor Hours	Machine Hours
			Costs Related to Direct Inputs		
P1	Small	10 (Low)	60	5	5
P2	Small	100 (High)	600	50	50
P3	Large	10 (Low)	180	15	15
P4	Large	100 (High)	1800	150	150
Amounts consumed			2640	220	220
Overhead ($)			264	2200	3300
Aggregated overhead ($)	—	—	5764		

Product	Number of Setups	Number of Orders	Times Handled	Costs Related to Number of Parts ($)	Total Overhead Costs ($)
	Setup-Related Costs				
P1	1	1	1	1	
P2	3	3	3	1	
P3	1	1	1	1	
P4	3	3	3	1	
Amounts consumed	8	8	8	4	
Overhead ($)	960	1000	200	2000	
Aggregated overhead ($)	—	—	2160	2000	9924

Note: 5764 + 2160 + 2000 = 9924

(2) the number of orders, and (3) the times handled. The final cost category, the costs related to the number of parts, has no further information available. This cost category includes costs of handling the finished products, sending them to storage, and so on.

Look at the way a volume-based costing system would report these costs. In Table 4.14, the results are shown. As usual, direct labor has been chosen as an allocation base, but in this example it would not make any difference if another one was used. That is because a 1:10:3:30 ratio exists for the material costs, direct labor hours, and machine hours for all the products. What makes the difference here is the volume-based approach only considers direct input allocation bases and also for the other overhead costs.

The overhead rates are found by dividing the total overhead cost ($9,924) by the total number of direct labor hours (220 hours). The allocated costs are then found by multiplying the direct labor hours by the overhead rate for each product, as shown in Table 4.14.

We see that the volume-based costing system assesses the unit costs of P1 and P2 to be equal and roughly three times lower than the unit costs for P3 and P4, which are also estimated to cost the same. If we think carefully about those findings, we realize that it does not sound very convincing because how can P1 and P2, for example, cost the same when their needs for setups are 1:3, respectively? Something was obviously not right, and to provide an alternative cost assessment the management of XYZ asked us to implement ABC because they had heard about it and thought that it sounded interesting.

To employ ABC, we first need to break up the work processes into smaller units: activities. It turns out that many activities must be considered, but their product cost assignment is governed by three distinct activity drivers, as indicated in Table 4.13. Based on this insight, we divide the overhead costs into three cost pools, each associated with an activity driver, as shown in Table 4.15. To trace the costs of these cost pools, we use direct labor hours, the number of setups, and the number of parts as activity drivers, as shown in Table 4.15. Then we take the overhead costs associated with each activity driver and divide them by the total number

Table 4.14 Overhead Costs Reported by a Volume-Based Costing System

Product	Direct Labor Consumed (hour)	Overhead Rates ($/hour)	Costs Allocated ($)	Reported Unit Cost ($)
P1	5	45.11	225.55	22.56
P2	50	45.11	2255.50	22.56
P3	15	45.11	676.65	67.67
P4	150	45.11	6766.50	67.67
	220		9924.200	

Table 4.15 Overhead Costs Reported by an ABC System for a Company

	Costs Related to		
	Direct Labor	Number of Setups	Number of Parts
Total overhead costs ($)	5764.00	2160.00	2000.00
Total activity driver units	220.00	8	4
Consumption intensity	26.20 $/h	270.00 $/setup	500.00 $/part

of activity driver units. The result is the consumption intensity, which is the unit price of a driver unit. We see, for example, that a setup costs $270.

After calculating the consumption intensities, we multiply the various activity driver values for each product and for each cost pool, as shown in Tables 4.16 through 4.18, producing the traced costs for each product for each cost pool.

We sum up all the traced costs in the last column of Table 4.16 through Table 4.18 for each product, yielding the total costs traced in the second-to-last column in Table 4.19. Finally, we just divide the total costs traced by the number of units to compute the unit costs.

In Table 4.20, the difference between the volume-based approach and ABC is presented. Clearly, the difference is substantial, up to 300 percent. Imagine the consequences of XYZ pushing P1 at a $40-per-unit sales price as a part of a marketing strategy, for example. The company risks digging itself into red numbers while believing it is doing the right thing. All because the existing cost accounting system tells the company that it is making more than $17 per product unit sold. Clearly, making decisions based on a volume-based costing system is unwise, because volume-based costing systems grossly mistreat overhead costs.

You may think that such results are rare and that it occurred in this example by design, but the fact is that often companies lose money on roughly 80 percent of their products. If we include the costs of capital, the numbers are even worse. It is not an exaggeration to claim that companies survive despite their volume-based cost accounting systems. Think about all the times you have heard about companies growing their market shares while their profits remain the same or even decline. The good news is that this represents a major opportunity for those companies that understand their costs, because they can focus on capturing *profitable* market shares at a minimum expense while their competitors can have the rest.

ABC at WagonHo!

Implementing an ABC system can be done in many ways due to a variety of factors, such as budget, cost views (see Table 4.12), organizational complexity (see Figure 4.6), and actual decision support needs. This case illustrates one of the most

Table 4.16   Costs Related to Direct Inputs

Product	Direct Labor Hours	Consumption Intensity ($/h)	Costs Traced ($)
P1	5	26.20	131.00
P2	50	26.20	1310.00
P3	15	26.20	393.00
P4	150	26.20	3930.00

Table 4.17   Costs Related to Setups

Product	Setups	Consumption Intensity ($/setup)	Costs Traced ($)
P1	1	270	270
P2	3	270	810
P3	1	270	270
P4	3	270	810

Table 4.18   Costs Related to Part Numbers

Product	Part Numbers	Consumption Intensity ($/part)	Costs Traced ($)
P1	1	500	500
P2	1	500	500
P3	1	500	500
P4	1	500	500

Table 4.19   Total Overhead Costs Reported by an ABC System

Product	Costs Related to Direct Labor ($)	Costs Related to Setups ($)	Costs Related to Part Numbers ($)	Total Costs Traced ($)	Reported Unit Costs ($)
P1	131.00	270.00	500	901	90.10
P2	1310.00	810.00	500	2620	26.20
P3	393.00	270.00	500	1163	116.30
P4	3930.00	810.00	500	5240	52.40

Table 4.20   Reported Unit Cost Difference

Product	Traditional Costing Unit Cost ($)	ABC Unit Cost ($)	Difference
P1	22.56	90.10	299.4 percent
P2	22.56	26.20	16.1 percent
P3	67.67	116.30	71.9 percent
P4	67.67	52.40	−22.6 percent

common approaches, which is to use ABC as a single analysis for strategic usage. WagonHo! is in such bad shape that for them it is most important to get the big picture (strategy) right first before beginning to use ABC on a more continuous basis.

This approach is also usually smart no matter what, because it is very difficult —if not almost impossible—to go directly from traditional cost accounting practices to an integrated ABM system. To use ABC analyses for strategic purposes on an ad hoc basis is therefore good training to prepare the organization for the full-fledged version of ABM sometime later if they want that. Furthermore, it is a far less costly approach since it takes time for a company to get used to managing and acting according to ABC thinking.

Company Overview

WagonHo! is a toy manufacturer located in the computers at the Center for Manufacturing Information Technology (CMIT) in Atlanta, Georgia. In other words, WagonHo! is not a real company. CMIT uses it as a simulation company in which local companies can test out the latest information technology for manufacturing. However, CMIT *does* have a model factory built in the laboratory where it actually produces products.

The company experienced a $1.3 million loss last year, which is a highly unsatisfactory result, and the management is, of course, in dire need of decision support to turn this situation around. It operates in a somewhat price-sensitive niche market, so increasing prices are not the first thing to consider, but the demand is fairly good. Other problems are also pending, such as expected higher energy costs due to an energy shortage.

WagonHo! has 56 employees organized mainly in six production teams and indirect people. More specifically, the CEO is Samuel P. Stone and the plant manager is Mary Ann Chesnutt. The six production teams consist of a supervisor and six employees. Besides these production teams, the remaining 14 employees are indirect. The supervisors of the six teams are also considered indirect. In other words, 20 indirect people are employed in total.

The strategy is to target the high-price/quality market for children from affluent families. All the products are made of similar materials, that is, mainly plastics, steel screws, and wood. WagonHo! produces only three products.

The high-end product is the CW1000 wagon, referred to as CW1000 for simplicity. This is a wagon with four wheels and front steering (see Figure 4.10). The sales price of this product is $120; corrected for 12 percent sales rebates and 2 percent provisions, we get $103.20. Current production is 5,000 units per year. The simplest product is the CW4000 wheelbarrow. This is single-wheeled, without steering. It sells for $100, yielding a net sales price of $86. Current production is 3,000 units per year. The CW7000 garden cart is the middle product. This is a two-

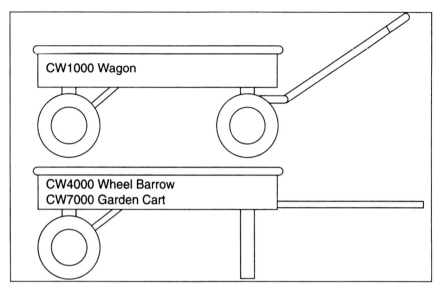

Figure 4.10 The products of WagonHo!

wheeled cart also without steering that sells for $105, giving a net sales price of $90.30. Current production is 2,000 units per year.

The shop floor is configured as shown in Figure 4.11 with six lathes (L), six milling machines (M), six subassembly (SA) stations, one kitting area, six final assembly and inspection (FA) stations, and one central conveyer. With this production line, the estimated aggregated production cycle times are 462, 247, and 259 minutes for the CW1000, CW4000, and CW7000, respectively. The cycle times are obviously long and clearly need improvement, but how? Also, an overall loss for the company is not a sustainable situation either, so that must also be improved.

WagonHo! is currently using Contribution Margin Costing, a volume-based costing system. But past experience has convinced management to try using ABC to give them better decision support. Table 4.21 presents the hourly labor costs of

Table 4.21 Hourly Labor Costs at WagonHo!

Labor Classifications	Labor Cost ($/h)
Mill operator	9.00
Lathe operator	8.50
Assembler	7.80
Kit maker	7.30
Inspector	11.30

Table 4.22 CW4000 Bill of Material (BOM)

Product Num.	Description	Parent Num.	Part Num.	Number Required	Estimated Time (h)	Unit Time (h)	Unit Cost	Ext. Cost	Comments
4000	**Wheelbarrow**		**CW4000**	**1**		**4.07**	**0.00**	**46.86**	**Complete**
4100	Labor, final inspection	4000		1	0.30	0.30	3.39	3.39	Labor
	Bed	4000	CW1373	1			6.54	6.54	Purchase assembled
4200	Screws	4100	SP4881	10			0.02	0.20	Purchase
4210	Labor, final assembly	4000		1	0.45	0.45	3.51	3.51	Assembly labor
4220	Labor, kit purch. parts	4000		1	0.30	0.30	2.19	2.19	Kitting labor
4300	Wheel assembly	4100		1			0.00	0.00	Subassembly
4310	Labor, assembly	4300		1	0.30	0.30	2.34	2.34	Assembly labor
4320	Axle bracket	4300	CW2019	2			0.87	1.74	Make
4330	Short axle	4300	CW3626	1			0.12	0.12	Purchase
4340	Wheel	4300	CW2314	1			0.73	0.73	Make
4350	Cotter pins	4300	SP6122	2			0.01	0.02	Purchase
4360	Labor, kit make part	4300		2	0.20	0.40	1.46	2.92	Kitting labor
4370	Labor, make part	4300		1	0.84	0.84	7.56	7.56	Machine part
4380	Raw material, wheel	4300	RM5784	0.5			0.78	0.39	Purchase raw
4390	Raw material, brackets	4300	RM5784	1			0.78	0.78	Purchase raw
4400	Leg/handle assembly	4100		1			0.00	0.00	Subassembly
4410	Labor, assembly	4400		1	0.15	0.15	1.17	1.17	Assembly labor
4420	Handle	4400	CW3908	1			0.47	0.47	Purchase
4430	Leg stand	4400	CW4240	1			0.95	0.95	Make
4440	Screws	4400	SP4881	6			0.02	0.12	Purchase
4450	Labor, kit make part	4400		2	0.20	0.40	1.46	2.92	Kitting labor
4460	Labor, make part	4400		1	0.93	0.93	8.02	8.02	Machine part
4470	Raw mat., leg stand	4400	RM5784	1			0.78	0.78	Purchase raw

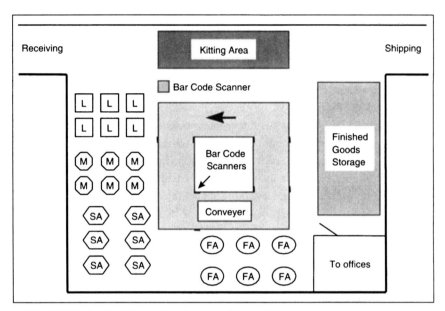

Figure 4.11 The initial shop floor layout at WagonHo!

the workers, and by multiplying the hourly labor cost with the estimated times, we get portions of the BOM, as shown in Table 4.22, which presents the BOM for the CW4000. The unit time in Table 4.22 is an estimated production time (h/unit).

The BOM should be read from bottom to top. Thus, for the CW4000, the total direct cost is $46.86 per unit while the unit production time is 4.07 hours per unit. We can also see the various subassembly numbers. For example, the product number for the bed is 4100 and its part number is CW1373.

Table 4.23 presents a summary of the BOM for the products, along with the aggregated production times, which currently serve as overhead cost allocation bases

Table 4.23 Summary of BOM and Aggregated Production Times for the Products

Product	Unit BOM ($/unit)	Aggregated Production Times (h/year)
CW1000 wagon	90.04	38,500
CW4000 wheelbarrow	46.86	12,210
CW7000 garden cart	57.40	8,640

in the company's volume-based costing system. The aggregated production times are found by multiplying the unit time for each product by the annual production of each product. These times will most likely also prove handy for the ABC implementation.

ABC Implementation

Since this chapter is about ABC in general, it is best to present here a common way of implementing an ABC model rather than presenting the way that provides the most decision support. It should be noted that this implementation is tailored to MS Excel and not to ABC software. Personally, I prefer MS Excel for strategic ABC analyses because such analyses are ad hoc and may require manual adjustments to give proper decision support; hence, the argument of the organization needing to maintain the model does not apply. Also, MS Excel provides a flexible implementation tool so that, for example, EP can easily be incorporated. Furthermore, in some cases executives have probing questions concerning the implementation and its results, and then an open ABC implementation is much more explanatory and trustworthy than the black boxes of software.

An MS Excel–based, strategic ABC analysis approach would typically consist of nine steps, some of which can be performed concurrently:

1. Create ownership of the ABC analysis in the organization and define the scope of analysis.
2. Review current cost accounting structures and clean out overhead costs from the direct costs if needed.
3. Get cost data from the General Ledger and aggregate them into cost categories.
4. Define the activity library.
5. Design the questionnaire and hold group interviews.
6. Calculate a Bill of Activities (BOA).
7. Define activity drivers and gather data. Also gather other relevant data such as sales data.
8. Aggregate the cost of activities that have the same activity drivers into separate cost pools.
9. Calculate product/customer costs and profitability.

It is important to include the customer perspective even though we are only interested in product profitabilities. The reason is that customer behavior often determines some costs and not product characteristics. An example of such costs is the invoicing costs; invoices are, after all, sent to customers and not to products. WagonHo! sells its own products to the end customers directly, and more important, 97 percent of its customers buy only one unit at a time, which makes the customer perspective redundant for practical purposes in this case.

Create Ownership and Define Scope

Creating ownership is very important in order to secure that once the ABC analysis has been performed, it will be followed up by action. For that reason, the ABC analysis should be championed by an executive with result responsibility, such as the CEO or COO. In WagonHo!, CEO Stone is the champion. Together with his team of managers, he defines the scope to be "assess the product profitability and identify possible improvements." Also, all costs are to be included in the model, even the facility-related costs. The ABC model is, in other words, a *full absorption* model. That is, we trace *all* the cost to the products. Full absorption costing is particularly useful in relation to pricing, outsourcing, sales promotion, and other improvement activities that require understanding the total costs.

Review Current Cost Accounting Structures and Cleanse Costs If Needed

As stated above, WagonHo! uses a volume-based costing system where estimated production times are used to assist the BOM calculations. Unlike the situation in many other companies, the direct costs in BOM are, in fact, direct costs. In other words, we do not need any cost cleansing. For many companies, however, cleansing the costs is needed because they often mix overhead costs such as production planning into their direct costs using simple rules of thumb, direct labor hours, or machine hours. Such mixed cost structures should in principle always be cleansed; that is, the overhead costs must be separated from the direct costs. For companies using standard costing, cost cleansing becomes substantially more complicated. In standard costing, various cost deviations are tracked, and some of these deviations must also be cleansed.

Get Cost Data and Aggregate Them into Cost Categories

From the General Ledger, we get all the cost data for the last 12 months. Table 4.24 shows how the costs are categorized. For completeness' sake, the direct costs found in BOM are also included although they will not be traced using ABC principles. In step 9, the direct costs will be subtracted from the sales, yielding the contribution margins of the various products.

From Table 4.24, we see that the total annual costs of WagonHo! are about $2.16 million, from which we understand that the company is small and that the employees are not paid well. This might be a result of earlier attempts to improve profits. We also see that the cost of the equipment is low (less than $75,000), which may indicate that the equipment is old and potentially inefficient. Finally, the building seems disproportionately expensive. Maybe WagonHo! should relocate to a cheaper part of town? These are just questions that arise while working with the cost data and are not particular to an ABC analysis.

Table 4.24 WagonHo! Costs

Cost Categories	Costs ($/year)	Cost Categories	Costs ($/year)
Building	261,000	BOM	694,900
Conveyer system	5,100	Support equipment	11,900
Kitting equipment	270	Indirect labor	1,081,250
Lathe machines	22,500	Office equipment	45,650
Milling machines	17,000	Inspection equipment	650
Assembly equipment	1,050		
Total			2,274,470

Define Activity Library

The activity library is defined by interviewing key personnel. During those interviews, it is important to keep in mind that it reduces the distortions if the activities and the cost categories match somewhat. But more important, it is crucial not to become overly detailed in the activity definitions, because it is pointless to be more detailed than warranted by the data. Basically, it is a matter of cost versus benefit. Consequently, creating an activity library can be done in different ways. The activity library developed for WagonHo! is shown in Table 4.25 as a hierarchy. This is not a common approach, but I find it helpful to provide tracing of the logic behind the activity library. The hierarchy also provides information aggregation structures.

The shaded cells in Table 4.25 represent the lowest-level activities for which we need to gather data. An important way to gather data is to interview people about their work.

Table 4.25 WagonHo! Activity Hierarchy

Level 1	Level 2	Level 3
Production A1	Logistics A11	Receive parts A111
		Run inventory A112
		Ship products A113
	Produce Products A12	Kit parts A121
		Run mill A122
		Run lathe A123
		Assemble products A124
		Inspect products A125
Product support activities A2	Design products A21	
	Sell products A22	Market/sell products A221
		Service customers A222
Facility support activities A3	Maintain facility A31	
Administration A4	Lead company A41	
	Run production A42	
	Process orders A43	
	Manage costs A44	

Design Questionnaires and Hold Interviews

The purpose of the questionnaires is to find out how the indirect people use their time. Based on their answers, we will trace labor costs and some other costs to the activities. The people are asked to think in terms of an annual average. You may think that this is crude, but what would be a better way for finding out how people use their time than asking them? Also, some people may be reluctant to tell us how they spend their time, particularly if they perceive the whole ABC analysis as a cost-cutting exercise. This emphasizes the need to thoroughly inform the organization about what is to take place, to create a sense of urgency, and to convey that the main objective is to increase profitability, not necessarily cut costs. This has worked well for me on several occasions when the employees were hostile to the ABC analysis. Still, some people will inevitably try to fix their answers, but because of the law of large numbers, such fixing will have little impact on the overall accuracy of the analysis.

Table 4.26 shows a sample of the answers. The times listed for a full-time employee add up to roughly 100 percent. The reason for saying roughly is that answers do not have to be accurate in order to be relevant. Moreover, it may seem odd that the total time of, for example, Activity A111 becomes 24.8 percent. The reason is that we often use tables to convert easy time concepts to percentages. For example, if an employee performs activity A111 1 hour a week, that would yield

Table 4.26 Sample Interview Answers

ID	Activity Name	Total (%)	Name, ID Number, and Department	Name, ID Number, and Department
A111	Receive parts	24.8		
A112	Run inventory	10.6		
A113	Ship products	24.8		
A121	Kit parts	254.9		5.0
A122	Run mill	447.8		20.0
A123	Run lathe	26.5		
A124	Assemble products	242.5		5.0
A125	Inspect products	221.2		
A21	Design products	83.2	25.0	
A221	Market/sell products	83.2	45.0	
A222	Service customers	123.9	10.0	
A31	Maintain facility	24.8		
A41	Lead company	49.6	20.0	7.0
A42	Run production	141.6		50.0
A43	Process orders	83.2		5.0
A44	Manage costs	157.5		8.0
Total		2000.0	100.0	100.0

an annual percentage of 48 hours divided by 1,800 hours, or 2.7 percent, assuming that the employee works 48 weeks and roughly 1,800 hours a year.

After the interviews are conducted and the aggregated time percentages (the Total (%) column in Table 4.26) are found, we proceed to calculate the BOA.

Calculate the Bill of Activities (BOA)

The first step in calculating the BOA is to determine the approach to use for the time percentages. The approach I prefer is to first normalize the numbers in Table 4.26 to produce Table 4.27. The normalization basically consists of dividing every activity time percentage by the total time percentage, which is 2,000 percent for WagonHo!

We must decide what to do about the cost categories in Table 4.24. Should we use resource drivers, only the time percentages as resource drivers, or a mix? A resource driver is a cause-and-effect measure between an activity and a resource. In Table 4.28, we see that only two such resource drivers exist: area and labor hours. The rationale behind area is that the more space an activity uses, the more building resources this activity consumes, which sounds logical. Labor hours works only as a resource driver for the indirect labor costs resource because labor costs will be caused by labor, but "labor hours" is not a resource driver for the "support equipment" resource because no clear cause-and-effect relationship exists. In this case, we use "labor hours" as an allocation. It is important that not too many allocations take place in an ABC model, because they reduce the quality of the model.

Table 4.27   Normalized Activity Time Percentages

ID	Activity Name	Time Percentage
A111	Receive parts	1.2
A112	Run inventory	0.5
A113	Ship products	1.2
A121	Kit parts	12.7
A122	Run mill	22.4
A123	Run lathe	1.3
A124	Assemble products	12.1
A125	Inspect products	11.1
A21	Design products	4.2
A221	Market/sell products	4.2
A222	Service customers	6.2
A31	Maintain facility	1.2
A41	Lead company	2.5
A42	Run production	7.1
A43	Process orders	4.2
A44	Manage costs	7.9
Total		100.0

Table 4.28 Resource Driver Definitions

Cost Categories	Costs ($/year)	Resource Driver Name
Building	261,000	Area
Conveyer system	5,100	A12x activities
Kitting equipment	270	Direct
Lathe machines	22,500	Direct
Milling machines	17,000	Direct
Assembly equipment	1,050	Direct
Support equipment	11,900	Labor hours
Indirect labor	1,081,250	Labor hours
Office equipment	45,650	Labor hours
Inspection equipment	650	Direct
Total	1,446,370	

Normally, I prefer that allocations govern less than 10 percent of the total overhead costs. In this case, it is 2.7 percent, which is very satisfactory.

Concerning the conveyer system, the costs are distributed equally among the A12x activities, that is, between activities A121 through A125. This is due to the fact that all A12x activities use the conveyer system equally because they are all interrelated via the production flow on the conveyer.

Direct is an even stronger relationship between the resource and activity. What this means is that, for example, the kitting equipment has a one-to-one relationship with the activity A121. This is the ideal situation of an ABC model because it reduces the distortion to zero, provided that the activities are defined in enough detail to provide any insight.

Note that in Table 4.28, BOM costs are excluded. That is because BOM costs are direct costs and therefore are simply included in the end of the ABC analysis only.

Given these resource driver definitions and the data as shown in Table 4.29, we can calculate the cost of the activities as found at the bottom of the table. One of the two 1,446,370 numbers is a control summation and should therefore be equal to the other (to the left). This is necessary when using MS Excel or any other open model.

Table 4.30 provides a summary of the BOA, listing all the activities. These results can be plotted in a graph, as shown in Figure 4.12. This figure can be helpful in identifying abnormal process costs or in identifying what activities are most important to either eliminate or reduce. We see, for example, that most of the overhead costs are in fact related to the core production activities (A12x), which may indicate that many problems must be solved or that the production layout requires a lot of follow-up.

The interesting question is: Can production costs be reduced significantly by streamlining the production? Because the cycle times are so long, it may seem that this is indeed the case.

Table 4.29 BOA Sample

Cost Categories	Costs ($/year)	Resource Driver	Total	Consumption Intensity	A122 Resource Driver	A122 Activity Cost	A44 Resource Driver	A44 Activity Cost
Building	261,000	Area	16,550	15.8	1,000 (ft^2)	15,770	100 (ft^2)	1,577
Conveyer system	5,100	A12x act.	5	1,020.0	1	1,020		
Kitting equip.	270	Direct	1	270.0				
Lathe machines	22,500	Direct	1	22,500.0				
Milling mach.	17,000	Direct	1	17,000.0	1	17,000		
Assembly equip.	1,050	Direct	1	1,050.0				
Support equip.	11,900	Labor hours	100%	11,900.0	22.4%	2,664	7.9%	937
Indirect labor	1,081,250	Labor hours	100%	857,200.0	22.4%	242,082	7.9%	85,164
Office equip.	45,650	Labor hours	100%	45,650.0	22.4%	10,221	7.9%	3,596
Inspection equip.	650	Direct	1	650.0				
Total	1,446,370			1,446,370		288,757		91,274

Table 4.30 BOA Summary

Activity	Activity	Cost	Percentage
A111	20,420	($/year)	1.4%
A112	163,753	($/year)	13.3%
A113	20,420	($/year)	1.4%
A121	162,181	($/year)	10.9%
A122	288,757	($/year)	19.5%
A123	54,403	($/year)	4.2%
A124	155,910	($/year)	10.5%
A125	143,412	($/year)	9.7%
A21	48,938	($/year)	3.2%
A221	48,938	($/year)	3.2%
A222	71,336	($/year)	4.7%
A31	15,689	($/year)	1.1%
A41	29,012	($/year)	1.9%
A42	82,988	($/year)	5.5%
A43	48,938	($/year)	3.2%
A44	91,274	($/year)	6.0%
Total	1,446,370	($/year)	100.0%

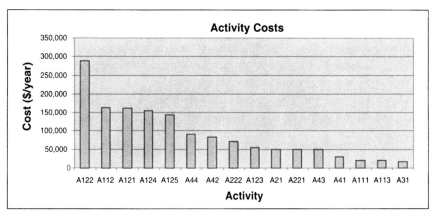

Figure 4.12 Cost of activities in descending order.

Define Activity Drivers and Gather Data

Table 4.31 shows the activities, including costs, and the corresponding activity drivers. Note that 11 different activity drivers are used. For example, "annual component use" is an activity driver that is used in three activities, namely, A111, A112, and A121. It seems reasonable to trace the cost of activities that involve product parts in some fashion using such an activity driver. What is important to remember is that the activity drivers must also be chosen according to what information is available.

Table 4.31   Activity Driver Definitions

Activity	Activity Driver	Cost ($/year)
A111	Annual component use	20,420
A112	Annual component use	163,753
A113	Annual production	20,420
A121	Annual component use	162,181
A122	Mill labor hours	288,757
A123	Lathe labor hours	54,403
A124	Assembly labor hours	155,910
A125	Annual production	143,412
A21	Number of products	48,938
A221	Annual sales	48,938
A222	Number of inquiries	71,336
A31	Annual production	15,689
A41	Annual sales	29,012
A42	Number of batches	82,988
A43	Number of orders	48,938
A44	Direct labor hours	91,274
Total		1,446,370

The activity drivers that probably most accurately reflect the true cause-and-effect relationships between products and activities are mill labor hours, lathe labor hours, and assembly labor hours. This is due to the fact that the production is manual with no usage of automation or batch production.

Other activity drivers also are used multiple times. To ease the analysis, we can aggregate all the costs that share the same activity drivers into cost pools, which is done next.

Create Cost Pools

Based on Table 4.31, cost pools based on activity driver similarity can be created as shown in Table 4.32. The benefit of doing this is that it reduces the model com-

Table 4.32   Cost Pools

Activity Driver	Cost Pools ($/year)	Activity Driver	Cost Pools ($/year)
Annual component use	346,354	Annual sales	77,950
Annual production	179,520	Number of inquiries	71,336
Mill labor hours	288,757	Number of batches	82,988
Lathe labor hours	54,403	Number of orders	48,938
Assembly labor hours	155,910	Direct labor hours	91,274
Number of products	48,938		
Total			1,446,370

plexity. Unfortunately, it may also reduce the accuracy of the model because it is tempting to create larger cost pools than warranted to save work and effort. Again, it is a matter of cost versus usefulness.

Calculate Product Costs and Profitability

The final step is to relate each cost pool to each product using the activity drivers and assigning values to them, as shown in Table 4.33. We see, for example, that the cost pool that relates to the "Annual comp. use" activity driver consumes in total $346,354 and that 190,000 components are consumed annually by all the products. The various products, however, do not consume an equal amount of components.

The CW1000 consumes 130,000 components annually and is by far the largest user, whereas the CW4000 and the CW7000 consume 36,000 and 24,000 components annually, respectively. These three numbers are then used to calculate the costs for each product in the following fashion:

- CW1000 annual component use cost = $346,354 \times (130,000/190,000)$ = $236,979
- CW4000 annual component use cost = $346,354 \times (36,000/190,000)$ = $65,625
- CW7000 annual component use cost = $346,354 \times (24,000/190,000)$ = $43,750

In this way, we calculate how the products consume all the cost pools and we sum up in the total OH costs row. Then, we subtract the direct costs (materials and direct labor) and sales rebates that are given to promote the products, which yields a total cost. By subtracting this total cost from the total sales, we get the profitability in the bottom row of Table 4.33.

These results are discussed further in the next section. But first, those of you who may have read about this case in earlier publications may notice that the total costs do not sum up exactly the same. That is because the standard version of ABC implementation ignores changes in inventory. This represents a minor distortion in the modeling, but as long as the inventory changes are modest, this omission of inventory changes will have little, if any, impact on the usefulness of the analysis. It is, therefore, important to be clear about the purpose of the analysis.

In this case, accurate profitability estimates were asked for that indicate that temporal changes in inventory, asset utilization, and so on should be ignored because we are interested in the true profitability of the products and not a mix of profitability and process efficiency. If we are interested in an ABC analysis that is to be used for process improvements, we should design the model to capture process inefficiencies. We must then include capacity and asset utilization and so on to best identify the hidden costs of the hidden factory[26] as it were.

Table 4.33 Product Cost and Profitability Calculations

Activity Driver Name	Activity Driver Value	Cost Pools ($/year)	Wagon CW1000		Wheelbarrow CW4000		Garden Cart CW7000	
			Activity Driver	Cost	Activity Driver	Cost	Activity Driver	Cost
Annual comp. use	190,000	346,354	130,000 (comp.)	236,979	36,000 (comp.)	65,625	24,000 (comp.)	43,750
Annual production	10,000	179,520	5,000 (units)	89,760	3,000 (units)	53,856	2,000 (units)	35,904
Mill labor hours	25,200	288,757	16,650 (h)	190,786	5,130 (h)	58,783	3,420 (h)	39,188
Lathe labor hours	7,000	54,403	3,500 (h)	27,201	2,100 (h)	16,321	1,400 (h)	10,881
Assem. labor hours	15,750	155,910	10,750 (h)	106,415	2,700 (h)	26,728	2,300 (h)	22,768
Number of products	3	48,938	1 (product)	16,313	1 (product)	16,313	1 (product)	16,313
Annual sales	1,110,000	77,950	600,000 ($)	42,135	300,000 ($)	21,068	210,000 ($)	14,747
Number of inquiries	5,400	71,336	2,000 (inquiries)	26,421	1,900 (inquiries)	25,100	1,500 (inquiries)	19,816
Number of batches	5,000	82,988	2,500 (batches)	41,494	1,500 (batches)	24,896	1,000 (batches)	16,598
Number of orders	2,700	48,938	1,200 (orders)	21,750	500 (orders)	9,063	1,000 (orders)	18,125
Direct labor hours	55,950	91,274	34,900 (h)	56,934	12,330 (h)	20,114	8,720 (h)	14,225
Total OH costs		1,446,370		856,189		337,866		252,315
Direct costs		694,900		431,450		149,010		114,440
Sales rebate		133,200		72,000		36,000		25,200
Total costs		2,274,470		1,359,639		522,876		391,955
Total sales		1,110,000		600,000		300,000		210,000
Profitability		-1,164,470		-759,639		-222,876		-181,955

Results

The results are normally not presented in the manner shown in Table 4.33. Often, the results are presented as shown in Table 4.34, in that the numbers are normalized by the sales volume, providing a Return on Sales (ROS) perspective. That is, we take, for example, the Margin 1 (sales − direct cost) of the CW1000 ($168,550) and divide it by the sales ($600,000), which produces the number 28.1 percent. A Margin 1 of 28.1 percent for the CW1000 essentially indicates that for every dollar sold, 28.1 cents is generated as a surplus toward covering rebates and overhead costs. Unfortunately, we see that the profitability of the CW1000 is −126.6 percent, or in other words, for every dollar sold, WagonHo! loses $1.266. In fact, all the products are highly unprofitable.

To improve the situation for WagonHo! we must investigate the results in Table 4.34 more thoroughly. We see, for example, that Margin 1 is quite low for the CW1000, which may indicate that the CW1000 either is priced too low or has cycle times that are too long. In this case, probably both are the case, particularly the latter.

We also see that all products generate too many overhead costs (over 100 percent for all products). This may indicate that simply too many overhead resources are included compared to the production volume and/or that the production volume is too low. Since laying people off is not a popular measure, the management at WagonHo! would like to pursue increasing the production volumes significantly, but as mentioned earlier, the cycles times are very long. In other words, the manufacturing system must be reconfigured to either lower direct costs and/or reduce cycle times.

From Table 4.31, we see that the lathes in Activity A123 generate little overhead costs, yet WagonHo! has as many lathes as mills, for example. This seems to indicate that too many lathes exist (too much capacity). An audit revealed that five of the lathes could be sold without any further consequences.

Conversely, for Activity A122 (milling), excessive usage of overhead resources is taking place. This may indicate that the milling operations have many problems, so we decide to do something about the mills. After conducting an audit of activity A122, it became evident that if we had a saw that could cut some parts rapidly and if the workers got to run extra mills, they could significantly increase output.

It also became clear that introducing cell manufacturing would reduce the probability of reworking because all the workers would understand the entire manufacturing operation and not just their part of it. In addition, the subassembly step should include quality control, rather than the final assembly step as before. That is, Activities A124 and A125 are merged. Furthermore, cell manufacturing will reduce activity A121 significantly. The freed resources can be used in the increased milling operations. After implementing these suggestions, the cycle time is

Table 4.34   ABC Results

Product ID	Product Name	Dir. Cost	Sales	Margin 1		Rebates	Margin 2		ABC OH Costs		Total Costs		Profitability	
		694,900	1,110,000	415,100	37.4%	133,200	281,900	25.4%	1,446,370	130.3%	2,274,470	204.9%	-1,164,470	-104.9%
CW1000	Wagon	431,450	600,000	168,550	28.1%	72,000	96,550	16.1%	856,189	142.7%	1,359,639	226.6%	-759,639	-126.6%
CW4000	Wheelbr.	149,010	300,000	150,990	50.3%	36,000	114,990	38.3%	337,866	112.6%	522,876	174.3%	-222,876	-74.3%
CW7000	Garden C.	114,440	210,000	95,560	45.5%	25,200	70,360	33.5%	252,315	120.2%	391,955	186.6%	-181,955	-86.6%

reduced with over 50 percent for all products, as shown in Table 4.35, and the shop floor layout is changed, as shown in Figure 4.13.

However, we also suggest *increasing* the price for the CW1000 significantly to *cut* demand for it. The reason is that the CW1000 actually costs a lot more to produce than was reflected before in its traditional cost accounting system, and this capacity can be more profitably employed for the two other products. For example, the CW1000 is the only product that consumes the A123 activity (lathes). On top of that, the CW1000 is basically a more complex product. WagonHo! therefore increases the price from $120 to $225 for the CW1000, and sales have fallen by 50 percent.

After making all these changes, we reestimated the previous estimated times and they fell a lot. The new improved cycle times (see Table 4.35) will hopefully make it possible to produce the products more resource-efficiently than before. A secondary effect is that the production volumes can be increased, which will provide an economies-of-scale effect for all the products.

What the management of WagonHo! is particularly proud of is that all these changes were made without firing a single person. Only a couple of early retirements were needed.

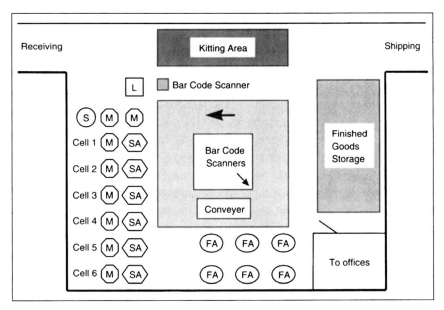

Figure 4.13   New shop floor layout for WagonHo!

Table 4.35   Cycle Time Reductions at WagonHo!

Product	Old Cycle Time (Min.)	New Cycle Time (Min.)	Improvement
CW1000 wagon	462	192	58.4%
CW4000 wheelbarrow	244	103	57.8%
CW7000 garden cart	259	113	56.4%

Discussion

As mentioned at the beginning of this section, this case is a functional one. Most real cases are much more complex, often having hundreds of products and customers. However, that is why this case is so suited for illustrative purposes; we can concentrate on the essential parts. Also, the processes in WagonHo! were apparently poorly configured as some of them had quite a massive amounts of surplus capacity. Most companies would manage to solve some of the problems of such gross production resource misallocation as shown in the case here. The point, however, is that they would have little, if any, aid from their cost management system. Here, in contrast, we see that with ABC the production managers in this case will get significant decision-support. ABC is basically an excellent attention-directing tool, and that is what I hope you will learn from this case.

In this case, we focused a lot on production issues. That is due to the available data from CMIT, which after all is preoccupied with manufacturing information technology. However, even in this case, we can provide marketing with useful information regarding pricing issues. In fact, in real-life situations, marketing people can benefit quite rapidly from an ABC analysis due to the immediate relationship between total costs and pricing. However, ABC analyses have the greatest impact on manufacturing and other costly processes, but the road toward harvesting results is longer and requires more diligent work.

Finally, it is important to keep in mind the cost view of the ABC analysis, as exemplified in Table 4.12. In this case, a strategic approach was chosen. This is the approach I would recommend for companies that have just started on the journey toward modern cost management practices for several reasons.

First, the company should first evaluate its strategies, because these strategies have an enormous impact on long-term profitability. Second, such ad hoc analyses provide more than enough decision support the first five to six years. Third, a more subtle reason is that one cannot jumpstart the organizational learning process; it is important to take it step by step. Finally, due to the initial uncertainties of the organization's execution capabilities and the costs of implementation, a simple, flexible, cost-effective approach should be chosen to reduce the costs committed and to increase the organizational learning. ABC is, after all, a very logical approach, and companies that want to explore it should not be hindered by black boxes and unnecessary committed costs.

Later, when a company feels comfortable with ABC, it can begin to use ABC for financial cost views (refer to Table 4.12). This will require the use of ABC software and managers who understand ABC sufficiently to avoid being dictated by the software. After all, who would trust major decisions to software engineers who have no stake in the company whatsoever and hardly understand ABC themselves?

The final stage in the learning process toward world-class cost management is to use ABC for operational purposes (see Table 4.12). In fact, we no longer talk about ABC, but ABM and nonfinancial performance measurements, including Balanced Scorecard, Activity-Based Budgeting (ABB), and so on. Such solutions must be embedded in an Enterprise Resource Planning (ERP) system or a similar system, but they require excellent managers that understand what they do. Otherwise, the company runs the risk of "delivering distorted information every single day"[27] to managers who do not understand what they see.

From this discussion, it follows that although ABC has great potential for use in all companies, it is important to implement it step by step to ensure sufficient organizational learning. Using ABC for LCC purposes, as discussed in this book, does not raise the risks of integrated ABM systems because LCC is ad hoc in nature, at least for the time being. Activity-Based LCC therefore is a sound next step up from traditional LCC and the hindsight of cost management in general. Its theory is discussed in Chapter 5.

Finally, I would like to thank Research Engineer Greg Wiles at CMIT in Atlanta for his cooperation and the data he provided, which made this case study possible.

FROM THE TRENCHES

In this chapter I have described ABC theoretically and used examples to illustrate the costing system, but undoubtedly real-world problems that have made people skeptical should be addressed. In my opinion, such skepticism is unwarranted, caused by the fact that ABC has too often been implemented unwisely, rather than the concepts themselves being faulty.

ABC is an advanced approach for improving the performance of companies, and like all advanced tools, ABC requires understanding and proper implementation to work as desired. Furthermore, it requires a change in mindset to avoid the business-as-usual syndrome, as pointed out in the controversial paper on activity-based panaceas, "It's Time to Stop Overselling Activity-Based Concepts," written by H. Thomas Johnson in 1992. The problem often lies not in the way ABC results are used, but rather in the way they are generated. Too often, ABC has been implemented as an improved cost allocation mechanism, while the important analyses of processes, value creation, and cause-and-effect relationships are largely ignored. Basically, managerial tools must be coupled with sound judgments to provide the desired results, but this is not always done.

On one hand, we have those ABC implementations that have gone astray by digging themselves into a ridiculous level of detail. I have heard of implementations with hundreds of activities and drivers, and even worse, those who did the job are proud of it. Such implementations become costly, ineffective, and excessively bureaucratic. On top of that, they tend to inhibit action because the decision-makers lose interest as the level of detail goes beyond what they consider relevant. On the other hand, we find some implementations that are so simple that they miss many of the distortions that ABC is supposed to handle. Both cases result from a lack of understanding.

Unfortunately, consultants push for sales, and their customers push back to cut the fees of the consultants, and the performance of ABC, BPR, or whatever managerial tool is used suffers. Consultants sometimes push ABC and associated IT solutions onto customers that either do not need ABC altogether or do not need an IT solution because of certain organizational characteristics. Companies sometimes purchase costly IT solutions then try to save pennies on training, proper up-front work, and assistance in performance improvement. Thus, it is no wonder that in the literature we sometimes hear the sound and fury of practitioners, consultants, and academics.

For ABC to work, it is absolutely crucial that consultants and other implementers understand an organization's characteristics (see Figure 4.6) and implement ABC accordingly; companies also must stop trying to save pennies while wasting these larger amounts. As Michaela Driver writes, "Like organizational learning, ABC is most useful, in terms of effective organizational performance, as a process rather than a product."[28] Furthermore, we must understand that ABC can be "described more as a cognitive tool for understanding systemic problems and conducting root-cause analysis than a cost reporting tool."[29] Basically, we must learn to walk before we can run, and it is important that both consultants and managers realize this and do not push implementations beyond the maturity level of the organization.

Consequently, I always recommend that the companies I work with first conduct ABC as an ad hoc, strategic analysis (see Table 4.12) without even using any software except MS Excel. Excel is great for both enabling the managers to understand the structure of an ABC model and providing detailed and thorough answers to skeptics who may try to cast the results into doubt.

When the managers have become fluent in using such cost information, we can proceed to the next step, which is to introduce software and do annual analyses.

My impression is that shortcutting this learning process is more often the rule than the exception. It is no wonder that some companies become disappointed, and claim that ABC is just another passing fad.

In my opinion, ABC is no passing fad. ABC represents the return to basics in the sense that processes, measures, and causalities determine the cost allocation and not some arbitrary allocation bases that are chosen more out of habit than anything else. Furthermore, ABC is a great cost accounting tool, but its true value lies in its learning potential and focus on causality. In this sense, the Balanced Scorecard and similar approaches in which causality is one of the main points can be seen as an offspring of ABC.

Cost management has invariably been the art of hindsight and cutting costs after they are incurred. However, ABC as an organizational learning tool opens up for proactive cost thinking and the identification of cost causalities. The next step should therefore be to turn the entire cost management process around and focus more on the cost causalities and less on the actual cost estimates, because it is only by understanding the cause-and-effect relationships among cost objects, processes, and resources can we truly manage costs. Once the cost causalities are understood, cost management can become forecasting oriented and proactive, and that is what Activity-Based LCC is all about.

NOTES

1. The example is adapted from P.L. Brooks, L.J. Davidson, and J.H. Palamides, "Environmental Compliance: You Better Know Your ABC's," *Occupational Hazards,* February 1993, pp. 41–46.
2. The full case description is found in R. Cooper, "Activity-Based Costing: Theory and Practice," *Handbook of Cost Management,* ed. B.J. Brinker. Boston, MA: Warren, Gorham & Lamont, 1997, pp. B1.1–B1.33.
3. For more details on this matter, see R. Cooper, "Explicating the Logic of ABC," *Management Accounting* (UK), November 1990, pp. 58–60.
4. P.B.B. Turney, "What an Activity-Based Cost Model Looks Like," *Journal of Cost Management,* Winter 1992, pp. 54–60.
5. According to a survey in 1987, 94 percent of the companies use labor hours to allocate overhead costs.
6. For more details, see J.W. Hardy and E.D. Hubbard, "ABC: Revisiting the Basics," *CMA Magazine,* November 1992, pp. 24–28.
7. A thorough discussion on this is provided in H.T. Johnson and R.S. Kaplan, *Relevance Lost: The Rise and Fall of Management Accounting,* Boston, MA: Harvard Business School Press, 1987, p. 269.
8. According to E.M. Goldratt in "Cost Accounting: Number One Enemy of Productivity," *Proceedings of the APICS Conference,* 1983, pp. 433–435.

9. According to R.S. Kaplan in "Yesterday's Accounting Undermines Production," *Harvard Business Review,* July/August 1984, pp. 95–101.

10. See note 6.

11. According to R. Fox in "Cost Accounting: Asset or Liability," *Journal of Accounting and EDP,* Winter 1986, pp. 31–37.

12. R.S. Kaplan, "In Defense of Activity-Based Cost Management." *Management Accounting,* November 1992, pp. 58–63.

13. It is necessary to separate the two because Generally Accepted Accounting Principles (GAAP) do not enable many of the adjustments that must be made in order to fully process-orient a costing system.

14. L.R. Dolinsky and T.E. Vollmann, "Transaction-Based Overhead Considerations for Product Design." *Journal of Cost Management for the Manufacturing Industry* 5, No. 2, Summer 1992, pp. 7–19.

15. P.F. Drucker, "Managing for Business Effectiveness." *Harvard Business Review,* May-June 1963, pp. 54–55.

16. J.G. Miller and T.E. Vollmann, "The Hidden Factory." *Harvard Business Review,* September-October 1985, pp. 142–150.

17. P.B.B. Turney, "How Activity-Based Costing Helps Reduce Cost." *Journal of Cost Management for the Manufacturing Industry* 4, No. 4, Winter 1991, pp. 29–35.

18. "Back to Basics: A Survey of Management," *The Economist,* 2002, p. 18.

19. P.T. Finegan, "Making Planning Relevant: The Real Role of Corporate Finance Reengineering." *Corporate Finance Review* 3, No. 3, November/December 1998, pp. 6–15.

20. According to W.W. Hubbell, Jr., "Combining Economic Value Added and Activity-Based Management," *Journal of Cost Management,* Spring 1996, pp. 18–30.

21. Gordon Shillinglaw at Colombia and George Staubus at Berkeley had articulated activity-based concepts by the early 1960s. Also in the early 1960s, General Electric accountants may have been the first to use the term *activity* to describe work that causes costs. However, the process of codifying the concept to what ABC is best known for today is mainly attributable to Robin Cooper at the Harvard Business School. For more details, see H.T. Johnson's "It's Time to Stop Overselling Activity-Based Concepts," *Management Accounting,* September 1992.

22. J.Y. Lee, *Managerial Changes for the 90s.* New York: Addison-Wesley, 1987.

23. For more details, see P.F. Drucker, "The Theory of the Business," *Harvard Business Review,* September-October 1994.

24. J.A. Miller, "Designing and Implementing a New Cost Management System." *Journal of Cost Management for the Manufacturing Industry,* Winter 1992, pp. 41–53.

25. W. Skinner, "The Productivity Paradox." *Harvard Business Review,* July-August 1986, pp. 55–59.

26. The term *the hidden factory* has been attributed to the seminal paper by J.G. Miller and T.E. Vollmann, "The Hidden Factory," published in the *Harvard Business Review,* September-October 1985, pp. 142–150.

27. R. Cooper and R.S. Kaplan, "The Promise—and Peril—of Integrated Cost Systems." *Harvard Business Review*, July/August 1998, pp. 109–119.

28. M. Driver, "Activity-Based Costing: A Tool for Adaptive and Generative Organizational Learning?" *The Learning Organization* 8 (3), 2001, pp. 94–105.

29. M. Lebas, "Which ABC? Accounting Based on Causality Rather than Activity-Based Costing." *European Management Journal* 17 (5), 1999, pp. 501–511.

5

ACTIVITY-BASED LIFE-CYCLE COSTING

> The expectations of life depend upon diligence; the mechanic that
> would perfect his work must first sharpen his tools.
>
> Confucius

Activity-Based Life-Cycle Costing (LCC) is an approach that was developed from the more comprehensive Activity-Based Cost and Environmental Management approach[1] that Professor Bert Bras and I developed in the latter half of the 1990s. Although Activity-Based Cost and Environmental Management deals with cost and environmental dimensions (energy and waste in particular), Activity-Based LCC only includes costs. Activity-Based LCC, however, has an improved structure and is more comprehensive with respect to costs.

Does that mean that Activity-Based LCC cannot be used in an environmental setting? On one hand, cost as a measure has many advantages over environmental measures, as discussed in the "LCC in the Environmental Domain" section of Chapter 2. On the other hand, many environmental effects cannot be captured as costs because they are externalities (see Glossary). We therefore must be careful using costs as an environmental measure in general. As with most management and engineering tools, we must strike a sound balance between theory and practice.

In this chapter, the theory of the Activity-Based LCC method is explained as concisely as possible. This will be done by going through each of the 10 steps depicted in Figure 5.1. Note that the first seven steps are modeling steps, whereas the latter three steps are for calculation.

STEP 1: DEFINE THE SCOPE OF THE MODEL AND THE CORRESPONDING COST OBJECTS

Step 1 is generic to almost any assessment; that is, define the scope of the model. The scope should include as a minimum the objectives of the model, its system boundaries, and its perspective.

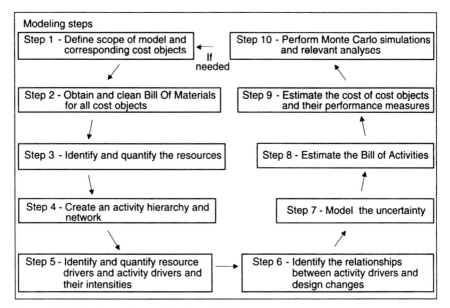

Figure 5.1   Implementing activity-based LCC.

It is crucial to define the objectives of the model because this determines what type of model one should build. Two options concern whether one should build a back-casting model or a simulation/forecasting model. LCC models are almost by definition forecasting models, but often one must build a back-casting model before one can build a good forecasting model. Alternatively, one can include the last year in the forecasting model to provide a 100 percent baseline and then use this year's costs to check whether the forecasting is good enough.

In a back-casting model, we would start with the resources. We would then, via the model, determine the costs of activities and the costs of the cost objects. This is a top-down approach at least as far as the cost assignment goes. Simulation models, however, are bottom-up models where we start with the process data, product demand, and so on and calculate the resources needed to run the operation. Alternatively, we can follow the target costing idea and end up with a target cost, which is what the operation can cost. However, in order to perform a simulation model, one must in general start with a back-casting model to determine the "as-is" situation. Then from the as-is situation, changes can be made and the future simulated, so to speak.

A more relevant distinction between models for this book is the difference between *cost accounting* models and *ad hoc* LCC analyses. LCC cost accounting models take a broad view of the situation and are applied to managing future costs by predicting them and managing their drivers, as shown in Chapter 8. Basically, they provide relevant decision support to numerous managerial issues as constrained and partly defined by a system boundary. In other words, the system boundary is an important driver for cost accounting models and ultimately limits which cost objects are relevant.

Ad hoc LCC analyses, as discussed in Chapter 2, are tailored toward specific decisions or cost objects. They provide decision support as defined by the cost object(s) that constrains the system boundary choice. The ad hoc analyses are therefore focused on a specific cost object(s), whereas the cost accounting models focus on the system boundary and understand what is inside it. Ad hoc analyses are consequently more narrow in scope than cost accounting models, usually tailored toward specific decisions, and the system boundaries are different. Traditional LCC is ad hoc and often focuses on one cost object at a time, whereas in Activity-Based LCC many cost objects are handled simultaneously when employed as either ad hoc analyses or cost accounting models.

Concerning the system boundary, we must distinguish between the system boundary for cost accounting models and for ad hoc models, as mentioned. For cost accounting models, it is important that the boundary is defined to minimize the number of transactions across the boundary. The length of the life cycle must also be defined by convention, such as by 1 year, 10 years, a strategic planning time horizon, or the life cycle of a product line. Ideally, the physical system boundary should be a Strategic Business Unit (SBU), a company, or an entire organization/corporation. At the very minimum, the business unit under study must have clearly identifiable cost accounts or cost information in a format that can be used. For example, making a cost model of a department in a company can be greatly inhibited if that department does not possess clearly identifiable cost accounts *and* if substantial interaction does not exist between that department and other departments. In such a case, it is usually less work to include the entire company in the cost model than to try to create proper system boundaries. Of course, once the system boundaries are defined, we need not study every part of the system with equal diligence. In other words, we can focus on one particular department if we want. Thus, once the scope of the modeling is determined, the cost objects will be defined by default in an LCC cost accounting model.

Conversely, in an ad hoc LCC model where the cost objects are defined first, the system boundaries are defined with respect to both time and physical extension. They are primarily designed to follow the length of the life cycle of the cost object(s) and include all conceivable costs and revenues.

Traditionally, the ad hoc approach has been associated with engineering, while the cost accounting approach has been associated with managers. In Activity-Based LCC, the difference no longer exists, except when it comes to defining the system boundaries.

When it comes to the perspective of the model—that is, whose point of view the model represents—several perspectives are possible. The most common perspective is the *SBU perspective*, which is the perspective of the SBU where the cost objects belong. Such a perspective will typically revolve around the operating costs and possible liability costs in the future. Another perspective that has gained much popularity in recent years is the *shareholder perspective*. The shareholder perspective is similar to the SBU perspective, but it also includes the cost of capital or something similar. A perspective that is popular in LCC models used in environmental management is the *stakeholder perspective*. The stakeholder perspective includes all the costs as seen by many stakeholders. In such models, it is vital to state for what stakeholder each cost assessment is made because a cost for one stakeholder is revenue for another and so forth.

STEP 2: OBTAIN AND CLEAN BILL OF MATERIALS FOR ALL COST OBJECTS

For LCC cost accounting models, it is important to assure that the existing costing system does not mingle overhead costs with direct costs in the Bill of Materials (BOM). Unfortunately, mixing up overhead costs with direct costs is a common practice, rooted in an attempt to allocate as many costs to products as possible. For an activity-based approach (such as Activity-Based Costing or Activity-Based LCC) to function well, it is important that the BOM does not contain any overhead costs that are not volume related in order to reduce possible distortions to a minimum.

If overhead costs and direct costs are mixed, which they usually are, the BOM must be cleansed for overhead costs and the costs must be transferred back to respective overhead accounts or to new accounts needed for the analysis. Doing so takes just as much craftsmanship and art as anything else, but with one single objective: Reduce cost assignment distortion. Typically, reviewing the cost accounting structures is useful but not sufficient, particularly for organizations with Standard Costing systems because all the deviations must be identified and handled.

It should be noted, as explained later in the "Step 3 Issues: The Role of the General Ledger" section, that these problems disappear if the General Ledger is disassembled and regrouped in an object-oriented manner. This involves a lot of work but always yields an overall better analysis. It is usually worth doing only if the results from the analysis are to be used in process or product design or major decisions.

STEP 3: IDENTIFY AND QUANTIFY THE RESOURCES

Identifying the resources implies listing *all* the resources within the system boundary and according to the objectives of the model. For example, a company can be the system boundary for an LCC model. The objectives may include a complete life cycle, a decade, or another time frame, but the point is that we must include the relevant costs given the appropriate perspective. For a company, the perspective will usually either be an SBU or shareholder perspective.

If the LCC model is to be used in scenario planning or any other activity where costs (and revenues for that matter) may or may not appear, it is important to include all possible costs, but more important to decide how to handle such costs. If we assign probability estimates to the costs, we implicitly assume that the Expected Monetary Value (EMV) approach is suitable, but cases occur where this would be highly misleading.

For example, if a cost either does or does not occur (with no intermediate values), then EMV will produce the average between occurring or not. The only problem is that this average will *never* occur; hence, it is misleading. For large costs, this can become inappropriate, and in such cases it is best to use indicator variables (variables that take the value of either 0 or 1) or step functions (functions that produce only discrete outcomes such as 0, 1, 2, 3, and so on). Then assign probability values to the values in the step function. This will essentially be similar to using a decision tree but without computing a grand, weighted average.

Resources can be refined into smaller and smaller resource elements. For example, a building is a resource that can be split up into the resource elements such as rent, cleaning, electricity consumption, depreciation (note that depreciation and other calculated costs can be calculated in several ways) and insurance, which in turn can be refined into smaller resource elements depending on what is useful with respect to meeting the objectives of the model. Thus, we can produce resource hierarchies, but these are virtually impossible to comprehend due to the vast number of resource elements most companies possess. Consequently, resource hierarchies are used.

While performing Step 3, the resources should be identified and quantified *if possible*. The identification only requires the name of the resource and type, such as depreciation, house rent, insurance, and so forth. Proper identification is important so that the resources can be identified during the analysis. The reason for emphasizing "if possible" is that resources directly related to the production volume and other volume-related variables will not be completely known until Step 9 is completed in simulation models.

In Figure 5.2, three different types of resources, as they relate to the production of products P1, P2, and P3, are illustrated:

1. Volume-related resources, which in reality are only materials and possibly but not necessarily transportation and direct labor costs.
2. A mixture of resources, which in essence are resources that are somewhat volume related such as labor and production planning. These resources are often in need of proper cleansing.
3. Pure overhead resources, which are typically finance, payroll, and the like.

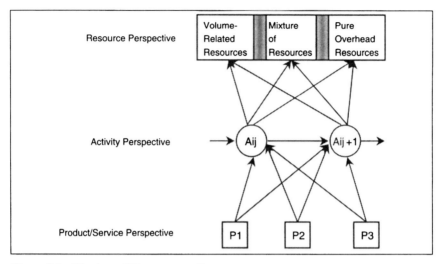

Figure 5.2   The three different types of resources.

Note that the dividing lines between the three resource categories are blurred. This is to signify that no 100 percent clear-cut distinction exists between the three types of resources, not even for materials. The types of resources overlap. However, Figure 5.2 serves as a *mental map* during implementation because the nonvolume-related resources will be known *only after* Step 9 is completed in simulation models. The mixed resources will mostly be known before Step 9 is completed, while the only resources that will be completely known at Step 3 are the pure overhead resources.

That this may sound difficult and even unclear is nothing to be alarmed by; it is not without reason that the volume-based costing systems lost their relevance as they were financially and structurally oriented. They were basically too simplistic and too aggregated to capture the reality of businesses. This goes to show that understanding resource consumption is not as easy as taught in school. In fact, many textbooks do not offer definitions and proper explanations of resources, costs, capacity, and expenses, let alone the differences. One reason might be that the traditional cost accounting systems are incapable of distinguishing between these terms, but for activity-based approaches it is important.

For example, when simulating the costs for a machine that is currently underutilized, but for which utilization will increase, it is important to realize that although the resource consumption of the machine will increase, the expenses will remain the same (except volume-related expenses). The reason the expenses remain the same is that the capacity is the same. In this way, the simulation model will correctly point out the fact that the economics of the machine will improve because the expenses stay the same, while the cost of surplus capacity decreases. In other words, the hidden factory or the waste has decreased. This example concerns just a machine, but the same line of argument holds for an entire corporation.

For advanced models, it is consequently important to distinguish between the resource dimension and the capacity dimension, as just explained and further expanded on in Chapter 4. This is, however, beyond the scope of this book because this distinction is mostly fruitful for implementations used on a continuous basis and provided that management in the SBU is capable of utilizing such information. Utilizing such information may sound simple but it is actually quite challenging because one must, in addition to understanding costing, also understand enough statistics to estimate whether changes in, for example, supply and demand are statistically significant or not. Organizations where statistical quality control is used should have an advantage at this because statistical cost control, as we may call what was just described, is conceptually the same.

In activity-based frameworks, resource consumption is managed by the activity consumption, which can occur in many different ways. In theory, it is said that activities are consumed on four levels: (1) unit level, (2) batch level, (3) product level, and (4) facility level, as discussed in the previous chapter. This is a simplification because product-line levels, brand levels, department levels, and so on are not included. In Activity-Based LCC, models of more than four levels are employed *if needed*. Hence, although Figure 5.2 is crude with respect to resource classification, it is more representative of reality than the classification into four activity levels. But again this discussion is related to distortion problems and one must choose a balance between accuracy and distortion, and cost and usefulness, which can be determined only from case to case.

STEP 4: CREATE AN ACTIVITY HIERARCHY AND NETWORK

In this step, every process within the system boundary is broken down into more and more detailed processes (activities), and thereby an activity hierarchy is created. The activities should be defined in enough detail to get *reliable* information. How to do this breakdown is an art. The most important point is that the breakdown does not proceed too fast; that is, the delineation from the top activities to the detailed activities should progress in a logical manner step by step and be consistent, as illustrated in the case studies provided in this book.

It is important to relate the level of detail to the objectives of the modeling. For example, a model for strategic analysis requires less detailed activity definitions than a model for product design. Basically, a model not intended for any design purposes can be less detailed than a model intended for design. The reason is that a model for design must be capable of capturing the links between activity drivers and design characteristics, as explained later in the "Step 6: Identify the Relationships between Activity Drivers and Design Changes" section. Other models are more purely attention-directing ones. Regardless of circumstances, activities should not be defined in more detail than the available information allows.

When identifying the activities, each activity should be labeled in a special manner (see Figure 5.3). This method makes it easy to see where the activities belong in the activity hierarchy and it saves a lot of space. Also, naming activities in a meaningful way is important. The names should be expressed as verbs plus an object. For example, an activity should be called Package Product and not Product Packaging or simply Packaging. This may seem like semantics, but it is in fact important for one reason: "a verb as attention director signals that continuous improvement is the new paradigm for the company."[2] Verbs also better describe what is actually being done. Using nouns to describe an activity easily hides the real content of the activity.

The activity hierarchy looks like any other hierarchy, as shown in Figure 5.4. It is important to note that the activity hierarchy shown in the figure is not easy to use for large models because the hierarchy does not fit on a single page or a computer screen. Activity hierarchies are therefore commonly presented as tables, as shown in the case studies in this book. Such tables, however, should be interpreted just like a hierarchy.

When the activity hierarchy is set up, the lowest level of activities, A_{11} through A_{nm}, is represented in an activity network, as shown Figure 5.5. The purpose is mainly to show which products consume which activities, the order of consumption, and important decisions involved. This is important to know when designing the model because otherwise the wrong products may be associated with the wrong activities or wrong decisions, which would cause fundamental errors in the model.

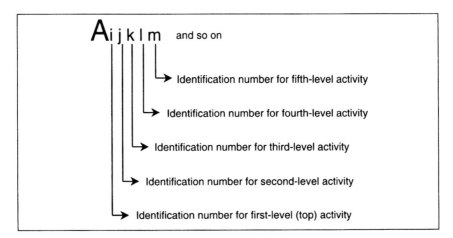

Figure 5.3 Activity notation.

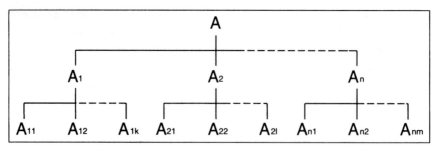

Figure 5.4   Generic activity hierarchy.

Also, the activity network can help identify what a decision (the diamond-shaped node) is really about. For example, if Product A is associated with a Yes in Decision Node A, we see immediately that Product A will incur Activity A_{1k} and then activities A_{21}, A_{22}, A_{2k}, A_{n2}, and A_{n3}.

The activity network in Figure 5.5 is not detailed, yet it suffices for most cases. In cases where detailed process mapping is required or desirable, it is probably better to use IDEF0 charts for the most critical parts of the process. The preferred approach, particularly for design purposes, is to use action charts.[3]

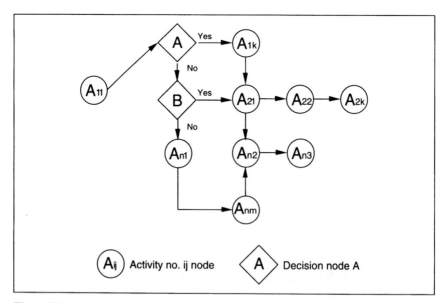

Figure 5.5   Generic activity network.

STEP 5: IDENTIFY AND QUANTIFY RESOURCE DRIVERS, ACTIVITY DRIVERS, AND THEIR INTENSITIES

The purpose of resource drivers is to trace how the activities consume resources, while activity drivers are to trace how the cost objects consume activities. When identifying these drivers, it is crucial that they are chosen to represent as closely as possibly the *actual* consumption as described by cause-and-effect relationships. That is, the drivers are to represent cause-and-effect relationships between activities and resources and between cost objects and activities. However, it is important to keep in mind that the cost of implementation versus the simplicity/accuracy of the implementation must be decided. Basically, the more accurate the implementation, the more costly and more troublesome it is to maintain if that is an issue.

Note that in cases where only one cost object is studied, only resource drivers are needed because all activities are related completely to a single cost object. When the drivers are identified, the consumption intensities must be identified when possible. Two types of consumption intensities exist: fixed and variable. A fixed consumption intensity is a consumption intensity that does not vary as the magnitude of the drivers (such as the material prices) changes. This is typically the case for direct costs.

A variable consumption intensity, in contrast, varies as the magnitude of the drivers varies, such as the machine-hour price. This is found by dividing the total resources associated with that driver by the total number of driver units. For example, if an activity costs $10,000 and 200 direct labor hours are associated with it, the consumption intensity becomes $50 per direct labor hour. Variable consumption intensities therefore usually are not known until the model is finished and they typically belong to overhead costs.

STEP 6: IDENTIFY THE RELATIONSHIPS BETWEEN ACTIVITY DRIVERS AND DESIGN CHANGES

In this step, we need to distinguish between two different design approaches. The simplest is when we want to select from several options. Here no relationships are needed since we are not interested in *changing* the design, only selecting. The most common case, however, is that some relationships take place.

Relationships can be anything from explicit *mathematical functions* to *action charts*. Mathematical functions are very accurate but are equally difficult to establish. Hence, mathematical functions are rarely used.[4] When the relationships are modeled as mathematical relationships, the Activity-Based LCC model becomes a mix that includes an LCC cost accounting model and the three other ways of performing LCC discussed in the "Four Ways of LCC" section in Chapter 2, particularly engineering cost methods.

At the other end of the scale are action charts where *no* explicit relations exist between design parameters and activity drivers. This gives greater flexibility, and action charts are therefore superb at directing *attention* toward *any* design changes in general, not just product changes. Action charts are also useful tools for performance measurements such as quality and time since they are time based and quality measures such as the scrapping percentage and the like can be easily facilitated.[5]

The action charts used in Activity-Based LCC are modified from action charts found in the literature.[6] Action charts are discussed in more detail later in the "Step 4 Issues: Building Submodels" section.

STEP 7: MODEL THE UNCERTAINTY

Chapter 3 discussed the various ways of modeling uncertainty (and risk). What is important to emphasize is that Monte Carlo methods, or simulation techniques, enable the most versatile handling of uncertainty.

In Activity-Based LCC Monte Carlo simulations, techniques are employed to find numerically how the assumption cells (where the uncertainty is modeled in the spreadsheet model) affect the forecast cells. An assumption cell can be viewed as a source variable (any design or process parameter can be an assumption cell) whose variability (modeled as uncertainty distributions) inflicts changes in the forecast cell(s). A forecast cell is essentially a response variable whose response is measured statistically.

The response is measured statistically because a Monte Carlo simulation is a numerical approximation method. The problem with measuring the response statistically is that the number of trials in the simulation and the sampling technique affect the reliability of the model due to unwanted random effects. The larger the models, the more care must be exercised, but it is no problem as long as a few simple guidelines are followed, as shown in the case studies.

To explain further, consider the example in Figure 5.6. The model in this example is simply Product Cost = Direct Labor + Material, where Direct Labor and Material are assumption cells and Product Cost is the forecast cell. Direct Labor is modeled as a triangular uncertainty distribution with a mean of $12 and lower and upper bounds of $4 and $20, respectively. Material is modeled as an elliptical uncertainty distribution with a mean of $10 and lower and upper bounds of $5 and $15, respectively.

The key issue is how these two assumption cells will affect the forecast cell. To find out, we run a Monte Carlo simulation. We see the three first trials: $4 + $6 = $10, $12 + $8 = $20, and $20 + $15 = $35. The numbers in the assumption cells are picked randomly *within* the modeled distribution. This means that if we picked

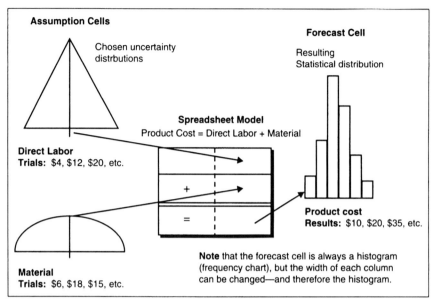

Figure 5.6   A SRS Monte Carlo simulation example. Source: B. Bras and J. Emblemsvåg, "Designing for the Life-Cycle: Activity-Based Costing and Uncertainty," *Design for X*, ed. G.Q. Huang. London: Chapman & Hall, 1996, pp. 398–423.

infinite numbers from Direct Labor, and afterward drew a histogram, the histogram would look exactly like the triangular distribution. After all the trials have been run, a histogram of the forecast cell is created; this is a graphical view of the forecast cell and how *it is numerically approximated to vary as a response to the uncertainty in the assumption cells.* Each estimate for the Product Cost is stored in the computer and an ordinary statistical analysis is performed on these stored values as if they were obtained by a real-life experiment. In other words, we are running a virtual experiment in a virtual world, where the virtual world is defined in the model as assumption cells, forecast cells, and model relationships.

We have so far discussed how to design the Activity-Based LCC model. The remaining three steps are calculation steps. Note that in a simulation model, Step 9 proceeds Step 8 for the reasons explained at the beginning of this chapter.

STEP 8: ESTIMATE THE BILL OF ACTIVITIES

To estimate the cost of an activity, the resource driver is multiplied by its consumption intensity. This is done for all the activities and then is summed up to produce the total cost of all the activities, which is the Bill of Activities (BOA). Tables 4.30 and 4.31 in Chapter 4 are good illustrations of this step.

STEP 9: ESTIMATE THE COST OF COST OBJECTS AND THEIR PERFORMANCE MEASURES

Step 9 works the same way as Step 8. The only difference is that in Step 8 resources are traced to activities, whereas in this step activity costs are traced to cost objects. From this, it is evident that Step 8 is the first step in an ABC system, whereas Step 9 is the second step. A good illustration for this step is Table 4.34 in Chapter 4.

When it comes to choosing performance measures, Economic Profit (EP) is highly recommended in most cases. Even without using EP as a performance measure, we must nonetheless have an idea about which discount factor should be used in the Net Present Value (NPV) calculations when they are applicable (see Glossary). This discount factor is also known as the discount rate, interest rate, or Minimum Attractive Rate of Return (MARR) in the literature.

The purpose of using discount factors is that earning a dollar today is better than earning a dollar tomorrow. Basically, discount factors take into account the alternative or opportunity cost of capital, including time and risk. In some cases, however, other considerations should come before the time cost of capital, such as the future. For example, if we are to investigate environmental issues, particularly from a public organization's point of view, we cannot discount the future because all generations must be treated equally. One cannot discount the future if one seriously seeks sustainability. The overriding objective in choosing discount factors must be that the choice is coherent with the overall mission of the organization. Otherwise, discord will exist between objectives and their decision support.

Cost of Capital in For-Profit Organizations

For-profit organization capital has many sources, such as:

- Cash advances (typical in the construction industry)
- Bank loans (short and long term)
- Loans against inventory
- Loans against accounts receivable
- Delaying payment on accounts payable
- Bond issues
- Preferred stock issues
- Common stock issues
- Retained earnings

Most of these are, however, usually small compared to the two main sources: equity and debt. The cost of capital should reflect this. A sound measure for the cost of capital in for-profit organizations, therefore, is the Weighted Average Cost of Capital (WACC). Table 5.1 shows the calculation of WACC. It has two struc-

Table 5.1   Example of Calculating WACC

Description	Value	Definition
Cost of equity:		
Risk-free rate	6%	Current long-term government bond rate
Beta (β)	1.1	Individual stock volatility versus market
Market risk premium (Mp)	6%	Fifty-year average
Cost of equity	**12.6%**	= Rf + (β × Mp)
Cost of debt:	7%	Company's current weighted average borrowing rate (short and long term)
Tax cost	2.8%	Assumes 40 percent marginal tax rate
After tax cost of debt	**4.2%**	
Capital structure:		
Equity	70%	Equity/(equity + debt)
Debt	30%	Debt/(equity + debt)
WACC	**10.1%**	= Equity × cost of equity + debt × after tax cost of debt

tures, namely, the cost of equity and the cost of debt. WACC is simply a weighted average of these two main costs. The cost of debt is the interest rates paid for the various loans.

The cost of equity, however, is a more interesting topic to discuss. We should be aware of a couple of facts concerning determining the cost of equity:

- Using the long-term government bond rate is only one of two common approaches. It is used in Table 5.1. Another approach is to use treasury bills, which are more risk free than government bonds, but bonds have a distinct advantage in that they better reflect expected future interest rates than treasury bills.[7] In the United States, many companies use the 10-year U.S. Treasury bond.[8]
- To infer investors' expectations for the market risk premium, one must look at periods longer than a year, and "conventional wisdom suggests one should select the longest period possible."[9]

The cost of capital is subsequently found by multiplying WACC by the *net assets* employed, which is defined as the net working capital plus the net fixed capital. Thus, if a company has $100 in net assets and a WACC of 10.1 percent, the cost of capital, or capital charge, is $10.10.

Many in the literature discuss many more discounting factors, such as the borrowing rate offered by banks. However, they do not emphasize that for a company, all capital is capital. You can borrow money to finance a project, but ultimately it will be difficult to say that certain capital is borrowed while the other capital is equity or other loans. The reason is that everything is interrelated in an organization. It would be like saying that eating breakfast provides nutrition for the arm and leg muscles while lunch is for the brain, and so on.

Some may argue that in for-profit organizations we can also use an external measure of the cost of capital such as the rate of borrowing capital in the marketplace. I strongly disagree, because such external measures implicitly assume that placing capital externally is a viable opportunity, or alternative, for the decision maker. Thus, such practices effectively drain the company of capital and thereby reduce its capability to create value over time. External measures are only financially viable in the short term; they ruin the company in the long run. In my opinion, for-profit organizations should use internal, consistent measures of the cost of capital, such as WACC, because such organizations must generate profit by their own business processes and capital.

Cost of Capital in the Public Sector

The public sector has features that make the for-profit discount factors unsuitable, at least without adaptation. Three main types of discount factors are used in the public sector:

1. **The long-term government bond rate**   This represents the rate paid by the government in order to acquire capital from sources other than taxes. For public organizations that cannot issue bonds, this is close to the rate of borrowing capital in the marketplace.
2. **The social opportunity cost rate**   This is the rate whereby government projects generate a return at least equal to the private sector projects displaced by the government applying funds to the investment.
3. **The social time preference rate**   This discount rate reflects the rate of return by the community at large to forgo the current consumption for future generations. The government project is thus only undertaken if, in the eyes of the community, it provides an acceptable trade-off between current and future costs.

The long-term government rate obviously does not reflect the alternative cost of capital well on a project level; it is more a reflection of macroeconomic government policy. The two other approaches are more subject to politics because they are not so clear-cut. Some may argue that if the public sector cannot do a job with less funding than the private sector, the private sector should do the job (the second type in the list above). Others may think that one should find an acceptable discount factor whereby a sound trade-off between current and future costs can be made (the third type). Of these three approaches, only the second type actually represents an alternative cost, while the third is more a trade-off cost; that is, we cannot decide which alternative to choose.

We could, however, also apply the WACC principles to the public sector. Instead of using equity, since the public sector has no equity, we could, for example, use taxes (corporate and individual) as capital with a cost equal to the annual inflation in the economy. The debt works the same way in both the public and private sectors. Then a project would be acceptable if it could provide a return higher than the weighted average cost of capital of taxes and debts.

A final but crucial issue is the fact that the public sector, at least in Norway, does not follow the same accounting principles as the private sector. The underlying assumption of all use of discounting factors (one dollar today is better than one tomorrow) may not be relevant. The reason is that most organizations in the public sector spend their funds according to their budgets. This means that time is close to irrelevant in the public sector; the only thing that matters is the size of their budgets this year because that is what they can spend. In a situation like this, using discount factors becomes somewhat artificial because one dollar today is one dollar tomorrow or whatever the politicians decide.

Before discussing how to handle inflation, it should be noted that in nongovernmental organizations (NGO), which are nonprofit organizations, discount rates should be chosen from case to case. The reason is that NGOs play a role that they define themselves, and the chosen role should be reflected in their choice of discount factors.

Handling Inflation

Before we can talk about handling inflation, we must first learn a little bit about it. Inflation may be defined as "persistent increases in the general level of prices."[10] Furthermore, "it can be seen as a devaluing of the worth of money." To exemplify the concept, if the annual inflation is 5 percent through the year 2000, then a $100 bill in the beginning of January 2000 will be worth $95 one year later in terms of purchasing power despite the fact that the bill is still a $100 bill. In other words, the usefulness of the $100 bill as a means to exchange goods and services has decreased by 5 percent. Over a long time, this will lead to the $100 bill having virtually no value. For this reason, and the consequences it leads to, "inflation ranks with unemployment as one of the two major macroeconomic diseases."[11] Note that inflation usually differs from industry sector to industry sector and between goods. If we talk about a certain item and the price increase associated with it, that is often called price escalation, or simply escalation, rather than inflation although the same mechanism is behind it.

Inflation has numerous causes. The most popular arguments are that inflation is caused by:

- Excess demand in the economy—demand-pull inflation
- High costs—cost-push inflation
- Excessive increases in the money supply—monetarism

Regardless of the causes behind inflation, it reduces the value of money. For organizations, this is important to take into account; otherwise, an apparently profitable project may become unprofitable. Organizations must look out for at least three situations:

1. The revenues are fixed in, for example, dollar terms. This represents a potential loss for the organization because the costs may rise while the revenues associated with the costs do not. The profit is therefore steadily declining and may easily become negative if inflation increases enough, since many companies have modest operating margins.
2. Their financial assets (bonds, or equities in other companies) produce less than inflation. Then a net decrease in value takes place. This is mostly a problem for retirees, financial institutions, or anybody else who has substantial financial assets.
3. The costs are fixed in, for example, dollar terms. This can produce an upside for the organization if its suppliers (of raw materials, labor, and capital) have fixed contracts and inflation is unexpectedly high.

Because inflation is a well-known phenomenon for the marketplace, most market participants calculate a certain amount of inflation into fixed price contracts. Thus, inflation is only a problem as long as it is not too high (although expected) or when it is unexpected. When it is unexpected, it leads to a reshuffling of wealth and this is generally considered economically unfair. This represents a major risk for fixed contracts because inflation produces economic uncertainty.

When inflation is neither too high nor unexpected, it can be dealt with in different ways. This is done by introducing a *real rate* of the object of discussion. For example, as shown in Figure 5.7, if you borrow money from the bank at 8 percent per annum and the inflation is 3 percent, the *real interest rate* is 5 percent. If the inflation turned out to become 10 percent that year, however, the real interest would be -2 percent. The bank would actually *give* you purchasing power although you paid the bank 8 percent, provided you had a fixed contract with the bank.

For LCC purposes, the previous first and third bullets are those most commonly considered. The simplest case occurs when we assume that revenues and costs are affected the same way by inflation. In other words, the ratio of real costs and revenues remains constant. In such cases, we do not need to worry about inflation in the model. This is a sound assumption when no long fixed price/cost contracts are to be considered *and* when no significant time lag exists between costs and revenues. If either prices or costs are fixed, or if a significant time lag exists between the costs incurred and the revenues received, inflation must be included in the LCC models.

If a time lag exists but no fixed prices or costs, the easiest way of dealing with inflation is to adjust the discounting factor using the principle shown in Figure 5.7. That means one must *add* the inflation rate to the discounting factor so that the net

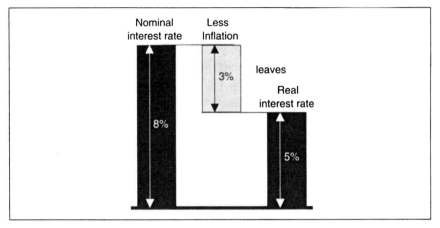

Figure 5.7   Nominal and real interest with 3 percent inflation.

effect over time is the discounting factor. This is important to remember for all types of equivalence calculations, such as when we calculate the value of future cash flows to an equivalent present value.

If prices/costs are fixed for a period, the easiest way to handle the situation that is to reduce the value of the prices/costs by a factor of 1 − inflation rate. That is done by simply multiplying the prices/costs in question by that factor. Then it is implicitly assumed that year 0 is the base year for the calculations.

Consequently, two approaches must be used when dealing with inflation:

1. Calculate future costs and revenues using nominal dollars, that is, money not adjusted for inflation, and then use a real discounting factor (a discounting factor adjusted for inflation). This approach is probably easiest to apply when a time lag exists but no fixed prices or costs. However, this approach has a drawback, namely that inflation is assumed to be constant, and that is simply not the case, particularly if the LCC spans many years.

2. Calculate future costs and revenues in real dollars, or money adjusted for inflation, and then use a nominal discounting factor, which is a discounting factor that is not adjusted for inflation. This approach is the safest to use in most situations because inflation will change over time and this approach allows us to handle inflation with complete flexibility.[12]

When it comes to the actual calculations, I would recommend using the same practical approach to the calculations as accountants do, which is to use spreadsheets and do each step of the LCC in a step-by-step manner. The safe accountant's approach is much easier to validate than formulas. The accountant's approach is also recommended even when inflation is not included in the calculations.

Finally, tax effects can also be included. This is most easily and safely done by multiplying the appropriate numbers by a factor of $1 - $ tax rate and using the previous real dollars calculation approach. If WACC is used as a discounting factor, caution must be exercised because WACC is normally already tax adjusted. It is also important to be aware of the fact that organizations have many ways to evade tax (legally) that are difficult to model well. Thus, when tax considerations are included in a model, it is more to give an idea than to calculate the exact amount.

Using Economic Profit as Performance Measure

Economic Profit (EP) or Economic Value Added (EVA®), as Stewart Stern & Company in New York has trademarked EP, is an old but sound concept. As the CFO of General Motors, Donaldson Brown, described it in 1924: "The objective of management is not necessarily the highest rate of return on capital, but . . . to assure profit with each increment of volume that will at least equal the economic cost of additional capital required."[13] Thus, a cost object must be capable of producing enough profits to also pay for its use of capital; otherwise, the company will have to get additional funding to replace assets as they depreciate and increasingly require more maintenance and so forth. Whatever profit is left after the cost object has secured enough profits to replace assets is a direct measure of the value the company has generated, an economic value added. Mathematically, EP is found as follows:

> *Revenues − Operating costs and expenses*
> *= Net operating profits before tax − Taxes*
> *= Net operating profits after tax (NOPAT) − Cost of capital*
> *= Economic profit*

The cost of capital is frequently calculated using WACC since a company cannot distinguish debt from equity in reality. The WACC is explained in the "Cost of Capital in For-Profit Organizations" section.

Positive economic profit will therefore increase the book value of the company because profits after tax are greater than the cost of capital. Over time it is believed that systematically increasing the book value also will increase the market value. Stewart Stern & Company has found a 44 percent correlation between the stock price and EP, which is well above common financial measures such as Return on Equity (24 percent) and Return on Capital (35 percent). Thus, to some extent we can say that positive EP over time increases the likelihood of increasing the market value.

But others disagree, stating that "neither EP nor EVA is remotely related to shareholder *wealth creation*, unless of course shareholders happened to have invested at book value."[14] This statement is too bold in my opinion, but it does have some merit because market value is often defined as:

$$Market\ value = Book\ value + Intellectual\ capital$$

Thus, the more knowledge-intensive the company is, the more likely it is that the market value/book value (M/B) ratio is large. For example, in November 1996, the M/B ratio of Microsoft was 91.93, whereas for IBM at the same time it was 4.25. In any case, the perceived value of the intellectual capital by far dominates the book value in the market. This might also be due to the fact that both Microsoft and IBM are in industries that move more rapidly than other industries, and hence the need for innovation, which by nature requires a steady flow of new knowledge, is larger. Companies in such industries will therefore be priced more according to expectations than according to past performance. Another reason is that for knowledge-intensive companies the balance sheet reflects their true capital base only to a minor degree. The majority of the capital is in fact in their employees' heads and in the IT systems.

Apparently, the link between EP and market value is somewhat unclear, at least for some companies. But that does not deny the fact that if EP is positive, the company is generating a net positive economic value, whereas if EP is negative, economic value is destroyed. EP is therefore probably a good indicator for many companies, while for some companies it has more limited value. But one thing is sure: EP cannot be significantly negative over time without having negative consequences for the market value.

The destruction of economic value is in principle due to two distinct but not mutually exclusive reasons: (1) the cost objects do not generate sufficient profit to maintain the capital base (the net assets[15]), and/or (2) the capital base is too costly. In the former case, a company must become more cost effective and/or generate higher net revenues, while in the latter case, the company needs to sell some assets, preferably ones that produce little, if any, operating profit.

To include EP into an Activity-Based LCC model, we rely on two critical points:

1. The identification and use of *capital* drivers whose purpose is to trace the cost of capital. The term *capital driver* is analogous to resource drivers and activity drivers found in activity-based frameworks and works the same way.
2. The computation of the cost of capital, as discussed earlier.

This section has discussed what EP is, how to calculate it, and how to interpret it, but how does EP compare to NPV? NPV calculations are safe approaches to use in LCC and in general, because they always produce consistent and "correct" answers. Interestingly, the present value of future EP is identical to the NPV, however, whereas "the total NPV of the project . . . helps one understand whether the entire project is value creating or not. In contrast, EVA is NPV by period and helps one understand the pattern of (economic) value creation throughout the project life."[16] EP is therefore also more suitable for identifying risks. However, the cash flow analysis that NPV is based on can provide additional insight to better understand the project's funding requirements and cash generation patterns.

The Moving Baseline

Discounted cash flow methods, such as NPV, implicitly assume that the cash flow remains constant if an investment is not made. In many industries, however, this is simply not the case. A minimum degree of progress is simply needed just to remain competitive in the marketplace, and this is in essence what the theory of *the moving baseline* acknowledges.

According to the theory, an "incremental cash flow attributable to a capital investment decision is higher than the capital investment model dictates because a company's cash flow without the investment is unlikely to remain constant. Therefore, the incremental cash flows that should be built into the capital investment model should be based on an assumption of *declining* cash flows in the future."[17] Figure 5.8 attempts to illustrate this theory. Of course, whether the declining baseline is linear or nonlinear is not the point here; the point is that it is declining and that this must be taken into account. The nonlinear curves in Figure 5.8 are possible cash flow scenarios. The more comprehensive the innovation, the higher the potential improvement, and the longer the time for positive cash flow to occur.

This illustrates a well-known problem with the commonly applied year's payback method. The accept criteria—which is normally a maximum payback period—can miss good long-term investments if the highest positive cash flows come late in the project. Payback methods should therefore not be applied in LCC at all since many LCC projects have a long-term scope.

Once the discount factors (if applicable), performance measures, and baselines are chosen, we can finally run the Monte Carlo simulations using commercially available software if the model is implemented in MS Excel.

STEP 10: PERFORM MONTE CARLO SIMULATIONS AND RELEVANT ANALYSES

How the Monte Carlo simulations and the accompanying analyses, such as sensitivity analyses, work is explained extensively in Chapter 3 and will therefore not be repeated here. This section will rather discuss some important engineering analyses that may greatly affect life-cycle costs and how to decide whether we should iterate the model implementation or not.

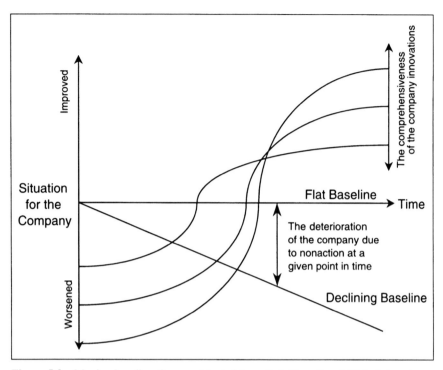

Figure 5.8 Moving baseline. Source: Adapted from R.A. Howell and W.A. Schwartz, "Asset Deployment and Investment Justification," *Handbook of Cost Management*, ed. B.J. Brinker. Boston, MA: Warren, Gorham, & Lamont, 1997, pp. D4.1–D4.32.

Some Engineering Analyses

Engineering analyses may come into play because things fail, and they rarely fail on schedule. LCC calculations that ignore such issues will therefore miss costs and risks and hence present an erroneous reality. In this book, these issues are only briefly discussed, but they are, however, important background information for the design of the maintenance program for the Platform Supply Vessels (PSVs) discussed in Chapter 7.

The life-cycle cost of a product, or system, is closely related to the effectiveness and efficiency of the product and vice versa. This is particularly true for large systems that are open and have a long life-span. In engineering-related LCC literature, they particularly focus on effectiveness, and the system effectiveness equation is:

$$System\ Effectiveness = \frac{Effectiveness}{Life-Cycle\ cost} \tag{5.1}$$

Although cost is a resource measure, system effectiveness is a measure of the value received, particularly value in an engineering sense. Effectiveness in

Equation 5.1, which can also be thought of as a performance measure, can be further specified as follows:

$$Effectiveness = Availability \times Reliability$$
$$\times\ Maintainability \times Capability \qquad (5.2)$$

These four performance measures have values in the interval (0, 1) and are typically defined as:

$$Availability = \frac{Uptime}{(Uptime + Downtime)} \qquad (5.3)$$

$$R(t) = e^{-\lambda t} \qquad (5.4)$$

$$M(t) = 1 - e^{-\mu t} \qquad (5.5)$$

$$Capability = \frac{Actual\ ouput}{Practical\ output} \qquad (5.6)$$

where:

- Uptime is the time the system is up and functioning. Downtime is basically the opposite.
- $R(t)$ is the reliability as a function of time.
- λ is the failure rate and is defined as the reciprocal of the mean time between failures.
- $M(t)$ is the maintainability as a function of time.
- μ is the maintenance rate and is defined as the reciprocal to the mean time to repair.
- Practical output is the maximum practical output of the system.

These issues are discussed in greater detail by Barringer and Weber.[18] However, it should be noted that reliability and maintainability are time functions. This fact is an important reason to include the cost of capital in the model because a time will come when purchasing new assets becomes less costly than maintaining old assets. Only LCC models where the cost of capital and engineering analyses are conducted can provide decision support in this matter. Unfortunately, I have been unable to provide a case study to illustrate this. It is, however, quite straightforward once you understand the cost of capital and engineering analyses.

Check Model and Iterate If Needed

Whether the model is satisfactory or not is a matter of how it responds to changes, the degree of meaningfulness of the results, and whether it actually meets the objectives specified in the beginning of the implementation. Three issues must be considered here:

1. Check if the model meets the objectives specified in the beginning. This is obvious but nevertheless important.
2. Go through the model to check if any *computational* errors have been made, which is done by using control sums. If the control sums are equal, no computational errors exist, which are the first type of errors.
3. The second type of errors is *logical* errors. These are much more difficult to identify, and here sensitivity charts can be used to see if any illogic tracings take place. Also, we sort the results in sequences to identify any weird results, such as excessively costly products. If we find such results, we backtrack in the model and often we find either a minor computational error or a logical error. More important, however, is the way the implementation is done. That is why it is important when implementing activity-based systems in general that the implementation procedure is systematic and that the people implementing the model know what they are doing.

If the model is deemed *unsatisfactory*, then depending on what failed the appropriate steps must be iterated until the model is satisfactory. Once the model is satisfactory, it can be used as specified initially.

FURTHER EXPLANATION REGARDING SOME STEPS

Some steps are more difficult or more important than others. In the following sections, I try to provide more detail about the more important steps in this process.

Step 2 Issues: Data Availability

Most organizations have too much data available, but often not the data we want. The more comprehensive LCC model we try to build, especially accounting-type LCC models because they require more consistent information than other LCC types, the more likely it is that we will end up in a situation where we lack the data we ideally would like to have. Several pitfalls or challenges must be avoided if possible or addressed and stated as possible limitations in the analysis.

First, and quite commonly, the availability of data may change substantially from one year to another in organizations where new information systems have recently been installed. It is important to avoid data from the year in which this installation process took place, because most likely these data are hard to export from the system in the format we want. It is better to have reliable data from a half-year than hard-to-export data from another year.

Second, information systems that are up and running may be difficult to export data from if the system utilizes several databases or if there have been mergers of information systems within the overall information system. For example, one company I worked with had eight databases from which it was impossible to export any useful nonfinancial information. Because of this, we could not perform the ABC analyses we were supposed to do.

Third, if information systems have merged within the overall information system, this may present some unexpected problems. For example, one company I worked with had just merged two accounting systems for two divisions into one single accounting system. This was no problem in general for the analysis, but it did add extra work to ensure that the information we had was consistent. The only real challenge was that it became difficult to trace parts of the material costs of some products that were manufactured in both divisions.

Fourth, be aware that information systems are set up in certain ways and that exporting data from them in ways they were not intentionally set up for may introduce challenges. Most of these challenges can be solved by having a skillful database administrator. However, sometimes the data we want has been destroyed or is simply too difficult to get. In such cases, we must find other information we can use. One company I worked with installed an Enterprise Resource Planning (ERP) system a couple of years ago. Unfortunately, the system had been installed in such a way that all batches that ran over 24 hours were assigned new batch numbers. Thus, it became impossible to find out how many batches of a certain product, particularly high-volume products, were produced in a year.

These are some of the potential pitfalls and challenges we may face when performing economic analyses in general. Most often they are solved by either choosing a different year on which to perform the base calculations or by making some additional assumptions. However, if we cannot make any viable or sound assumptions, we have a problem. If the problem is large enough, the whole analysis may have to be planned differently than originally thought. For this reason, it is important to identify data availability problems as early as possible.

However, a particular approach may be useful if we are only interested in the relative difference between certain items and have no better alternative. For example, let's say we have three products and want to know their relative consumption of a machine in order to assign the correct process costs to these products, but we lack data. In such cases, or whenever we want to establish relative rankings, we can use an approach called Analytic Hierarchy Process (AHP) that Thomas L. Saaty developed in the late 1960s. AHP is a tool to aid decision processes, but its matrix system of pair-wise comparisons can be used to subjectively establish the relative importance, or weight, between objects, criteria, or whatever we want. Even though AHP is based on subjective statements from groups of people, experts, and so on, it has an indispensable feature that other subjective methods lack, namely an internal, logical consistency check. AHP, in other words, produces logically consistent answers. Whether this logic is consistent with reality is, of course, an entirely different issue that only the practitioners of the method must judge.

From the discussion in this section, it is evident that finding which data to use, how to get the data, how to find replacement data, and so forth is not straightforward. It is possibly the most difficult part of the entire analysis because it is not only a challenge in its own right, but it also directly affects activity definitions, driver definitions, and even, in the worst cases, cost object definitions. The overriding principle of data availability is consequently the cost of obtaining the data versus the benefit of the data. As a rule of thumb, it is therefore wise to avoid too many activities and drivers in the LCC model because the number of activities and drivers is the primary origin of data needs.

Step 3 Issues: Role of the General Ledger

The role of the General Ledger is important to be aware of. Ideally, the General Ledger should be object oriented and not function oriented as today. For example, one account may be Depreciation, which should be related to the various processes that are depreciated. A better solution is therefore an object-oriented General Ledger where depreciation is accounted for by the various assets, such as equipment. Hence, when implementing Activity-Based LCC, the General Ledger should ideally be disassembled and reorganized to fit an object-oriented resource hierarchy. This will ensure a perfect fit among capacity, demand, and cost information, but unfortunately it a lot of work to reassemble the General Ledger in such a manner.

The approach chosen by several commercial ABC software vendors is to take the General Ledger directly as is and then break it down into various cost centers. From the previous discussion, it is clear that it is not ideal to use the General Ledger as it is, particularly when the results are to be used for any design purpose. If the model is to be used for purposes where understanding the process view is not so important, such approaches will suffice, as shown in the case in Chapter 4.

This discussion is also closely linked to the discussion on data availability, and we realize that no single way of implementing an Activity-Based LCC model exists; it is a matter of the objectives of the model.

Step 4 Issues: Building Submodels

One issue is particularly important to be aware of when implementing Activity-Based LCC for large systems: Various model configurations must be employed when handling large problems. Then one model may feed into another, which may affect the activity definitions. Some reasons for this are:

- A corporation wants models for the various plants, which are separate business units, and models on division levels and on corporate levels. Hierarchical models[19] can be employed here.

- Several plants are tightly cooperating but are separate judicial entities and make decisions on their own. In this case, relational models[20] can be employed.
- Software limitations can make it necessary to split up models into several models. This is the situation where either submodels or relational models suffice.

In the LCC context, only submodels are applicable, so we only discuss these here.

Submodels are simply models within a governing model where the governing model communicates one way with the submodels. The sole purpose of submodels is therefore to give particular attention to a defined area within the governing model. This can be done either by using action charts or by using mathematical functions to describe the processes. In my experience, using action charts is by far the most versatile approach.

In both cases, however, the governing model provides the submodel with the resource elements and other system boundaries, and then the submodel provides insight into the part of the governing model that needs particular attention. A submodel is therefore like a magnifying glass, as illustrated in Figure 5.9, where we show how an activity (Aij) can be studied in detail by investigating the actions that it consists of.

Figure 5.10 shows how to design a submodel. The first step concerns how to use the governing model in setting the system boundaries for the submodel(s). The system boundaries should include at least cost objects, activities, and their associated actions. It should be noted that action chart models can be built per cost object because the governing model ensures proper cost assignment between the various cost objects.

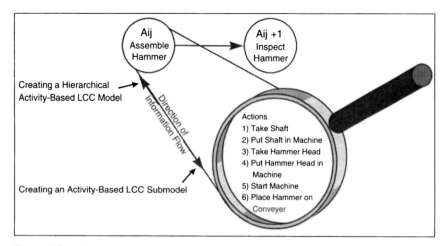

Figure 5.9   How submodels magnify aspects of the governing LCC model.

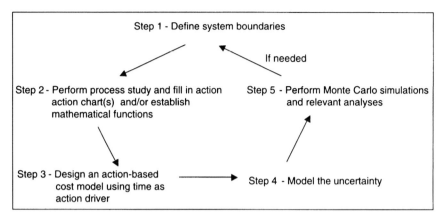

Figure 5.10   Creating submodels.

Step 2 focuses on the detailed process study needed to gain further insight. The process study should include the cost object structure, which is usually more detailed than BOM, action sequences, time estimates, and process parameters for use in conjunction with mathematical functions. In addition, quality measures and links to product characteristics can be useful in relation to product design. IDEF0 charts can also be used in the process study if desired.

Steps 3, 4, and 5 are similar to Steps 7 through 10 in the governing model. The resulting model is like a small Activity-Based LCC model with time as the only driver.

Step 5 Issues: Choosing Drivers

Choosing drivers is one of the most important aspects when implementing any activity-based framework. Three situations are shown in Figure 5.11 and they occur in the resource activity cost assignment and in the activity cost object cost assignment.[21] The ideal situation occurs when, for example, a resource matches an activity one to one and an activity matches a cost object, which can be referred to as direct attribution. This ensures a 100 percent correct tracing due to the one-to-one match. This always occurs with material costs that can be traced to an exact product unit. If the General Ledger is object oriented, this would be much easier to achieve than is usually the case. This must also be taken into account when defining the activities, resources, and cost objects.

The other extreme, the last resort so to speak, is *allocation* in a traditional sense (see Glossary). This is simply a way to distribute costs arbitrarily, such as allocating production planning costs using the number of units. Clearly, this is allocation since the planning costs are not related to the number of units produced. Allocation must *never* occur for activities with high costs because that will lead to significant distortion.

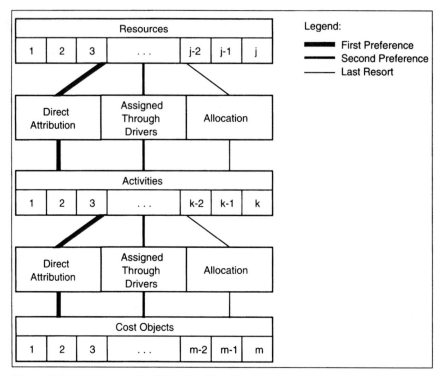

Figure 5.11   Preferences for driver identification. Source: Adapted from M.R. Ostrenga, "Activities: The Focal Point of Total Cost Management," *Management Accounting*, February 1990, pp. 42–49.

In between these two extremes, we have assignments by drivers called tracing, the second preference in Figure 5.11. When choosing drivers, three issues must always be considered:

1. The ease of obtaining data required by a particular driver
2. The correlation between the consumption of an activity implied by that driver and the real consumption
3. The behavioral effects a driver can induce

It is important to be aware of the fact that sometimes drivers cannot be identified using a single measurable variable, such as labor hours. One must simply be creative and come up with a combination of measurable variables and combine them to form a driver in a way that gives a high correlation between the driver and the actual consumption. This can be difficult particularly for support activities, ones not directly related to production.

In one project, this was done for a purchasing activity: The ideal driver would be the number of purchase orders per product, but this information was not readily available, so a second-best solution was found—identifying the total number of purchase orders and how many articles were checked for every order. This information was combined as Purchase Order Articles. Then how many of the various articles a product consumed were identified, thereby creating a quite reliable driver, although it had no physical meaning.

It is extremely important that the drivers, activities, and resources are defined so that the distortion in the model is as low as economically feasible (due to budget constraints). It is therefore vital to work with the best and brightest who know their organization thoroughly. Activity-Based LCC models, as well as ABC systems, perform rather differently depending on the level of skills of those implementing them.

To ensure the high quality of the implementation of activity-based systems, some rules of thumb can be useful, given a certain implementation budget:

- **Secure ownership of the system**   Preferably, this should be someone at an executive level who can directly use the results in his or her own work.
- **Ensure that the implementation team contains at least one person who has a holistic picture of the cost objects, such as a plant manager or a similar employee**   Also, people with thorough knowledge of the various functions and processes in the company need to be involved. Specifically, there should invariably be people from management, marketing, production, and design.
- **Define activities, resources, and drivers so that as many one-to-one matches as possible can be achieved**   Then concentrate on finding good drivers for all the significant resource elements. This is crucial in order to minimize distortion of the system. Allocating up to 10 percent of the total overhead costs is acceptable if it is difficult to identify drivers at a reasonable cost.
- **Address the issues of maintaining the model early**   That is, *never* implement a model that is impossible to maintain within an acceptable budget. Keep in mind the good advice from Robin Cooper: "The premise for designing a new ABC system should be: 'It is better to be approximately right than exactly wrong.'"[22]

All Steps: Think Continuous Improvement

Even when a satisfactory solution is found, the constantly changing market conditions make it important to continuously improve whatever processes must undergo enhancements. It is also vital to keep in mind that success stems from the famous Total Quality Management (TQM) dictum "do it right the first time." Hence, the improvement efforts must be directed toward where they make the most difference. That is the primary goal of activity-based approaches in general and of Deming's concept of "profound knowledge."

Profound knowledge signifies that gathering the right data from the right sources at the right time, and then using the right resources to make the right interpretations, leads to the right actions to improve quality.[23] Deming understood at least by the 1950s the importance of continuous improvement, and central in his thinking was what later became known as the Deming Cycle (see Figure 5.12), which is essential in continuous improvement thinking as well.

The four sectors—Simulation, Proactive, Assessment (or Accounting), and Reactive—relate the Deming Cycle to Activity-Based LCC directly. Simulation and assessment provide attention direction for the other two sectors.

The Deming Cycle consists of four steps:

1. The company should *plan* what to accomplish over a period of time and what it is going to do to get there. Activity-Based LCC can be helpful in this process in terms of simulation capabilities so that the critical success factors can be known up front and the impact of uncertainty can be assessed.
2. The company should then *do* what furthers the goals and strategies developed previously. The identification of the critical success factors is crucial in this stage because it allows proactive management of what is critical.
3. The company should then *check* the results of its actions to ensure a satisfactory fit with the goals. This is the easiest way to employ Activity-Based LCC because it is a simple after-calculation, or backcasting.
4. The company should then *act* to eliminate possible differences between the actual performance and the goals stated up front. This reactive way of acting is not discussed in the case studies.

It is important to realize that continuous improvement applies not only to products, services, and systems but also to measurement systems such as an Activity-

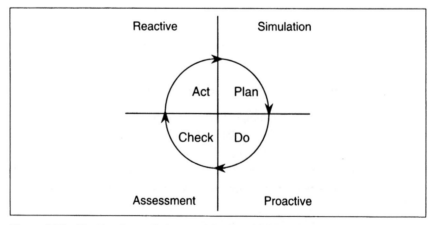

Figure 5.12   The Deming cycle in an activity-based LCC context.

Based LCC model. Spending too much time on making the perfect model is usually counterproductive because the owners of the model typically need results, not lengthy explanations of why the model is not yet finished. Also, most models require changes after their initial design, either to answer questions about functions other than what the models were originally designed for or because their logic must be refined.

The second implementation of Activity-Based LCC will most likely be better than the first implementation and so on. It is therefore important not to pursue perfection in the beginning because it is too time consuming. Rather, seek perfection over time in understanding, application, and improvement. As Chan (Zen) Master Jiantang Ji said:

Who has no faults? Excellence is a matter of reforming them.

And the reformation takes time, as this Zen saying indicates:

Those in a hurry do not arrive.

NOTES

1. This approach is the result of my Ph.D. work and has been published in numerous papers and in a book, *Activity-Based Cost and Environmental Management: A Different Approach to the ISO 14000 Compliance*, by J. Emblemsvåg and B. Bras, Boston: Kluwer Academic Publishers, 2000.
2. J.A. Miller, "Designing and Implementing a New Cost Management System." *Journal of Cost Management,* Winter 1992, pp. 41–53.
3. For further details, see J. Emblemsvåg, "Activity-Based Life-Cycle Assessments in Design and Management." Ph.D. Dissertation. Atlanta, GA: George W. Woodruff, School of Mechanical Engineering, Georgia Institute of Technology, 1999, p. 600.
4. A case where mathematical functions were employed is in the design of a vehicle for handicapped persons discussed in J. Emblemsvåg's master's thesis, "Activity-Based Costing in Designing for the Life-Cycle," Atlanta, GA: George W. Woodruff, School of Mechanical Engineering, Georgia Institute of Technology, 1995, p. 300.
5. In my Ph.D. dissertation (see note 3), I have discussed this in detail and also provided a good case from a furniture manufacturer in Norway.
6. Specifically, the action charts in W. Beitz, M. Suhr, and A. Rothe's, "Recyclingorientierte Waschmachine," Berlin: Institut für Machinenkonstruktion—Konstruktiontechnik, Technische Universität, 1992. This report is in German.
7. For more details, see E. Dimson, P. Marsh, and M. Staunton, "Risk and Return in the 20th and 21st Centuries," *Business Strategy Review* 11 (2), 2000, pp. 1–18.
8. According to S. Godfrey and R. Espinosa, "A Practical Approach to Calculating Costs of Equity for Investments in Emerging Markets," *Journal of Applied Corporate Finance*, vol. 9, Fall 1996, pp. 80–89.
9. Dimson, Marsh, and Staunton, "Risk and Return."

10. G. Bannock, R.E. Baxter, and E. Davis, *Dictionary of Economics*. London: Penguin Books, 1999, p. 439.

11. P. Wonnacott and R. Wonnacott, *Economics*. New York: John Wiley & Sons, 1990, p. 804.

12. S.K. Fuller and S.R. Petersen, *Life Cycle Costing Manual for the Federal Energy Management Program*. Washington, D.C.: U.S. Government Printing Office, 1996, p. 210.

13. A.P. Sloan, *My Years at General Motors*. New York: Doubleday, 1990, p. 472.

14. D.B. Kilroy, "Creating the Future: How Creativity and Innovation Drive Shareholder Wealth." *Management Decision* 37 (4), 1999, pp. 363–371.

15. The gross asset value must be corrected for depreciation because depreciation is included in the operating costs and we must avoid double-counting. Be aware of the fact that depreciation is a calculated cost and three main avenues exist for calculating it:
    - *Linear depreciation*, which implies that the asset loses an equal amount of value per period. This is the most common and crudest approach.
    - *Accelerated depreciation* in which the value loss of the asset accelerates according to its age. This approach has several variants.
    - *Activity-based depreciation*, where the value of the asset is reduced by the ratio between the actual use of the asset and the estimated useful life of the same asset.

16. For more details, see T. Gandhok, A. Dwivedi, and J. Lal, "EVAluating Mergers and Acquisitions: How to Avoid Overpaying." Mumbai, India: Stern Stewart & Co., 2001, p. 8.

17. R.A. Howell and W.A. Schwartz, "Asset Deployment and Investment Justification." *Handbook of Cost Management*, ed. B.J. Brinker. Boston, MA: Warren, Gorham & Lamont, 1997, pp. D4.1–D4.32.

18. H.P. Barringer and D.P. Weber, "Life Cycle Cost Tutorial." Fifth International Conference on Process Plant Reliability, 1996. Houston, TX: Gulf Publishing Company and Hydrocarbon Processing.

19. See note 3.

20. See note 3.

21. Note that cost objects consume activities, which in turn consume resources as measured by costs. Thus, strictly speaking, no direct cost assignment exists between an activity and a cost object, but rather an activity consumption assignment indirectly produces a cost assignment.

22. R. Cooper, "Implementing an Activity-Based Cost System." *Journal of Cost Management*, Spring 1990, pp. 33–42.

23. S.M. Hronec and S.K. Hunt, "Quality and Cost Management." *Handbook of Cost Management*, ed. J.B. Edwards. Boston, MA: Warren, Gorham & Lamont, 1997, pp. A1.1–A1.42.

6

CASE STUDY: LIFE-CYCLE COSTING AND TIRE DISPOSAL[1]

Randi Carlsen
Sagex Petroleum AS

Continue to contaminate your bed and you will one night suffocate in your own waste.

Chief Seattle (Sealth)

All around the world car tires are worn out in massive quantities every year—Norway is no exception. Some places have systems that collect and dispose, recycle, and/or reuse the tires, whereas other places lack such systems. Depending on whether such a system exists or not, tires can be either a useful resource or a major waste problem.

When tires are treated as waste, problems arise from the fact that tires are bulky and difficult, if not impossible, to compress and keep compressed. In turn, this creates a superb breeding ground for rodents and insects while simultaneously causing stability problems for the disposal sites. Also, the possibility of fire and the associated environmental hazards makes tires unwanted material for disposal sites.

Managing tires at the end of their life is therefore important. This case study investigates what can be done if a system is lacking and a large pile of tires is waiting in the forest, so to speak. The case presented here is a reworking and extension of a project that Randi Carlsen and Jon-Arve Røyset did during the spring of 2000 at the University of Oslo in Norway.

Two disposal sites for unwanted tires are located in the county of Ullensaker, north of Oslo. The largest site is the one at Østli, which contains roughly 100,000 tires, while the site at Borgen is somewhat smaller. Since 1992, Ullensaker officials, the Statens Forurensingstilsyn (SFT),[2] landowners, the Sessvollmoen military base, and other neighbors have wanted to remove the tires (and other scrap) from Østli, but it took about 10 years before the tires were removed.

The question was what should be done about the disposal site, and if the tires were to be removed, what would be the best way of removing them from Østli? The chosen approach must incur the least possible overall damage to the environment and inconvenience to humans. Equally important, the solution must be as effective as possible from a macroeconomic point of view. Because of pending ownership and legal issues, the solution had to balance these with the economic and environmental aspects. In other words, this case had three dimensions (economic, environmental, and legal), of which this book focuses on the economic aspects. The environmental and legal factors are included only to the extent that they have an economic impact.

These issues were discussed thoroughly and possible solutions were found by Carlsen and Røyset in their report to which interested readers are referred.[1] In the next section, we discuss the decision in more detail, but first we describe the history of this project.

First, we discuss how the traditional Life-Cycle Costing (LCC) approach can be implemented. We also include an uncertainty analysis using uncertainty distributions and Monte Carlo methods. Second, how the Activity-Based LCC approach can be employed is shown. Third, a discussion of the case study is provided.

Note that the currency in Norway is *Norske Kroner* (NOK). The exchange rate between NOK and U.S. dollars is roughly 8:1 over the last couple of years; that is, $1 equals NOK 8. To make the discussion less confusing, I have simply replaced NOK with USD ($) without correcting for the exchange rate and purchasing power differences. To make real cost comparisons, both exchange rate differences as well as purchasing power differences must be included, but that is not done here because those vary from year to year.

Environmental and legal issues of economic importance will be explained as needed as the case study proceeds. It should be mentioned that a legal disagreement exists concerning who should pay for cleaning up the site. In this case, it is assumed that the county of Ullensaker is paying. The alternatives are therefore formulated from the perspective of Ullensaker.

WHAT THE DECISION IS ABOUT

Several decisions must be made in this case, but primarily a decision-maker in Ullensaker must consider three possible major options. The first is to continue as before, that is, to do nothing. This option, which is the baseline, is denoted as Alternative 1. But just because nothing is done, that does not mean that nothing will, or may, happen. For example, what if the tires catch fire, what if toxic substances leak into the groundwater reservoir beneath, which is Norway's largest, and what if an accident occurs due to the fact that children often play in the site?

A fire will increase the risk of environmental hazards. A large amount of black, toxic, and polluting smoke and ash will be released during a fire. The pollution will consist mainly of substances like carbon monoxide (CO), soot, sulfur dioxide (SO_2), and substances that increase the risk of cancer. In addition to these environmental hazards, the thick smoke may force the nearby Oslo Gardermoen

International Airport to close until the fire is extinguished. Closing the airport will naturally have substantial economic effects. Finally, the rubber in the tires is a resource that can be used, but in Alternative 1 it is wasted. Evidently, doing nothing can have substantial negative consequences. The only upside of doing nothing is that the expenses are few and known, at least in the short run.

The second option, Alternative 2, is to recycle the tires to reclaim rubber. This alternative involves removing and transporting the tires away from their current location, sending them to a recycler, recycling the rubber, and eliminating all the risks. Although this option is potentially the most costly for Ullensaker, it is possibly the best option from a macroeconomic perspective.

The third option, Alternative 3, is to put the tires in a proper depot. This is essentially the same as Alternative 2 except that the tires are transported to a proper waste depot where the environmental risks are controlled and the impact of a fire is mitigated. The potential risk of shutting down Oslo International Airport is practically eliminated; however, the rubber is still wasted and the legal issues around using a depot to dispose of tires remain. Alternative 3 might, in fact, turn out to be nonviable due to legal issues.

The three options are summarized in Table 6.1, which lists strengths and weaknesses. Opportunities can become future strengths, while threats are potential problems that may follow each option.

Table 6.1 Three Decision Options

Alt.	Strengths	Weaknesses	Opportunities	Threats
1 Do nothing	Money saved in the short term.	A resource is wasted. The site is illegal.		Environmental hazards. Risk of closing Oslo Gardermoen Int. Airport.
2 Recycle tires	All risks are eliminated.	May prove costly for Ullensaker.	Overall macroeconomic benefits from tire recycling.	Lack of funding.
3 Dispose of tires properly	Environmental risks are prevented. Impact of fire is mitigated. The risk of closing down Oslo Gardermoen Int. Airport is eliminated.	A resource (rubber) is wasted.		The risks are prevented but not eliminated. Possible legal issues may render the alternative infeasible. Lack of funding.

We see that Alternative 2 is the best from a risk management perspective because the risks are eliminated, while Alternative 3 is basically a major risk management exercise. Doing nothing has potential large liabilities but costs nothing right now. Thus, Ullensaker faces a classic choice between short-term spending and long-term benefits.

TRADITIONAL LCC IMPLEMENTATION

The traditional LCC approach to decision-support problems of this kind is to first identify all cost and revenue elements associated with each option. Then identify potential risks and find a suitable discounting factor and time horizon. The overall economic performance is calculated as a Net Present Value (NPV).

This is what was done here too, and each option is discussed in the following three sections. To find the best alternative, we perform an uncertainty analysis, and investigate what value it can provide to the decision makers.

But first we should clarify what perspective we use; costs and revenues are after all only a matter of perspective in a value chain. We have chosen to perform the analysis using Ullensaker's point of view. Also, we have chosen to include costs that are, strictly speaking, external to Ullensaker, but for which it can be argued that Ullensaker is liable. This includes costs that may be associated with accidents and shutting down Oslo Gardermoen International Airport.

Alternative 1: Do Nothing

If we do nothing, 100,000 tires will still be lying around 20 years from now. This will have three consequences: (1) accidents, (2) fires, and (3) environmental problems. These three categories, which represent possible future liability costs, are discussed in more detail below.

Possible Costs of Accidents

A mountain of old tires is often an interesting playground for children, but the inherent instability of the tires may cause accidents, even fatal ones. Even though this may sound sinister, in an LCC we must try to quantify these costs too. For the parents involved, this is impossible, but we must try to make an assessment.

It is particularly children between the ages of 7 and 15 who may find this tire site interesting. The neighborhood has about 35 children in that age group. Although children are unaware of all the dangers involved, they are somewhat aware that they must be careful in the dump. The accidents that may take place are therefore normally less dangerous. The costs of such accidents are difficult to assess because they depend heavily on the type of accident.

In our cost assessment, we therefore limit ourselves to fatal accidents. To calculate the costs of a lost life, we need to introduce the concept of a *statistical life*. As Schelling put it, "It's not the worth of human life I shall discuss, but of 'life-savings,' of preventing death. And it is not a particular death, but a statistical death." In Norway, Elvik has calculated the value of a statistical life in relation to traffic deaths to be $10 million. We use the same number for our purpose, but we need to assess the chance of occurrence—the probability—of a life being lost as well. According to Ståle Navrud, the probability can be set to roughly 0.1 percent or 1 death in 1,000 lives.

To estimate the cost of losing a statistical life, we simply multiply the value of a statistical life by the chance of occurrence, which yields $10,000. What we essentially have done is calculate the Expected Monetary Value (EMV) of a life and then explain that a loss of life will occur in 1 out of 1,000 times.

Possible Costs of Fires

Anybody who has witnessed a rubber fire will never forget the immensely thick and black smoke. Neither will those who lived near Østli during the 1995 fire, when 20,000 to 30,000 tires went up in smoke. Luckily, due to the rapid response of several fire corps in the vicinity, the fire was contained and extinguished after only five hours. The fire, however, reemerged twice during the week that followed.

The cost of these operations amounted to $208,000, but there were also costs not possible to quantify, such as the costs of inconvenience for all the inhabitants and businesses in the area. In this case study, these costs are ignored in the calculations but acknowledged. Our cost estimate is therefore slightly optimistic.

Since Østli first was utilized for disposal purposes in 1975, there has been one major fire, and that can be used as a premise for quantifying the probability of the future occurrence of fires. It should be noted that there were arson investigations, but the evidence was inconclusive and the case was closed. Nevertheless, if we assume that fires in the future will occur as often as in the past, we can say that in 1 out of the 20 years there was a fire. In other words, there is a 5 percent probability of fire.

If we utilize the EMV concept as before, we find that the annual cost is 5 percent of $208,000, or $10,400. Today, however, the costs are likely to be much higher because in 1996 the new national airport of Norway opened just a few miles away. This airport, Oslo Gardermoen International Airport, has about 300 arrivals and departures every day. If a fire like this took place today, it is virtually guaranteed that air traffic will be affected. How much the air traffic would have been affected, however, is very difficult to quantify since it depends significantly on the weather and the time of the day and week. But in the worst case it would be a complete shutdown, which would cost the airlines roughly $180 million per day according to the air traffic controller at Oslo Gardermoen. Weather reports from

Det Norske Meteorologiske Institutt (the Norwegian Meteorological Institute) indicate that the weather is likely to be unfavorable 20 percent of the time.

If we combine the weather probability with the fire probability, we see there is a 1 percent chance of fires that will affect the airport significantly (shutdown). This yields an EMV of $1.8 million. The overall EMV is then simply the sum of the aforementioned EMVs, or $1,810,400.

Possible Costs of Other Environmental Problems

Some of the obvious problems are that this tire disposal site is ugly, it reduces the value of the surrounding natural habitats and housing areas, and it can be a source of both accidents and fires. However, there are numerous other environmental aspects to the threat presented by this mountain of decaying tires.

Since we do not possess comparable data for disposal costs in Norway, we can utilize data found in a study done in the state of California.[3] In that report, it is esti-mated that it costs roughly $2.50 to $3.00 per tire per year for low-standard dis-posal sites (no fencing, wastewater removal, and so on). That means that Østli's 100,000 tires incur a cost of roughly $250,000 annually. This is probably a low estimate since the weather conditions in California are much more favorable than in Norway. Add to that the lack of wastewater removal and its potential impact on the aquifer below, the largest underground freshwater reservoir in Norway.

Cost Savings

Because we do nothing, we save on costs. These mostly concern two issues: (1) the removal of the tires and recycling them, and (2) cleaning the soil where the tires are burnt.

To remove the tires, we have looked at the less costly scenario. It includes pay-ing a local sports club $40,000 for loading the tires onto trucks and then using sol-diers to transport the tires to a recycler. The reason we think the tires will have to be recycled some time in the future, as a consequence of delaying a decision to act now, is that current trends, which are growing day by day, point toward a future where recycling will be more important than it is today. Furthermore, SFT in Norway has been very restrictive about disposing tires in waste sites.

The soldiers come as an offer from Major Øyamo of the Norwegian Army as he has offered to do the freight free of charge as part of the training of recruits in the logistics regiment. The value of this offer is around $60,000. If Ullensaker does not act now, it may lose this opportunity.

The price the recycler at Moreppen charges depends on whether the tires are cleaned or not. Clean tires cost $1,180 per metric ton, whereas tires that also need cleaning cost $1,400 per metric ton. Roughly, 125 tires are in a metric ton, and if we assume that 10 percent of the tires need cleaning, the total cost of recycling the tires amounts to $965,000.

After the fire in 1995, some soil was seriously polluted, and this needs to be cleaned up. Deconterra, a local company that cleans soil, charges $600 per metric ton to clean up the soil. According to Major Øyarno, the burnt area is roughly 25 × 25 × 1.5 meters, or 1,700 metric tons. The total cleanup cost will therefore be around $1,020,000.

LCC Calculation

If we compile the information in the last sections, we get the following costs and savings shown in Table 6.2. We see that the margin is negative all the years, which means that this alternative is not a good idea from an economic perspective. Even if we ignore the fact that the Oslo Gardermoen International Airport can be seriously affected by fire, the sum of the annual margins will still be negative. But due to the principle that it is better to earn a dollar today than one tomorrow, we should also compute a NPV—or should we?

Traditionally, we would compute an NPV despite the fact that the idea behind it is to discount the future, an approach that is not compatible with sustainable development and environmental management ideas. This is particularly true when the decision makers are politicians and public officials, because they are by default servants of the people and also future generations. In any case, to compute the NPV we must first find a discounting factor. As discussed in Chapter 5, several premises exist for doing so.

When the decision maker is a public organization, it may operate according to accounting principles that, for example, *ignore* depreciation; everything is pure spending. In this light, the time-value of money has no meaning because it is only the present that counts. The discounting factor should therefore be 0 percent, but that is not what is commonly done. Traditionally, the discounting factor is set equal

Table 6.2 Costs, Savings, and NPV of Alternative 1

Annual Costs	Year 1	Year 2	. . .	Year 20	Sum	NPV (6%)
Accidents	10,000	10,000		10,000	200,000	121,581
Fire, airport	1,800,000	1,800,000		1,800,000	36,000,000	21,884,610
Fire, crew	10, 400	10,400		10,400	208,000	126,444
Environment	250,000	250,000		250,000	5,000,000	3,039,529
Free transport lost opportunity	60,000				60,000	60,000
Total costs	**2,130,400**	**2,070,400**		**2,070,400**	**41,468,000**	**25,232,164**
Annual savings			. . .			
Loading tires	40,000				40,000	40,000
Recycling tires	965,000				965,000	965,000
Cleaning of soil	1,020,000				1,020,000	1,020,000
Total savings	**2,025,000**				**2,025,000**	**2,025,000**
Annual margin	**−105,400**	**−2,070,400**	. . .	**−2,070,400**	**−39,443,000**	**−23,207,164**

to a market interest rate, as if investing in the market were an alternative option for the decision maker, which in the public sector it is not. In their project, Carlsen and Røyset chose this to be 6 percent.

With a discounting factor of 6 percent, we get an NPV of −$23.2 million. In other words, the economics of doing nothing is highly negative almost regardless of what discounting factor is chosen. In fact, already in the first year, the annual margin is negative (see Table 6.2). This is largely due to the risk of shutting down Oslo Gardermoen International Airport. However, if that risk is ignored, the NPV will still be negative (−$1.3 million) during the period. Thus, to do nothing about the tire disposal site is outright uneconomic. Add to that the potential loss of human lives, degrading the natural environment, and a loss in real-estate value.

The next step in the analysis is to include uncertainty and perform sensitivity analyses. Traditionally, the values of the discounting factors and some other crucial parameters are changed systematically, and the changes in the result, NPV in this case, are recorded manually. Here we have chosen a more efficient solution by running a Monte Carlo simulation (it took only 103 seconds). The NPV with the associated uncertainty is shown in Figure 6.1. The choice is clear: Something *must* be done. In the worst case, doing nothing can inflict a cost of potentially up to $39 million, but more likely $25.1 million, or Ullensaker can hope for $11.2 million in costs. In any case, the NPV is very negative. What is interesting to note is that the deterministic NPV of −$23.2 million is higher than the mean of the Monte Carlo simulation (−$25.1 million). This indicates that the uncertainty has most likely a *downside*. In other words, the uncertainty is generally unfavorable; hence, the more risky it is to not act.

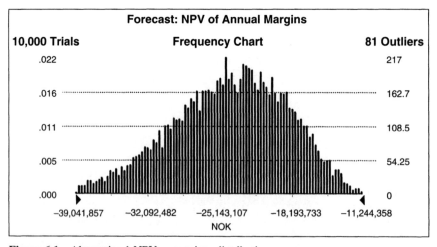

Figure 6.1 Alternative 1 NPV uncertainty distribution.

Alternative 2: Recycling

If the county of Ullensaker chooses to recycle the tires, all the cost and savings elements are in fact the same as before. They just turn up differently on the balance, as shown in Table 6.3.

The reason that Table 6.3 is almost like a negative image of Table 6.2 is that the baseline in Alternative 1 is recycling due to the likelihood of recycling becoming the most feasible alternative some time in the future. The biggest difference is therefore that recycling eliminates many potential liabilities and that makes recycling a very economically sound alternative with an estimated NPV of $23.2 million. If we think about the uncertainty involved, we can use Figure 6.1 and simply remove the minus signs.

Alternative 3: Proper Disposal

Alternative 3 is the only option that is truly different in terms of the cost and savings structure. Although many of the costs and savings will be as before, some unique elements occur.

Not far from the tire disposal site is a high-standard waste management site called Dal Skog, but a complicating factor is that this site does not accept tires, due to regulations. This is not the end of the road, however, because if Ullensaker applies for a one-time permit to SFT and gets a positive reply, Dal Skog has agreed to accept the tires. However, the probability of a positive reply is small because in similar cases SFT has been very restrictive. For example, when the county of Hitra

Table 6.3   Costs, Savings, and the NPV of Alternative 2

Annual Costs	Year 1	Year 2	. . .	Year 20	Sum	NPV
Loading tires	40,000				40,000	40,000
Recycling tires	965,000				965,000	965,000
Cleaning of soil	1,020,000				1,020,000	1,020,000
Total costs	**2,025,000**	**0**		**0**	**2,025,000**	**2,025,000**
Annual savings			. . .			
Free transport	60,000				60,000	60,000
Accidents	10,000	10,000		10,000	200,000	121,581
Elim. fire threats, airport	1,800,000	1,800,000		1,800,000	36,000,000	21,884,610
Eliminating fire threats, crew	10,400	10,400		10,400	208,000	126,444
Elim. environmental problems	250,000	250,000		250,000	5,000,000	3,039,529
Total savings	**2,130,400**	**2,070,400**		**2,070,400**	**41,468,000**	**25,232,164**
Annual margin	**105,400**	**2,070,400**	**. . .**	**2,070,400**	**39,443,000**	**23,207,164**

applied to dispose of 1,700 tires, it was denied a permit. Nonetheless, if such a permit is granted to Ullensaker, Dal Skog will accept all the tires at a cost of $850,000.

This cost, however, is probably too low to reflect the actual costs incurred at Dal Skog because the cost of disposing tires is two to three times higher than disposing of other municipal waste.[4] In other words, Dal Skog is subsidizing Ullensaker because it simply does not charge Ullensaker for what the service costs. Most likely, Dal Skog itself does not account for the total costs.

Because Dal Skog has a high standard, the environmental costs of disposing the tires there will be lower than at their current location. Such sites have an estimated environmental cost of $0.60 per tire per year.[5] This gives an annual cost of $60,000, which is considerably less than the annual costs of $250,000 that is incurred at Østli. Hence, from a societal perspective, it makes much more sense to let Dal Skog handle the tires than Østli. Thus, we get the costs and savings for this alternative, as presented in Table 6.4.

We see that the overall picture is quite similar to the recycling scenario. The biggest difference is that disposing of the tires is less costly for Ullensaker than recycling them. The NPV of Alternative 3 is therefore slightly better than for Alternative 2, $23.3 million versus $23.2 million, respectively.

Interestingly, this is a direct consequence of the fact that Dal Skog is pricing its services too low. If Dal Skog charged $2 million, which would probably better reflect the true costs, the situation would be turned around. This clearly illustrates the dangers of subsidies with respect to solving environmental problems. As pointed out in numerous publications, this is not an exception; it is rather the rule in the world today. From this we understand that LCC as a concept can hold great promise in relation to environmental management as well as cost management.

Table 6.4 Costs, Savings, and NPV of Alternative 3

Annual Costs	Year 1	Year 2	. . .	Year 20	Sum	NPV
Loading tires	40,000				40,000	40,000
Disposing tires	850,000				850,000	850,000
Cleaning of soil	1,020,000				1,020,000	1,020,000
Total costs	**1,910,000**	**0**		**0**	**1,910,000**	**1,910,000**
Annual savings			. . .			
Free transport	60,000				60,000	60,000
Accidents	10,000	10,000		10,000	200,000	121,581
Eliminating fire threats, airport	1,800,000	1,800,000		1,800,000	36,000,000	21,884,610
Eliminating fire threats, crew	10,400	10,400		10,400	208,000	126,444
Eliminating environmental problems	250,000	250,000		250,000	5,000,000	3,039,529
Total savings	**2,130,400**	**2,070,400**		**2,070,400**	**41,468,000**	**25,232,164**
Annual margin	**220,400**	**2,070,400**	**. . .**	**2,070,400**	**39,558,000**	**23,322,164**

The preferred alternative for Ullensaker is nonetheless Alternative 3, disposing of the tires at Dal Skog. But due to the regulatory constraints imposed by SFT, it is an unlikely option. Also, knowing that Dal Skog, a company that Ullensaker co-owns with other counties in the area, has priced itself too low, the overall best choice for Ullensaker is undoubtedly to recycle the tires.

A look at how uncertainty impacts the two alternatives indicates that our conclusion also holds under the presence of uncertainty because the alternatives are virtually identical since the two distributions overlap almost completely (see Figure 6.2). In other words, it is not the economic performance of these two alternatives that makes the difference for Ullensaker; it is the legal and environmental issues, and recycling scores the best on both. Thus, recycling is the preferred alternative.

Uncertainty Analysis of the Preferred Alternative

Looking 20 years ahead involves, of course, some uncertainty, and so does the quantification of many of the different cost estimates, such as the costs of accidents and fire and their associated probabilities. This can be done in many ways, but some are definitely better than others.

We start by performing an uncertainty analysis of Alternative 2 using modern technology in traditional approaches. Then we take the next step into the world of Monte Carlo simulations, and as will be evident, that is the way to go.

Traditional Uncertainty Analysis of Alternative 2

As shown in Chapter 3, a way of dealing with uncertainty would be to use the what-if technique. This technique is especially adapted to performing uncertainty/sensitivity analyses manually, but today computers can do this in a straightforward

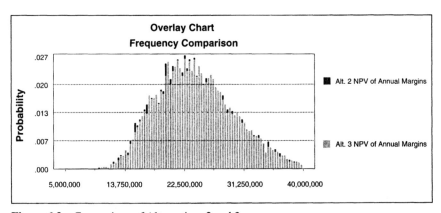

Figure 6.2   Comparison of Alternatives 2 and 3.

manner. The fundamental shortcomings of the approach persist, however. The analyses done in this book utilize Crystal Ball® 2000 where applicable.

A computerized what-if analysis of Alternative 2 can be done using a tornado chart approach, as shown in Figure 6.3. This particular tornado chart is generated by varying each variable one by one by ±10 percent, *ceteris paribus*.[6] We see that the single most important variable is the cost associated with fire and its impact on Oslo Gardermoen International Airport because it is located on top and has the widest bars. We also see that an increase in this variable has an upside effect with respect to the forecasted variable (Alt. 2 NPV of Annual Margins). This is because if the fire costs turn out to be higher than expected, Ullensaker will save more money than expected because it avoided the cost by choosing Alternative 2. The values beside the bars (such as 2,095,010) are the maximum values of those particular variables when the forecast variable had its highest value within the ±10 percent variation span of the assumption cells.

We also see that the NPV is, as expected, sensitive to the chosen discounting factor, the market interest rate in this case. If the market interest rate becomes 7 percent, the corresponding NPV is roughly $21.5 million.

The good thing about the tornado chart is that it can provide clear answers to questions concerning how much the forecasted variable will change as a consequence of a change in an input variable. This is unfortunately a deceptive ques-

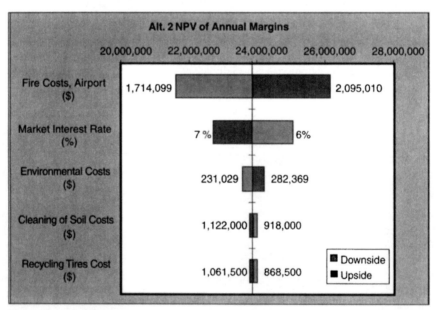

Figure 6.3 Deterministic tornado chart for Alternative 2.

tion because it relies on an assumption that everything else remains constant; by testing a one-by-one variable, interactions are ignored. Furthermore, the approach is sensitive to the base case, that is, the values that were put in the spreadsheet initially. So even though the tornado chart is a tempting tool, it is deceptive if you rely too much on the numbers in it. Thus, we apply it only in special cases.

Another way of presenting essentially the same information is the spider chart shown in Figure 6.4. The spider chart, however, is easier to follow, and it does not present numerical values that pretend they are measures of how important the variable is with respect to the forecast. For example, we see that if Fire Costs, Airport ($) is 10 percent below the base case, the NPV will be roughly $21.5 million.

Whereas the importance of a variable in the tornado chart is illustrated by the width of the associated bar, in a spider chart it is the slope of the line that counts: the steeper the slope, the more the impact. The spider chart does, however, suffer from the same problems as the tornado chart, but it is less deceptive because it shows that we only look at deviations from the base case and exclude interactions. Also, the traditional approaches are simply incapable of producing an uncertainty distribution, as shown in Figures 6.1 and 6.2. They can only provide a very limited number of discrete points, as shown in Figure 6.3, and that has obvious limitations.

Next, we use Monte Carlo methods to perform an uncertainty analysis of Alternative 2 because Monte Carlo simulations have significantly reduced the shortcomings of the other approaches.

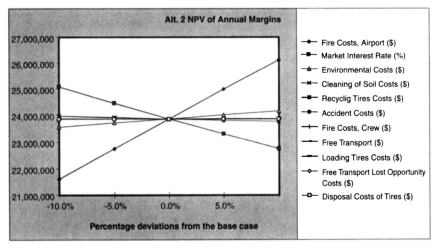

Figure 6.4 Deterministic spider chart for Alternative 2.

Monte Carlo Methods in an Uncertainty Analysis of Alternative 2

By employing Monte Carlo simulations and statistical sensitivity analyses, we have a much wider array of tools that not only are more effective but also are virtually free of deception. In order to use Monte Carlo methods, we must first identify the variables that are uncertain and model the uncertainty as either uncertainty distributions or fuzzy numbers and intervals. As explained in Chapter 3, Monte Carlo methods are completely insensitive to the difference between uncertainty distributions and fuzzy numbers and intervals because the difference lies mainly in interpretation and not in the shape of the distributions. Uncertainty distributions, fuzzy numbers, fuzzy intervals, and possibility distributions are therefore collectively referred to as uncertainty distributions in this book.

The NPV model of Alternative 2 is very small, with only nine input variables, but to illustrate the approach, it is sufficient to show and discuss briefly four distinctly different ways of modeling the uncertainty (see Figure 6.5). We can start with the most common approach, which is the *normal* distribution in the lower-right corner. We typically choose to model uncertainty in the shape of a normal distribution if:

- We have hard data from which the distribution can de derived, but that is not the case here.
- We have reason to believe that the variable will exert normal behavior over time and/or in the future.

In the upper-left corner, we see an interesting version of a normal uncertainty distribution. We know that the market interest rate over time will behave as a nor-

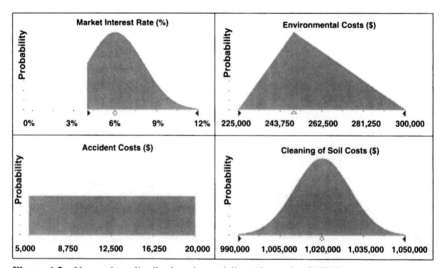

Figure 6.5   Uncertainty distributions in modeling Alternative 2 NPV.

mal distribution, but at the same time we are quite sure that the market interest rate will never drop below 4 percent in Norway. Hence, we chop the distribution off at 4 percent. At the other end of the distribution, we think that it is very unlikely that the interest rate will pass 12 percent. The last time that happened was in the mid-1980s, but that was under a more socialistic monetary regime. Given the trend in Norwegian politics during the last 30 years, it is unlikely that Norway will ever go back to such regimes. Also, a return to a socialist monetary regime is unlikely in light of the worldwide globalization process.

In the upper-right corner, we see a *triangular* uncertainty distribution. We prefer to model the uncertainty as triangular distribution if we suspect the variable to be normally distributed, but the uncertainty is quite large. When the uncertainty is quite large, a normal distribution tends to emphasize too little on the ends of the distribution, and that is not desirable if we are very unsure. Also, triangular distributions handle asymmetry better than normal ones.

But if we are highly uncertain about a variable and have virtually no preference for even an expected value, the *uniform* distribution is chosen. We see that in this case even though the deterministic value of the accident cost is $10,000, we have no idea concerning the real cost of an accident; we just know that it will probably lie in the range of $5,000 to $20,000.

This way of handling uncertainty is clearly far more realistic than being forced to come up with a single number or even a range of numbers. But more importantly, because uncertainty can be handled with such ease, we can concentrate on finding likely uncertainty distributions instead of chasing the wind after the one magic number. Thus, we increase the mathematical uncertainty in the model but reduce the risk of giving bad or wrong decision support.

After deciding how to model the uncertainty, we proceed to the second step in the Monte Carlo method, namely identifying the forecast variables. The forecast variables are the variables we want to study; hence, they could be of any sort. These variables are important to name properly so that after the simulation, it is easy to find the results for them and interpret them. This is, of course, crucial in large models with several hundred forecast variables.

The next step is to choose a sampling procedure and how many times the simulation is going to recalculate the model (trials). In this step, it is important to identify the capabilities of the computer first. Five years ago, it was often our experience that the computer had to stop too early (with respect to keeping the random error low) because the Random Access Memory (RAM) was too small. Today, however, RAM is so affordable that this is no longer an issue for Monte Carlo simulations used for LCC purposes. We therefore always choose the best sampling procedure, which is Latin Hypercube Sampling (LHS) despite the fact that it demands much more RAM than Simple Random Sampling (SRS). The advantage is that we do not need as many trials as before to achieve a certain level of confidence, but again, due to the power of modern computers we always run a high number of trials (10,000). In fact, the last time we were forced to cut down on the number of trials due to computer limitations was in 1996 when the case presented in Chapter 7 was first run. Then a Pentium 120 MHz Laptop computer with 16 MB of RAM and utilizing a SRS Monte Carlo method had to stop at around 4,000 trials.

When the sampling procedure and number of trials have been chosen, the simulation is run. Depending on the size of the model and the usage of logical tests and macros, a simulation can take anywhere from 10 seconds to several hours.

In Figures 6.1 and 6.2, we see the results of such a simulation. From Figure 6.1, we see that the uncertainty distribution of Alternative 1 is skewed toward the left, which means that it is more likely that the NPV will be higher (than the mean) than lower. This is good news for Ullensaker because it shows that if it acts now, it can benefit from this likely upside.

From the sensitivity chart in Figure 6.6, we see that the possible elimination of liability costs associated with fire and its impact on Oslo Gardermoen International Airport is the primary reason for this upside. This is evident from that fact that if the fire cost increases, the NPV increases. In plain words, the higher the fire costs, the happier Ullensaker should be since it has avoided the liabilities (as a consequence of recycling the tires). Also, the way we modeled the market interest rate plays a significant role in the skewness as well as the overall amount of uncertainty. The market interest rate is unfortunately beyond Ullensaker's control. This is a factor that Ullensaker will just have to live with and adjust to.

Unlike the tornado and spider charts presented earlier, the sensitivity chart in Figure 6.6 is generated by measuring the statistical response (in this case by the rank correlation method) of the forecast variable given the uncertainty in *all* the input vari-

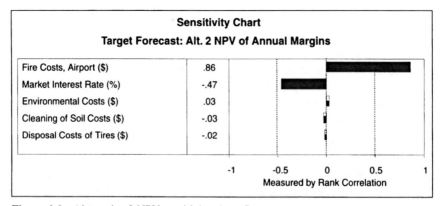

Figure 6.6   Alternative 2 NPV sensitivity chart, first run.

ables (to the left in the chart). It has therefore none of the limitations that the tornado and spider charts have. There is, however, a caveat for the untrained practitioner.

Since the sensitivity chart is generated using statistical information, random errors occur, as mentioned earlier. These errors are negligible for variables with a rank correlation coefficient larger than roughly 0.05 (or −0.05), such as the market interest rate whose rank correlation coefficient is −0.47. Therefore, the fact that environmental costs turn up in Figure 6.6 *might* be due to random errors because the rank correlation coefficient is only 0.03. To find out whether the ranking of environmental costs is real or due to randomness, we must remove the two dominating variables from the model and rerun it. Then the other variables will show up as in Figure 6.7.

From Figure 6.7, we identify another random effect we must be aware of when utilizing statistical approaches, namely variables that have absolutely nothing to do with a certain forecast variable that might show up. This is due to the fact that a statistical correlation took place during that particular simulation between the variable in question and the forecast variable. Luckily, such effects only appear for variables with a very low rank correlation coefficient (less than 0.05), such as for the disposal costs of tires in Figure 6.6, and will disappear or remain insignificant (see Figure 6.7) if we rerun the model once more after removing the most dominant variables. A dominant variable is a variable with a rank correlation coefficient of more than 0.10.

Both the aforementioned caveats are due to randomness. However, if you are aware of the effects randomness may produce, you cannot go wrong using

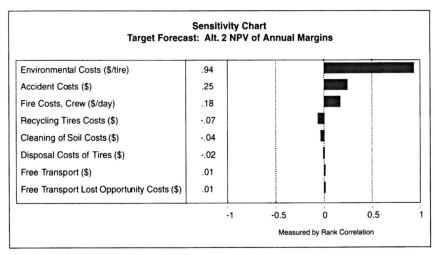

6.7   Alternative 2 NPV sensitivity chart, second run.

statistical sensitivity analysis. Just remember to rerun models after eliminating the dominant variables to check whether the variable that shows up is real or not.

Almost ironically, the same reason may present a problem for random effects, namely, that statistical approaches do not rely upon direct relationships between input variables and forecast variables, making statistical approaches the only ones capable of measuring relations between variables that are loosely coupled as in complex systems. That is why statistics play such an important role in many fields; setting up a system of equations is simply not possible due to the sheer complexity. This means that our way of performing an uncertainty analysis can handle not only cause-and-effect relations but also weak relations between multiple variables. This is something a tornado chart or a spider chart cannot do because they rely upon relations being modeled as systems of equations. This makes sensitivity charts the perfect tools for identifying critical success factors, which in this case are primarily to avoid fires. Thus, if Ullensaker decides not to act, it should at least make plans for a rapid response to fires. It cannot rely on the luck it had in 1995.

ACTIVITY-BASED LCC IMPLEMENTATION

Employing Activity-Based LCC in this simple case may seem to be overkill, and it is in many ways (no overhead costs, no product cost allocation, and so forth). But as we shall see, Activity-Based LCC will provide additional insight and value. In this particular case, this insight could also have been produced by traditional means, but nothing inherent in the traditional methods supports it. In Activity-Based LCC, such insight cannot be avoided because it is inherent in the system. That is the point because, as Robert Lutz puts it, "common sense . . . is not all that common."[7]

The analysis follows the same steps as always, as shown in Figure 5.1. But before we proceed to the modeling steps, we should define the goals of the implementation. The sole purpose of this implementation is to provide decision support concerning what to do about the Østli tire disposal site. In other words, we only need to find an answer to a one-time question, not to provide the continuous cost management. In a decision support model, we must include the time value of money if it is relevant. Because the decision maker, Ullensaker county, is a public organization that does not follow ordinary accounting procedures with depreciation and so forth, the time value of money and its risk has no meaning. More importantly, however, is that public organizations are obliged to think more broadly than private decision makers, and in this case the issue of sustainability is pertinent. Basically, county, state, government, or publicly elected or servicing bodies cannot discount the future or future generations. Unlike the traditional approach, Activity-Based LCC will therefore reject the notion of discounting factors in this particular case, even though it is a decision-support model.

Step 1: Define the Scope of the Model and the Corresponding Cost Objects

The scope was defined in the "What the Decision Is About" section and will not be repeated here. In this case, the cost objects are the possible alternatives because this Activity-Based LCC model is designed solely to provide decision support for choosing among those alternatives.

Step 2: Obtain and Clean the Bill of Materials for All Cost Objects

In a decision-support model, the cost object is the decision to be made. The assessment should therefore revolve only around what is needed in order to decide. In this case, Ullensaker must decide whether to do nothing or act, and if it acts, it must decide whether to recycle or dispose of the tires. This was discussed in detail earlier in the "What the Decision Is About" section.

Step 3: Identify and Quantify the Resources

Here we can directly use the data presented in the "Traditional LCC Implementation" section. For brevity, we show this information together with its drivers in Step 5 in Table 6.5. The reason is that the amount of information is so little that we really do not need to split Steps 3 and 5.

Step 4: Create an Activity Hierarchy and Network

In order to create an activity hierarchy, we must think about what activities are incurred as a consequence of the various decision alternatives. Start with the case's

Table 6.5   Activities, Their Resources, and Resource Drivers

Activity	Resource Consumption ($ 1 year)	Resource Driver
A11	10,400	Duration of fire × probability of fire
	1,800,000	Duration of fire × probability of fire and weather
A12	10,000	Life value × probability of accident
A13	250,000	Number of tires
A21	40,000	Number of jobs
A22	60,000	Number of loads
A23	1,020,000	Mass of contaminated soil
A241	100,000	Number of tires
	10%	Percentage of tires that need cleaning
A242	850,000	Number of tires

Table 6.6   Preliminary Østli Tire Disposal Site Decision Activity Hierarchy

Level 1 (Decision Level)	Level 2 (Consequence Level 1)	Level 3 (Consequence Level 2)
Do nothing **A1**	Tires may catch fire **A11**	
	Accidents may happen **A12**	
	The environment degrades **A13**	
Do something **A2**	Load tires **A21**	
	Transport the tires **A22**	
	Clean up site **A23**	
	Terminate the tires **A24**	Recycle the tires **A241**
		Dispose tires **A242**

basis, which is to do nothing, and then identify the various decisions. Conceptually, we can create a decision hierarchy that describes what decisions are involved, but that would be overkill for this case. Nevertheless, we see that essentially two decisions are involved (in Table 6.6, the corresponding activity hierarchy is presented):

1. The primary decision concerns whether or not Ullensaker should do something, denoted as D1.

2. We may have to decide how to remove the tires, this decision is denoted as D2.

Unlike an ordinary activity network whose purpose is to present the various routings and process options in relation to the cost objects, a decision activity network depicts the consequences of a decision in terms of the various routings and process options that may occur. It is a simple tool for understanding the process consequences of a decision.

The situation at Østli can be presented as shown in Figure 6.8, given the final activity definitions in Table 6.5. The activities between D1 and D2 are simply activities that are necessary for D2 to take place. These activities are therefore nonvalue added from the decision maker's point of view. The same is true for all base case activities.

It is important to realize that activity networks say nothing about the sequencing between decision nodes. In other words, activity A22 does not have to follow A21. In this case, it will, however, but we see that activities A241 and A242 are mutually exclusive because only one will follow after decision D2 because they are the two possible outcomes of decision D2. In other words, all activities that are downstream to a decision are consequences of that particular decision.

The decisions that incur the highest number of activities are therefore more risky than those with few activities in the sense that more things can go wrong. However, this says nothing about the potential impact. In this case, we clearly see this difference because although recycling has more activities attached to it, it is less risky than doing nothing, because of the potential impact of activity A11 (tires may catch fire) overshadows all other activities.

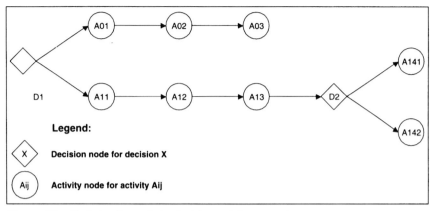

Figure 6.8 Østli tire disposal site decision activity network.

Step 5: Identify and Quantify Resource Drivers, Activity Drivers, and Their Intensities

The resource data are collected for convenience in Table 6.5. The resource drivers track how changes in activity levels affect the resource consumption. For example, the cost of A23 depends on the size of the area that is contaminated and therefore needs to be cleaned up. Given the current area, this is estimated to cost $1.02 million.

Since all costs are associated with one cost object, we do not need activity drivers. Furthermore, the consumption intensities (see Glossary) are fixed because they are price quotes from other organizations.[8] We use the same probability estimates as earlier to estimate the EMVs. Also, the concept of statistical life is used to assess the value of a life.

Given these assumptions, we can set up the consumption intensities and the values of the resource drivers as shown in Table 6.7. If we multiply the driver values with the intensities, we get the resource consumption in Table 6.5.

Step 6

Step 6 is omitted because neither design issues nor activity drivers are used in this case. We therefore have all the input data we need in order to set up the model. We just need to model the uncertainty first, which is done next.

Step 7: Model the Uncertainty

How we model the uncertainty discussed in the "Monte Carlo Methods in an Uncertainty Analysis of Alternative 2" section. We therefore simply present how we modeled the uncertainty in Table 6.8 without any further discussion. It should be noted that we normally just keep this information in an MS Excel® spreadsheet

Table 6.7 Resource Drivers and Their Consumption Intensities

Resource Driver	Resource Driver Value	Consumption Intensity
Duration of fire × probability of fire	1 day × 5%	208,000 $/day
Duration of fire × probability of fire and weather	1 day × 5% × 20%	180,000,000 $/day
Life value × probability of accident	0.1%	10,000,000 $/life
Number of tires	100,000	2.50 $/tire
Number of jobs	1 job	40,000 $/job
Number of loads	200 loads	300 $/load
Mass of contaminated soil	1,632 metric ton	625 $/metric ton
Number of tires	100,000	9.50 $/tire
Percentage of tires that need cleaning	10%	3.00 $/tire
Number of tires	100,000	8.50 $/tire

because there is too much information to present, but this model is so small that here the uncertainty distributions can be presented without problems.

In addition to modeling the uncertainty as accurately as possible, we use symmetric, bounded, and ±10 percent triangular uncertainty distributions for tracing purposes. We introduce uncertainty into the model in order to trace the actual importance of the various assumption cells (input variables). This is important with respect to finding the critical success factors regardless of whether they are uncertain or not.

We can then proceed to the results that are generated during Steps 7 through 9. First, however, we should evaluate the quality of the modeling and decide whether we must iterate (Step 10) or not.

We think that the current model captures all the relevant economic aspects of decisions D1 and D2 and consequently fulfills Ullensaker's needs. The greatest weakness of the analysis is the amount of uncertainty surrounding the potential liabilities, but we can't do anything about that except model the uncertainty as accurately as possible.

Step 8: Estimate the Bill of Activities

In this case, the Bill of Activities (BOA) is simple compared to the other two cases in this book. The BOA is found in Table 6.9. Because we use a frequency interpretation of probability the time frame is somewhat important. Activities that have a time frame of one year are performed only once, in the beginning in the period.

We see, for example, that the five activities A11, A13, A23, A24, and A242 dominate BOA. A11 is particularly large and should therefore be avoided. It should be noted that only the deterministic values are shown; how we modeled the uncertainty is not shown.

Table 6.8 How the Uncertainty Is Modeled

Uncertainty Distributions	Rationale
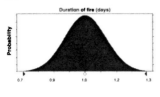	We assume that if there is a fire, it will take roughly a full working day to extinguish it on average. It may, however, only take 0.7 days or as much as 1.3 days in the worst case. We have chosen a normal shape because time-related variables are usually normally distributed.
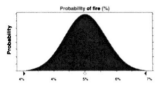	During the last 20 years only one fire has occurred. If we assume the future will be somewhat similar to the past, we assume that in 1 out of 20 years there will be a fire, that is, in 5 percent of the time. We use a normal uncertainty distribution because we think that matches the reality the best.
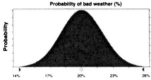	The expected value of 20 percent is based on weather reports, but we allow quite a substantial amount of uncertainty.
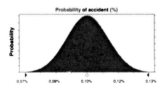	0.10 percent is a qualified guess obtained from Mr. Navrud; however, as with other probability estimates we allow for some added uncertainty. Basically, we say that there are probabilities around the probability estimate.
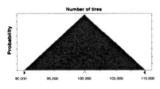	Estimating the number of tires in a big mountain of tires is not easy, but we are quite confident that there are not more than 110,000 tires and no less than 90,000. We use a triangular shape to signify that we have an idea about the mean, but that we are quite unsure.
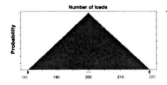	The rationale is similar as for the number of tires.
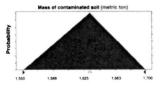	To estimate the mass of soil theoretically is quite straightforward, but in practice no site will be dug out as accurately as planned.

(continues)

Table 6.8   How the Uncertainty Is Modeled (*Continued*)

Uncertainty Distributions	Rationale
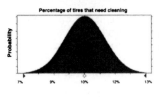	How many tires need to be cleaned is not easy to estimate, but by investigating some tires up front we expect 10 percent of the tires to need cleaning. An investigation is like an experiment and hence a normal shape is warranted.
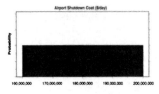	To estimate the costs of shutting the Oslo Gardermoen International Airport down is associated with large uncertainties. We must therefore use the uniform shape, because we have virtually no preference among the range of estimates.
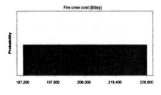	The same logic applies here as for the Oslo Gardermoen International Airport shutdown costs.
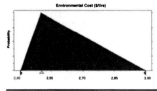	The environmental costs associated with landfills are in the range of $2.50 to $3 per tire according to studies abroad. We think that $2.50 is probably the most likely, and maybe even a little lower, but we open up for quite a substantially higher cost than anticipated.

Step 9: Estimate the Cost of Cost Objects and Their Performance Measures

In this case, the various alternatives are directly related to the various activities, as shown in Table 6.10. Hence, the costs and savings of the cost objects are found simply by summing the costs and savings for the activities incurred by the various alternatives. Note that all numbers are deterministic.

Step 10: Perform Monte Carlo Simulations and Relevant Analyses

The Monte Carlo simulation is performed using commercially available software: MS Excel and Crystal Ball. The Crystal Ball software is employed to handle the uncertainty in the model and, more importantly, to trace the critical success factors.

Table 6.9 Bill of Activities

Activity	Time Frame (Years)	Resources
A11	20	$36,208,000
A12	20	$200,000
A13	20	$5,000,000
A21	1	$40,000
A22	1	$60,000
A23	1	$1,020,000
A241	1	$965,000
A242	1	$850,000

The Results

First, we compare the various alternatives to decide which is the best before we can discuss the best alternative in greater detail. From Figure 6.9, we see that Alternative 1 is vastly inferior to the two others, which are virtually identical.

The reasons for this can be seen from the sensitivity chart in Figure 6.10. Alternative 1 is simply associated with too many liability risks. It may be that none of these risks materialize; that is, no fires or unfavorable weather occur, but we do not know.

However, which is better: Alternative 2 or 3? It turns out that Alternative 3 has a slightly better margin than Alternative 2. However, recall that Ullensaker has to apply for a special permit from SFT to dispose of the tires at Dal Skog and that permit is unlikely to be granted. Also, since Ullensaker partially co-owns Dal Skog, it would be unwise to use a disproportionately amount of capacity in the disposal site when the potential savings are minor. Alternative 2 therefore appears to be the overall best alternative.

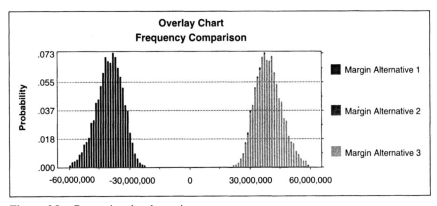

Figure 6.9 Comparing the alternatives.

Table 6.10 Cost ($) of Cost Objects

Alternative	A11	A12	A13	A21	A22	A23	A241	A242	Costs
1	36,208,000	200,000	5,000,000		60,000				41,468,000
2				40,000		1,020,000	965,000		2,025,000
3				40,000		1,020,000		850,000	1,910,000

Alternative	A01	A02	A03	A11	A12	A13	A141	A142	Savings
1				40,000		1,020,000	965,000		2,025,000
2	36,208,000	200,000	5,000,000		60,000				41,468,000
3	36,208,000	200,000	5,000,000		60,000				41,468,000

Alternative	Margin	Ranking
1	−39,443,000	3
2	39,443,000	2
3	39,558,000	1

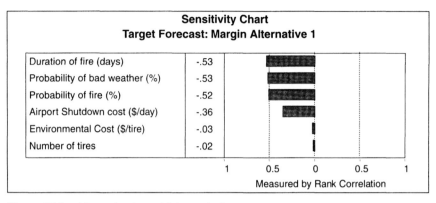

Figure 6.10 Alternative 1 sensitivity analysis.

Uncertainty Analysis of Alternative 2

The purpose of an uncertainty analysis in this case is to ensure that when all the uncertain elements are included in the model, the margin of Alternative 2 is still satisficing (see Glossary). If that turns out to not be the case, we must be able estimate the likelihood of a positive margin.

From Figure 6.11, we see the uncertainty distribution of Alternative 2. The margin is always positive with a solid margin of more than $21 million. In other words, Alternative 2 is an economically viable option under all conceivable circumstances.

Because Alternative 2 is the negation of Alternative 1 by definition in this case, the uncertainty sensitivity chart of Alternative 2 will look like a mirror of Figure

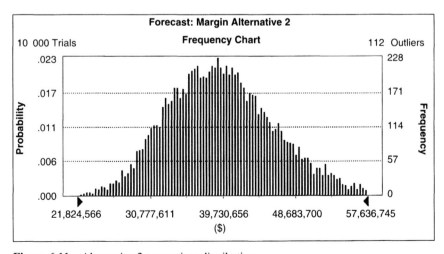

Figure 6.11 Alternative 2 uncertainty distribution.

6.10; that is, the rank correlation coefficients that are negative in Figure 6.10 are positive for Alternative 2 and vice versa. Therefore, the chart is omitted here.

Managing Alternative 2

In order to ensure that Alternative 2 indeed becomes the best option, Ullensaker must manage its resources well. To assist it in that, we can employ the sensitivity chart in Figure 6.12.

Unfortunately, Ullensaker can actually influence only one factor, namely the duration of a fire. Ullensaker can also intensify the surveillance of the Østli disposal site in order to prevent fires from starting until it has recycled all the tires, thus reducing the probability of occurrence as well as the duration.

Recall from earlier discussions that the reason major costs such as airport shutdown cost ($/day) show up with *positive* rank correlation coefficients is that they are potential liability costs of doing nothing. Hence, if you recycle the tires, you avoid these potential future liabilities completely, and that has a positive economic value. The reason this line of argument may seem confusing is that often the base case is implicitly assumed to be zero; this is, however, a faulty assumption in most cases, as explained in the "Moving Baseline" section in Chapter 5. Also note that we now look at the effect of the time frame, that is, the effect that extending or shortening the time span has on the margins. We see that the longer the time horizon is, the larger the margins. This is evidently sensible because the longer the time horizon, the more likely it is that a liability will occur.

If we summarize our findings, we see that the greatest benefits to Ullensaker arise from doing something, not necessarily doing "the right thing." The point is that Ullensaker must do everything in its power to prevent fires from occurring due

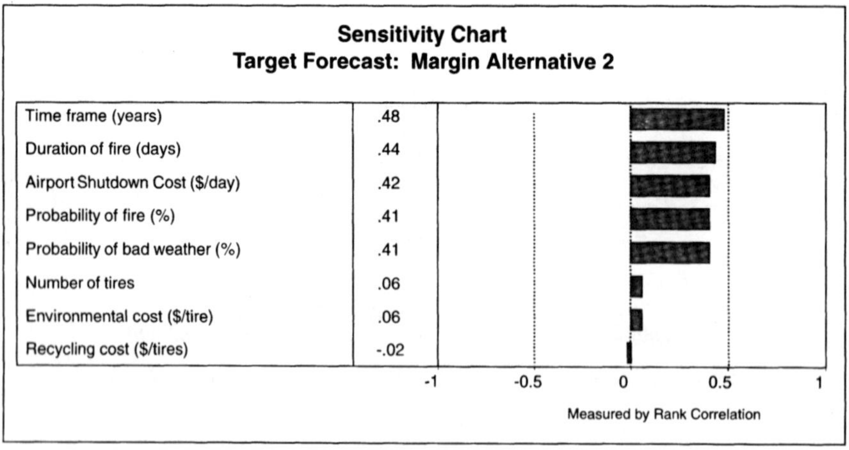

Sensitivity Chart
Target Forecast: Margin Alternative 2

Time frame (years)	.48
Duration of fire (days)	.44
Airport Shutdown Cost ($/day)	.42
Probability of fire (%)	.41
Probability of bad weather (%)	.41
Number of tires	.06
Environmental cost ($/tire)	.06
Recycling cost ($/tires)	-.02

Measured by Rank Correlation

Figure 6.12   Alternative 2 tracing sensitivity chart.

to the major potential liabilities, particularly if the weather is unfavorable, so that the airport does not suffocate in smoke. The only way to do this is to act, and the sooner the better.

Whether it should recycle the tires or dispose them seems to be a less clear question to resolve, but our analysis indicates that the most feasible option is to recycle them. The reasons are twofold:

1. Significant ownership, legal, and regulatory difficulties may arise in disposing of the tires.
2. Recycling the tires is almost as economically viable as disposing the tires. The difference in the deterministic case is only $115,000, but this estimate excludes the cost of wasting capacity at Dal Skog. If we include the uncertainty, it will be somewhere between $102,000 and $128,000 (see Figure 6.13).

DISCUSSION

The discussion of this case has four main purposes. The primary purpose is simply to illustrate how LCC can aid decision making concerning issues in the public sector. Since the public sector expands when societies become more affluent because "as countries grow richer, they want to spend more of their incomes on it (social spending), and can afford to,"[9] the public sector becomes increasingly difficult to manage. Yet the tools they have at their disposal were designed for times when the public sector consisted only of the bare bones: defense, police, schools, hospitals, and so forth. But what is the cost of a new school today? Politicians and

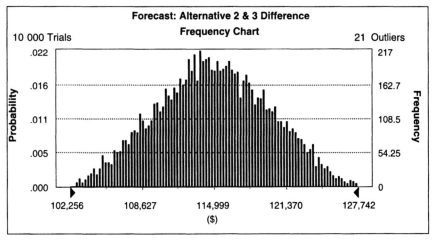

Figure 6.13 Economic differences between Alternatives 2 and 3.

other decision makers today typically discuss in great depth the construction costs but give downstream costs little, if any, notice. The airtight walls between the various budget posts further enhance such thinking; the construction costs would be in one budget post while maintenance would be in another post, not to mention the costs of wages that would probably be in a third post. The result is that decision makers miss the total costs and nobody is responsible for them. It is the perfect recipe for wasteful spending or, perhaps more often, for misplaced spending or cost cutting.

A perfect example of this is the Norwegian nursing home system. Due to the poor economy of many counties, they try to save money where they can, and the nursing homes must take their share. I was fortunate enough to work with one nursing home in becoming more competitive as the city of Ålesund opens up for private nursing home initiatives. The nursing home had a process cost of $24.7 million in addition to direct costs related to food, medicine, and so on that amounted to roughly $3 million. In another city, they tried to save money by no longer feeding the elderly hot dinners. But for the nursing home that participated in the project in Ålesund, more than $1.2 million (5 percent of the total process costs) was spent on just making reports and in total 17 percent ($4.2 million) was overhead costs. However, according to the General Ledger, overhead costs should not be around $1.5 million. Thus, significant hidden overhead costs exist, even in such a small organization. In addition, *all* the meals combined only cost $900,000. Thus, no longer serving hot dinners in order to save costs is bad management, to put it mildly. It also illustrates the danger of focusing on direct costs.

The question, of course, is why such things take place so often in the public sector. A part of the answer is simple: Decision makers are aided by accounting schemes where labor, food, and electricity are typical accounts, but no accounts exist for either the processes or for the services provided. Furthermore, no costing system is utilized beyond the General Ledger. In other words, no reliable product cost estimates take place; even the old volume-based costing systems would represent a massive improvement over today's situation.

Hence, when costs are cut, the largest costs are axed first with no concern for the product or processes. As in the previous example, food is a separate account and therefore easy to spot, whereas no process cost estimates were made (until I made them). The process costs are simply hidden, particularly the labor costs that dominate the cost structure. With no costing system, such costs are completely intangible for the manager of the nursing home. It is, in other words, very difficult to improve the process efficiencies beyond reducing the inputs, and it is not feasible to cut labor costs. The logical conclusion is to try cutting somewhere else, but this yields such bizarre results as trying to save costs by no longer serving hot meals. Luckily, LCC ignores the artificial boundaries made by organizations. For

Activity-Based LCC, only actual, total costs count and the boundaries are set by what actually goes on (the process), regardless of what department does what. This is exactly what the public sector needs to produce a holistic picture.

A secondary purpose of this case study is to show how uncertainty analysis can be carried out as discussed in this book. Also, we compare it to more traditional ways of handling uncertainty. In the literature, many talk about handling uncertainty, but very few actually do it, and in the industry even fewer do it. This may be so, because the traditional ways of managing risk and uncertainty are so simplistic that decision makers do not trust them. Another explanation might be that these methods are too laborious to produce reliable decision support.

The fact that the traditional methods are very simplistic is beyond doubt since they rest upon a very dangerous assumption, namely that "everything else remains constant," or *ceteris paribus* in Latin. This is an assumption that is virtually never true. The only question is to what extent it is faulty, but that is exactly the type of question that makes a decision maker distrust the approach because he or she has spent money on it but is left with a major question that is unresolved. Resolving this question adequately using traditional approaches is very laborious because we must try out many different scenarios *manually*, and if the model is large with several hundred variables, this task is daunting.

A totally different approach is to use the Monte Carlo methods. They are very simple yet sample the entire solution space without a *ceteris paribus* constraint. So, instead of wasting time on trying to find one single variable's impact, we just vary all the variables, store the results, and perform a statistical analysis in the end. We perform in many ways a virtual experiment in a virtual world described by the model and then perform an analysis in the end. Basically, the computer picks numbers in the input variables and stores the results of the corresponding forecast ariables. It is apparently a crude method, which is why it was, and still is by many, considered a "stupid" approach. However, it is, in our opinion, an ingenious method because it is simple, efficient, reliable, and highly effective. Or as it was said in a Chinese fortune cookie: "Simplicity of character is the result of profound thought."

The efficiency of the Monte Carlo methods comes partially from the fact that they are simple, but also from the fact that they can so easily be implemented in computers. We simply model the problem as accurately as possible and crank it through a Monte Carlo simulation; it does not matter much whether the number of variables in the model is 100 or 1,000. Afterward we can spend time on understanding and implementing the results. We do not have to waste time on thinking out smart ways of simplifying problems, solving complicated mathematics, or wondering about whether our model is valid or not. Because Monte Carlo methods are reliable, we can concentrate on solving the *actual* problem and not on solving a fancy, but possible deceptive, mathematical formulation of the actual problem.

Because of the comprehensiveness (many variables, many trials, little need for simplifying the problem, and so on) of Monte Carlo methods, they are effective as well. Monte Carlo methods simply enable us to spend time on making the decision because the mathematics and problem formulation parts are solved so straightforwardly and with a minimum of assumptions. In this respect, this case was not an ideal one because we could not contrast the power of Monte Carlo methods to the traditional approaches. In many ways, the case was so simple that even the traditional approaches were feasible. That is, however, the point of using this case to illustrate the ways uncertainty can be handled: It is so simple, so easy to follow, that we can show both the traditional approaches and the Monte Carlo methods and discuss all approaches in relation to the case. Now you just have to imagine a more complex case with maybe 100 or 1,000 variables and then ask yourself how you would handle the uncertainty. We all would agree that the way to go is with the Monte Carlo methods.

The third purpose of this case study is to illustrate two important aspects of Activity-Based LCC: the process orientation and the use of drivers. The traditional approaches lack a systematic process orientation and drivers. They do not incorporate any explicit way of securing process orientation, and drivers are usually forgotten. The traditional approaches are basically too cost focused, and the drivers behind costs are largely ignored. That is not easy to see in this case, but it can be seen, for example, from the fact that the traditional approach does not explicitly consider the duration of a fire. It rather focuses on the cost of a certain time period. Activity-Based LCC, however, focuses on the duration of the fire *and* the unit price of the duration, that is, the cost of one day. Then, by multiplying the duration by the unit price of the duration, the cost is found. Activity-Based LCC is in other words a more systematic and general approach that disseminates complex cost structures into relevant elements (drivers, resources, cost objects, and activities) that are interrelated in a web of cause and effect.

The process orientation is obvious in Activity-Based LCC because we are forced to define the various decisions and processes or activities that may take place. By doing this, we discovered, for instance, that two decisions are to be made: one concerning to do something or not, and one concerning what to do if we choose to do something. This is useful because it divides up a bigger problem into smaller, more easily graspable problems.

In a large and complex case, these seemingly academic differences have a huge impact on the outcomes of an analysis, but that will be discussed later in Chapter 9. Here it suffices to acknowledge that these differences exist and that they have had some impact even in this little, simple case.

The fourth, and last, purpose of this case study is to illustrate how LCC can be used purely in providing decision support. In the rest of the book, however, the

LCC models are mostly used for cost management purposes. The difference is that LCC models for decision making are attuned toward a specific purpose: providing decision support for a specific decision or a set of decisions; however, managerial LCC models have a broader view, a distinction that will become clearer in later chapters.

CLOSURE

Things are not always what they seem, particularly if your cost information is irrelevant or highly distorted for the issue under investigation. For the county of Ullensaker, it may seem tempting to do nothing about the tire disposal site at Østli. After all, no costs result from having it there, according to the country's accounting system. Removing the tires will therefore be an act of benevolence or, at worst, a response to threats from the local population, industry, and others.

Luckily, LCC discovers a more interesting and challenging truth. The fact is that although no costs exist in the books associated with the disposal site, hidden, potentially large costs can be unleashed by a little child, a small flame, or simply bad luck. These costs are liability costs, imaginary today, but maybe very real tomorrow. After all, parents may sue Ullensaker for not securing a well-known hazardous area close to residential areas. Airline companies may demand compensation from Ullensaker in case of fire because Ullensaker should have prevented fires because the disposal site is so close to Oslo Gardermoen International Airport. Thus, Ullensaker should have acted accordingly. The local population may hold Ullensaker responsible for environmental degradation. All such potential costs, and more, are simply not included in ordinary accounting practices, but they lie at the very center of LCC and in this case they make all the difference. The LCC analysis in this case, regardless of approach, discloses that doing nothing is outright risky and very uneconomic. As John F. Kennedy said:

> *There are risks and costs to a program of action, but they are far less than the long-range risks and costs of comfortable inaction.*

The analysis of what should be done about the tires is less clear: The choice is between recycling and disposal. Disposal is slightly more profitable, but that may also be due to the apparently erroneous underpricing of disposing of the tires, as discussed earlier. The difference in the margin of the two options is consequently miniscule and probably lies within the range of the inherent uncertainty of the modeling. Therefore, the decision of what to do about the tires will probably be determined according to other considerations rather than economic ones. Because disposing of the tires requires special permits that are hard to obtain and disposing of such voluminous objects uses a disproportionate amount of valuable landfill capacity, recycling the tires is probably the overall best solution.

EPILOGUE

After Carlsen and Røyset made the county of Ullensaker fully aware of the pending legal, environmental, and liability issues it faced, Ullensaker acted quite swiftly. Both LCC models clearly pictured the potential economic consequences of further delay in the matter. The new and creative environmental consultant at Ullensaker, Mari Kristel Gederaas, subsequently gained support and the tires were removed right before snowfall in November and December of 2001.

RagnSells AS, the company now responsible for operating the tire return system, took on the job for about $250,000. The low fee was attached to the condition that Ullensaker would find a use for the shredded tires within the county within one year. Currently, there are some pending issues concerning the fact that it is illegal to dispose of shredded tires, and the rules and regulations concerning potential applications of shredded tires are far from clear. Once these issues are resolved, the disposed tires at Østli will finally be relegated to history.

The case illustrates that proper decision support can be a catalyst for effective decision making because it is much easier to act on facts than relying on anecdotal guesstimates or worse.

NOTES

1. I would like to thank Randi Carlsen for providing this case study and her valuable contributions to it. For a complete overview of the project, see R. Carlsen and J.A. Røyset, "Dekkdeponiet På Østli: Uønsket Nabo" (The Tire Disposal Site at Østli: Unwanted Neighbor), Oslo University, Oslo, 2000, p. 78. The report is written in Norwegian.

2. The Norwegian Pollution Control Authority (SFT) is a directorate under the Ministry of the Environment and was established in 1974. Its main goal is to promote sustainable development. It is the Norwegian equivalent of the U.S. Environmental Protection Agency (EPA).

3. For more details, see Tellus Institute's "Disposal Cost Fee Study: Final Report," Boston, MA, 1991.

4. According to a study by Mepex Consult.

5. According to the aforementioned report by the Tellus Institute.

6. This is a common condition in all traditional approaches and it implies that "all else remains the same or constant" except the single variable whose value is being changed.

7. R.A. Lutz, "Lutz's Laws: A Primer for the Business Side of Engineering." Atlanta, GA: George W. Woodruff Annual Distinguished Lecture. Georgia Institute of Technology, 1998.

8. The details of price quotes and so on are found in the report (see note 1).

9. "Globalisation and Its Critics: A Survey of Globalisation." *The Economist*, 2001, p. 34.

7

ACTIVITY-BASED LIFE-CYCLE COSTING FOR PLATFORM SUPPLY VESSELS[1]

> If you need a machine and don't buy it, you pay for it without getting it.
>
> Henry Ford

As organizations become increasingly aware of both environmental costs and customer service costs, life-cycle costs will become more and more important to assess, predict, and trace. This growing concern led to a project between Møre Research and Farstad Shipping ASA (Farstad for short) in which the operation of a Platform Supply Vessel (PSV) that operates in the North Sea was studied. In this project, the economic and environmental aspects of the PSV were analyzed. We also looked at the choice of propulsion machinery and support systems. The choice of fuel is particularly important due to the tradeoffs between low fuel costs and high maintenance costs. In this chapter, only the costing part is discussed.

Note that all the input information is from 1995 and is probably not accurate anymore, so the results are outdated. The purpose of this case study is therefore to illustrate a complete Activity-Based Life-Cycle Costing (LCC) implementation for a large and complicated system (the PSV). This case is, however, quite simple in terms of, for example, overhead cost allocation and product-mix complexity because it covers only one product.

Before we discuss the LCC modeling and its results, we must first understand a little bit more about operating a PSV, which is the next issue.

OPERATING A PLATFORM SUPPLY VESSEL

Operating a platform supply vessel (PSV) profitably is not easy because competition is very stiff. Farstad's technical manager, Jan Henry Farstad, illustrated this by telling me that the company once lost a bid because MAERSK offered the customer a contract that was NOK 50 cheaper (roughly $8 at the time) per day. The margins are squeezed to the maximum, and very little room exists for error.

A further complicating factor is that the contracts are of different lengths. Due to the tight margins in the industry, only a high degree of utilization of their vessels translates into a high profitability for the shipowners. The most sought after contracts are therefore the long ones (five years or so) because they offer less uncertainty and revenue risk. The short-term contracts, or spot contracts, are more profitable, but it is difficult to secure a high-enough degree of utilization. Spot contracts are therefore the last resort.

Even with stable revenues, significant problems related to the maintenance, service, and repair costs exist. The maintenance, service, and repair activities are defined as:

- **Maintenance**   All maintenance activities that can be done while the vessel is in service, or operating as planned.
- **Service**   Planned maintenance activities that require the vessel being out of service. This happens every time the vessel is docking. How often the vessel docks depends on the policy of Farstad, but the vessel has to be docked every at least once every five years to renew its classification with Det Norske Veritas (DNV).
- **Repair**   Unplanned service.

The aforementioned challenges usually translate into a few crucial questions, such as:

- How can the amount of off-hire be reduced? Off-hire occurs whenever the vessel is incapable of fulfilling the contract and it results in a direct revenue loss. In the contract between the shipowners and the charter group, off-hire conditions are specified in detail. Planned services on dock (kept within the lay days) are *not* considered off-hire. The lay days are the number of days specified in the contract between the shipowners and charter group when necessary repair, service, and maintenance can be done without any revenue loss.
- How can the life-span costs be reduced?
- How can profitable contracts be acquired?

Depending on the contract, off-hire will occur in different situations. For FAR Scandia, which is the PSV followed in this case, the contract states that:

- Planned service on dock is not considered off-hire.
- Unplanned repairs are considered off-hire.
- The shipowners are given one lay day per month, but the maximum annual aggregated number of lay days is set to be six. Hence, the annual service time that exceeds six days is considered off-hire.

Because of this situation, it is important for shipowners to project the costs as reliably as possible so that they know what their margins are in bidding situations. The life-span costs (the total costs of the operational phase) must therefore be predicted many years ahead before negotiating with an oil company or a charter group, or before new ships are designed. During contract negotiations, the primary issue is therefore what price the shipowner should offer the charter group, which usually pays the fuel costs, particularly on longer contracts. This is beneficial for the shipowner because it eliminates the substantial risk of fuel price fluctuations.

When new ships are designed and built, however, the issue is far more complex. Typically, the shipowner would only order a new ship if it had a solid first contract. The problem is that these contracts may last only up to 5 years, but the life span of a PSV is about 20 years before it is sold. Thus, 15 years are completely uncertain. During these 15 years, the PSV may change from being used in a time charter to a line charter or vice versa.

A time-charter contract is a contract under which the shipowner puts the PSV at the charter group's full-time disposal for a certain period of time, whereas in a line charter, the PSV performs a certain transportation job for a charter group from point A to point B. The difference between these two contract types is that a time-charter contract typically is longer, involves less activity for the main machinery because much of the time is usually spent waiting either at the oil platform or onshore (see Table 7.5), and the fuel costs are paid by the charter group. This means that the fuel consumption is relatively lower than on a line-charter job, but the shipowner must carefully manage the maintenance costs to avoid off-hire and too high costs that would erode margins. The shipowner will therefore typically prefer Marine Gas Oil (MGO), which is a fuel that keeps maintenance to a minimum.

In a line-charter job, on the other hand, the fuel consumption is high, the fuel costs are incorporated in the bid, and the shipowner manages the maintenance costs (as always). In this situation, it is advantageous for the shipowner to have machinery that balances fuel costs and maintenance costs. Typically, heavy fuel oil (HFO) is dirt cheap but causes many maintenance costs because such fuel is very thick, almost like asphalt. Hence, HFO is only profitable when the fuel consumption is high, such as on a line-charter job. In this light, it is clear that the machinery installed in a new PSV can greatly alter the profitability depending on the contracts the shipowner may acquire in the future.

In the project, the use of tributyltin (TBT) Self-Polishing Copolymer antifouling paint on the hull was also discussed. This paint has very positive cost effects. According to studies,[2] the savings compared to other painting types is "at the very least £700 million annually (or roughly $1.1 billion) for the Deep Sea fleet due to lesser fuel costs, lower repair costs, and less time in dock." Unfortunately, TBT causes environmental problems, such as imposex of the dogwhelk snail, *Nucella Lapillus* (female snails develop a penis), and reduced growth and enhanced mortality of larvae of bivalves.[3] The costs of such environmental problems are unfortunately impossible to estimate because they affect animals that have no economic value[4] to humans. Due to the difficulty of evaluating the environmental impacts of TBT, the whole issue of hull paint was dropped in the project between Møre Research and Farstad. In this book, the costing part also excludes the paint issue for the same reason. Before looking into the Activity-Based LCC implementation, the problem must be defined.

PROBLEM STATEMENT AND SYSTEM BOUNDARIES

In the previous section, many of the problems that shipowners of PSVs face were discussed. Farstad wanted to shed more light on two problems. First, the stiff competition makes a model that can predict the total costs of operating a PSV up to 10 years ahead very valuable because it can be used actively in negotiations. Second, under what circumstances will machinery that runs on HFO be preferable to machinery that uses MGO? This question is also important in negotiations, but it is possibly more important when purchasing new ships because that is when the type of machinery (HFO or MGO) is determined. Of course, purchasing a new ship may indeed become an issue during negotiations.

Therefore, Farstad needs a cost model that can predict and trace life-span costs. Also, the costs and benefits of using a type of HFO called IF 40 instead of the current fuel, MGO, should be addressed. The decision concerning a fuel type is for simplicity denoted as design decision A.

The tracing of significant cost contributors, or critical success factors, enables improvement through design. Basically, the critical success factors can be used to direct attention toward where the shipowners should focus their data collection for further analysis and improvement efforts.

To provide data for the analysis, an overall representative PSV is chosen as the base case. The chosen PSV is called FAR Scandia, a PSV of the UT 705 type. An additional PSV, FAR Service, has provided data for an IF 40—an HFO—operation. The UT 705 PSV is a specific type of platform supply vessel designed by Ulstein International AS capable of:

- Transporting pipes, cement, equipment, and goods to and from pipeline barges, oilrigs, and ships
- Loading a pipeline barge under North Sea conditions with approximately 4.6-meter-high waves and a tidal current of roughly 3.5 knots

Because an UT 705 PSV is a large and complex system, the analysis was constrained, in agreement with Farstad, to the most significant subsystems (see Figure 7.1). The subsystems are grouped according to the SFI grouping system, which is provided in Appendix B. The analysis is constrained to SFI groups 27, 28, 60, 63, 70, 71, and 71. These SFI groups therefore define the system boundaries. Also recall from the previous section that we have not included the cost of issues that we know exist but whose impact is noneconomic.

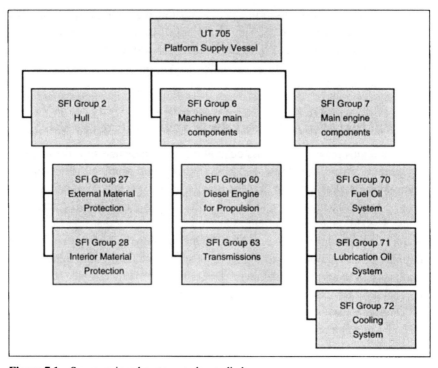

Figure 7.1   Seven main subsystems to be studied.

Before describing how the Activity-Based LCC model was built, the information sources are discussed.

INFORMATION SOURCES

Many types of information are needed to design a reliable Activity-Based LCC model for Farstad. Table 7.1 presents an overview of the information sources and their contributions. This gives an idea of the comprehensive amount of information that must be gathered for this costing model.

ACTIVITY-BASED LCC MODEL IMPLEMENTATION AND RESULTS

When developing the Activity-Based LCC model, only the operational phase of the PSV is handled just as in the project. In Figure 5.1, a 10-step description of the method is given, and the implementation of the Activity-Based LCC model will follow these steps.

Table 7.1 Information Sources

Information Source	Type of Information
Farstad Shipping ASA, Ålesund	• Maintenance and service plans and respective costs. • Overhead costs. • Insurance and crew costs. • Vessel specifications and some technical information.
Farstad Shipping Ltd., Aberdeen	• Maintenance plans and respective costs. • Fuel (HFO) information.
International Maling AS	• Paint prices. • Product data sheets. • Analysis of tin antifouling versus other coatings.
Ulstein Bergen AS	• Environmental performance of machinery.
FAR Scandia	• Use pattern. • MGO consumption.
Møre Research, Ålesund	• General information regarding the operational phase of ships.
Different Shipyards	• Waste streams. • Cost information.
ESSO—Mørebunkers AS	• Fuel prices.
Castrol	• Lubrication oil prices.
Ulstein International AS	• Technical specifications for an UT 705 vessel.
FAR Service	• HFO consumption.

Source: A.M. Fet, J. Emblemsvåg, and J.T. Johannesen, *Environmental Impacts and Activity Based Costing during Operation of a Platform Supply Vessel.* Ålesund, Norway: Møreforsking, 1996.

Step 1: Define the Scope of the Model and the Corresponding Cost Objects

The scope of the model was defined in the "Problem Statement and System Boundaries" section and will not be repeated here. The object of investigation, the cost object, in this case is a UT 705 PSV owned by Farstad Shipping ASA. The model does not concern any specific UT 705 PSV but rather attempts to look at the UT 705 PSV as an object. Data are, however, obtained from specific but representative UT 705 PSVs, as mentioned earlier.

Step 2: Obtain and Clean Bill of Materials for All Cost Objects

Obtaining and cleansing the Bill of Materials (BOM) is relevant when several cost objects are in the model and consequently may consume overhead resources disproportionately. In this case, however, only one cost object is used and the step is therefore omitted.

Step 3: Identify and Quantify the Resources

For brevity, only selected resources are presented (see Table 7.2). The revenues are also omitted since they may indicate the bargaining power of Farstad. Note that in 1995 $1 U.S. equaled NOK 6.50. In this chapter, as previously, I have simply converted the amount from NOK into U.S. dollars without correcting for differences in exchange rates and purchasing power.

The maintenance costs for the tanks and the machinery are computed using a job as basis. A job is a basic element in the maintenance program such as "wash wing tanks (components 238.10.1 through 238.10.12)." When MGO fuel is used, the maintenance spreadsheet contains 149 different jobs, whereas HFO IF 40 demands 198 different jobs. Each job is associated with a job number, an activity number, a service interval (how often it should be performed), a machine component (where the job should be done), a component number, component costs, and labor hours.

Table 7.2   Sample Resources

Resource	Costs ($/year)
Various types of insurance	620,000
Crew costs	6,697,600
Fuel costs (MGO)	3,774,000
Classification costs (annual average)	71,392

Step 4: Create an Activity Hierarchy and Network

Step 2 starts by forming an activity hierarchy (see Table 7.3). The activity hierarchy was mostly established by interviewing technical managers Jan Henry Farstad and Bjarne Nygaaren. The maintenance programs for FAR Scandia (regarding MGO fuel) and FAR Service (concerning HFO IF 40 fuel) provided detailed information concerning activities A13 and A14. An important premise for defining the activities is to balance accuracy versus the cost of obtaining information when it comes to both activities and drivers.

From the activity hierarchy in Table 7.3, we see three main activities: (A1) Use, (A2) Service on Dock, and (A3) Repair. All the activities under A1 (Use) sustain production of service hours, which is essentially what the charter group pays for. Activities A2 (Service on Dock) and A3 (Repair), however, are activities the

Table 7.3 Life-Span Activity Hierarchy for the UT 705 PSV

Activity Level 1	Activity Level 2	Activity Level 3	Activity Level 4
Use **A1**	Operate ship **A11**	Load ship **A111**	
		Be in service **A112**	
		Stand by **A113**	
		Service platform **A114**	
		Be out of service **A115**	
	Entering harbor **A12**		
	Maintain tanks **A13**	Wash **A131**	
		Test **A132**	
		Check **A133**	
	Maintain machinery **A14**	Maintain SFI group 6 **A141**	Check **A1411**
			Test **A1412**
			Lubricate **A1413**
			Get fluid sample **A1414**
			Survey/control **A1415**
			Overhaul **A1416**
			Honing **A1417**
			Replace comp. **A1418**
		Maintain SFI group 7 **A142**	Check **A1421**
			Test **A1422**
			Replace components **A1423**
			Survey/control **A1424**
			Lubricate **A1425**
	Certify class **A15**		
Service **A2** on Dock	Dock ship **A21**		
	Service hull **A22**	Sand-blast hull **A221**	
		Paint hull **A222**	
		Clean hull **A223**	
	Service machinery **A23**	Check **A231**	
		Change oil **A232**	
		Service cooling system **A233**	
	Change anodes **A24**		
	Service tanks **A25**	Sand-blast tanks **A251**	
		Paint tanks **A252**	
		Clean tanks **A253**	
Repair **A3**	Tow ship **A31**		
	Quay ship **A32**		
	Dock ship **A33**		
	Repair machinery **A34**		
	Repair propellers **A35**		

Table 7.4   Repair Activities Information

Activity	Occurrence Frequency	Expected Repair Cost ($)	Expected Loss of Time (h)	Expected Repair Costs ($)
A31	1.0	130,000	10.0	130,000
A32	2.0	1,400	5.0	2,800
A33	1.5	18,312	20.0	27,468
A34	2.0	500,000	5.0	1,000,000
A35	1.5	50,000	10.0	75,000

shipowner needs to provide the PSV service. The difference between A2 and A3 is that Activity A2 is according to the contract, whereas A3 is extraordinary and hence results in off-hire and therefore loss of revenues for Farstad.

Also, the activities have four different levels. For example, the Repair activity (Activity A3) consists of five level 2 activities: Tow Ship (A31), Quay Ship (A32), Dock Ship (A33), Repair Machinery (A34), and Repair Propellers (A35). The five level-2 Repair activities are far from the only unwanted incidents that may occur, but according to historical data, these unwanted incidents occur relatively frequently compared to other incidents like fire, collision, and war. The system boundary of the project also limits which incidents to consider.

In Table 7.4, the information used for the Repair activities is shown. Note that the occurrences are projected for a 10-year period.

After the hierarchy is made, an activity network is designed as shown in Figure 7.2. The circular nodes are activities, while the diamond-shaped nodes are design-

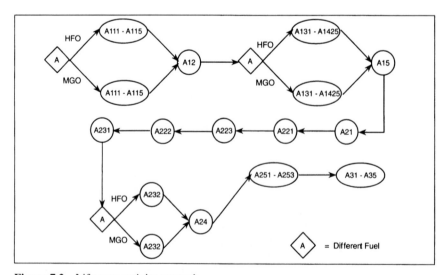

Figure 7.2   Life-span activity network.

decision nodes. The letter in the decision nodes represents a specific design decision. In the activity network, we use the lowest-level activities from the activity
hierarchy in Table 7.3, that is, the shaded cells.

Step 5: Identify and Quantify Resource Drivers, Activity Drivers, and Their Intensities

The Activity-Based LCC model is extensive, as indicated by the information
requirements. Hence, presenting all the drivers and consumption intensities (when
known) is unfeasible. The most important resource drivers are:

- **Direct labor**   This resource driver is used mostly to capture the maintenance and service activities performed by the crew and the workers at shipyards. Shipyards split direct labor into four resource drivers: (1) ordinary
  direct labor, (2) 50 percent overtime direct labor, (3) 100 percent overtime
  direct labor, and (4) shift direct labor. The direct labor resource driver related
  to maintenance is not believed to affect the choice between the different fuel
  types for the machinery. In Figure 7.3, the resource driver for activity A1416,
  Job 0.61 for components 601.1–2.01 is modeled. The unit is hours/year,
  (h/year).
- **Number of components**   This resource driver is normally employed to capture the cost of replacing components in the machinery and is highly affected
  by different fuel types for the machinery. It is therefore a design-dependent
  driver.
- **Running hours**   This resource driver is used to determine the use pattern
  of the vessel, and it plays a key role (along with the days in dock resource
  driver) in determining when the vessel is off-hire. Furthermore, running

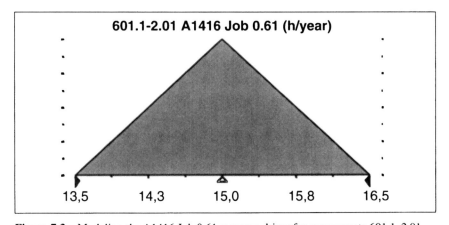

Figure 7.3   Modeling the A1416 Job 0.61 resource driver for components 601.1–2.01.

hours is the resource driver the overhead is distributed by, but it will not be significantly affected by any design changes.

- **Fuel consumption**   This resource driver keeps track of the fuel costs for the vessel, is highly affected by different fuel types, and is consequently a design-dependent driver.

Note that since only one cost object exists in this model, the UT 705 PSV, activity drivers are not needed.

Step 6: Identify the Relationships between Activity Drivers and Design Changes

Since this model has only one cost object, the resource drivers will capture the design changes. Due to the fact that the consumption of activities depends on a variety of resource drivers, it is convenient to use historical data when available as a basis from which the relationships can be determined. This is unfortunately associated with more uncertainty than the use of mathematical equations. However, it is the most feasible and probably the most reliable approach, because the variety of known and unknown resource drivers is virtually impossible to model realistically as a set of equations.

The historical data is obtained by asking the crew on FAR Scandia, Bjarne Nygaaren (Farstad Shipping ASA, Ålesund) and Jim Watt (Farstad Shipping Ltd., Aberdeen), to fill out some forms and by using invoices up to four years old from different shipyards. Some data were also from FAR Service, which runs on HFO.

Table 7.5 presents the historical data obtained from FAR Scandia. In this fashion, we see how historical data is used to quantify a cost driver, which is fuel consumption in this case. The "% Run. Hrs." is employed as a basis for the computation of the running hour resource driver.

Step 7: Model the Uncertainty

The model consists of 501 assumption cells, or input variables, in which the uncertainty is modeled. Most of them are modeled as either triangular distributions (see Figure 7.3), whereas others are modeled as normal distributions. For our purposes here, it is sufficient to acknowledge that the uncertainty is modeled as realistically as possible without going into further details. The case in Chapter 6 illustrated the considerations that must be taken into account when modeling the uncertainty.

Step 8: Estimate the Bill of Activities

Keeping track of the assumptions is vital in order to trust the computations. In general, two types of assumptions are made: user-defined and inherent. The user-

Table 7.5 Typical FAR Scandia Mission in 1995

Operational Mode	Run. Hrs.	% Run. Hrs.	Speed (nm/h)	Fuel Consumption (1,000kg/day)
In port	9.3		0.0	1.0
Stand vy	0.0	0.0	0.0	4.0
Economic speed	2.1	5.4	10.0	14.3
Full speed	15.3	39.3	14.0	21.4
Service platform	21.5	55.3	0.0	4.8

defined assumptions are uncertainty distributions that are needed to model the uncertainty, and they can be changed whenever the user wants to. In this model, many user-defined assumptions[5] are made, but only a small sample is presented (see Figure 7.3 and Table 7.5) for brevity.

The inherent assumptions are made by the designer of the model (that is, me) to simplify the modeling based on the user preferences and budget. These assumptions are therefore embodied in the framework of the model and thus cannot be easily changed. In this model, only a few of these assumptions are made:

- The historical data are used as a good guideline for the future development. That is, we assume the future will proceed similarly to the past, a common assumption in all forecasting, as discussed in Chapter 1.
- Real revenues and costs are assumed constant. In other words, inflation is not an issue.
- The maintenance program for the vessels is followed accurately so that the jobs in the maintenance program are done as listed. According to technical manager Jan H. Farstad, these programs are followed meticulously. The model nonetheless allows ±10 percent variability.
- The technical condition of the machinery and hull remains adequate as long as maintenance and service programs are followed. Thus, costs other than depreciation due to aging will not exist. Since only the first 10 years of the life span were considered, this assumption has very little influence on the results. For vessels older than 20 years, the situation may be significantly different.

With these assumptions and design decision A embodied in the model, the Monte Carlo simulations took place using the commercially available software Crystal Ball®, which adds into Microsoft Excel as a macro. A high number of trials are used in the simulations to reduce the random error to a minimum.

Step 9: Estimate Cost Objects' Cost and Their Performance Measures

Since only one cost object is used in the model, the cost of consumption of the objects is the same as the cost of consumption of the activities. See the "Review the Results and Iterate If Needed" section below for the actual results. Since this was a pure costing exercise, no additional performance measures are done, except risk measures, which are discussed in the "Identifying the Major Operational Risks" section at the end of this chapter.

Step 10: Perform Monte Carlo Simulations and Relevant Analyses

During the Monte Carlo simulations, statistical sensitivity analyses were the only additional numerical analyses performed in this case due to the scope of the project. The corresponding sensitivity analysis results are presented along with the other results in the next section.

Review the Results and Iterate If Needed

The results and the discussions are divided into four main parts:

1. Using the results to check the model
2. Using trend charts to predict and trace future costs and revenues
3. Identifying the critical success factors for the shipowner
4. Investigating design scenario A

But first it is important to clarify how the profitability is determined because two perspectives are possible. The first is the shipowner's perspective. Farstad, as a shipowner, has some expenses covered by the charter group, such as the fuel costs, as long as the PSV is on a time-charter contract. While the PSV is on a line-charter contract, Farstad must pay all the expenses. This latter perspective, where all costs are included, is referred to as the vessel's point of view.

The shipowner perspective is, as the name indicates, the perspective that the shipowner mostly cares about because it is the bottom line for the shipowner. The vessel's perspective, in combination with the shipowner's perspective, is more interesting from a product design perspective because the shipowner would like to reduce the total costs. After all, the vessel will sooner or later have to operate on line-charter contracts, and potential charter groups will appreciate lower fuel costs.

Checking the Model

Many issues must be checked when validating a model.[6] Briefly stated, these can be summarized into two main concerns that are discussed in subsequent sections: (1) the internal logic of the model and (2) the degree to which the model reflects reality.

Internal Validity. The most basic element in checking the internal validity of the model is to evaluate its logic. In other words, has the model been built using all available information as logically as possible while making sound assumptions? The project group has every reason to believe so because technical managers Jan Henry Farstad and Bjarne Nygaarden were closely involved in explaining the logic of their business while at the same time supervising how it was used.

The internal logic of the model can also be checked using the results. For example, the distribution of uncertainty in Figure 7.4 seems strange because the amount of uncertainty is distributed very uncommonly[7] and ought to be investigated. To find out if this is a problem or in fact logical behavior, the sensitivity chart in Figure 7.5 is studied.

It is evident that the different maintenance intervals and the annual running hours play a major role in the sense that they determine the periods in which costs are incurred. Or to put it another way, depending on when a certain maintenance job is performed, it can be reported in year 6, 7, or 8.

Therefore, let us investigate what happens if the service intervals and annual running hours are kept constant, that is, with no uncertainty in the corresponding assumption cells. Figure 7.6 shows the effect: A nice bell-shaped distribution appears. The abnormal distribution in Figure 7.4 evidently arises because the registration of costs depends on when the activity is performed, thus producing this large uncertainty in the forecast cells. This fact may be important with respect to liquidity management, but that is not a topic of this book. Nevertheless, the behavior is logical and the model is therefore deemed reliable. Next, we must find out if the model seems to represent reality in a fair way.

External Validity. The external validity of the model can best be investigated by showing the model to technical managers Farstad and Nygaarden because they know their business very well, have extensive experience both technically and eco-

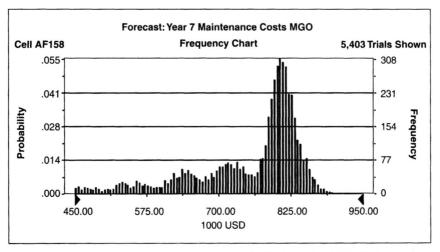

Figure 7.4   Year 7 maintenance cost uncertainty distribution using MGO fuel.

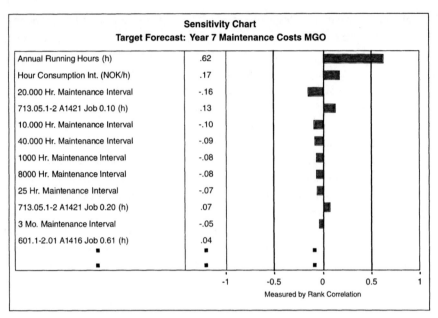

Figure 7.5   Year 7 maintenance cost sensitivity chart using MGO fuel.

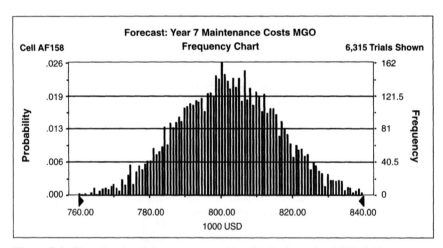

Figure 7.6   Year 7 maintenance cost uncertainty distribution using MGO fuel.

nomically, and have been involved in the project from start to finish. We met and presented the model and its results to them and they asked questions. They were very pleased with the model because they found it logical, sound, and matched well with their experience. Thus, we had every reason to believe that the model captures the real issues well. After checking the model for internal and external validity, the next step is to predict future costs and revenues.

Predicting Future Costs and Profitabilities

The predictions of future costs and profitabilities are, of course, greatly affected by the logic of the model and how well the uncertainty is modeled. Concerning the logic of the model, we can assume that it will remain valid because the overall logic of operating will not change substantially within the period of time the predictions concern. Modeling the uncertainty, however, is much more difficult because nobody can tell the future. For example, what is the exchange rate between U.S. dollars and Norwegian kroner in five years? Essentially, we must rely on guesswork when it comes to modeling the uncertainty. Here an important principle applies: Invite those who know the business to provide "guesstimates." Technical managers Farstad and Nygaarden played a major role is this part of the project as well.

Given these limitations, the Activity-Based LCC model can predict future costs, revenues, or profitabilities. In Figure 7.7, for example, we can see how the main-

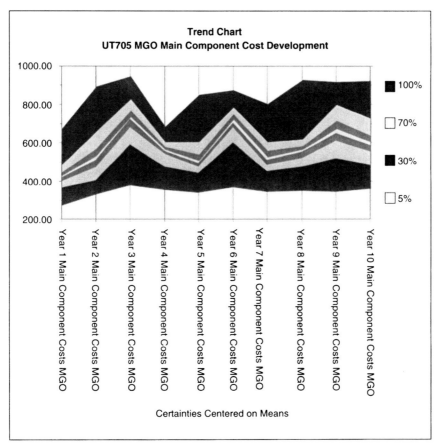

Figure 7.7   Maintenance cost predictions (unit is $1,000).

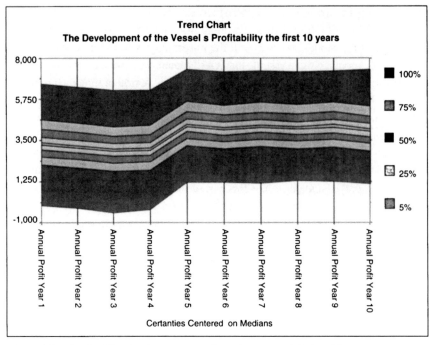

Figure 7.8   Profitability for the vessel the first 10 years (unit is $1,000).

tenance costs for the main components fluctuate from approximately $400,000 to over $800,000 per year. If we look at the 70 percent confidence interval, for example, we see it has a certain repetition, every three years being the most costly from a maintenance point of view. This is not strange since the machinery has certain maintenance and service intervals that involve more work than others. Again, this seems to indicate that the model is sound.

However, the trend chart in Figure 7.8 shows that these fluctuations have little effect in the overall profitability for the PSV. The shift in profitability from year 4 to year 5 is due to the refinancing of the Farstad fleet in 1995.

Of course, predicting the future is nice, but the real strength of Activity-Based LCC does in fact not lie in superior predicting and uncertainty analysis capabilities. It lies in the process orientation and use of drivers because that enables us to find the future critical success factors. When we have identified the critical success factors, it is much easier to work toward future goals because now we know what matters most.

In my opinion, too much effort is wasted every year in most organizations on chasing "how much" and "how to do it" when they really should be concerned about "what to do" and "why." It is as Drucker says:[8]

Not in a very long time—not, perhaps, since the late 1940s or early 1950s— have there been as many new major management techniques as there are today: downsizing, outsourcing, total quality management, economic value analysis, benchmarking, reengineering. Each is a powerful tool. But, with the exceptions of outsourcing and reengineering, these tools are designed primarily to do differently what is already being done. They are "how to do" tools.

Yet "what to do" is increasingly becoming the central challenge facing managements. Especially those of big companies that have enjoyed long-term success.

Although activity-based techniques in general are mainly "how to do it" tools, they also incorporate a "what to do" aspect in that they direct attention toward what drives the business. Activity-Based LCC directs attention even better than standard ABC due to improved forecasting and simulation capabilities and tracing mechanisms. The critical success factors for Farstad is discussed next.

Identifying the Critical Success Factors for the Shipowner

The beauty of Monte Carlo simulations is that not only are their forecasting and uncertainty-handling capabilities superb, but an equally important side effect occurs: a large sample of statistical data. These data are used in statistical sensitivity analysis. Figure 7.9 presents a sensitivity chart that allows us to identify the most significant cost and revenue contributors, or drivers, to the life-span profitability.

The drivers are:

- **Daily revenue**   This is the only driver that contributes to the revenues and is consequently paramount to the profitability.
- **Crew cost**   This is the second most important contributor to the profitability.
- **Fuel-related drivers**   All these contribute significantly in a negative direction; that is, an increase in these resource drivers will result in a decreased profitability.
- **Annual running hours**   If the number of annual running hours is increased, the profitability will decrease. This is evident because the more a vessel is running, the more fuel and maintenance are required, but the revenue remains the same.
- **Annual investment overhead** (An.Inv. Overhead)   This factor determines Farstad's annual cost of capital for this vessel and is therefore important.

The other drivers in Figure 7.9 are also significant cost contributors. However, since the correlation coefficients are low, we should be careful with using them right away because the method is based on a numerical approximation technique that is susceptible to random errors.

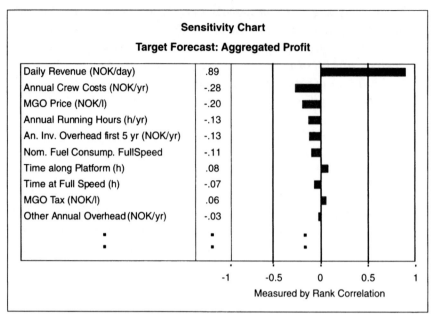

Figure 7.9   Sensitivity analysis for the aggregated life-span profitability.

For the shipowner, however, the situation is slightly different, because the charter group provides the fuel. The difference between the vessel's profitability and the shipowner profitability is roughly $3.5 million, or the annual fuel costs. It should be noted that not all the costs are included due to the system boundaries, as was discussed in the "Problem Statement and System Boundaries" section.

So what is determining the profitability for the shipowner? For Farstad, the profitability sensitivity chart is shown in Figure 7.10. Compared to Figure 7.9, we see that the main drivers are more or less the same, except that the fuel-related drivers have dropped out in Figure 7.10.

However, the sensitivity chart in Figure 7.10 may be unreliable, except for the top three contributors, because how can anything with fuel affect the profitability when the fuel cost is not included in the shipowner's profitability? The reason for the unreliable identification of the small critical success factors in Figure 7.10 is that the top three are very dominant, especially daily revenue, whose correlation coefficient is 0.94. To eliminate this problem, all the large critical success factors already identified are eliminated:

- Daily revenue.
- Interest rate.
- Crew costs.

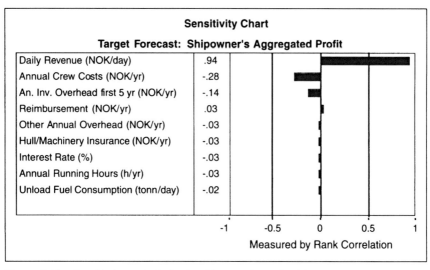

Figure 7.10   Sensitivity analysis for the shipowner's profitability.

- Fuel-related drivers (if the shipowner pays the fuel as in line chartering).
- Annual running hours.
- All the different maintenance and service intervals. These do not affect the total costs for the 10-year period significantly, but they highly affect the periodicity of the costs, as mentioned earlier.
- Reimbursement for the usage of Norwegian seamen.
- Insurance.

The model is run once more and the results are presented in Figure 7.11. Now the less important critical success factors can be identified.

Table 7.6 presents the 20^9 expected largest cost and revenue factors to the shipowner's profitability. The table starts with the expected largest. Note that:

- The ordering of the critical success factors may be slightly wrong, and there may be other factors that should have been listed instead of some of the contributors listed at the end of the table due to random effects in the Monte Carlo simulation. Nevertheless, the listed critical success factors are always important.
- All the cost factors from the A3 Repair activity are excluded due to the large amount of inherent uncertainty in those activities. Farstad simply cannot manage a vessel to avoid, say, a collision. Farstad can only launch some programs that can reduce the risk of a collision.

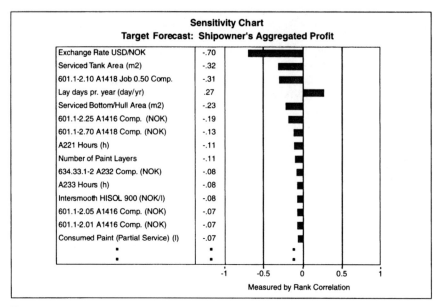

Figure 7.11 Sensitivity chart for the shipowner's aggregated life-span profitability after eliminating the largest factors.

Table 7.6 Twenty Most Critical Success Factors for the Shipowner's Aggregated Life-Span Profitability

Ranking	Cost/Revenue Contributors	Type
1	Daily revenue	Revenue
2	Capital cost	Cost
3	Crew cost (included reimbursement)	Cost
4	Annual running hours	Cost
5	Other annual overhead costs	Cost
6	Insurance	Cost
7	Different maintenance and docking intervals	Cost
8	Classification (exchange rate USD/NOK)	Cost
9	Serviced tank area	Cost
10	601.1–2.10 A1418 Job 0.50 component cost	Cost
11	Lay days per year	Revenue
12	Serviced bottom/hull area	Cost
13	601.1–2.25 A1416 component cost	Cost
14	601.1–2.70 A1418 component cost	Cost
15	A221 hours	Cost
16	Number of paint layers	Cost
17	634.33.1–2. A232 component cost	Cost
18	A233 hours	Cost
19	Intersmooth HISOL 900	Cost
20	601.12.05 A1416 component cost	Cost

Only two revenue factors, daily revenue and the number of annual lay days, can be identified from Table 7.6. During negotiations with a possible charter group, the different daily revenue and the number of annual lay days options can be simulated using the model presented here. Farstad can then, aided by a trend chart as in Figure 7.8, determine which option is preferable, or Farstad can determine before negotiations how low daily revenue can be and what are the fewest lay days it can agree upon. In both cases, some of the strength of the model presented here, compared to ordinary LCC models concerning prediction, is that future uncertainties can be modeled realistically and taken into account during the negotiations. Table 7.6 can furthermore be used to identify potential areas of saving. After studying the model and identifying the critical success factors, the effect of using different fuel, MGO versus IF 40 HFO, is investigated.

Investigating Design Decision A

As can be seen from the activity network in Figure 7.2, design decision A, IF 40 versus MGO, affects mainly the cost of fuel consumption and the cost of the maintenance activities. Figure 7.12 presents the uncertainty distribution for the aggregated savings of using IF 40 (versus MGO).

The model estimates an expected $(USD)711,000 savings over a 10-year period, but as can be seen from Figure 7.12, if IF 40 is chosen, the vessel still has approximately 40 percent probability of increasing the costs. The choice is therefore difficult; IF 40 is only *expected* to be more cost effective. However, as can be seen from Figure 7.13, the fuel prices, the fuel consumption, and the annual running hours play a major role. Thus, the IF 40 choice depends on favorable fuel prices, high fuel consumption, and low number of annual running hours. From the shipowner's perspective, however, using IF 40 is highly unprofitable because the consumption of machinery components increases by several hundred percent while the benefits of lower fuel prices cannot be harvested since the fuel is provided by the charter group.

The sensitivity chart in Figure 7.14 pinpoints the most important maintenance cost factors. Those with a negative correlation coefficient drive the cost associated with using IF 40, and those with a positive correlation coefficient drive the cost associated with MGO. Hence, an IF 40 system incurs much more maintenance costs than an MGO system, and we can also see that the difference is mainly due to a higher consumption of components.

From the discussion above, we understand that:

- From the vessel's point of view, use IF 40 when (otherwise not):
  - The IF 40 price is expected to be favorable in the period. Favorable means that the IF40 fuel price is as low as now or even lower.

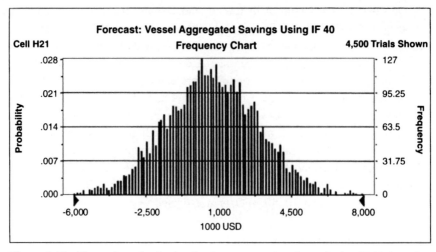

Figure 7.12   Uncertainty distribution for the aggregated savings of using IF 40 from the vessel's perspective.

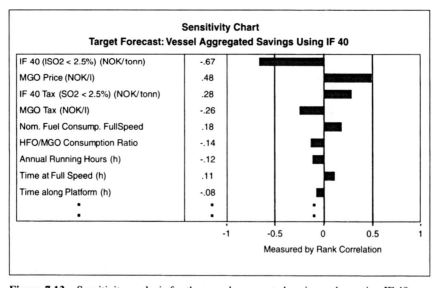

Figure 7.13   Sensitivity analysis for the vessel aggregated savings when using IF 40.

○ The vessel will be running steadily with a high fuel consumption. This can only be achieved when the vessel is going back and forth on full speed, because then the positive effect of high fuel consumption will dominate the negative effect of more annual running hours.

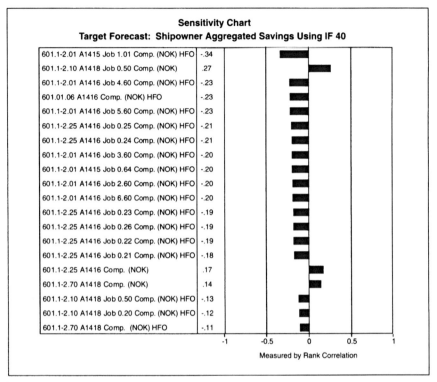

Sensitivity Chart
Target Forecast: Shipowner Aggregated Savings Using IF 40

601.1-2.01 A1415 Job 1.01 Comp. (NOK) HFO	-.34
601.1-2.10 A1418 Job 0.50 Comp. (NOK)	.27
601.1-2.01 A1416 Job 4.60 Comp. (NOK) HFO	-.23
601.01.06 A1416 Comp. (NOK) HFO	-.23
601.1-2.01 A1416 Job 5.60 Comp. (NOK) HFO	-.23
601.1-2.25 A1416 Job 0.25 Comp. (NOK) HFO	-.21
601.1-2.25 A1416 Job 0.24 Comp. (NOK) HFO	-.21
601.1-2.01 A1416 Job 3.60 Comp. (NOK) HFO	-.20
601.1-2.01 A1415 Job 0.64 Comp. (NOK) HFO	-.20
601.1-2.01 A1416 Job 2.60 Comp. (NOK) HFO	-.20
601.1-2.01 A1416 Job 6.60 Comp. (NOK) HFO	-.20
601.1-2.25 A1416 Job 0.23 Comp. (NOK) HFO	-.19
601.1-2.25 A1416 Job 0.26 Comp. (NOK) HFO	-.19
601.1-2.25 A1416 Job 0.22 Comp. (NOK) HFO	-.19
601.1-2.25 A1416 Job 0.21 Comp. (NOK) HFO	-.18
601.1-2.25 A1416 Comp. (NOK)	.17
601.1-2.70 A1418 Comp. (NOK)	.14
601.1-2.10 A1418 Job 0.50 Comp. (NOK) HFO	-.13
601.1-2.10 A1418 Job 0.20 Comp. (NOK) HFO	-.12
601.1-2.70 A1418 Comp. (NOK) HFO	-.11

-1   -0.5   0   0.5   1

Measured by Rank Correlation

Figure 7.14   Sensitivity chart for the aggregated savings of using IF 40 from the shipowner's perspective.

- From the shipowner's point of view, it is favorable to use MGO, except when the shipowner must pay the fuel *and* the previous points occur. This situation is only likely to occur when the vessel is on line-charter contracts.

In summary, for the shipowner, MGO is best in most cases (unless the charter group specifies something else). The only case where IF 40 will in general benefit the shipowner is when the vessel is on line-chartering *and* the IF 40 price is expected to be favorable.

It is important to understand that the way design decision A was investigated is not for procurement/design purposes in the sense that we did not try to find out what were the financial consequences of purchasing/installing machinery that used HFO. If that was the purpose, we should have used a discounting factor because the initial investment would be on the other end of the time-line than the operation costs and benefits. The purpose was rather to find out under what operating circumstances HFO is preferable to MGO on a general and continuous basis. If we had used discounting factors, we would have distorted the sensitivity analysis in

Figure 7.14, which would have led to erroneous conclusions regarding the critical operating factors. Thus, understanding the purpose of the LCC model is pivotal. Before we close this case, a few issues about risk management should be mentioned since any LCC inherently is about future profitability, which is associated with risks.

IDENTIFYING THE MAJOR OPERATIONAL RISKS

The most important point regarding risk management is that sensitivity charts are indispensable when it comes to identifying the risks because we should identify the risks in relation to the critical success factors and the overall objectives. Since the critical success factors will inevitably relate to the overall objectives, if the model is built correctly, it is sufficient to identify the risks of the critical success factors. Some of the critical success factors are operational risks in themselves because they produce cost variances such as fuel consumption.

For Farstad, Table 7.7 represents a compilation of the critical success factors found in the sensitivity charts as argued earlier, which can be used in conjunction with a group session with Farstad representatives to identify the risks for each of those critical success factors. Table 7.7 shows some of the risks related to three of the most critical success factors. Note that risks involve not only bad things happening but also good things not happening, as explained in Chapter 3.

Table 7.7 Three Most Critical Success Factors for the Shipowner's Aggregated Life-Span Profitability and Their Risks

Ranking	Cost/Revenue Contributors	Risks	Type
1	Daily revenue	• Contract is discontinued for various reasons. • Poor customer-relationship management inhibits contract extension.	Revenue
2	Capital cost	• Fixed interest rates inhibit interest rate reductions. • Market premium risk increases/decreases. • Farstad Shipping ASA beta increases/decreases. • Interest on long-term government bond increases/decreases.	Cost
3	Crew cost (included reimbursement)	• Social costs increase/decrease. • Wages increase. • Regulations require more employees.	Cost

The rest of what constitutes sound risk management practices can be done quite straightforwardly, as briefly explained in Chapter 3.

CLOSURE

The results from the Activity-Based LCC model include much more information than presented here. But the results presented *do* illustrate the comprehensiveness and the effectiveness of Activity-Based LCC, which is the main purpose of this chapter. That Activity-Based LCC works well should be beyond any doubt.

The big question that *may* arise after reading this case is why no discounting factors were used. Clues to the answer can be found in the the "Problem Statement and System Boundaries" section, where the twofold problem statement is presented. Basically, Farstad wanted a LCC model that would provide decision support concerning:

- The total costs of operating a PSV up to 10 years.
- Under what circumstances will machinery that runs on HFO be preferable to machinery that uses MGO?

The point is that both issues are related to the continuous operation of a PSV. In such a situation, we simply cannot discount the future because operational/management issues are continuous in character and the time value is consequently the same regardless of where you are in a timeline. That is, it is just as important to operate a PSV well in year 5 as in year 1 provided that Farstad is interested in being in business after year 5.

It is also important to find out how rapidly the industry is moving. The offshore shipping industry is a mature industry and one year in it is therefore not comparable to one year in a rapidly changing industry such as the IT industry. For Farstad, a lag of one month between costs and revenues does not warrant using discount factors except in extraordinary circumstances. Thus, what is continuous and what is not is a matter of industry characteristics and the relative size of the costs or the cash flows. All such issues should be considered when considering discounting factors. Be sure that the assumptions that accompany the usage of discounting factors represent the reality of the case.

In what kind of situation could discount factors rightfully be used? For Farstad, many investments (financial and real) can be supported by an Activity-Based LCC model, but it all boils down to whether a significant time difference exists between costs and revenues. For example, if Farstad decides to rebuild a PSV by changing machinery from using MGO to HFO, it would have an initial cost that must be recovered from a series of annual profitability improvements. Then it would be necessary to use a discounting factor because the company has spent resources today that will produce benefits for years to come. If Farstad simply wants to know how to increase its annual profitability, it would be wrong to use a discounting factor because then it would be a matter of improving the daily operation, a continuous activity where costs and revenues follow each other.

NOTES

1. I gratefully acknowledge the very good cooperation and financial support from Farstad Shipping ASA and Møre Research in Ålesund, Norway, that made the work presented in this chapter possible. I would particularly like to mention that unless I had been fortunate enough to be invited by Annik Magerholm Fet to participate in the project, I would never have had the opportunity to present this case in the first place. The project is described fully in A.M. Fet, J. Emblemsvåg, and J.T. Johannesen, *Environmental Impacts and Activity-Based Costing during Operation of a Platform Supply Vessel* (Ålesund, Norway: Møreforsking, 1996).
2. See, for example, J. Brown, "Copolymer Antifoulings: Look Beneath the Surface," *Propeller Direct* 3 (1), 1996, pp. 1–5.
3. For more information, see S.K. Bailey and I.M. Davies, "The Effects of Tributyltine on Dogwhelks (Nucella Lapillus) from Scottish Coastal Waters," *Journal of Marine Biology Association UK* 63, 1989, pp. 335–354, and A.R. Beaumont and M.D. Budd, "High Mortality of the Larvae of the Common Mussel at Low Concentrations of Tributyltin," *Marine Pollution Bulletin* 15, 1984, pp. 402–405.
4. Because something has no economic value does not imply that it is worthless in itself. It simply indicates that the current transactions in the economic system do not include it because there is no market for it.
5. There are 501 assumption cells and 65 forecast cells. The term *cells* is used because the model is implemented in MS Excel. A more generic term would be *variable*.
6. See, for example, K. Pedersen, J. Emblemsvåg, R. Bailey, J.K. Allen, and F. Mistree, "Validating Design Methods and Research: The Validation Square," the 2000 ASME Design Engineering Technical Conference, Baltimore, Maryland, ASME.
7. Due to the Central Limit Theorem, the common would approximately be a bell-shaped curve, a normal distribution.
8. P.F. Drucker, "The Theory of the Business." *Harvard Business Review,* September-October, 1994.
9. By running more simulations and eliminating the most dominant factors in each simulation, this table could have been expanded to capture all the 501 assumption cells.

8

ACTIVITY-BASED LIFE-CYCLE COSTING AT WAGONHO![1]

There are risks and costs to a program of action, but they are far less
than the long-range risks and costs of comfortable inaction.

John F. Kennedy

In Chapter 4, WagonHo! was discussed extensively within the context of identifying ways to improve the company. In this chapter, a complete Activity-Based Life-Cycle Costing (LCC) implementation for all WagonHo!'s products, and for the entire product life cycle, is discussed. That is, the Activity-Based LCC model will include all the stages shown in Figure 2.1 from manufacturing to use/service to downstream.

The primary purpose of this chapter is to illustrate how Activity-Based LCC can be implemented to cover an entire product life cycle. A simple case like WagonHo! is ideal for several reasons:

- Very few organizations are doing such exercises. Most organizations use LCC for procurement and design. A very limited number of for-profit organizations include end-of-life issues, as far as I know.
- A complete real-life case would have been too large and complex to comprehensibly present in a book format. For example, in one of the projects I worked on recently, the model had about 4,000 variables, 100-plus product lines, about 50 activities per manufacturing site, of which there were three, and so forth. The model provided detailed decision support for deciding between four major restructuring scenarios for a $150 million manufacturing company and several process and product outsourcing alternatives. Because of the complicated information system in the company combined with simulating the introduction of three new major product lines, we spent 14 days checking and tuning it, which is twice the normal time usually spent. Clearly, presenting such a case in a comprehensible manner to someone who does not know the company would be virtually impossible.

- The WagonHo! case has all the elements needed (multiple products, detailed process information, substantial overhead costs, and so on) to illustrate the points, yet it is simple enough to provide value to the readers.

Since WagonHo!, Inc. was discussed in Chapter 4, where much background information was presented, this chapter starts by reiterating some of the most important issues. It then discusses how to implement Activity-Based LCC and presents the results.

WAGONHO!'S NEW STRATEGY AND BUSINESS IDEA

WagonHo!, Inc. is a small toy manufacturer in the computers of the Center for Manufacturing Information Technology in Atlanta, Georgia.[2] It manufactures carts and wheelbarrows for children. Its products are high quality and cater to a market segment for children whose parents are well off. It has been facing hard economic times, mostly because it has not been able to manage its costs well, but after implementing a new strategy, it turned a $1.3 million loss into a $225,000 profit.

To further increase profits, the company decided to implement a totally new business idea. It was no longer going to just sell its products; it was also going to buy the products back in order to reuse and remanufacture the parts and recycle materials. That could potentially cut its material costs substantially and therefore make the company more profitable. An initial idea was to stop selling and instead lease its products, but this strategy proved too difficult for WagonHo! to finance at the present time. This strategy must therefore be adopted at a later stage.

Reusing and remanufacturing components and recycling materials are indeed interesting ideas, but what are the economic realities? How is the company going to implement the strategy? To provide decision support, the chief executive asked me to implement Activity-Based LCC, which is discussed in the next section.

As a first step, the company decided to keep products (including prices) as before, as shown in Figure 8.1:

- *CW1000 wagon*, referred to as CW1000. This is a wagon with four wheels and front steering.
- *CW4000 wheelbarrow*, which is denoted CW4000. This is a single-wheel wheelbarrow, without steering.
- *CW7000 garden cart*, which we simply call CW7000. This is a two-wheeled cart also without steering.

The products are mainly made of plastics, steel screws, and some wood. Since these materials are easy to recycle and possibly reuse depending on how they have been handled by previous owners, the main challenge is the take them apart (demanufacture or disassembly) fast enough to be economically viable.

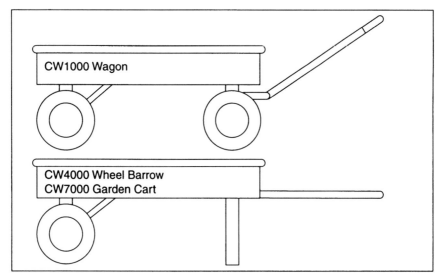

Figure 8.1 Products of WagonHo!

Later, however, redesign of the products may also become an option, but for now management realizes that it cannot make too many big changes. More details concerning products, the Bill of Materials (BOM), hourly labor rates, and so on were discussed found in Chapter 4.

DEVELOPING AN ACTIVITY-BASED LCC MODEL

The steps for implementing Activity-Based LCC models are given in Figure 5.1. In the following sections, each step is discussed in relation to WagonHo!

Step 1: Define the Scope of the Model and the Corresponding Cost Objects

Since WagonHo! has no experience concerning its new business idea, it is important that the Activity-Based LCC model provides decision support regarding the most uncertain issues. At the time of implementation, the most notable uncertainties were:

- What drives the profitability at WagonHo!?
- What products are profitable and why?
- What organization is needed to run the downstream operations after manufacturing?
- What are the risks associated with the new business idea?

To facilitate decision support of these issues and more, both a costing model and a cash flow model must be built. The reason for making a cash flow model is that during the transition phase, it is important to keep track of liquidity to avoid insolvency.

The Activity-Based LCC model implemented at WagonHo! is a *full absorption* model. That is, *all* the costs are traced to the products. Such full absorption models are particularly useful with respect to evaluating the pricing of the products.

To provide the decision support needed for the downstream operations, we must in addition to estimating the costs and profitabilities of the three products also assess the costs of the main processes, as depicted in Figure 2.1. These generic processes are:

1. Mining (raw material extraction)
2. Material processing
3. Product manufacture
4. Distribution
5. Use and service
6. Product take-back
7. Product demanufacture and disassembly, including the remanufacturing of reusable components and the reprocessing of recycled materials
8. Materials demanufacturing, including energy recycling, fuel production, and materials regeneration
9. Disposal

The first four processes are already covered in the standard ABC model presented in Chapter 4. The main focus of the Activity-Based LCC model is therefore processes 5 through 9 to the degree they are applicable. It is crucial to realize, however, that since the product properties are established early in the product life cycle yet have large consequences for the entire life cycle, the Activity-Based LCC model must include *all* applicable processes. To give decision support with respect to organizational issues, the model must therefore treat every activity as a cost object.

Step 2: Obtain and Clean Bill of Materials for All Cost Objects

The Bill of Materials (BOM) has been obtained (see Figure 8.2) where the CW4000 BOM is found. We see that only material costs and direct labor costs are included. Since no significant batch production is done at WagonHo!, we can use the direct labor estimates. In other words, cleaning the costs is not needed.

Model:			CW4000			Number of Components:			12
List Price									100
Net Price									88
Product				Parent	Part	**Num**		Unit	Ext
Num			Description	Num	Number	**Required**		Cost	Cost
4000			Wheel Barrow		CW4000				7.24
	4100		Bed	4000	CW1373	1	0.5	6.54	3.27
	4200		Screws	4100	SP4881	10		0.02	0.20
	4300		Wheel Assy	4100					2.28
		4320	Axle Bracket	4300	CW2019	2	1	0.87	0.87
		4330	Short Axle	4300	CW3626	1	0.5	0.18	0.09
		4340	Wheel	4300	CW2314	1	0.5	1.45	0.73
		4350	Cotter Pins	4300	SP6122	2	1	0.01	0.01
		4380	Raw Material - Wheel	4300	RM5784	1	0.25	0.78	0.20
		4390	Raw Material - Brackets	4300	RM5784	1	0.5	0.78	0.39
	4400		Leg/Handle Assy	4100					1.49
		4420	Handle	4400	CW3232	1	0.5	1.12	0.56
		4430	Leg Stand	4400	CW4240	1	0.5	0.95	0.48
		4440	Screws	4400	SP4881	6	3	0.02	0.06
		4470	Raw Material - Leg Stand	4400	RM5784	1	0.5	0.78	0.39
Direct Labor			Activity		Measured in	Price		Amount	Total
Kit Parts			A121		Minutes	0.12		12	1.46
Run Mill			A122		Minutes	0.15		56.0	8.40
Run Lathe			A123		Minutes	0.14		0.0	0.00
Assemble Product			A124		Minutes	0.13		30.0	3.90
Inspect Products			A125		Minutes	0.19		5.0	0.94
Direct Labor Costs								103	14.70

Figure 8.2 CW4000 BOM.

Step 3: Identify and Quantify the Resources

In a costing model, resources are defined as cost elements that are consumed by the performance of activities. To run the demanufacturing process, WagonHo! has hired five more employees: a supervisor and four workers (see Table 8.1). We see that by Year 3, all new people are fully employed at an annual expense of $121,800.

The new strategy will produce both negative changes in the cash flow as well as positive changes. The negative changes in the expense levels are shown in Table 8.2. The purchase of new equipment, for example, represents an increase in expenses of $65,000 for new equipment in Year 0. After the initial three-year period, the increased expense level for added equipment (due to the purchase of new equipment) depreciation and maintenance, as well as the new employees, will be $174,425.

But since materials and components are recycled, the benefits will start materializing when the old products are taken back and reused or recycled, which is discussed later. Thus, savings yield a positive cash flow and reduced expense levels, as shown in Table 8.3.

Finally, since a considerable amount of time takes place from when the initial investments are committed in Year 0 until the strategy is fully implemented, infla-

Table 8.1 Hiring Plan

Personnel	Year 0	Year 1	Year 2	Year 3
Supervisor	14,450	28,900	28,900	28,900
Truck driver		8,950	17,900	17,900
Worker 1		13,000	26,000	26,000
Worker 2				24,500
Worker 3				24,500
Total	14,450	50,850	72,800	121,800

tion could be included. However, the inflation will affect both expenses and savings in a similar fashion in this particular case, because the relative difference remains the same as before. To make life simple, inflation is therefore omitted.

The changes in expense levels combined with the old cost structure have produced the current cost base, as shown in Table 8.4, after the three-year transition period following the investment. Each cost element is broken further down into greater detail in the model to fit the activity definitions as closely as possible. In other words, the standard General Ledger, which is organized according to cost categories (depreciation, direct labor costs, indirect labor costs, rent, and so on) has been rearranged and become object oriented. This makes the distortion from the resource level to the activity level in the model as small as possible. More importantly, however, the object orientation makes process cost assessments easier and more accurate, and cause-effect relations are easier to identify.

The manufacturing costs were quantified using information from the BOM and the existing cost accounting system. The cost of demanufacturing resources is based on guesswork with respect to the kind of personnel needed and what processes and activities are needed to sustain a viable demanufacturing process. Even though this is guesswork, the point is that the Activity-Based LCC model makes it possible to investigate the consequences (costs and risks) and what the critical success factors are regarding the entire demanufacturing process. All equipment costs are handled as depreciation to which the annual maintenance costs have been

Table 8.2 Increase in Expense Levels

Expense Elements	Year 0	Year 1	Year 2	Year 3	Year 4	Year 5
Equipment	65,000	5,000	5,000	5,000	5,000	5,000
Buildings	47,625	47,625	47,625	47,625	47,625	47,625
Labor	7,225	50,850	72,800	121,800	121,800	121,800
Total expenses	119,850	103,475	125,425	174,425	174,425	174,425

Table 8.3   Saved Expenses

Savings	Year 0	Year 1	Year 2	Year 3	Year 4	Year 5
Saved energy		1,417	2,833	4,250	4,250	4,250
Materials savings		79,497	158,993	238,490	238,490	238,490
Total savings	0	80,913	161,827	242,740	242,740	242,740

added. The building is an aggregated resource that includes the annual gas and electricity costs. The resources in Table 8.4 also include all new employees.

In this case, it is important to notice that since the products are estimated to have an expected life in the market of three years before WagonHo! can take them back, there will be a transition period of roughly three years. Note that Year 0 appears two years after the new strategy has been implemented. The reason is that it takes three years before any products are taken back due to the life expectancy and the expiration of leasing contracts. To monitor this period, a cash flow model is needed to avoid liquidity problems.

The cash flow model is a comparative model; that is, it compares the cash flow of the new strategy to not implementing the new strategy, and not to the total cash flow in the company. This suffices in this case, and in most investment analyses, the baseline is the "do nothing" option. This is a commonly chosen baseline, but it is rarely the correct one because doing nothing has hidden implications. The reason is that the baseline is always moving; the business environment as well as the organization itself is always evolving, and doing nothing therefore means the

Table 8.4   Resources After a New Strategy Is Implemented

Resource Elements	Costs
Administration labor costs	490,095 ($/year)
Demanufacturing building	47,625 ($/year)
Demanufacturing equipment	12,275 ($/year)
Demanufacturing labor costs	98,680 ($/year)
Design equipment	3,500 ($/year)
Facility overhead costs	80,000 ($/year)
Logistics equipment	2,900 ($/year)
Manufacturing building	238,125 ($/year)
Manufacturing labor costs	1,102,226 ($/year)
Material, design	2,500 ($/year)
Material, maintenance	3,000 ($/year)
Material, production	246,260 ($/year)
Office equipment	45,650 ($/year)
Production equipment	46,570 ($/year)
Truck for take-back	8,000 ($/year)
Total	2,427,406 ($/year)

situation will get worse, as explained in Chapter 5's "Moving Baseline" section. For WagonHo!, however, the new strategy will most likely have a positive impact. Doing nothing as a baseline will therefore be a conservative choice because the future reality will most likely be better than today since WagonHo! has already undergone substantial positive changes the last two years, as discussed in Chapter 4.

Step 4: Create an Activity Hierarchy and Network

To create the activity hierarchy, we simply break down all the operations performed at WagonHo! and group them into activities. How to gather them depends on what is most useful in terms of data gathering, accuracy, process understanding, and so on. Consequently, an activity hierarchy can be created in different ways. The activity hierarchy developed for WagonHo! is shown in Table 8.5.

Table 8.5 WagonHo! Activity Hierarchy

Level 1	Level 2	Level 3
Manufacture products **A1**	Provide logistics support **A11**	Receive parts **A111**
		Run inventory **A112**
		Ship products **A113**
	Produce products **A12**	Kit parts **A121**
		Run mill **A122**
		Run lathe **A123**
		Assemble products **A124**
		Inspect products **A125**
	Design products **A13**	
	Sell products **A14**	Sell products **A141**
		Service customers **A142**
		Renew leasing contract **A143**
	Maintain facility **A15**	
Demanufacture products **A2**	Take-back products **A21**	
	Inspect products **A22**	
	Disassemble products **A23**	Remove fasteners **A231**
		Take products apart **A232**
		Sort components **A233**
		Clean good components **A234**
	Recycle materials **A24**	Send metals to recycler **A241**
		Incinerate nonmetal parts **A242**
Manage company **A3**	Lead company **A31**	
	Run production **A32**	
	Process orders **A33**	
	Manage costs **A34**	

It should be noted that based on earlier implementations, as shown in Chapter 4, some improvements have already been made. Basically, this model has been simplified in some respects. Note that because no costs are associated with using the products and no need exists for servicing them, no activities are required in the use and service process category.

In Figure 8.3, the activities in the gray shaded cells are linked together in an activity network but not necessarily in the order of the process. If possible, however, the actual process flow should be mapped in the activity hierarchy and network.

The main purpose of the activity network is to give a visual but simplified process view. It is important to relate the right products to the right activities in order to avoid errors. We see, for example, that CW1000 is the only product that uses the lathe. Similarly, in the demanufacturing process (activities A2xx), we see that following the clean good components activity (A234) a decision is made concerning what to do about the good components and the rest. The good components are sent to the kit parts activity (A122) from which they enter the production process. The rest of the material is recycled either by being sent off to a recycler (A241) or being incinerated locally (A242) to provide heat for WagonHo!, Inc.

Since the processes now include a demanufacturing process, more space must be rented in the Atlanta Technology Center. Studies indicate that roughly 20 percent more space is needed to facilitate the demanufacturing process. Figure 8.4 shows the new factory layout.

The factory is designed to minimize internal transportation needs, and as can be seen, virtually no internal transportation takes place other than moving products, components, or materials from one activity to an adjacent one. In other words,

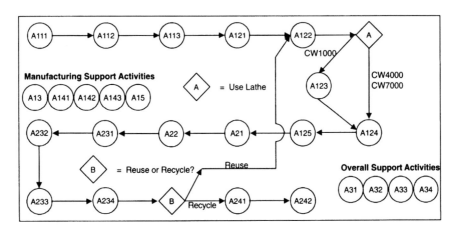

Figure 8.3 WagonHo! activity network.

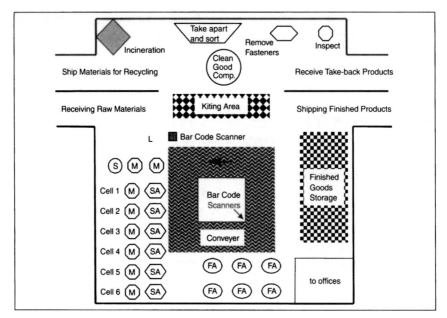

Figure 8.4 New factory shop floor.

WagonHo! does not need any internal, dedicated transportation system other than the conveyer system.

Step 5: Identify and Quantify Resource Drivers, Activity Drivers, and Their Intensities

Table 8.6 shows the resource drivers employed in the Activity-Based LCC model at WagonHo! Direct means that the resource element matches the activity completely. This is preferable since the associated distortion is zero. Area, which is a measure of the floor space, traces the consumption of the building. The larger the area a particular activity uses, the more building costs are traced to that particular activity.

The material costs, such as "material, production," are not traced to any activity because they are the material costs of the products. Finally, the facility overhead costs are allocated to the activities using activity labor costs as an allocation base. The reason that this is an allocation is that the facility overhead costs are not really related to the labor costs of the activities; it is just an arbitrary cost assignment. Hence, the words *allocation* and *allocation base* are used.

Similar to Table 8.6, Table 8.7 provides the details of the second stage of the cost assignment in Activity-Based LCC. Compared to standard ABC, we note that

Table 8.6 Resources, Resource Drivers, and Consumption Intensities at WagonHo!

Resources	Resource Drivers	Resource ($/year)	Consumption Intensity
Atlanta Technology Center:			
Manufacturing building	Area	238,125	14.39 ($/ft^2)
Demanufacturing building	Area	47,625	14.39 ($/ft^2)
Logistics equipment:			
Fork lift	Labor hours	2,900	1.53 ($/h)
Truck for take-back		8,000	
Production equipment:			
Conveyer system	Direct	5,100	
Disassembly equipment	Labor hours	5,275	1.00 ($/h)
Kiting equipment	Direct	270	
Lathe machines	Direct	3,500	
Milling machines	Direct	36,000	
Assembly equipment	Direct	1,050	
Incinerator	Direct	7,000	
Inspection equipment	Direct	650	
Design equipment	Direct	3,500	
Material, design	Direct	2,500	
Material, maintenance	Direct	3,000	
Material, production	*See BOM*	246,260	
Manufacturing labor costs	See *Resources*	1,102,226	
Demanufacturing labor costs	See *Resources*	98,680	
Administration labor costs	See *Resources*	490,095	
Office equipment:			
Computer systems	Acquisition Costs	39,500	0.23 ($/$)
Furniture and so on	Acquisition Costs	4,000	0.12 ($/$)
Reception	Number of Communications	2,150	0.03 ($/comm.)
Facility overhead costs	Labor costs	80,000	0.05 ($/$)

no cost pools exist other than the activities themselves. Also, many activities have two activity drivers. One is related to the variable activity consumption, such as labor hours, whereas the other is related to the fixed activity consumption, such as area usage.

It should also be noted that because production at WagonHo! is not automated or performed in large batches, many activity drivers are volume related. One might argue in such a situation that a volume-based costing system would suffice. The reality is, however, that the existing volume-based costing system does not provide correct enough cost assignments and is insufficient in providing decision support in terms of what to do about the situation.[2] Thus, even in a situation where the cost estimates of a volume-based system and an ABC system are the same, the ABC

Table 8.7 Activities, Activity Drivers, and Consumption Intensities at WagonHo!

Activity	Activity Driver	Total Activity Costs	Consumption Intensity	
A111	Annual comp. use	19,852	0.05	($/comp.)
	Annual production	5,755	0.21	($/unit)
A112	Annual production	9,425	0.34	($/unit)
	Annual comp. use	143,882	0.39	($/comp.)
A113	Annual products sold	20,157	0.73	($/product)
	Annual production	5,755	0.21	($/unit)
A121	Material cost	246,260		
	Labor hours	88,489	16.09	($/h)
	Annual production	14,388	0.52	($/unit)
A122	Labor hours	405,665	14.53	($/h)
	Annual production	14,388	0.52	($/unit)
A123	Labor hours	23,313	31.08	($/h)
	Annual production	14,388	0.52	($/unit)
A124	Labor hours	210,112	12.96	($/h)
	Annual production	14,388	0.52	($/unit)
A125	Labor hours	70,598	29.73	($/h)
	Annual production	14,388	0.52	($/unit)
A13	Labor hours	120,456	2.28	($/h)
	Annual production	1,439	0.05	($/unit)
A141	Number of batches	123,032	47.32	($/batch)
	Annual production	1,439	0.05	($/unit)
A142	Number of inquiries	115,430	21.38	($/Inquiry)
	Annual production	576	0.02	($/unit)
A143	Annual products sold	18,197	0.66	($/unit)
A15	Annual production	25,027	0.91	($/unit)
A21	Annual demfg. units	39,260	1.50	($/unit)
A22	Annual demfg. units	4,251	0.16	($/unit)
A231	Number of screws	38,888	0.09	($/screw)
A232	Annual comp. use	9,127	0.03	($/comp.)
A233	Annual comp. use	11,403	0.03	($/comp.)
A234	Annual comp. use	29,718	0.08	($/comp.)
A241	Number of screws	14,876	0.03	($/screw)
A242	Nonmetal costs	16,725	0.07	($/$)
	Annual demfg. units	7,000	0.27	($/unit)
A31	Number of comp.	64,626	1,292.52	($/comp.)
A32	Number of batches	211,902	42.38	($/batch)
	Annual production	2,158	0.08	($/unit)
A33	Annual products sold	90,323	3.25	($/unit sold)
	Annual production	1,439	0.05	($/unit)
A34	Total labor hours	157,472	2.99	($/h)
	Annual production	1,439	0.05	($/unit)

system would still be preferable due to its superior tracing capabilities, which are essential for providing decision support.

Step 6: Identify the Relationships between Activity Drivers and Design Changes

In this model, no explicit relationships exist between activity drivers and design variables. Potential product design changes, however, can be found by simply identifying the weaknesses of each product. The design team can then improve the design by eliminating or reducing these weaknesses. When it comes to process design and organizational changes, these are directly related to the activity costs and activity drivers, and thus they are always incorporated into an activity-based framework.

Step 7: Model the Uncertainty

Since WagonHo! embarks on a totally new strategy, it is difficult to say how sales will be affected. However, since prices will be a little lower, it is safe to assume that sales will not *decrease*. Thus, if sales are kept constant in the model, the model is conservative.

Due to the fact that cash flow is a particularly important issue in this case, it is necessary to model the uncertainty as realistically as possible. Then we can give sound predictions, or forecasts, about possible cash flow scenarios. The same benefits also apply to profitability and cost forecasts. How this can be done is explained extensively in the latter half of Chapter 3, and in Figure 8.5 two sample assumption cells are shown. The "Products that Can Be Demanufactured (%)" is chosen to be normal because such variables tend to be normally distributed and WagonHo! is quite confident that it will manage to demanufacture about 95 percent of the products it takes back on average. When it comes to the "Nonmetallic Parts that Can Be Reused (%)," it is much more uncertain. In fact, the management at WagonHo! does not even want to guess on a most likely outcome. Hence, a uniform uncertainty distribution is chosen. In other words, all we know is the degree of reuse concerning nonmetallic parts will be somewhere between 45 and 55 percent.

For the management of the company, however, it is more important to identify what drives costs and what are the critical success factors than to study the uncertainty in detail. To do that, another model is made where all the key input data are modeled as bounded and symmetric distributions. More specifically, the variables are modeled as triangular uncertainty distributions, where the upper and lower bounds are ±10 percent of the mean. The purpose of this is to perform sensitivity analyses and to trace the effects of changes.

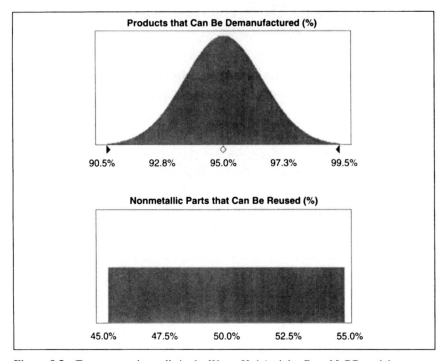

Figure 8.5   Two assumption cells in the WagonHo! Activity-Based LCC model.

Step 8: Estimate the Bill of Activities

The computation of the cost of activities is the first stage in the overall cost assignment process. Table 8.8 presents only the two first activities, but the rest of the activities are treated in the same way. Note that the leftmost columns, including consumption intensity, are the same as in Table 8.6.

Also notice that the lightly shaded cells in the spreadsheet, the assumption cells, are where the uncertainty is modeled. The darker cells are forecast cells whose responses, caused by the uncertainty in the assumption cells, are measured statistically. The last issue to notice is that for every activity, there is a set of activity drivers. The cost associated which each activity driver (for example, the costs associated with the annual component usage of activity A111 is $19,852) is input to the next stage in the cost assignment, which is discussed next.

Step 9: Estimate the Cost Objects' Cost and Their Performance Measures

The logic behind the second-stage assignment, which is the assignment of activity consumption from activities to cost objects (products CW1000, CW4000, and

Table 8.8 First-Stage Cost Assignment for the Two First Activities

Resources	Resource Drivers	Total Resource	Consumption Intensity	A111 Resource Driver	A111 Activity Cost	A112 Resource Driver	A112 Activity Cost
Atlanta Technology Center:							
• Manufacturing building	Area	238,125	14.39 ($/ft^2)	400.0 (ft^2)	5,755	10,000.0 (ft^2)	143,882
• Demanufacturing building	Area	47,625	14.39 ($/ft^2)				
Logistics equipment:							
• Fork lift	Labor hours	2,900	1.53 ($/h)	800.0 (h)	1,221	100.0 (h)	153
• Truck for take-back		8,000					
Production equipment:							
• Conveyer system	Direct	5,100					
• Disassembly equipment	Labor hours	5,275	1.00 ($/h)				
• Kiting equipment	Direct	270					
• Lathe machines	Direct	3,500					
• Milling machines	Direct	36,000					
• Assembly equipment	Direct	1,050					
• Incinerator	Direct	7,000					
• Inspection equipment	Direct	650					
Design equipment	Direct	3,500					
Material, design	Direct	2,500					
Material, maintenance	Direct	3,000					
Material, production	See BOM	246,260					
Manufacturing labor costs	See Resources	1,102,226		17,000		7,500	
Demanufacturing labor costs	See Resources	98,680					
Administration labor costs	See Resources	490,095					

(continues)

Table 8.8 First-Stage Cost Assignment for the Two First Activities (*Continued*)

Resources	Resource Drivers	Total Resource	Consumption Intensity	A111 Resource Driver	A111 Activity Cost	A112 Resource Driver	A112 Activity Cost
Office equipment:							
• Computer systems	Acquisition costs	39,500	0.23 ($/$)	3,000.00 ($)	685	5,000.00 ($)	1,142
• Furniture and so on	Acquisition costs	4,000	0.12 ($/$)	500.00 ($)	62	1,000.00 ($)	123
• Reception	No. of communi-cations	2,150	0.03 ($/com.)	2,500 (comm.)	80	4,800 (comm.)	153
Facility overhead costs	Labor costs	80,000	0.05 ($/$)	17,000 ($)	804	7,500 ($)	355
Total activity cost:		**2,427,406**	Activity drivers		**25,607**	Activity drivers	**153,307**
			Annn. comp. use		19,852	Ann. production	9,425
			Ann. production		5,755	Ann. comp. use	143,882

CW7000 in this case), is exactly the same as the first-stage assignment. The only differences are what is being assigned, how it is being assigned, and to what:

- In the first stage, resources ($) are assigned to activities using resource drivers.
- In the second stage, activity consumption (various measures of activity levels) is assigned to cost objects using activity drivers. Cost objects are therefore assigned costs *indirectly*.

With this in mind, we see the similarity between Table 8.8 and Table 8.9. Note that Table 8.9 should also include the two other products, cost objects CW4000 and CW7000, but due to space constraints this is not possible.

An additional performance measure in this model is the Net Present Value (NPV) of the cash flow. As explained earlier, in the current situation for WagonHo!, keeping track of cash requirements is important to avoid insolvency. It is also the chosen measure for the management at WagonHo! to decide whether to invest in the new business idea or not.

Note that at the bottom of Table 8.9 we see the deterministic results for WagonHo!, Inc. as a whole (to the left) and for CW1000 (to the right). The results should be used with care because they are deterministic. Basically, the results do not take uncertainty into account. To do that, we must run a Monte Carlo simulation, as discussed next.

Step 10: Perform Monte Carlo Simulations and Relevant Analyses

The Activity-Based LCC model for WagonHo! is modeled in commercially available software: MS Excel and Crystal Ball. The Crystal Ball software is employed to handle the uncertainty in the model and, more importantly, to trace the critical success factors. The Crystal Ball software performs the Monte Carlo simulations.

The sensitivity analysis measures statistically how the uncertainty of the different assumption cells affects the uncertainty of the forecast cells using rank correlation as measure. The assumption cells with the largest absolute magnitude of the correlation coefficient are the most critical success factors.

To provide more decision support regarding the use of their capital, Economic Profit (EP) has been implemented in parallel with the more standard Activity-Based LCC model. To do that, the Weighted Average Cost of Capital (WACC) must also be found. Other pertinent numerical analyses include the computation of the NPV of the net cash flow, but before that can be done, a discounting factor must be chosen. As argued in Chapter 5, WACC is a suitable discounting factor to use, and for WagonHo! it is 8.9 percent.

Table 8.10 shows the balance sheet of WagonHo!, and Figure 8.6 presents the computation of WACC. With respect to finding WACC only, the equity-and-debt

Table 8.9   Second-Stage Cost Assignment for the CW1000

Activity	Activity Driver	Total Activity Costs	Product: Consumption Intensity		Wagon CW1000 Activity Driver		Driver Costs	Activity Cost
A111	Annual comp. use	19,852	0.05	($/comp.)	65,000	(comp.)	3,535	4,058
	Annual production	5,755	0.21	($/unit)	2,500	(unit)	523	
A112	Annual production	9,425	0.34	($/unit)	2,500	(unit)	857	26,480
	Annual comp. use	143,882	0.39	($/comp.)	65,000	(comp.)	25,623	
A113	Annual products sold	20,157	0.73	($/product)	2,550	(product)	1,852	2,375
	Annual production	5,755	0.21	($/unit)	2,500	(unit)	523	
A121	Material cost	246,260					33,925	43,277
	Labor hours	88,489	16.09	($/h)	500	(h)	8,044	
	Annual production	14,388	0.52	($/unit)	2,500	(unit)	1,308	
A122	Labor hours	405,665	14.53	($/h)	4,583	(h)	66,602	67,910
	Annual production	14,388	0.52	($/unit)	2,500	(unit)	1,308	
A123	Labor hours	23,313	31.08	($/h)	750	(h)	23,313	24,621
	Annual production	14,388	0.52	($/unit)	2,500	(unit)	1,308	
A124	Labor hours	210,112	12.96	($/h)	1,875	(h)	24,306	25,614
	Annual production	14,388	0.52	($/unit)	2,500	(unit)	1,308	
A125	Labor hours	70,598	29.73	($/h)	292	(h)	8,670	9,978
	Annual production	14,388	0.52	($/unit)	2,500	(unit)	1,308	
A13	Labor hours	120,456	2.28	($/h)	8,000	(h)	18,268	18,399
	Annual production	1,439	0.05	($/unit)	2,500	(unit)	131	
A141	Number of batches	123,032	47.32	($/batch)	1,000	(batch)	47,320	47,451
	Annual production	1,439	0.05	($/unit)	2,500	(unit)	131	
A142	Number of inquiries	115,430	21.38	($/Inquiry)	2,000	(Inquiry)	42,752	42,804
	Annual production	576	0.02	($/unit)	2,500	(unit)	52	
A143	Annual products sold	18,197	0.66	($/unit)	2,550	(unit)	1,672	1,672
A15	Annual production	25,027	0.91	($/unit)	2,500	(unit)	2,275	2,275

(continues)

Table 8.9 Second-Stage Cost Assignment for the CW1000 (*Continued*)

Activity	Activity Driver	Total Activity Costs	Product: Consumption Intensity	Wagon CW1000 Activity Driver	Driver Costs	Activity Cost
A21	Annual demfg. units	39,260	1.50 ($/unit)	2,375 (unit)	3,569	3,569
A22	Annual demfg. units	4,251	0.16 ($/unit)	2,375 (unit)	3,569	3,569
A231	Number of screws	38,888	0.09 ($/screw)	40,000 (screw)	3,535	3,535
A232	Annual comp. use	9,127	0.03 ($/comp.)	65,000 (comp.)	1,625	1,625
A233	Annual comp. use	11,403	0.03 ($/comp.)	65,000 (comp.)	1,625	1,625
A234	Annual comp. use	29,718	0.08 ($/comp.)	65,000 (comp.)	1,625	1,625
A241	Number of screws	14,876	0.03 ($/screw)	40,000 (screw)	1,352	1,352
A242	Nonmetal costs	16,725	0.07 ($/$)	32,475 ($)	2,277	2,914
	Annual demfg. units	7,000	0.27 ($/unit)	2,375 (unit)	636	
A31	Number of components	64,626	1,292.52 ($/comp.)	26 (comp.)	33,605	33,605
A32	Number of batches	211,902	42.38 ($/batch)	2,500 (batch)	105,951	106,147
	Annual production	2,158	0.08 ($/unit)	2,500 (unit)	196	
A33	Annual products sold	90,323	3.25 ($/unit,sold)	2,550 (unit,sold)	8,300	8,431
	Annual production	1,439	0.05 ($/unit)	2,500 (unit)	131	
A34	Total labor hours	157,472	2.99 ($/h)	8,000 (h)	23,882	24,013
	Annual production	1,439	0.05 ($/unit)	2,500 (unit)	131	

Total product-related costs:	2,427,406				508,927
Total revenues:	2,715,913				494,802
Result WagonHo!:	288,507				−14,125
Product unit profitability					−6
Product unit profitability vs. result WagonHo!			−4.90 %		
Product unit profitability vs. product sales			−2.85 %		

Table 8.10 Balance Sheet of WagonHo!

Assets	Purchase value	Depreciation	Net value	Cost of Capital
Fixed capital				
Ford Taurus	17,500	17,500	0	0
Ford F150	20,000	20,000	0	0
Computer systems	105,000	70,000	35,000	3,123
Furniture and so on	17,500	7,000	10,500	937
Reception	6,000	2,000	4,000	357
Design equipment	30,000	12,000	18,000	1,606
Fork lift	10,000	6,000	4,000	357
Truck for take-back	15,000	3,000	12,000	1,071
Conveyer system	50,000	35,000	15,000	1,338
Kiting equipment	750	750	0	0
Lathe machines	30,000	21,000	9,000	803
Milling machines	320,000	224,000	96,000	8,566
Assembly equipment	5,000	5,000	0	0
Inspection equipment	1,500	1,500	0	0
Disassembly equipment	50,000	5,000	45,000	4,015
Incinerator	50,000	5,000	45,000	4,015
Sum fixed capital	**728,250**	**434,750**	**293,500**	**26,190**
Working capital				
Cash			74,678	6,664
Accounts receivable			171,591	15,311
Work in process			9,768	872
Inventory			10,572	943
Sum working capital			**266,609**	**23,790**
Sum assets			**560,109**	**49,980**

Debt and Equity	
Short-term debt:	
Credits	11,240
Short-term loans	97,565
Other	450
Sum short-term debt	**109,255**
Long-term debt:	
Long-term loans	157,654
Unpaid tax	24,750
Other	34,600
Sum long-term debt	**217,004**
Sum debt	**326,259**
Equity:	
Shares	233,850
Sum equity	**233,850**
Sum equity and debt	**560,109**

side of the balance sheet is used. That is evident from Figure 8.6, where we can see that we need data on the average cost of debt, both short-term and long-term, and the cost structure, which is found by dividing total equity by the sum of equity and debt, and likewise for total debt. In addition to those numbers, some macro-economic numbers are needed, such as the tax rate, the return on long-term government bond, the beta, which is 1 for WagonHo! because it is not a publicly listed company, and the market-risk premium.

The computations are:

- Cost of equity = long-term government bond + (beta × market-risk premium) = 13 percent
- Average cost of debt = ((avg. cost of short-term debt × sum short-term debt) + (avg. cost of long-term debt × sum of long-term debt)) ÷ sum debt = ((8 percent × $109,255) + (9 percent × $217,004)) ÷ $326,259 = 8.3 percent
- Avg. cost of debt after tax = (1 − tax rate) × avg. cost of debt = (1 − 28 percent) × 8.3 percent = 6 percent
- Cost structure, equity = sum equity ÷ sum equity and debt = $233,850 ÷ $560,109 = 41.8 percent
- Cost structure, debt = sum debt/sum equity and debt = $326,259 ÷ $560,109 = 58.2 percent
- WACC = (cost of equity × equity) + (average cost of debt after tax × debt) = (13.0 percent × 41.8 percent) + (6 percent × 58.2 percent) = 8.9 percent

Average cost of short-term debt	9.0 %
Average cost of long-term debt	8.0 %
Long-term government bond	6.0 %
Beta (market volatility)	1
Market-risk premium	7.0 %
Tax rate	28.0 %
Cost of equity	13.0 %
Average cost of debt after tax	6.0 %
Cost structure	
Equity	41.8 %
Debt	58.2 %
WACC	8.9 %

Figure 8.6 Computation of WACC.

Note that the 8.9 percent includes the newly purchased equipment. In general, the purchase of assets and financing them by loans is likely to decrease the WACC somewhat because equity normally produces a higher WACC than debt. The reason is that most investors expect around a 15 percent return on equity, whereas the interest on debt is usually less than 10 percent, at least in countries with a sound economic policy.

The side of the balance that lists the assets is used to compute the cost of capital, which could have been used to compute the EP, or the Economic Value Added (EVA), as Stern Stewart & Company in New York call it. For WagonHo!, the calculation would have been as follows:

WagonHo! operating profit, found in Table 8.9 = $288,507
− Taxes (assumed to be 28 percent)   = $ 80,782
− Cost of capital, found in Table 8.10   = $ 49,980
= Economic Profit (EVA)   = $157,745

An economic profit of $157,745, or 5.8 percent in terms of sales, is very good for WagonHo!, because as long as the EP is larger than zero it indicates that shareholder value is generated. We should, however, not be overly joyous concerning the result because WagonHo! is labor intensive and the cost of capital is consequently low. Also, since the cost of capital is so low compared to the annual profits, it is not necessary to include EP calculations on a product and process level. If we did, however, we would expect all products to become less profitable according to their use of capital, in which case the CW1000 would probably become more costly than the two others.

In any case, with a WACC of 8.9 percent, a time horizon of five years, and net cash flows, as shown in Table 8.11, we get an NPV of $81,012 (deterministically). This NPV suggests that the investment in new equipment and the process is worth pursuing because it provides a higher return than WACC.

RESULTS AND HOW TO USE THEM

Many results can be discussed from this Activity-Based LCC implementation. Since WagonHo! has made both an investment and a change of business strategy,

Table 8.11   Net Cash Flows and NPV

	Year 0	Year 1	Year 2	Year 3	Year 4	Year 5
Net cash flow ($/year)	−119,850	−22,562	36,402	68,315	68,315	68,315
Net present value ($)	81,012					

it is important to consider future risks and uncertainties as well as to understand what drives the performance, and that is done as follows:

- Cash flow and NPV
- Critical success factor of the NPV
- Activity costs
- Profitability and uncertainty
- Profitability and tracing

Concerning the profitability, all cost objects are discussed.

Cash Flow and NPV

The cash flow of the new strategy is shown in Figure 8.7. As is evident, the cash flow is mostly negative the two first years, but then positive the third year and onwards. Normally, the cash flow would not stabilize this year (after only three years), but in this case it does. The reasons are that new people are all employed by Year 3, all purchases are done in Year 1, and the conservative modeling (no sales increase) is used, even though prior to this WagonHo! made substantial changes that led to the products being more profitable.

The net cash flow in Figure 8.7 can also be used as a measure of risk because as long as the net cash flow is negative, a probability of loss exists. Most of the

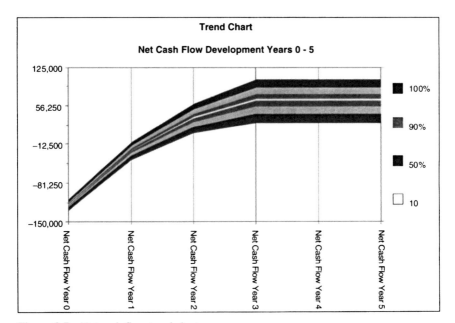

Figure 8.7   Net cash flow trend chart.

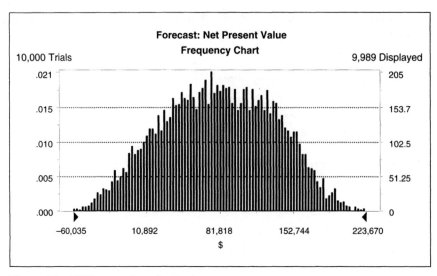

Figure 8.8 NPV uncertainty distribution.

Table 8.12 NPV 10 Percent Percentiles

Percentile	NPV ($)
0%	−74,775
10%	8,197
20%	31,169
30%	49,343
40%	66,068
50%	81,569
60%	97,530
70%	114,404
80%	131,784
90%	152,655
100%	225,296

time, luckily, is not associated with any risk. But to assess whether this cash flow is sufficient or not in generating enough positive cash flow, the NPV is computed.

Table 8.11 shows that the NPV is positive in the deterministic case, and from Figure 8.8 we can see the uncertainty distribution of the NPV. The NPV is clearly positive most of the time; that is, a small probability exists that the NPV will be negative. To better investigate the NPV, we turn to Table 8.12 where the percentiles are shown. Clearly, the probability of loss is a little less than 10 percent. The potential upside, however, is very substantial: If everything went as well as possible, the NPV would in fact reach about $220,000.

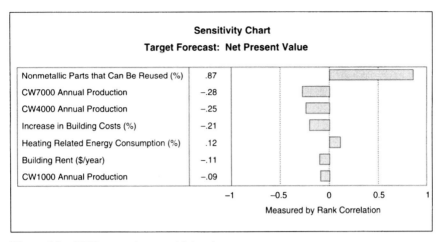

Figure 8.9   NPV uncertainty sensitivity chart.

The risk situation should be acceptable to WagonHo!, but to enhance the chances of doing better than the expected value (which is $81,569) the sensitivity chart in Figure 8.9 is used.

Using statistical sensitivity analyses and charts is an efficient, but most of all, effective way of keeping track of all the factors that are uncertain and that directly impact the cash flow. Interestingly, the single most important factor for the entire strategy in terms of the uncertainty of the cash flow is the degree to which the nonmetallic parts can be reused. The second factor that is uncertain in a positive way for the NPV is the degree to which energy is used for heating purposes. The higher degree of the energy bill that is used for heating, the better the cash flow is due to incinerating nonreused materials as an energy-recycling measure. It is also interesting to note that as the production levels increase, the NPV decreases. That is due to the fact that when production increases, the material costs increase and hence the NPV decreases. Also, an increase in the uncertainty in the production levels results in an increase in the uncertainty of the NPV because an increase in uncertainty will always result in a higher uncertainty regardless whether or not it is positive. The increase in building costs is a consequence of needing more area due to the new demanufacturing process and will therefore reduce the NPV.

In any case, the most important finding for WagonHo! is that the uncertainty of the degree of reuse is crucial for the overall cash flow uncertainty. If WagonHo! wants further insight into the future, it should consequently spend money on reducing the uncertainty concerning the reuse of components and materials. Then it could try to reduce the uncertainty regarding the production levels.

Next, the most important factors that determine the value of the NPV, or the expected value of the uncertainty distribution, are determined.

Critical Success Factors of the NPV

The critical success factors of the NPV are those factors that impact the value of the NPV, and these are presented in Figure 8.10. To put it another way, although the factors in Figure 8.9 determine the bandwidth (or degree of uncertainty) of Figure 8.8, the factors in Figure 8.10 determine the expected value of the NPV in Figure 8.8. The factors in Figure 8.10 are therefore critical when it comes to performance, whereas the factors in Figure 8.9 are critical with respect to uncertainty and risk in the sense of the unknown. The factors in Figure 8.10 are also important with respect to risk not in the sense of being unknown, but rather in the sense of being mismanaged or ignored.

Clearly, the degree of reuse is less important from an improvement point of view than an uncertainty and risk point of view, but it is still the largest factor by far and is therefore the most important in all respects. Hence, WagonHo! should probably introduce a Design for Manufacturing (DFM) and a Design for Disassembly (DFD) to redesign their products so that an even higher proportion of components and materials can be reused than suggested in their business plan. However, as the analysis shows, the plan is economically viable now.

This finding is further supported by the fact that the production levels are more important than believed, because a redesign effort may also have a positive impact

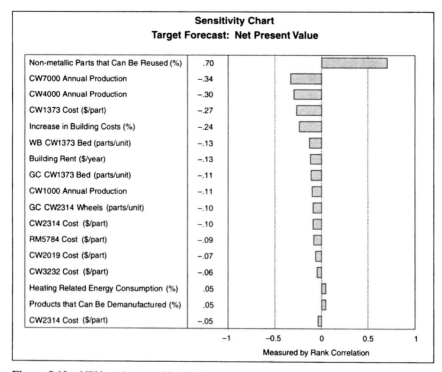

Figure 8.10   NPV tracing sensitivity chart.

on material costs. From Figure 8.10, we can even identify which components are most important to redesign, such as the CW1373 bed.

The last important thing to notice is that although the degree of heating-related energy consumption introduces large amounts of uncertainty into the model (refer to Figure 8.9), it is not an important variable because the rank correlation coefficient is only 0.05. Further work, if initiated, should therefore not include the issue of heating. It simply will not pay off, although it is a very uncertain issue.

The analysis so far suggests that the new strategy is an economically sound strategy in the sense that the cash flows and NPV will be satisfactory. In the next two sections, costs and profitability are discussed, but first the activity costs are discussed.

Activity Costs

All activity-based frameworks consist of two stages in the cost assignment. The activity costs are an intermediate stage when it comes to estimating cost and profitabilities of products, for example. However, the activity costs can provide a useful insight into business process reengineering, process design, and other process-focused efforts.

Figure 8.11 presents a profile of the activity costs that includes the uncertainty. Normally, it would have been organized according to descending activity costs, but in a simulation model that is not feasible. In any case, what we would normally look for are the highest costs, which in this case are associated with

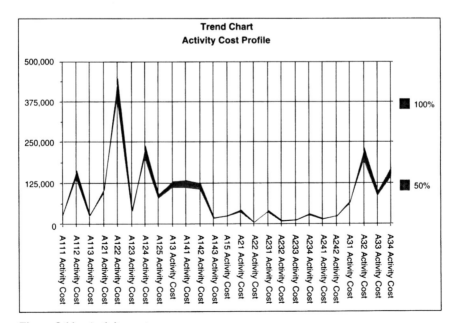

Figure 8.11 Activity costs.

Activities A122, A124, A32, and so on. Then we can investigate more closely whether ways exist for reducing the costs of all value-adding activities, such as A122 and A124. The nonvalue-added (NVA) activities such as A32 should ideally be eliminated. But everybody knows that we need some production management and other NVA activities. Anyway, Figure 8.11 is useful in identifying activities to start improving.

Often the sum of the activity costs for a certain process is different from what we might expect, based on the organizational chart. For example, many companies may have a few people in their organization working with taking orders from customers, but once the activity costs for that process are added up, the costs are several times larger than what those few people could cost. What is detected by the ABC system is that many people work with customers' orders in some fashion throughout the organization. Such costs are useful to identify because they are good indications of misallocated capacity, or most often they indicate that the system does not work as planned and that people have to make telephone calls and so on to correct errors, find missing information, and so on. For WagonHo!, a similar problem may exist because activity A32, run production, is very large: Is it sensible to spend over $200,000 annually on managing the production for such a small company? This may indicate severe system problems and further investigations should be undertaken.

Finally, it should be noted that the trend chart is somewhat misguiding in this context because it may look like there are costs between the activities. That is, of course, not the case. The reason for using a trend chart for this purpose at all is that it provides a simple overview of the activity costs.

Profitability, Uncertainty, and Risk

The most interesting profitability estimate for the management at WagonHo! is undoubtedly the overall profitability, which is the operating result of WagonHo! (see Figure 8.12). Evidently, the expected result is roughly $300,000 annually. That is good news for WagonHo! However, on one hand, Table 8.12 indicates that a small chance of loss exists, roughly 3 percent, while on the other hand, the upside is very substantial with a possible profitability of $600,000 according to Figure 8.12 and $709,000 according to Table 8.13. The reason Table 8.13 contains a wider range (from −$62,906 to $709,229) than the uncertainty distribution in Figure 8.12 ($0 to $600,000) is that the probabilities of the −$62,906 to $0 range and the $600,000 to $709,229 range are so minute that they are negligible.

From the previous discussion, it is evident that due to the inherent uncertainty of the matter, the possible uncertainty range of the WagonHo! result is almost $800,000. It is therefore useful to understand how to reduce this uncertainty and

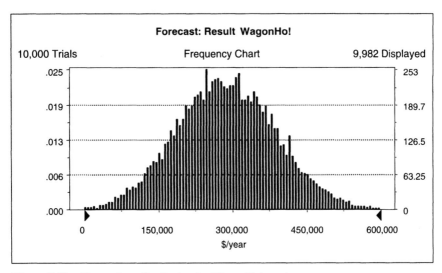

Figure 8.12 Uncertainty distribution for WagonHo! results.

Table 8.13 WagonHo! Result Percentiles

Percentile	WagonHo! Result ($/year)
0%	−62,906
10%	159,697
20%	202,760
30%	234,020
40%	261,087
50%	286,889
60%	313,449
70%	342,301
80%	373,811
90%	417,661
100%	709,229

manage the risks. That can be seen in Figure 8.13. We see that the six largest contributors to the uncertainty are all related to sales-related factors (price and sales volume). Unfortunately, we cannot do much about the prices because the market is the master, but we can try to manage the operational risks associated with the CW4000 production volume. One way of doing that is to ensure that, for example, the CW4000 has a production priority above the two other products.

Another risk is related to the sales rebates. We see from Figure 8.13 that if the sales rebates increase, the profitability decreases. Here we are in a classical dilemma. Salespeople are often rewarded based on volume because a substantial body of research from decades ago shows that a strong correlation exists between

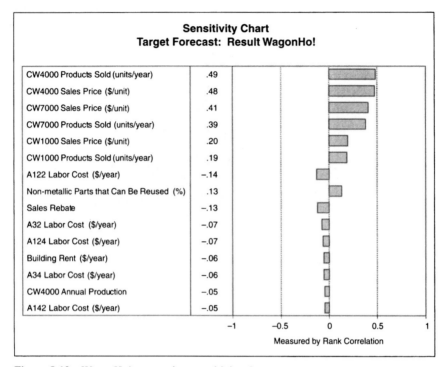

Figure 8.13   WagonHo!, uncertainty sensitivity chart.

market share and Return on Investment (ROI).[3] This has, however, been taken to the extreme in many cases, and the result is that salespeople push volume without thinking of profitability. To manage this risk, however, WagonHo! should reward salespeople using profit incentives and not volume incentives.

It might be tempting to reduce the uncertainty of such variables in the model in order to narrow down the forecast. However, if we reduce the uncertainty without reducing the real uncertainty, we increase the risks of making the decision support deceitful, and that can be a major decision risk.

Of the factors we can do something about, we see that the A122 labor cost is substantial, as is the degree of reuse of nonmetallic parts. The latter is also paramount for the NPV. Other important factors are the A32, A124, A34, and A142 labor costs. You may wonder how labor costs can be such important sources of uncertainty, but the fact is that costs, like quality, are statistical in nature. Just think of all the factors that may impact the labor costs: wage increases, overtime, layoffs, use of temporary employees, illness, and so on. All these factors are unknown prior to the cost estimation.

When costs are statistical on the aggregate level, imagine how much more statistical they are on the product level, which is evident from Figure 8.14. The costs

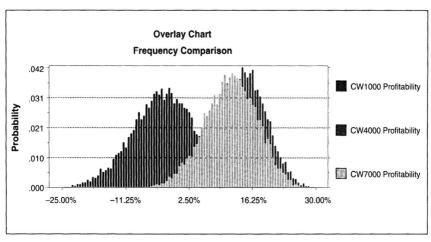

Figure 8.14 Product profitability uncertainty distributions.

on the product level cannot, as on the aggregate level, be simply summed up. The costs on the product level must first undergo a cost assignment process, as shown in the "Step 7: Model the Uncertainty" and "Step 8: Estimate the Bill of Activities" sections, which use resource and activity drivers, whose nature is also statistical. The entire cost assignment process is highly statistical combined with a statistical input (the resources that are measured as costs).

From this, we understand that to estimate costs with a single number is a major simplification that ignores the fact that costs are statistical. The result is that decision-makers overtrust or reject the cost estimates and instead use gut feelings as a gauge. Needless to say, when we have ways of presenting costs as they are, we should use them, because guessing about such important fundamentals of companies is gambling with shareholder values to an unacceptable extent.

In any case, the profitability of the products of WagonHo! are associated with substantial amounts of uncertainty. As Table 8.14 shows, if everything went really badly, all the products would go into the red (unprofitable). Luckily for WagonHo!, the probability of that occurring is small (less than 5 percent) for both CW4000 and CW7000.

According to Table 8.9, the profitability of the CW1000 is −2.85 percent in the deterministic case. However, from Table 8.14 we see that in fact a 30 percent probability of positive profitability exists, which should be good news for the management of WagonHo! A substantial downside must be avoided, however, and to do that the sensitivity chart in Figure 8.15 is helpful.

Finally, it should be noted that the CW1000 is also associated with the largest uncertainty range (43.54 percent). This indicates that the CW1000 is also the most

Table 8.14   Product Profitability Percentiles

Percentile	CW1000 Profitability	CW4000 Profitability	CW7000 Profitability
0%	−27.30%	−7.78%	−11.58%
10%	−11.80%	6.53%	4.27%
20%	−8.70%	9.09%	6.90%
30%	−6.55%	10.87%	8.82%
40%	−4.69%	12.45%	10.39%
50%	−3.02%	13.98%	11.89%
60%	−1.29%	15.35%	13.28%
70%	0.49%	16.75%	14.82%
80%	2.44%	18.39%	16.63%
90%	4.93%	20.52%	18.93%
100%	16.24%	30.17%	28.87%

difficult product to manage. In fact, the Japanese quality guru Genichi Taguchi devised a loss function where the variability of a factor is viewed as an important measure of quality. The larger the variability, the worse the quality, given the same expected value. Eliminating the variance in all significant processes is also a major objective in the successful Six Sigma approach, which is essentially a Total Quality Management (TQM) methodology that focuses heavily on statistical measures.

If we apply that idea to the CW1000, we soon understand that the CW1000 is inherently more difficult to make profitable, since costs are also statistical due to the higher uncertainty range than the two others. This, like earlier findings, supports the advice to significantly redesign the CW1000. Simply too many things can go wrong, which means that too many resources are spent ensuring that they do not go wrong, which ultimately leads to poor profitability.

So far, the uncertainty of the profitabilities has been discussed; next the underlying factors that determine the profitability is identified and discussed.

Profitability and Tracing

The operating result of WagonHo! is estimated to be around $300,000 annually after implementing the new business idea. The corresponding critical success factors that should be attended and managed are shown in Figure 8.15. It is strikingly similar to the uncertainty sensitivity chart shown in Figure 8.13. That indicates that the uncertainty surrounding the result of WagonHo! is not particularly great because the tracing sensitivity chart in Figure 8.15 appears by simply modeling all assumption cells in the spreadsheet as triangular uncertainty distributions with a ±10 percent uncertainty range, which is not much. This is also good news for the management team at WagonHo!, because it means that they do not need to worry about managing the uncertainty especially. They simply need to concentrate on managing the company, and the most important factors for that are found in Figure 8.15. The overall impression of Figure 8.15 is that WagonHo! needs to do mainly three things to improve the profitability:

1. Sell more product units. To increase the prices seems tempting, but given that they are already at the high end of the market, it is not smart to push prices further.
2. Reduce labor costs and/or increase the output, as mentioned previously. This can most easily be achieved if the products are redesigned to consume less direct labor. Other options may include process redesign, as mentioned in the "Activity Costs" section.
3. Increase the degree of reused nonmetallic components. Again, as mentioned many times already, the path goes through product redesign.

Finally, a factor in Figure 8.15 has not been mentioned at all so far. WagonHo! offers a 12 percent leasing rebate to its customers, which results in over $200,000 lost revenue annually. Are sales rebates really necessary? Since its customers are used to these sales rebates, it may be difficult to do anything about them at this stage, but once the products are redesigned, it will be easier to change the pricing strategy.

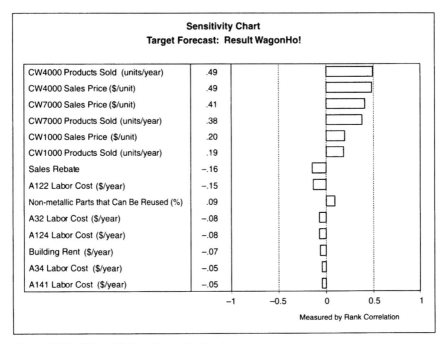

Figure 8.15 WagonHo! result sensitivity chart.

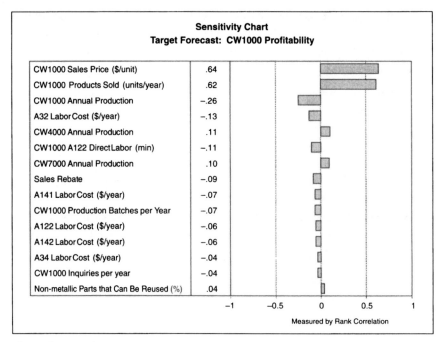

Figure 8.16 CW1000 profitability sensitivity chart.

Thus, the products must be redesigned also in order to change the leasing strategy to eliminate the use of rebates altogether. For that to happen, WagonHo! must most likely be capable of arguing that its new redesigned products are better than before. How that can be achieved is unclear, at least for the time being.

Due to the similarity of the products, it suffices to discuss the two extreme points: the most unprofitable CW1000 and the most profitable CW4000. The sensitivity chart for the CW1000 is shown in Figure 8.16. As expected, sales price and sales volume are the most important factors. The reason annual production turns out negative is that the model handles inventory changes and then an increase in production will result in reduced profitability because it is the number of units sold that counts. Of course, over time production and sales must match.

It is interesting to note that an increase in the production levels of the CW4000 and the CW7000 increases the CW1000 profitability. This is the good, old economies-of-scale effect; basically, the more units produced, the less overhead costs will be traced to each unit on average. Another interesting factor to note is the relatively low importance of the degree of reused components. This is due to two factors.

First, the CW1000 has many special components and screws that make reuse less feasible than for the two other products. Second, but more important, the other costs in Figure 8.15 are large and substantial, so the reuse of components there-

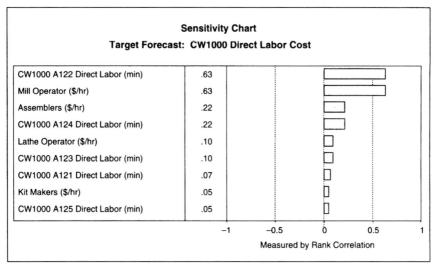

Figure 8.17   CW1000 direct labor cost sensitivity chart.

fore plays a *relatively* lesser role although substantial enough to result in an overall improvement of the WagonHo! result of roughly $75,000 annually. Many of the
labor costs are very substantial and significantly impact the profitability of the
CW1000 as is shown in Figure 8.16. These costs can be studied in greater detail
in Figure 8.17.

Three main sources for the costs exist:

1. The time it takes to manufacture the CW1000 is too long, particularly the milling
   activity (A122) and the assembly activity (A124). This is a further indication of
   the need to redesign the CW1000 completely both with respect to the way the
   parts are manufactured (milling) and the way they are joined (assembly).
2. The CW1000 uses too many overhead resources, particularly production
   planning and so on (A32). This is a result of the CW1000's complexity,
   which calls for product redesign via simplification.
3. The cost of the workers is important, but not easy to do anything about. The
   best that can be done is to try to automate some particularly time-consum-
   ing tasks. To do that, so-called action charts can be deployed,[4] as explained
   briefly in Chapter 5's "Step 3 Issues: Role of the General Ledger" section.

The reason for not using action charts in this particular implementation is that
the products need a complete redesign and not just improvements with respect to
some functions or tasks.

The most profitable product is, as stated earlier, the CW4000, and Figure 8.18
presents the corresponding sensitivity analysis. As usual, sales-related factors are

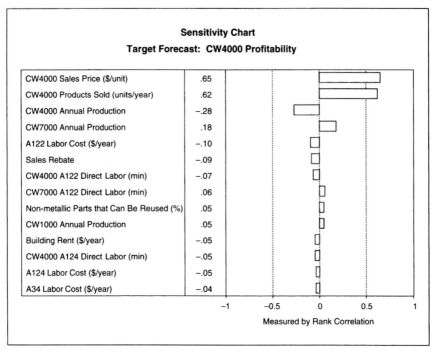

Figure 8.18   CW4000 profitability sensitivity chart.

crucial, but compared to the CW1000 sensitivity chart in Figure 8.16, we see three major and interesting things concerning the CW4000 in contrast to the CW1000:

1. It is relatively less labor intensive. The fact that the CW4000 is less labor intensive gives a direct improvement on the profitability because labor is a direct cost.
2. The degree of reused components plays a relatively more significant role. This means that the direct materials become less costly because they are reused to a significant extent.
3. The use of overhead resources is significantly less despite the absolute volume being several times larger (2,500 CW1000 units versus 14,000 CW4000 units). That the CW4000 production is more than five times larger also gives it a better economies-of-scale effect, which is of course highly beneficial for the unit cost of the CW4000, but not necessarily for the overall CW4000 cost unless the CW4000 is a simpler product, which it is in this case.

All in all, the CW4000 seems to be a much better product than the CW1000, although the price and traditional margin are less. The CW4000 goes through the company without any extra work, complicating parts, procedures, and so on, and that translates into lower costs and better profitability. The CW4000 is, however, also plagued by the sales rebate.

The CW7000 product is somewhat between the CW1000 and the CW4000 in most respects. That is important because it shows that if WagonHo! embarks on a total redesign of all products to eliminate complexities (to cut overhead resources), to reduce manufacturing times (to cut direct labor costs), and to make the products easier to disassemble and reuse (to cut direct material costs), the rewards will be positive. If it manages to redesign the products sufficiently, it may even get around the sales rebate problem, because sales rebates are often signs of products being not quite what customers want. The potential for the WagonHo! result will be, in other words, much better than what it is today. By implementing the new business strategy and then embarking on the redesign program, as shown in this this Activity-Based LCC analysis, major profitability improvements can be made.

CLOSURE

This case study is special since it concerns a simulated company and not a real one. On one hand, this has bearing on the reliability of both the input information and the way the output from the model is interpreted. On the other hand, the case study is illustrative enough to point out several issues concerning LCC in general and Activity-Based LCC in particular. For this book, the latter is more important than the former, particularly as other real-world case studies are presented elsewhere in the book. In any case, what can be learned from this case study is worth discussing, and that is done in the next two sections.

LCC in General

As explained in Chapter 2, most LCC approaches are not costing methods but cash flow methods. In this case study, both a cash flow analysis and a costing analysis have been conducted.

The cash flow analysis is clearly useful in that it provides insight concerning liquidity, the NPV of the investment, and the financial risk exposure. It cannot, however, provide any insight in the profitability of the products, the company as a whole, or the underlying success factors. In this case, as often, the success factors of cash flows and operating profits are somewhat related. Both the costing analysis and the cash flow analysis point out the degree of reuse as relatively important, although it is relatively much more important for the cash flow than the operating costs; however, the cash flow analysis totally misses the labor costs and most of the overhead costs.

This goes to show that a cash flow analysis will not, and cannot, substitute for a costing analysis. Unfortunately, many, particularly in the environmental management domain, believe that cash flow analyses *are* costing analyses. As shown here, they are not. The consequences of that misinterpretation are that significant areas of improvements *can be* missed.

One may, however, argue that the cash flow analysis in this case study was only comparative and not absolute; that is, not all cash flows were incorporated in the model. That is true in the sense that if all cash flows were incorporated, the cash flow model would have had a wider scope, but many costs are simply not represented by cash flows and would have been missed in any case. Also, costs represent the demand for jobs to be done, whereas cash flows represent some of the capacity for doing the jobs. Good management practice is to match capacity to demand, and that cannot be achieved by a cash flow model.

Several Features of Activity-Based LCC

This case study is complex enough to illustrate several novel features about Activity-Based LCC that cannot be shown when only one cost object is discussed. First, Activity-Based LCC can handle multiple products and other cost objects simultaneously. This is absolutely necessary if overhead costs are to be given credible attention. Most LCC analyses either forget overhead costs altogether or grossly mistreat them. It is also shown that the profitability of one product is closely intertwined with the performance of another product. See, for example, Figure 8.16 where the production volumes of the CW4000 and CW7000 impact the CW1000 profitability almost to the same extent as the CW1000 production volumes. Performing an LCC product by product introduces large distortions but, as shown here, Activity-Based LCC overcomes such problems.

Second, Activity-Based LCC can address the entire cost structure of the company and any other cost objects. Even the cost of capital can be introduced, as shown here. Whether or not to include the cost of capital issues should be decided from a cost/benefit perspective. If the cost of capital is large, this must be included; however, for WagonHo!, that is not the case.

Third, due to the inherent flexibility of activity-based approaches, a number of specialized analyses can be done easily . For example, cash flow analyses can be easily incorporated because the basic information already exists in the system. To put it another way, it is far easier to make a cash flow model using a costing model as a basis than vice versa. Our case study also showed how economic profit considerations can be included.

Fourth, the use of uncertainty distributions and Monte Carlo simulations offers an unconstrained flexibility in handling uncertainty and risk, along with a greatly enhanced tracing capability using statistical sensitivity analyses. In this way, uncertainty can really become a manager's or an engineer's best friend, and not just because uncertainty is used by will in Monte Carlo simulations. More importantly, since costs are statistical in nature, making precise cost estimates is not only a waste of time but is actually wrong and deceptive. As Zadeh's Law of Incompatibility states (see Chapter 3):

> *As complexity rises, precise statements lose meaning and meaningful statements lose precision.*

From this discussion, it is evident that Activity-Based LCC eliminates many problems that other LCC methods either cannot address or overly simplify or completely mistreat. This was shown in the case study, and it is the rule rather than the exception.

NOTES

1. I would like to thank research engineer Greg Wiles at the Center for Manufacturing Information Technology in Atlanta for his cooperation and the data he provided, which made this case possible.
2. This has been discussed extensively in J. Emblemsvåg and B. Bras, "ISO 14000 and Activity-Based Life-Cycle Assessment in Environmentally Conscious Design and Manufacturing: A Comparison," 1998 American Society of Mechanical Engineers (ASME) Design Engineering Technical Conference, Atlanta, GA.
3. According to F. Allvine, *Marketing: Principles and Practices,* Boston, MA: Irwin/McGraw-Hill, 1996.
4. See, for example, J. Emblemsvåg and B. Bras, "The Use of Activity-Based Costing, Uncertainty, and Disassembly Action Charts in Demanufacture Cost Assessments," 1995 American Society of Mechanical Engineers (ASME) Advances in Design Automation Conference, DE-Vol. 82, Boston, MA, pp. 285–292.

9

FROM HINDSIGHT
TO FORESIGHT

It's better to begin in the evening than not begin at all.

English Proverb

Life-Cycle Costing (LCC) is a tool for engineers, managers, and others who care about downstream costs and total costs. As with most tools, the success of LCC models is the result of balancing understanding on the one hand and craftsmanship on the other. I have tried to find a suitable balance in order to avoid lengthy discussions about academic differences and also to avoid presenting many examples with little reflection and insight. Experience without reflection is not worth much; in fact, it can be outright dangerous. As Confucius said (*The Analects*, 2:16):

Study without thinking, and you are blind; think without studying, and you are in danger.

Thus, some theoretical foundation is clearly needed to clarify what LCC is and what it should be, what the difference is between traditional LCC and Activity-Based LCC, and so forth. Similarly, the three cases were chosen to complement each other and to complement the presented theory as well. This book should therefore provide a practical guide to a new, powerful method of conduction LCC, risk management, and uncertainty analysis that opens up many new avenues for engineers, managers, and others.

ACTIVITY-BASED LCC REVISITED

Activity-Based LCC is in many ways a synthesis of Activity-Based Costing (ABC), LCC, and Monte Carlo methods. In fact, Activity-Based LCC can be described in terms of three layers, as shown in Figure 9.1.

These layers have great implications for the characteristics, the benefits, and the pitfalls of Activity-Based LCC. These issues are discussed in the three subsequent sections.

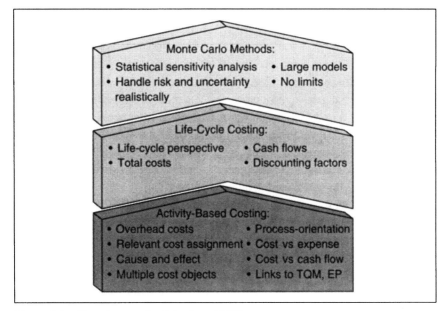

Figure 9.1   Three layers of activity-based LCC.

Characteristics

Characteristics refer to what is novel about Activity-Based LCC, both in relation to traditional cost management as a whole and to traditional LCC approaches in particular. As already discussed, these characteristics are closely linked to the three layers of Activity-Based LCC, as shown in Figure 9.1.

Activity-Based LCC and ABC

As the name implies, Activity-Based LCC is an offspring of ABC. It shares the common characteristics of ABC on the conceptual level, that is, the use of:

- Activity definitions to model the value chain and to report process costs.
- Resource drivers to trace how activities consume resources.
- Activity drivers to trace how cost objects consume activities.
- Cost drivers to measure nonfinancial process performance.

Chapter 4 explained in detail what these similarities imply. This chapter will concentrate on the differences. The two major differences are explained in the following two sections. In addition, other differences revolve around the focal point of implementation.

In ABC implementations, the cost of the cost objects is often the focal point. The inclusion of the process perspective and the definition of the drivers are viewed as hurdles to overcome in order to get to the results. In Activity-Based LCC, however, it is almost the opposite. True, the cost of the cost objects is important, but since they often are associated with significant uncertainties, ballpark answers are usually good enough. The definition of the drivers, however, is crucial because they allow us to identify the critical success factors, which are important for most design and management processes. The process perspective is also important in Activity-Based LCC as we try to predict the future, and many processes materialize in the future. Understanding the costs of future processes can therefore be very useful information, for example, when planning future organizational capacity. In fact, understanding the processes and their cause-and-effect relationships are crucial for good forecasting.

It is not that these issues are unimportant for standard ABC implementations, but they rarely get the attention they need because ABC is often employed as just another cost-cutting tool.[1] In Activity-Based LCC, these largely ignored aspects of ABC play a more crucial role due to their ability to predict and understand future costs and risks. In other words, while ABC is a backcasting tool, Activity-Based LCC is a backcasting *and* a forecasting tool, and that requires a different focal point: from an accurate calculation and interpretation of past costs and events to an approximate prediction and understanding of future costs and risks based on an understanding of the processes and their cause-and-effect relationships to both cost objects and resources.

Activity-Based LCC and Traditional LCC

The only aspect of traditional LCC that Activity-Based LCC shares is the idea of estimating costs throughout the life cycle of a system. Other than that, the two approaches are different. We can at least identify five major differences:

1. Activity-Based LCC handles both costs and cash flows.
2. It is process oriented.
3. It relies on the establishment of cause and effect relationships.
4. It handles overhead costs.
5. It estimates the costs of all cost objects of a business unit simultaneously.

First, traditional LCC often is cash flow oriented, and Activity-Based LCC handles both cash flows and costs. It should, however, be noted that cash flow analyses have a limited scope and hence need not be activity-based to provide relevance.

Second, traditional LCC is structure oriented and hence follows the traditional cost breakdown, that is, variable cost, fixed costs, and costs organized according to functions, attributes, or characteristics. Activity-Based LCC, however, is purely process oriented and variable, and fixed costs have a different meaning (see Glossary) because the traditional interpretation of fixed and variable costs is meaningless in activity-based frameworks.

Third, traditional LCC does not emphasize the need for establishing cause-and-effect-relationships to the extent that Activity-Based LCC does. This is partly a consequence of the fact that traditional LCC is not process oriented. Therefore, identifying cause-and-effect relationships is limited to issues such as material and labor costs and product characteristics. Activity-Based LCC, in contrast, is systematically built up from definitions of activities, resources, and cause-and-effect relationships (resource drivers, cost drivers, and activity drivers). Needless to say, this gives an entirely different push toward understanding the cause-and-effect relationships.

Fourth, traditional LCC ignores overhead cost. This was not a major problem in the 1960s when it was invented by the U.S. Department of Defense, but today when many companies face 30 to 40 percent overhead costs, the need for handling such costs is obvious. Handling overhead costs realistically is one of the strong sides of Activity-Based LCC and other activity-based frameworks. The fact that traditional LCC ignores overhead costs makes it less useful as systems today become increasingly capital intensive and require more support.

Fifth, traditional LCC is incapable of handling several products at the same time. This is because it is rarely attempted, but more importantly because traditional LCC is unable to handle overhead costs realistically, it simply cannot handle multiple products. The problem with this product-by-product approach is that it can, and often does, lead to suboptimization. Although the products may have a satisfactory life-cycle cost when estimated in isolation, when put together, the overall product line, product family, or product portfolio will have an unnecessary complexity in terms of unique parts and practices and is therefore still too costly. For Activity-Based LCC, handling many products is no problem at all. In fact, activity-based frameworks are rarely used on a single product because that would be overkill. That said, it should be mentioned that the process perspective of activity-based frameworks adds value that the traditional concepts cannot, as shown in this book.

Traditional LCC has many shortcomings that make the concept increasingly unsuitable for management purposes and engineering. For example, as technologies grow increasingly complicated, the need for support and capital increases. The time when engineers could design a system or product without giving much thought to the impact on overhead costs is gone. Likewise, the inability of traditional LCC to establish cause-and-effect relationships renders it incomplete in providing relevant decision support. Thus, I feel confident in claiming that the characteristics of Activity-Based LCC outlined previously clearly indicate that it is a more effective and efficient approach than traditional LCC. In fact, due to the aforementioned five characteristics, the use of Monte Carlo methods becomes much more potent than it would otherwise be.

Activity-Based LCC and Monte Carlo Methods

Activity-Based LCC can work effectively without any Monte Carlo simulations, but it would be less efficient. The Monte Carlo methods are, in many ways, the turbo of Activity-Based LCC.

The handling of uncertainty would be much more troublesome without the Monte Carlo simulations since the uncertainty distributions used to model the uncertainty are numerically approximated. To perform numerical approximations manually is basically too tedious work.

However, a more important factor that ties Activity-Based LCC to Monte Carlo methods is the fact that without Monte Carlo simulations to trace the critical success factors, it would be practically impossible to use statistical sensitivity analyses. The identification of the critical success factors is crucial because they are basically the significant cause-and-effect relationships, and it is important to understand these in order to continuously improve the performance of the cost objects and manage visits.

Having said that, it is important to emphasize that without the characteristics of Activity-Based LCC outlined in the previous section, the use of Monte Carlo simulations would be less potent. Other methods use Monte Carlo simulations, but they lack its sting as the underlying structure of the models is traditional and hence subject to the limitations pointed out previously. This is not to say that such models and applications of Monte Carlo are inferior; they are simply limited to a smaller area of application.

Activity-Based LCC and Monte Carlo methods therefore mutually reenforce each other. They offer a great way to harness the benefits of uncertainty for the good of decision-support relevance. As we saw in the review of LCC approaches in Chapter 2, most LCC approaches lack a powerful way of handling uncertainty and have diminishing relevance to decision support. This is a natural consequence of technological development, which has increased overhead resource use, which in turn makes it necessary to handle all products and the entire organization in LCC. Traditional LCC simply cannot match Activity-Based LCC.

Benefits

The "absolute" benefits of Activity-Based LCC arise from the individual characteristics of Activity-Based LCC as well as their totality, whereas the benefits of traditional LCC are due to the five differences explained in the "Activity-Based LCC and Traditional LCC" section. Since this book is about LCC and not cost management in general, the discussion will be limited to benefits in comparison to traditional LCC.

In the literature, many practitioners and researchers discuss cash flow and costs as if they were the same thing. Cash flow and costs are, however, different, as explained in Chapter 2. Cash flows concern liquidity, financial measures, and financial risk exposure; they are therefore important in cases where a significant time difference exists between expenses and revenues. Costs, however, concern resource consumption and determine the profitability for a given level of revenues. Naturally, it can be useful to present both perspectives in order to provide decision-makers with wide support regarding liquidity, net present value, profitability, and other important economic measures of performance. Activity-Based LCC facilitates both perspectives. This versatility makes the approach useful in a wide array of economic considerations even beyond life-cycle thinking.

The process orientation of Activity-Based LCC ensures a close link to other well-established process-oriented methods, such as Business Process Reengineering (BPR), Total Quality Management (TQM), Six Sigma, and so on. Moreover, the process orientation is important because we cannot manage costs directly; we can only manage them indirectly, by understanding how the activities (processes) impact costs, as explained in Chapter 4. Also, process orientation has numerous more subtle benefits that are beyond the scope of the discussion here.[2]

The primary need for process orientation is to establish reliable cause-and-effect relationships. Process orientation would be worth little if it were not for the fact that causes are almost by definition found in the production processes, the work processes, or the management processes. The reliance on cause-and-effect relationships is crucial because it ensures accuracy and, more importantly, relevance. After all, we cannot find a root cause unless we have some ideas about causes and effects. We can measure the effects, but it is the causes we must manage. The benefits from this characteristic are numerous: They include accurate cost assignment, accurate cost estimates, the correct handling of overhead costs, the tracing of critical success factors/root causes, a clearer understanding of the underlying causes of cost formation, and superb forecasting capabilities. Activity-Based LCC is an attention-directing tool. Unless attention is paid to the causes, relevant decision-support information will never materialize. Thus, the systematic usage of cause-and-effect relationships is at the very core of effective and efficient design and management.

Due to the rapid increase in technology fueled by modern capitalism and technological innovations, the whole economy is changing to what many refer to as a "knowledge economy." The capital base of a company including intellectual capital is becoming an increasingly larger part of the company's wealth. For example, even though the book values of IBM and Microsoft are *only* $16.6 billion and $930 million, respectively, their market values are $70.7 billion and $85.5 billion.[3] The difference can largely be attributed to the perceived value of their intellectual capital and its ability to generate future profits. The effect of these changes on all forms of cost management is that it has become increasingly important to understand the formation of overhead costs and assign such costs to cost objects. Otherwise, decision-making would be based on an increasingly smaller part of the total picture, thus increasing the risk of deceptive analyses and erroneous conclusions. Activity-Based LCC is tailor-made in this respect because its root, ABC, allows the effective handling of overhead costs, as discussed in Chapter 4.

Overhead costs are like a big clump of gel on top of the processes in an organization. By simply removing a product or an activity without any further reduction in the overhead costs, the gel will simply flow over onto the remaining products and activities. This is the malaise of the traditional approaches; they simply focus on the direct costs and ignore the overhead costs. Similarly, estimating the cost of a product in isolation to the other products induces gross errors because every product in an organization is ultimately related to the other products in that they share a common overhead cost structure and processes. Activity-Based LCC avoids such problems by estimating the costs for all products and all activities in a given business unit at the same time. Thus, we get the whole picture established simultaneously and no room is left for costs to hide (at least in principle).

These benefits translate into a profound advantage, namely, the fact that Activity-Based LCC provides decision-makers with the relevant information they need to make better decisions. Traditional cost management and traditional LCC are both too fragmented to provide relevant decision support. Activity-Based LCC incorporates all costs, all cost objects, all activities, and the entire business unit—basically, a complete cost picture.

We have all heard the story about the group of blind people who tried to describe an elephant. Each person felt a different part of the animal and had a different fact about it. It was only when these facts were combined that the full picture could be seen. Activity-Based LCC provides the sight, but the decision-makers must decide what to do about what they see.

Disadvantages and Pitfalls

As we have seen, Activity-Based LCC has many benefits, but it also has pitfalls and disadvantages. One disadvantage is that Activity-Based LCC requires more data than the traditional LCC approaches. The reason is that Activity-Based LCC handles all products in one model and it always includes a complete process perspective. Another is that even though it is more logical than other LCC approaches, it is easier to get lost during the implementation because it is important to strike a suitable balance between the level of detail and the usefulness of the details, which is not always that easy.

In fact, one of the greatest pitfalls of activity-based approaches in general is the ease of designing very accurate models. But it is important to resist the temptation of indulging oneself in accuracy because excessive accuracy often comes at the expense of usefulness, costs, and even *true* accuracy. We simply must accept that an inherent uncertainty exists in both the model and the numbers in the model. Making a model more accurate than what is reasonable only makes the model more deceptive.

It is important is to put time and effort into defining the activities—the resource drivers and activity drivers— in order to provide as much useful information as possible to reduce the inevitable distortion in the model. This can best be achieved by having drivers and activities that match one to one so that the need for a driver is eliminated. The drivers that are needed should follow cause-and-effect relations. Naturally, not all costs and activities can be well matched to driver definitions. In my opinion, it is good enough if such allocations constitute less than 5 percent of the costs. Sometimes we can be even less precise; this depends on the complexity of the organization and the available data. Thus, as with most methods, it is necessary to use good judgment to produce good results and avoid the famous "garbage in, garbage out" syndrome.

Another potential pitfall is the failure to understand the effect of randomness on the statistical sensitivity charts. Monte Carlo simulations produce a lot of numbers, according to some input constraints and the model relationships, that are handled statistically to produce the sensitivity charts. A side effect is that, in the bottom of the sensitivity charts, many factors appear that are statistically insignificant. Basically, they either should not appear or they have appeared with the wrong sign. As a rule of thumb, only rely upon factors with a rank correlation coefficient of 0.05 or larger. This avoids the whole problem.

IDEAS FOR THE FUTURE

Predicting the future in terms of costs and risks should by no means be limited to LCC exercises. In fact, I believe it should become the standard in both budgeting/prognosis making and cost management. After all, would it not be smarter to eliminate costs before they are incurred than to try to cut them afterwards?

Looking ahead is always an interesting exercise. After writing this book, I realized that there is even more to the idea of combining ABC with other concepts than described here. Activity-Based LCC is, as the name indicates, an LCC approach, but what is really the core difference between LCC and budgeting?

Many companies waste substantial amount of resources every year trying to figure out how to allocate next year's capacity. Even worse:

Corporate budgeting is a joke, and everybody knows it. It consumes a huge amount of executives' time, forcing them into endless rounds of dull meetings and tense negotiations. It encourages managers to lie and cheat, lowballing targets and inflating results, and it penalizes them for telling the truth. It turns business decisions into elaborate, exercises in gaming. It sets colleague against colleague, creating distrust and ill will. And it distorts incentives, motivating people to act in ways the run counter to the best interests of their companies.[4]

Often the whole budgeting exercise is a simple increase from last year's budget by some percentage points. Some of the most progressive companies have already left the old ways of doing budgeting and embraced a new forecasting-oriented approach where the company only estimates capacity for the next quarter or so. However, the basic problem is more or less the same, namely, that we chase numbers about future issues based on hindsight. One advantage of the new approach is that it makes it easier to update the prognoses because we only forecast one quarter at a time. This is definitively a step forward for industries undergoing rapid change. The main problem, however, persists: Errors in budgeting will only be detected when it is too late, and cost management becomes a matter of damage control.

If we use the ideas presented in this book, we can greatly reduce the chance of budget errors and unforeseen financial troubles. The overall objective of a budget is to ensure that economic and financial goals are met. In the traditional budgeting world, this is achieved by controlling spending, or so it is believed. The problem is that a company is an open system that interacts with an environment where changes are frequent and surprises lurk around the corner. The greatest obstacle to reaching budgeted goals is not a company's control of spending, but rather its lack of control over risks. Truly effective budgeting should therefore be risk-based; hence, we can talk about Risk-Based Budgeting (RBB).

With the RBB idea in mind, we can introduce a second idea: Activity-Based Budgeting (ABB). ABB was originally developed by consultants Coopers Lybrand Deloitte.[5] Its root is obviously in ABC, but it also brings in aspects from other established techniques as appropriate, including Zero-Based Budgeting (ZBB) and Priority-Based Budgeting. It focuses the budgets on activities "by defining the activities underlying the financial figures in each function and using the level of activity to determine how much resource should be allocated, how well it is being managed and to explain variances from budget."[6] One major objective and benefit of ABB is its ability to provide an ideal[7] interface between long-term planning and budgetary control, but it is data intensive and it lacks risk capabilities. Hence, a conceptual merger between RBB and ABB would produce a truly viable solution.

To further boost performance while at the same time reducing the need for accurate numbers, Monte Carlo simulations should be used. Monte Carlo simulations, as shown in this book and elsewhere, offer the great benefit of turning uncertainty into an asset and not a liability.

This way of doing budgeting or continuously updating forecasts will greatly reduce the costs of performing the budgeting/forecasting tasks because:

- They no longer rely on accuracy but on relevance and on understanding cause and effect.
- They become far less data oriented and more risk- and process-oriented.
- The use of Monte Carlo simulations enables us to turn uncertainty into an asset.

All this translates into a more effective, relevant, and less costly budgeting/forecasting process. With a risk-based budgeting process, the next step would be to also make some of the cost accounting information risk-based. Of course, the cost accounting activities revolving around calculating the costs after the fact need not be risk-based; they should, however, incorporate measures of uncertainty.

What I am talking about is when the Bill of Materials (BOM) and Bill of Activities (BOA) are set up before production. Then it would be useful to understand which risks are present in terms of either underestimating the costs prior to production or increasing the costs during production. Such information is largely ignored today, and all the missed budgets should therefore come as no surprise. Organizations simply do not operate according to plans, either because of internal problems and variations or external factors. In any case, it would be helpful to think about risks before it is too late so that the worst problems can be either prevented or mitigated.

So far, this is only an idea. Future research may prove it wrong or right, or something in between. My feeling is that it may well prove useful, because after all it is not a particularly novel idea; it is simply a matter of applying a body of knowledge from one field to another field and making some minor adjustments. It is time to stop restricting risk management ideas to engineering and finance, and to employ them on a wider basis where they can add value. Cost management seems to be one obvious place, and some people have probably already thought about it to some extent.

However, the greatest impact from introducing risk management is probably on the management process itself, because the management process is the pivotal point of all major decisions in organizations. As Peter F. Drucker said:

The first duty of business is to survive and the guiding principle of business economics is not the maximization of profits—it is the profit of loss.

Avoiding loss is the primary objective of risk management. Thus, risk management must become an integral part of the entire management process—from the definition of objectives and strategies to the follow-up part. By using the approach discussed in this book, significant decision support can be provided, but this is not just a question of management tools. Risk management also requires education and a change of mind-set. As Dag Hammarskjold said:

The longest journey is the journey inward.

SOME THOUGHTS AT THE END

For those who want to learn a subject well, writing a book about it is an effective way of learning. After considering what I have learned so far, I realized that uncertainty is the decision maker's best friend if managed wisely. It would, of course, be nice to know the future, but that is simply impossible, so we might as well embrace uncertainty instead of rejecting it. The fact is that uncertainty is inherent in many systems and situations. This is obvious, yet we keep chasing accurate cost estimates, as management equivalents of Don Quixote; we make elaborate strategies and so on as if the future were a game of chess. Take, for example, the well-known Balanced Scorecard method developed by Kaplan and Norton that is used to help organizations stay strategy focused; I still have not seen a Scorecard that deals with uncertainty and risk. This is also why I do not consider chess to be an interesting strategy game; no surprises can occur other than those your opponent devises. A supercomputer will therefore always win simply because it can calculate the highest number of moves ahead. Similarly, the company with the most rationally devised strategy and Balanced Scorecard should in principle become market leader, but does it?

I believe it is time to take the consequence of uncertainty and seek relevance rather than accuracy and foresight rather than hindsight. It is better to know which causes and factors determine a cost than to calculate the cost accurately after the fact. Responsiveness to uncertainty and future risks is more important than optimization based on past performance. In fact, it is impossible to calculate a cost accurately because, as every ABC practitioner knows, the cost estimates depend on the choice of activity drivers, activity definitions, and so on. Optimization is useless in open systems because we cannot control the environment.

Managing a company, designing a product, or being a leader in an organization are complex affairs. That is, no definite links exist between cause and effect. A strategy may fail because it did not take into account a seemingly unimportant issue, such as when IBM chose to outsource software development to Microsoft and chip manufacturing to Intel because it believed the future, like the past, lay in hardware design and manufacturing. A product may fail because the customers turned out to love the product except when it has your brand name on it, as happened wih the New Coke flop by Coca-Cola. A cost estimate may turn out to be way too low because hidden costs and risks were not considered, such as when Exxon chose to use single-hull tankers to save money and ended up paying billions in cleanup and fines. These are all examples of a small, unpredictable issue turning a situation upside down. Numerous examples exist; what they all have in common is that the complexity of the situation was not considered well enough prior to the catastrophe. In hindsight, it is easy to see what went wrong. IBM failed because they assumed the future would be like the past (a common assumption in most forecasting), Coca-Cola thought that people bought Coke for the taste alone. A simple risk analysis would have shown Exxon the madness of its actions.

Unfortunately, no means exists for eliminating such erroneous analyses and decisions. However, I believe that one reason such problems arise is that many analyses tend to appear more precise than they are, so decision-makers believe they know more than they actually do. Such analyses focus on accuracy and answers rather than approximations and understanding. The result is organizational self-delusions and hidden assumptions become prolific. It is useful to think in terms of Zadeh's *Law of Incompatibility*:

As complexity rises, precise statements lose meaning and meaningful statements lose precision.

This is a profound insight. It implies that since uncertainty is inevitable, it is outright dangerous and deceptive to reduce the uncertainty, for example, in an analysis by making it appear precise. Similarly, grand plans of strategies and budgets are bound to fail because the more precise they are, the less meaningful they become. It is, for example, interesting to notice[8] that "CEO Superman"[9] Jack Welsh of General Electric (GE), during his 20-year reign, focused on relatively simple yet adaptable strategies without grand action plans and the like. Yet, according to Stern Stewart & Company's new Wealth Added Index™ (WAI), GE added the most wealth ($226.8 billion) of all listed companies in the world from 1996 to 2000. Instead of viewing uncertainty as an enemy, GE used uncertainty to its advantage by rapidly responding to new opportunities or threats. A good strategy is more concerned about what not to do than what to do, in my opinion. Similarly, a cost assessment should be carried out according to the succinct phrase: "It is better to be approximately right than exactly wrong." The point is that we should seek a reliable solution space (an approximation) and not a point solution (exact and accurate). After all, with a solution space, we know what is likely and what is not, whereas with a point solution, we have no idea except that it is definitely wrong.

The interesting thing is that, on the one hand, an Activity-Based LCC model is built up around cause-and-effect relationships, while on the other hand, the Monte Carlo methods actually introduce uncertainty on purpose. Hence, the uncertainty in the model is not a problem; it is a necessity since uncertainty is what makes Monte Carlo simulations and statistical sensitivity analyses possible. In turn, critical success factors are identified, uncertainty is modeled, and risks are identified in one shot.

In other words, the exploitation of uncertainty in a relevant performance measurement framework is one of the most potent characteristics of Activity-Based LCC. It thrives on the paradox that relevance and uncertainty coexist for mutual benefit. It makes the use of Monte Carlo methods possible, which in turn greatly enhances effectiveness by identifying the critical success factors and making handling uncertainty and risks realistically a breeze. When we understand the causes of something (the causes, or factors, of a cost), its approximate state (how much it costs), and its risks (what are the risks that impact the costs), what more can we ask for?

There is also, a more subtle benefit of systematically modeling uncertainty. This benefit is not pertinent to Activity-Based LCC but it is highly relevant for decision-makers and less quantitative management methods. Virtually all management methods implicitly assume that stakeholders are rational. This includes everybody who has a stake in the organization, such as customers, investors, managers, workers, and so on. Yet the results from Arrow's Impossibility Theorem[10] clearly show that even a group of 100 percent rational beings, if such existed, would still produce an irrational outcome. Since we cannot model irrationality, because if we could, it would not be irrational, our only option is either to purposely add uncertainty to the results or to make the results less precise. The point is to force decision-makers to decide under an explicit presence of uncertainty—to decide in chaos, so to speak. "Given the increasing complex and uncertain environment in which contemporary organizations operate, there is a need for being able to 'embrace complexity and learn how to handle uncertainty.'"[11] A method in which one can blend rationality with irrationality should therefore be useful. In the words of a commercial lender:

> *Basic credit decisions are often based solely on considerations of the heart (often biased), head (analytical) or gut instinct (experience). Using these guidelines, I have generally found that if my heart overrules my head, the loan has almost uniformly been a poor one. If my head overrules my gut instinct, the resulting loam may sometimes be a poor one. In looking back at poor loans, I should have followed my gut instinct more often.*[12]

The good thing about the approach presented in this book is that it allows us to model the gut instinct. This should be good news for all managers because managerial thinking (especially at the senior levels) requires intuition and the exercise of subjective judgment in all organizations. In fact, I believe that intentionally using uncertainty in general can open up many new avenues for management and engineering improvements, ranging from strategy work to technical assessments. That, combined with a diligent search for relevance, can prove to be a new way toward foresighted, relevance-based management whose hallmarks are approximations, cause-and-effect measures, responsiveness, and risk focus.

The future is unpredictable, but ignoring it will not help. We should learn from the past by analysis and experience but act toward the future, keeping in mind that things change. Hindsight is 20/20, but foresight is better.

NOTES

1. According to H.T. Johnson, "It's Time to Stop Overselling Activity-Based Concepts," *Management Accounting,* September 1992.
2. See, for example, J. Emblemsvåg and B. Bras, "Process Thinking: A New Paradigm for Science and Engineering," *Futures* 32 (7), 2000, pp. 635–654.
3. L.A. Joia, "Measuring Intangible Corporate Assets: Linking Business Strategy with Intellectual Capital," *Journal of Intellectual Capital* 1 (1), 2000, pp. 68–84.
4. M.C. Jensen, "Corporate Budgeting Is Broken: Let's Fix It," *Harvard Business Review* 79, No. 10, November 2001, pp. 94–101.
5. According to J. Brimson and R. Fraser, "The Key Features of ABB," *Management Accounting,* January 1991.
6. See M. Morrow and T. Connolly, "The Emergence of Activity-Based Budgeting," *Management Accounting,* February 1991.
7. According to M. Harvey, "Activity-Based Budgeting," *Certified Accountant,* July 1991, pp. 27–30.
8. J. Welsh and J.A. Byrne, *Jack: Straight from the Gut.* New York: Warner Business Books, 2001, p. 479.
9. According to P.F. Drucker, "The Next Society: A Survey of the Near Future," *The Economist* 361 (8246), 2001.
10. K.J. Arrow, *Social Choices and Individual Values.* New Haven, CT: Yale University Press, 1963.
11. D. Jankowicz, "Why Does Subjectivity Make Us Nervous? Making the Tacit Explicit," *Journal of Intellectual Capital* 2 (1), 2001, pp. 61–73.
12. S. Sailsbury, "Failures of My Lending Career," *Journal of Commercial Lending* 67 (2), 1984.

APPENDIX
A

MONTE CARLO SIMULATION EXAMPLE

> Do not put your faith in what statistics say until you have carefully considered what they do not say.
>
> William W. Watt

This appendix illustrates how Monte Carlo methods can be used to aid information management, uncertainty analysis (and consequently risk management), and cost management. To do that, a very simple example is used, which is structured in three parts: (1) definition, (2) what hypothesis to test, and finally (3) the results and discussion.

PROBLEM DEFINITION

Assume that Company X has two products, P1 and P2, with the costs of materials and labor as shown in Table A.1.

Company X wants to manage its costs from *three* different perspectives: uncertainty/forecasting, information management, and continuous improvement. To do that, Monte Carlo methods are employed in *two* different ways:

1. For cost management and the corresponding continuous improvement efforts, the assumption cells are modeled as shown in Figure A.1, where all the uncertainty distributions are modeled as triangular distributions with ±10 percent upper and lower bounds respectively. Note that it can, in principle, be any value; thus, ±5 percent triangular is just as good as ±10 per-

Table A.1 Material and Labor Costs for Company X

Product	Material Costs	Labor Costs	Total Costs
P1	1	1	2
P2	1	2	3

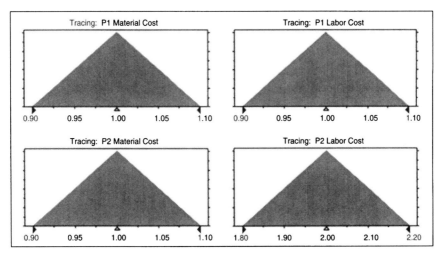

Figure A.1   Modeling assumption cells for cost and information management purposes.

cent triangular. The point is to be consistent and for the chosen distributions to be symmetric and bounded. The purpose is to find out which factors have the greatest impact on the total costs and what information is subsequently most critical (and should therefore be paid extra attention to) respectively. This is done by *tracing* the different contributors using sensitivity analyses. This case is consequently referred to as the tracing case.

2. For uncertainty analysis and the corresponding information management, we try to find out how the uncertainty affects the forecasts and what information should be pursued in order to reduce this uncertainty. In this case, which is referred to as the uncertainty case, we model the uncertainty as accurately as possible. In this example, we simply choose triangular distributions so that we can compare the two different ways of employing Monte Carlo simulations. From Figure A.2, we see that we have chosen two ±10 percent triangular distributions and two (–5 percent, 10 percent) triangular distributions.

We note that information management in the two cases has two distinct roles. In the tracing case, the information management revolves around the issue of what information is most crucial to have with respect to managing costs, while in the uncertainty case, the issue is what information generates the most uncertainty, and risk for that matter, in the model.

Next, we put forth some hypotheses that we intend to test using Monte Carlo simulations.

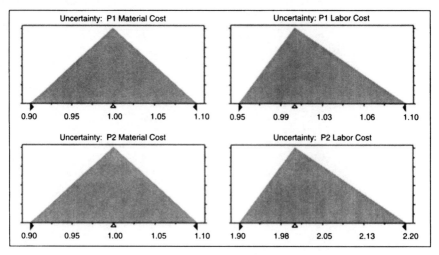

Figure A.2 Modeling assumption cells for uncertainty and information management purposes.

HYPOTHESES TO BE TESTED

The question is how will these two different ways of using Monte Carlo simulations affect the forecast cells? Since this example is simple, we pose the following four hypotheses:

1. For P1, in the tracing case, the material cost and the labor cost should be found equally important since the material cost is equal to the labor cost.
2. For P2, in the tracing case, the labor cost should be found twice as important as the material cost since the labor cost is twice the material cost.
3. For P1, in the uncertainty case, the material cost should be found more important than the labor cost since the material cost is equal to the labor cost in magnitude but associated with a larger uncertainty.
4. For P2, in the uncertainty case, the material cost and the labor cost should be found unequally important because the magnitudes and uncertainties are different.

Furthermore, in Monte Carlo simulations, the number of trials is very important for the accuracy. Hence, we put forth two more hypotheses:

5. When we increase the number of trials, the random effects that appear in the sensitivity charts should be reduced.
6. When we add two symmetric distributions, the forecast distribution should be symmetric as well. That is, the skewness should be zero.

If we find these six hypotheses to be fulfilled, we can conclude that the Monte Carlo methods can be employed as claimed, provided that we are aware of the fact that their accuracy is dependent on the number of trials performed. The results are discussed next.

RESULTS AND DISCUSSION

From the sensitivity chart in Figure A.3, we see that Hypothesis 1 is clearly supported because the correlation coefficients are close to equal (0.69 versus 0.70). The reason that they are not equal is that the Monte Carlo method is a numerical approximation technique where random effects occur. However, by increasing the number of trials from 10,000 to 100,000, these effects are not detectable any more (see Figure A.4). This clearly supports Hypothesis 5.

Similarly, we see that Hypothesis 2 is also valid. This is done in Figure A.5, but we see that $0.42 \times 2 = 0.84 < 0.89$. This is due to random effects. By running the model 100,000 times instead of 10,000, we reached $0.43 \times 2 = 0.86$ (see Figure A.6). In other words, 0.89 will be reached when the number of trials is substantially high, say 1,000,000 trials.

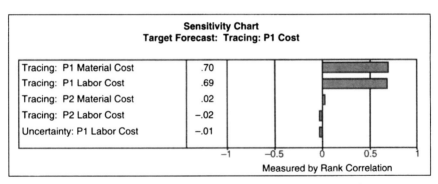

Figure A.3   Tracing P1 cost sensitivity chart with 10,000 trials.

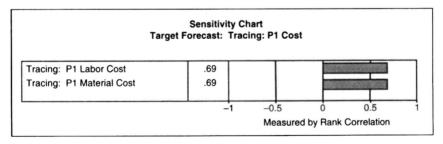

Figure A.4   Tracing P1 cost sensitivity chart with 100,000 trials.

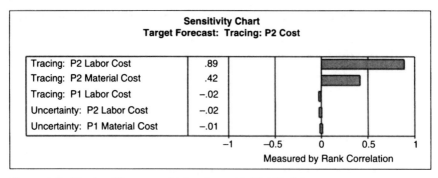

Figure A.5   Tracing P2 cost sensitivity chart with 10,000 trials.

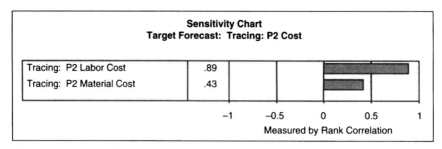

Figure A.6   Tracing P2 cost sensitivity chart with 100,000 trials.

Similarly, Hypotheses 3 and 4 can be proven using the sensitivity charts in Figures A.7 and A.8.

The last hypotheses to prove are Hypotheses 5 and 6, which concern the accuracy of the Monte Carlo simulation in terms of random effects and skewness respectively. This can be easily seen from the results in Table A.2. The most interesting results are in bold. Notice that the skewness of the tracing cases went from 0.02 to 0.00 and the range minimum and range maximum went from the asymmetric (1.83, 2.18) to the symmetric (1.81, 2.19).

We have now illustrated some of the points that were discussed theoretically in Chapter 3. It is clear that Monte Carlo methods are very powerful as they facilitate many different applications *at the same time*. However, we must remember that Monte Carlo simulations are dependent on the number of trials performed. This becomes more and more important the larger the models are.

Table A.2 How the Number of Trials Affects Random Effects and Skewness

Statistics	Uncertainty P1	P2	Tracing P1	P2	Uncertainty P1	P2	Tracing P1	P2
Trials	**10,000**	**10,000**	**10,000**	**10,000**	**100,000**	**100,000**	**100,000**	**100,000**
Mean	**2.02**	**3.03**	**2.00**	**3.00**	**2.02**	**3.03**	**2.00**	**3.00**
Median	**2.02**	**3.03**	**2.00**	**3.00**	**2.02**	**3.03**	**2.00**	**3.00**
Standard deviation	0.05	0.07	0.06	0.09	0.05	0.07	0.06	0.09
Variance	0.00	0.01	0.00	0.01	0.00	0.01	0.00	0.01
Skewness	0.07	0.18	**0.02**	**0.00**	0.05	0.18	**0.00**	**0.00**
Range minimum	1.86	2.83	**1.83**	**2.74**	1.86	2.81	**1.81**	**2.72**
Range maximum	2.18	3.28	**2.18**	**3.27**	2.19	3.29	**2.19**	**3.28**
Range width	0.32	0.45	0.35	0.53	0.34	0.48	0.38	0.56
Mean statistics error	0.00	0.00	0.00	0.00	0.00	0.00	0.00	0.00

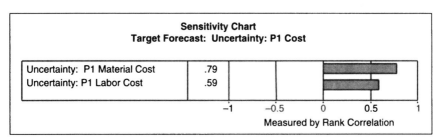

Figure A.7 Uncertainty P1 cost sensitivity chart with 100,000 trials.

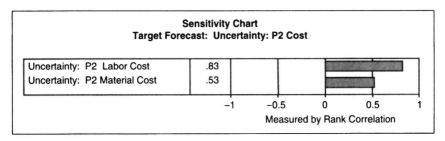

Figure A.8 Uncertainty P2 cost sensitivity chart with 100,000 trials.

Before we leave this topic, let's summarize the different models we can have:

- **Tracing models**   Models where uncertainty is added consistently using bounded and symmetric distributions only. The uncertainty distributions in tracing models provide information regarding the possible distortion problems in the models. The sensitivity charts are used to identify the critical success factors and what data are most important for the model in terms of cause and effect.
- **Uncertainty models**   Models where the true uncertainty is modeled as accurately as possible. The uncertainty distributions in uncertainty models give information with respect to how the uncertainty in the assumption cells affects the forecast cells. The sensitivity charts are employed to identify what information should be gathered to reduce the uncertainty in the model and what data are most uncertain.

Tracing models are important because they show that adding uncertainty to a model can make it more useful in identifying improvements. That is, by increasing the uncertainty, we can lower the risk of making ill-fated decisions.

In short, we do not need accurate data. We need satisfactory process descriptions that reflect the cause-and-effect relationships and data that are roughly correct.

APPENDIX
B

SFI GROUP SYSTEM

The SFI group system is used in the shipping industry to categorize vessel parts and components. SFI is distributed by Norwegian Shipping and Offshore Services AS, and it is the most frequently used system in Norway.

1 General Description	2 Hull	3 Equipment for Cargo	4 Equipment	5 Crew	6 Machinery, Main Components	7 Main Engine Components	8 Ship Systems
10 Specification, drawings	20 Construction and materials	30 Hatches and ports	40 Maneuvering	50 Lifesaving equipment	60 Diesel engine for propulsion	70 Fuel oil system	80 Ballast and bilge system
11 Insurance: fees and certificates	21 Afterbody	31 Equipment on deck	41 Maneuvering machinery and equipment	51 Insulation, partition, bulkhead, panels, and doors		71 Lubrication oil system	81 Fire and lifeboat alarm
12 Models	22 Engine and midship area	32 Special equipment for cargo handling	42 Communication equipment	52 Interior deck covers: stairs, ladders and so on		72 Cooling system	82 Air and sounding system from tanks
13 Rigging	23 Cargo area	33 Cranes	43 Anchoring, mooring, and towing equipment	53 External deck cover: stairs, ladders, and so on	63 Transmissions	73 Pressure system	
14 Launching	24 Forebody	34 Winches	44 Repair, maintenance, and cleaning equipment		64 Boilers, steam, and gas generators	74 Exhaust systems and air intakes	
15 Measurements, trials, and tests	25 Super-structure		45 Lifting and transport equipment		65 Generator sets for main electrical production		
16 Guarantee	26 Hull outfitting				66 Other aggregates		

1 General Description	2 Hull	3 Equipment for Cargo	4 Equipment	5 Crew	6 Machinery, Main Components	7 Main Engine Eomponents	8 Ship Systems
	27 Material protection, external						88 Common electrical system
	28 Material protection, internal						89 Electrical distribution systems

GLOSSARY

For reference information concerning the various definitions, contact the author of this book.

Action   The various units of work that activities are comprised of, such as individual tasks, jobs, steps, operations, or any other possible division of work.

Activity-Based Costing (ABC)   A methodology that measures the cost and performance of activities, resources, and cost objects. Resources are assigned to activities, and then activities are assigned to cost objects based on their use. ABC recognizes the causal relationships of cost drivers to activities. ABC also adopts an attention-focusing, long-term, resource-consumption orientation.

Activity-Based Management (ABM)   A discipline that focuses on the management of activities as the route to improving the value received by the customer and the profit achieved by providing this value. This discipline includes cost driver analysis, activity analysis, and performance measurement. ABM draws on Activity-Based Costing (ABC) as its major source of information.

Activity driver   A measure of the consumption of an activity by another activity or an assessment object. Activity drivers that measure the consumption by an assessment object are also referred to as *final* activity drivers, whereas activity drivers that measure the consumption of activities by other activities are called *intermediate* activity drivers. Examples of activity drivers are the amount of labor, the weight of a product, the number of products, and so on.

Allocation   1. An apportionment or a distribution. 2. A process of assigning cost to an activity or a cost object when a direct measure does not exist. For example, assigning the cost of power to a machine activity by means of machine hours is an allocation, because machine hours is an indirect measure of power consumption. In some cases, allocations can be converted to tracing by incurring additional measurement costs. Instead of using machine hours to allocate power consumption, a company can place a power meter on machines to measure actual power consumption. Note that considerable confusion about this topic exists due to the early descriptions of an ABC system by Robin Cooper and Robert S. Kaplan as a system to get "more accurate fully absorbed unit costs" when it in essence is a "contribution margin approach." The reason for this confusion is that allocation used in volume-based costing systems reflects an arbitrary assignment and is therefore irrelevant for decision-making, whereas in ABC it reflects an estimation. *See also* tracing.

Allocation base   Unit-level product characteristics. The term is used in discussing volume-based costing systems.

Assumption cell   A cell in a spreadsheet in which input is given with an associated, assumed uncertainty distribution representing a source variable.

Bill of activities (BOA)   A listing of the activities required (and, optionally, the associated costs of the resources consumed) by a product or other cost object.

Ceteris paribus   Latin for "everything else remains constant." This is a common condition in economic theories.

Consumption intensity   The unit price of a cost driver, an activity driver, or a resource driver.

Cost driver   Any factor that causes a change in the cost of an activity. Raw material quality, the number of vendors, employee training, and the complexity of assembly are examples of cost drivers. They are used in the process view of Activity-Based Costing and Management to identify the root cause of the work and cost of an activity.

Cost object   Anything for which we want separate cost information.

Critical success factor   The factors that have the greatest impact on the chosen performance measures.

Deterministic   The values of the variables are known with 100 percent certainty.

Effectiveness   A measure of the quality of a decision (correctness, completeness, and comprehensiveness) that is made by a designer.

Efficiency   A measure of how swiftly information, which can be used by a designer to make decisions, is generated.

Expected monetary value   The sum of the monetary values of each of a number of outcomes multiplied by the probability of each outcome relative to all the other possibilities. This definition is based on Daniel Bernoulli's definition of expected value.

Expected utility   A measure of the welfare accruing to a consumer from an asset that yields an uncertain flow of benefits. Computationally, it is calculated in the same way as an expected value but with the utility serving as the weighting factor.

Externality   A side effect of production or consumption that may be either positive (vaccinations) or negative (pollution). These effects are external to the economic system, hence the name, and can therefore only be very crudely estimated, if at all. Many people in the environmental management field use *externality* to denote what is here referred to as *societal cost*.

Fixed cost   This has two distinct definitions depending on whether the term is applied in either activity-based systems or in volume-based systems:

1. Fixed costs are costs that do *not* vary with the amount of output. Some refer to this as nonvariable costs. Fixed costs can be divided into two categories:
   - Programmed costs that result from attempts to generate sales volume
   - Committed costs required to maintain the organization
2. A cost element of an activity that does not vary with changes in the volume of cost drivers or activity drivers.

Forecast cell   A cell in a spreadsheet in which an output (result) with associated, resulting uncertainty distribution is given, representing a response variable.

Life-cycle accounting   A system for assigning specific costs to product systems within a physical life-cycle approach and is based on total cost assessment. *See* total cost assessment (TCA).

Open system   A system that coevolves with its environment over time and changes.

Product life-cycle   The life-cycle of a product system begins with the acquisition of raw materials and includes bulk material processing, engineered materials production, manufacture and assembly, use, retirement, and disposal of residuals produced in each stage.

Profitability   Assessed revenues minus assessed costs associated with the creation of the revenues. Profit, on the other hand, is actual revenues minus actual costs.

Remanufacturing   An industrial process that restores worn products to like-new condition. In a factory, a retired product is first completely disassembled. Its usable parts are then cleaned, refurbished, and put into inventory. Finally, a new product is reassembled from both old and new parts, creating a unit equal in performance to the original or a currently available alternative. In contrast, a repaired or rebuilt product usually retains its identity, and only those parts that have failed or are badly worn are replaced.

Resource An economic, energy-related, or waste/mass-related element that is consumed by the performance of activities. Resources, like activities, can be aggregated into hierarchies or one big hierarchy depending on what is useful. In special cases, such as waste, resources may be generated by activities instead of consumed.

Resource driver A measure of the quantity of resources consumed by an activity. An example of a resource driver is the percentage of total square feet of space occupied by an activity.

Risk Applies to situations of uncertainty (*see* uncertainty) for which the outcome involves potential loss but about which we have good probability information. Risk is, in other words, a subset of uncertainty.

Satisficing Not the best, but good enough. The use of this term in the context of optimization is first attributed to Nobel Laureate Herbert Simon.

Simulation A numerical technique for conducting experiments on a digital computer. It involves certain types of mathematical and logical models that describe the behavior of a business or economic system (or some component thereof) over extended periods of real time. However, in the context of Monte Carlo simulations, some differences occur:

- In the Monte Carlo method, time does not play as substantial a role as it does in stochastic simulation.
- The observations in the Monte Carlo method, as a rule, are independent. In simulation, however, we experiment with the model over time so, as a rule, the observations are serially correlated.
- In the Monte Carlo method, it is possible to express the response as a rather simple function of the stochastic input variations. In simulation, the response is usually a complicated one and can be expressed explicitly only by the computer program itself.

Societal costs Costs borne by society rather than those involved in a transaction.

Target costing A system of profit planning and cost management that is price driven, customer focused, design centered, and cross-functional. Target costing initiates cost management at the earliest stages of product development and applies it throughout the product life-cycle by actively involving the entire value chain.

Total cost assessment (TCA)   A comprehensive method of analyzing costs and benefits of a pollution prevention or design project. TCA includes:

- Full-cost accounting, a managerial accounting method that assigns both direct and indirect costs to specific products
- Estimates of both short- and long-term direct, indirect, or hidden, liability and less tangible costs
- Costs projected over a long horizon, such as 10 to 15 years

Tracing   Also known as direct tracing. This is the assignment of cost, energy consumption, or waste generation to an activity or an assessment object using an observable measure of the consumption of resources or the generation of waste by the activity or assessment object. Tracing is generally preferred to allocation if the data exists or can be obtained at a reasonable cost. For example, if a company's cost accounting system captures the cost of supplies according to which activity uses the supplies, the costs may be traced (as opposed to allocated) to the appropriate activities. *See also* allocation.

Trigger   The occurrence of an event that starts as an activity.

Uncertainty   Applies to situations about which we do not even have good probability information. Uncertainty is a superset of risk. *See* risk.

Useful life   Measures how long a system will operate safely and meet performance standards when maintained properly and not subject to stresses beyond stated limits.

Utility   The pleasure or satisfaction derived by an individual from being in a particular situation or from consuming goods and services. Utility is defined as the ultimate goal of economic activity, but it is not a label for any particular set of pursuits such as sensual pleasure or the acquisition and use of material goods. Thus, there is no single measure of utility.

Value chain   Three distinct definitions exist for this term:

1. A cost-reduction and process improvement tool that utilizes information collected about business processes and examines various attributes of the processes (diversity, capacity, and complexity). It is used to identify candidates for improvements efforts.
2. Any linked set of value-creating activities from basic raw materials through the ultimate end-use product or service delivered to the final customer.
3. The set of activities required to design, procure, produce, market, distribute, and service a product or service.

Value chain costing   An activity-based cost model that contains all activities in the value chain.

Variable cost   Two distinct definitions exist depending on whether the term is applied in volume-based systems or in activity-based systems:

1. Variable costs are costs that vary with the amount of output. Like fixed costs, variable costs are also divided into two categories:
   - The cost of goods sold, which covers materials, labor, and factory overhead applied directly to production
   - Costs that are not directly tied up in production but nevertheless vary directly with volume, such as sales commissions, discounts, and delivery expense
2. A cost element of an activity varies with changes in the volume of cost drivers or activity drivers.

Volume-based costing   An umbrella term for all costing methods that rely on the distinction of variable and fixed costs to determine the product costs. Because variable costs vary with the amount of output and only one single allocation base, it follows that the product costs strongly correlate with the production volume. Contribution margin costing and standard costing are two well-known volume-based costing methods.

ACRONYMS

Below is a list of acronyms used in this book.

Acronym	Explanation
ABB	Activity-Based Budgeting
ABC	Activity-Based Costing
ABM	Activity-Based Management
AHP	Analytic Hierarchic Process
AVA	Activity Value Analysis
BOA	Bill of Activities
BOM	Bill of Materials
BPR	Business Process Reengineering
CAP	Critical Assumption Planning
EMV	Expected Monetary Value
EP	Economic Profit
EU	Expected Utility
EVA	Economic Value Added
GAAP	Generally Accepted Accounting Principles
HFO	Heavy Fuel Oil
ISO (Greek for equal)	International Organization for Standardization
JIT	Just-in-Time
LCA	Life-Cycle Assessment or Life-Cycle Analysis
LCC	Life-Cycle Costing
LHS	Latin Hypercube Sampling
MGO	Marine Gas Oil
NPV	Net Present Value
NVA	NonValue Added
PSV	Platform Supply Vessel
QFD	Quality Function Deployment
SPC	Statistical Process Control
SQC	Statistical Quality Control
SRS	Simple Random Sampling
RF	Risk Function
TQM	Total Quality Management
VA	Value Added
WACC	Weighted Average Cost of Capital

INDEX

Lightning Source UK Ltd.
Milton Keynes UK
04 November 2010

162357UK00001B/37/P